PROPERTY

PROPERTY

ROGER BERNHARDT
Professor of Law, Golden Gate University

BLACK LETTER SERIES®

WEST PUBLISHING CO.
ST. PAUL, MINN.
1991

COPYRIGHT © 1983 WEST PUBLISHING CO.
COPYRIGHT © 1991 By WEST PUBLISHING CO.
  610 Opperman Drive
  P.O. Box 64526
  St. Paul, MN 55164–0526

Library of Congress Cataloging-in-Publication Data

Bernhardt, Roger.
   Property / Roger Bernhardt. — 2nd ed.
      p.   cm. — (Black letter series)
   Includes index.
   ISBN 0–314–86227–7
   1. Real property—United States—Outlines, syllabi, etc.
I. Title. II. Series.
KF570 .Z9B46 1991
346.7304′3—dc20
[347.30643]
                                        91–11786
                                           CIP

ISBN 0–314–86227–7

Bernhardt–Property, 2d BLS
2nd Reprint—1995

 TEXT IS PRINTED ON 10% POST CONSUMER RECYCLED PAPER

 PRINTED WITH SOY INK™

PUBLISHER'S PREFACE

This "Black Letter" is designed to help a law student recognize and understand the basic principles and issues of law covered in a law school course. It can be used both as a study aid when preparing for classes and as a review of the subject matter when studying for an examination.

Each "Black Letter" is written by experienced law school teachers who are recognized national authorities in the subject covered.

The law is succinctly stated by the author of this "Black Letter." In addition, the exceptions to the rules are stated in the text. The rules and exceptions have purposely been condensed to facilitate quick review and easy recollection. For an in-depth study of a point of law, citations to major student texts are given. In addition, a **Text Correlation Chart** provides a convenient means of relating material contained in the Black Letter to appropriate sections of the casebook the student is using in his or her law school course.

If the subject covered by this text is a code or code-related course, the code section or rule is set forth and discussed wherever applicable.

FORMAT

The format of this "Black Letter" is specially designed for review. (1) **Text.** First, it is recommended that the entire text be studied, and, if deemed necessary, supplemented by the student texts cited. (2) **Capsule Summary.** The Capsule Summary is an abbreviated review of the subject matter which can be used both before and after studying the main body of the text. The headings in the Capsule Summary follow the main text of the "Black Letter." (3) **Table of Contents.** The Table of Contents is in outline form to help you organize the details of the subject and the Summary of Contents gives you a final overview of the materials. (4) **Practice Examination.** The Practice Examination in Appendix B gives you the opportunity of testing yourself with the type of question asked on an exam, and comparing your answer with a model answer.

In addition, a number of other features are included to help you understand the subject matter and prepare for examinations:

Short Questions and Answers: This feature is designed to help you spot and recognize issues in the examination. We feel that issue recognition is a major ingredient in successfully writing an examination.

Perspective: In this feature, the authors discuss their approach to the topic, the approach used in preparing the materials, and any tips on studying for and writing examinations.

Analysis: This feature, at the beginning of each section, is designed to give a quick summary of a particular section to help you recall the subject matter and to help you determine which areas need the most extensive review.

Examples: This feature is designed to illustrate, through fact situations, the law just stated. This, we believe, should help you analytically approach a question on the examination.

Glossary: This feature is designed to refamiliarize you with the meaning of a particular legal term. We believe that the recognition of words of art used in an examination helps you to better analyze the question. In addition, when writing an examination you should know the precise definition of a word of art you intend to use.

We believe that the materials in this "Black Letter" will facilitate your study of a law school course and assure success in writing examinations not only for the course but for the bar examination. We wish you success.

The Publisher

SUMMARY OF CONTENTS

PART THREE: RIGHTS RELATING TO LAND

APPENDICES

*

TABLE OF CONTENTS

PART ONE: INTERESTS IN LAND

PART TWO: CONVEYANCING

PART THREE: RIGHTS RELATING TO LAND

APPENDICES

CAPSULE SUMMARY OF REAL PROPERTY

PART ONE: INTERESTS IN LAND

I. ADVERSE POSSESSION

If an owner of property fails to sue a person in wrongful possession of it within the time allotted by the statute of limitations for actions in ejectment, the possessor may acquire title to the property.

A. Background

Adverse possession operates to confirm the possessory claims of persons which have been asserted long enough and visibly enough. In most cases such claimants in fact believe themselves to be owners but their titles suffer from technical deficiencies.

B. Theory

A possessor of land, even though not an owner, may protect that possession against everyone in the world except the true owner. Although the true owner may bring ejectment against a person wrongfully possessing her property, her failure to do so in time, means that the possessor is then protected from ejectment by anyone, stranger or former owner. At this stage the possessor becomes, for all practical purposes, the owner.

1

C. Elements

1. Continuous and Uninterrupted

   An adverse possession must last for so long as the statute of limitations, on a cause of action in ejectment, runs. It must be continuous, so that the owner may have sued at any time during the period. It must be uninterrupted, so that no other person was possessing adversely to the adverse possessor during that period. The adverse possession of predecessors may be included (tacked) if there is privity between the possessors.

   a) Extenuating Features

      The statute of limitations does not run against future interests until they become possessory or are interfered with, nor does the statute commence running against possessory interests if, at the time of the wrongful entry, the owner is under a disability. However, subsequent disabilities or transfers by the owner do not extend the time period once the cause of action has already arisen.

2. Open and Notorious

   Lack of actual knowledge by an owner is no defense, but adverse possession must be sufficiently open and notorious as to give notice to any owner inspecting her land.

   a) Extent of Possession

      Only the property actually possessed is acquired by the adverse possessor, unless he has a color of title to a larger area and actually possesses some part of it, thereby establishing constructive possession of it.

3. Hostile; Ouster

   An adverse possessor must act like an owner with regard to others and permit them to be on the property only with his permission. He must be hostile to the true owner in that the adverse possessor must not believe that the owner's consent to his possession is necessary.

   a) Ouster; Where the Initial Possession Was Permissive

      Where a possession is undertaken permissively, there must be an ouster before it can become adverse to the owner, i.e., the owner must be advised that the possessor has repudiated her rights in the property.

   b) State of Mind

      Most jurisdictions do not require any particular state of mind if an adverse possessor; thus, it is irrelevant whether the adverse possessor is there by mistake or is hoping to "steal" the title.

D. Effect
Completion of a successful adverse possession gives the possessor an original title to the property, although it may not be marketable until so established in court. Such a title is only good as against those rights in the property which are extinguished by the statute of limitations; this does not include holders of future interests or nonpossessory interests. Nor, generally, is the government barred by the doctrine of adverse possession.

II. ESTATES
A. Present Estates
   1. Types
      a) Freehold
         Freehold estates have no ascertainable termination date. At common law a person in possession of a freehold estate was said to have seisin. A fee simple estate was created by a grant to a person "and his heirs"; these words of limitations indicated that the estate was inheritable and would not terminate on the death of the grantee. A fee tail estate was created by a grant to the person "and the heirs of his body"; this estate was inheritable only by the grantee's lineal descendants. A life estate was created when the grant did not include any words of inheritance; it ended upon the death of the grantee or whomever was used as the measuring life.

      b) Nonfreehold
         Nonfreehold estates all have ascertainable termination dates. They include the tenancy for a term, the periodic tenancy and the tenancy at will. If one of the above estates contains no additional provision for termination (other than death or expiration of the term) it is referred to as "absolute."

      c) Qualified Estates
         Any of the above mentioned estates can be made qualified (defeasible) rather than absolute. An estate is determinable if some condition is incorporated into its duration ("so long as . . ."); it then ends automatically if the event occurs. Alternatively, it is subject to condition subsequent if the grant states that upon the occurrence of a specified event it may be reclaimed by the grantor ("but if . . . then"); termination of the estate here is optional rather than automatic. If title is to pass to a third person rather than revert to the grantor, the estate may be called an estate subject to an executory limitation.

B. Future Interests

1. **Possibility of Reverter and Power of Termination**
   If the owner of an absolute estate conveys away a determinable estate, he retains a possibility of reverter; if he conveys an estate subject to a condition subsequent he retains a power of termination.

2. **Executory Interest**
   If a defeasible estate is conveyed to the grantee and the property is to go to a third person upon occurrence of the event, the future interest in the third person is called a (shifting) executory limitation. A future interest which is to go directly from the grantor to a third person in the future is called a (springing) executory interest.

3. **Remainder**
   A remainder is a future interest created in a third person. It takes effect upon the natural termination of a preceding estate rather than by cutting it short. Where a series of estates of less than fee simple are created, there may be a series of remainders. A remainder is vested if it is given to an ascertained person and is subject to no condition precedent (other than natural termination of the prior interest); a remainder is contingent if the taker is unascertained or if there is a condition precedent. A remainder may also be defeasible when it is made subject to a condition subsequent; it is then referred to as a remainder subject to divestment. It may be subject to partial divestment, where it is given to a class of persons whose individual interests are reduced as new members enter the class and claim their corresponding fractional shares.

4. **Reversion**
   A reversion is a future interest retained by the grantor whenever he gives away estates smaller than he held. It takes only upon the natural termination of the prior estate, rather than by cutting it short. It is always vested (although it may be subject to divestment) and requires no special creating language, arising by virtue of the grantor having conveyed less than he had. A grantor may retain both a reversion and a possibility of reverter or a power of termination when he conveys an estate which is both defeasible and smaller than the estate held.

C. Destructibility

At common law, a contingent remainder was destroyed if it had not become a vested remainder by the time the supporting estates terminated. It did not matter whether the preceding estates ended naturally or prematurely; thus a merger of a preceding estate into a vested future interest led to the destruction of any intervening contingent remainders. All other future interests were indestructible.

D. The Rule Against Perpetuities

This rule invalidates any contingent interests (contingent remainder or executory interests) which could conceivably vest or fail to vest more than 21 years after the end of some life in being at the creation of the interest. Thus, contingent remainders must be certain to either become vested remainders or fail, and executory interests must be certain to take possession or fail in less than that time or else they are immediately invalidated by the rule. It does not matter that the interest actually does vest in time, so long as there is a theoretical possibility that it might not. A remainder subject to open must be closed and vested as to every member within the time period or else the entire class gift is void. (There is an exception when both the present and future interests are given to charities.) When an interest is held invalid, it is stricken from the document and there is either a new reversionary interest created in the grantor, or the preceding estate is enlarged.

E. The Rule in Shelley's Case

At common law, if a freehold estate was given to a person and, in the same document, a remainder was given to her heirs, the remainder was treated as being a remainder in the ancestor rather than in the heirs. The remainder might then become vested rather than contingent and might also merge with the preceding freehold estate. The rule did not apply when one interest was legal and the other equitable.

F. The Doctrine of Worthier Title

At common law, an inter vivos gift of a future interest to the heirs of the grantor was void; it became, instead, a reversion in the grantor. At common law, a testamentary devise of an estate to a person who would otherwise take the same by descent if the testator had died intestate was also void.

G. Restraints on Alienation

A provision in a deed conveying a fee simple which absolutely prohibits the grantee from conveying the property is invalid. A restriction upon the power of a co-owner, a tenant, or the holder of some lesser interest in land is also invalid if it is written as a disabling restraint, but may be valid if it is a forfeiture or promissory restraint. A restraint may also be valid when it is partial as to time or to persons.

H. Marital Estates

1. Dower

Dower was the common law right of a wife to a life estate in one-third of all of the property of which her husband had been seised at some time during the marriage and which was inheritable by her issue.

2. Curtesy

At common law, immediately upon marriage a husband acquired a legal life estate in all property of which his wife was seised. (Jure uxoris.) As soon as issue were born alive his life estate was measured by his own life alone and was not dependent upon the continued survival of his wife. (Curtesy initiate.)   After her death the husband's life estate continued in its own right.   (Curtesy consummate.)

III.   CONCURRENT OWNERSHIP
A.   Types
1.   Joint Tenancy
A joint tenancy involves the principle of survivorship, whereby the surviving joint tenant takes the entire estate in preference to heirs or legatees of the deceased joint tenant.   There may be a joint tenancy among two or more persons, and it is not required that a fee simple absolute estate be involved.   A joint tenancy requires unity of time (that the persons take at the same time), unity of title (that they take by the same instrument), unity of interest (that they hold equal shares), and unity of possession (that they have equal rights to possess).   Since the modern presumption is against joint tenancy, it is generally required that it be specifically stated in the creating instrument.

a)   Severance
A joint tenancy may be severed and converted into a tenancy in common by a deed to a third person executed by either party. Sometimes there is severance when one of the parties has mortgaged, leased or contracted to convey the property.

2.   Tenancy in Common
A tenancy in common is created whenever no other special form of concurrent ownership has been designated.   There need not be unity of time or title or interest, but there must be unity of possession.

3.   Tenancy by the Entirety
This estate is a joint tenancy between husband and wife, which may not be severed or terminated except by death, divorce or mutual agreement.

4.   Community Property
In some of the western states, a community property system coexists with or replaces common law concurrent estates.   Most property acquired during marriage is held to be community property and may not be conveyed unilaterally by either party.

5.   Condominium
The owner of a condominium project has sole ownership of his or her individual unit but owns the common parts of the project as a tenant in common with other unit owners in the project.

6.   Cooperative Apartments
     In a cooperative apartment building, a corporation owns the building, and the tenants own shares in the corporation, generally entitling them to a particular apartment.

B.   Possession and Income

Each cotenant is entitled to possess all of the property, subject to the equal rights of all other cotenants to do the same. Neither may exclude the other, nor is the sole possession of one resulting from the voluntary absence of the other actionable. However a few states charge the tenant in sole possession a fractional share of the rental value. The Statute of Anne compels a cotenant who collects rent from third parties to account for them to the other cotenants. Rent from community property is itself community property.

C.   Payments

1.   Affecting Title
     Unequal contributions to the down payment may lead to acquisition of unequal interests by co-owners if they take as tenants in common. Joint tenants are required to hold equal interests. (Therefore, unequal contributions to a joint tenancy will be regarded as either a loan or a gift.) In community property jurisdictions, the character of the property may depend upon the nature of funds employed for its acquisition. The party asserting that the property is separate (not community) must prove, by tracing, that the property was purchased with her separate funds.

2.   Reimbursements
     A co-owner who makes payments necessary for the preservation of the title may sue the other co-owners for contribution or may have the payments recognized in an action for an accounting or partition. Sometimes there may be an offset for the value of a co-owner's sole possession. A party who pays for repairs to the property may not sue for contribution, but may have that expenditure recognized in an accounting or partition action; a party who pays for improvements to the property may recover for them only in a partition action unless they increase the rents from the property.

D.   Partition

Partition separates the undivided interests of co-owners into divided, separate interests. It is accomplished either by a physical division of the property or by a sale of the property and division of the proceeds. Covenants between co-owners not to partition the property are generally valid. Tenancy by the entirety may not be partitioned until after a divorce has converted it into a joint tenancy or tenancy in common. Community property is divided between the spouses as part of a divorce action.

E.   Transfers
1.   Inter Vivos
Tenants in common and joint tenants may freely convey their fractional interests; conveyance by a joint tenant severs the joint tenancy. Tenancy by the entirety and community property may be conveyed only by the joint act of the parties.

2.   Death Transfers
The principle of survivorship gives the surviving joint tenant or tenant by the entirety entire ownership of the property in preference to the claim of heirs or legatees. Tenancy in common and community property are subject to testamentary disposition as to half the property, but where a person dies intestate his community property share generally passes to his surviving spouse while his tenancy in common interests pass to his heirs.

IV. LANDLORD AND TENANT
A. Leasehold Estates
A leasehold is a nonfreehold estate in land, giving the tenant a present possessory interest and the landlord a future interest in the same property (a reversion). The fact that the tenant has possession distinguishes a leasehold from a license or an easement.

B. Types of Tenancies
1.   Tenancy for a Term
A tenancy for a term arises when the parties have agreed upon a termination date for the leasehold estate. If the term is to endure longer than one year, the statute of frauds usually requires a writing. Upon expiration of the term, the tenancy ends automatically.

2.   Periodic Tenancy
A periodic tenancy arises when the parties have agreed upon a regular payment of rent but have not established any termination date for the tenancy. It may arise by express agreement or by the bare fact of a person being in possession and paying a regular rent to the owner. The length of the period is established according to how rent is paid or calculated. A periodic tenancy is automatically renewed at the end of each period unless either party gives proper and timely notice of termination; at common law, notice was required to be given at least one period in advance (or six months in the case of a tenancy from year to year).

3.   Tenancy at Will
A tenancy at will exists whenever one party is in consensual possession of another person's land without any agreement as to either termination or payment of rent. It may be terminated at any time by either party.

4. **Tenancy at Sufferance**
A tenancy at sufferance arises once a tenant holds over past the expiration of his term and until the landlord elects either to treat him as a trespasser or a tenant for another period or term.

C. Possession
1. **Possession at Commencement**
Under the American Rule, a landlord is not responsible for the inability of the tenant to take possession arising from interference by strangers. The English Rule requires the landlord to deliver actual as well as legal possession to the tenant.

2. **Possession Throughout the Term**
The covenant of quiet enjoyment, which is implied in every lease, imposes upon a landlord the duty not to interfere with the tenant's possession during the term. A landlord is not responsible for interference with the tenant's possession caused by strangers, but is responsible if the tenant is evicted by a paramount title, by the landlord or by agents of the landlord. The tenant's obligation to pay rent is dependent upon the covenant of quiet enjoyment; a tenant is therefore excused from further rent liability once evicted by the landlord or a paramount title. At common law, destruction of the premises did not terminate the tenancy.

3. **Abandonment**
If a tenant abandoned the premises during the term at common law, the landlord was entitled to recover the rent as it fell due and had no duty to mitigate. Alternatively, the landlord could elect to treat the abandonment as an offer to surrender the leasehold estate and accept it as such by retaking possession for her own account. As a third remedy, the landlord could treat the abandonment as empowering her to act as agent for the tenant in reletting the premises for the tenant's account. The landlord could hold the tenant liable for the difference between the amount received on reletting and the rent due under the lease. Some jurisdictions now permit a landlord to sue the tenant, immediately following his abandonment, for damages equal to the lost benefit of the bargain (i.e., the difference between rent reserved and rental value for the balance of the term).

4. **Holding Over**
When a tenant wrongfully holds over after the expiration of his term, the landlord may elect to remove him or to compel him to remain for another term or period. If a landlord elects to treat the tenant as a trespasser, she is generally not entitled to use self-help to recover possession but must bring an action to evict the tenant. Statutory summary dispossess or unlawful detainer procedures are available in every jurisdiction to accomplish this purpose; these restore the landlord to possession and

award her damages for the tenant's wrongful holding over. Alternatively, the landlord may compel the holdover tenant to remain, usually as a periodic tenant based upon the original lease term or the method by which rent was paid or calculated. Until the landlord's election is made, the holdover tenant is a tenant at sufferance.

D. Rent

If a tenant in possession fails to pay the rent as required, the landlord may either sue for the rent or may terminate the tenancy and bring an action to evict the tenant. The landlord's right to retain an advance payment made by the tenant may depend upon whether it was a security deposit to cover actual losses, payment of advance rent to cover certain future periods, or merely a bonus given to the landlord in consideration of executing the lease.

E. Condition of the Premises

1. Common Law

A common law landlord had no duty to repair either preexisting or subsequently arising defects in the property, and was only required not to conceal hidden defects from the tenant. The tenant had an obligation to avoid waste, i.e., to make minor repairs in order to keep the premises windtight and watertight. If the premises were destroyed or significantly damaged by some outside cause, neither party had duties to repair or rebuild and neither was entitled to terminate the lease. The parties were free to alter their positions by covenants in the lease.

2. Constructive Eviction

If a landlord is obligated to repair the premises and fails to do so, and if the disrepair materially interferes with the tenant's enjoyment of the premises, then the tenant may claim that he has been constructively evicted and may quit the premises and terminate the lease. However, the tenant must show that the landlord was under an obligation to repair and that the disrepair was material. If the tenant is wrong, he has wrongfully abandoned the premises and continues to owe the rent.

3. Illegal Lease

Some courts hold that the rental of dilapidated premises constitutes an illegal agreement, which is therefore invalid, entitling the tenant to terminate at any time.

4. Statutory Duties

Many states now require the owner of residential premises to keep them habitable, and entitle the tenant to make the repairs himself (and deduct the cost from the rent), to withhold the rent until the repairs are made, or to have a receiver appointed to make the repairs. Many states prohibit a landlord from evicting a tenant in retaliation for exercising repair rights, or from requiring a tenant to waive these rights.

5. Implied Warranty of Habitability
    Many courts and statutes now declare that a landlord impliedly warrants the condition of residential premises for the duration of the term. If there is a breach of such warranty, the tenant is entitled to remain in possession and pay a reduced rent.

6. Tort Liability
    At common law, the fact that the tenant was the possessor of the premises meant that the landlord was not generally liable for personal injuries caused by defective conditions. Today, there are many exceptions: (1) A landlord is liable for personal injuries caused by latent defects known to her and not disclosed to the tenant; she may also be liable under this theory for injuries suffered by third persons; (2) A landlord is liable for injuries suffered by tenants and third persons in the common areas, which she is deemed to possess; this has recently been extended to include harm resulting from criminal activities occurring in the common areas; (3) A landlord is liable for negligently making repairs, or; (4) Failing to make repairs when she has covenanted to do so in the lease; (5) Many courts now treat local housing and building codes as safety ordinances for the protection of the public and hold a landlord liable for injuries arising from code violations; (6) A few courts now hold that a landlord, even though not a possessor, is required to exercise due care under the circumstances. Clauses in a lease exculpating the landlord from liability for injuries are often held invalid, and are not effective against third parties anyway.

F. Transfers

1. The Right to Transfer
    A leasehold interest is transferable unless the lease provides to the contrary. A landlord may prohibit transfers or may require that her consent first be obtained, and is then generally under no duty to act reasonably with regard to granting or withholding assent. A no-assignment clause usually operates as a forfeiture restraint, entitling the landlord to terminate the lease if an improper transfer has been made.

2. Kinds of Transfers
    A leasehold interest may be assigned or subleased. An assignment occurs when the entire estate is transferred; it is a sublease if an estate temporally smaller than what the tenant holds is transferred. In some jurisdictions the distinction is made according to the intent of the parties rather than the duration of the estate transferred. A landlord may also transfer the reversion, with or without transferring the right to receive the rents.

3. Effect of Transfer
    a) Assignment
        If a leasehold estate is assigned, the assignee is in privity of estate
        with the landlord and is subject to all covenants running with the
        land. Both tenant and assignee remain obliged to pay the rent,
        under privity of contract and privity of estate theories respectively.
        An assignee who further assigns is no longer liable for the rent
        unless he had also assumed the obligations of the lease.

    b) Subleases
        A sublease of premises creates neither privity of estate nor privity of
        contract between the subtenant and the landlord. The subtenant is
        not bound (nor benefitted) by the covenants in the master lease unless
        they have been assumed; however the subleasehold estate will be
        destroyed if the leasehold estate is terminated for nonpayment of rent
        by any party.

V.   EASEMENTS
A.   Definitions
An easement is a nonpossessory interest in land which someone else possesses.
The holder of the easement is the dominant tenant and his land is the
dominant tenement; the person subject to the easement is the servient tenant,
holding a servient tenement. An easement is appurtenant when it benefits
land; it is in gross when it benefits a person. A profit is involved when there
is a right to remove products of the soil. If the use is revocable at will, it is
a license. An affirmative easement entitles its holder to engage in otherwise
unprivileged activity affecting the servient tenement; a negative easement
entitles its holder to prohibit the holder of the servient tenement from
engaging in otherwise privileged activity.

B.   Creation
1. Express Language
    An easement may be granted to another person or may be reserved by a
    grantor of land over land being granted. If the easement is granted
    orally, it is merely a license, revocable at will, unless the grantor is
    estopped from so doing by virtue of detrimental reliance by the grantee.
    At common law an easement could not be reserved in favor of a third
    party.

2. By Implication or Necessity
    When one part of a parcel of land is already burdened for the benefit of
    another part of that parcel (such that, if these were separate parcels, the
    relationship would be considered an easement) then a severance of the
    parcel may lead to the creation of an easement by implication if the
    former quasi-easement was apparent, continuous and beneficial (or
    necessary, if an implied reservation is claimed). Where the severance

results in a landlocked parcel, an easement of necessity may be created even if there was no prior use.

3.   Prescription
     Adverse use of another's land, continued long enough, may create a prescriptive easement. Unlike adverse possession, it is not required that the prescriptive use have excluded all other activities on the property, so long as the use itself has been maintained long enough. Objections by the servient tenant do not interrupt a prescriptive use except in those jurisdictions which follow a lost grant theory. The use need not be continuous, but if it is limited or partial in time, the easement acquired will be similarly restricted. Some jurisdictions permit the public to acquire recreational easements through long continued use.

C.   Scope and Variation
1.   Express Easements
     The language of the document controls what a dominant tenant may do; where it is silent, the dominant tenant may engage in activities reasonably related to the easement (which includes changes due to the normal development of the dominant estate) and not unreasonably burdensome upon the servient tenement. However the dominant tenement may not be enlarged so as to benefit land which was not initially included.

2.   Implied Easements
     The same circumstances which led to the creation of an easement by implication are used to determine the scope of the easement.

3.   Prescriptive Easements
     The original activities which created a prescriptive easement also determine its scope. New and different activities themselves become privileged if engaged in long enough.

4.   Use by the Servient Tenant
     The servient tenant may engage in any activities on the land which do not unreasonably interfere with the easement. He may also permit third parties to engage in similar activities. He is not entitled to relocate an easement where its location is set forth in an instrument.

D.   Transfer and Subdivisions
1.   Burden
     The burden of an easement is transferred along with the servient tenement. If the servient tenement is subdivided, each parcel is subject to the burden, unless the easement has been geographically confined.

2. Benefit
   A transfer of the dominant tenement carries with it the benefit of all easements appurtenant. A subdivision of the dominant tenement subdivides the benefit amongst all the lots. At common law, an easement or profit in gross could not be transferred or subdivided, but this is now generally allowed when it is commercial or quantifiable or involves payments for its use.

E. Termination

An easement ends when its time period expires, or when it has been properly revoked, or when the underlying property has been destroyed, or when the necessity which created it ends. It is destroyed or superceded by a merger of the dominant and servient parcels. It is also terminated when the dominant tenant reconveys it to the servient tenant or properly abandons it. It may also be lost by prescription, or by forfeiture where it has been abused.

VI. COVENANTS
A. Nature

A covenant running with the land is a promise which may be enforced by the successors to the original covenantee, or against the successors to the original covenantor, or both. Its benefits or burdens run automatically without the need for an assignment of rights or delegation of duties.

B. Requirements

1. General Prerequisites
   A covenant will not run with the land unless it is an enforcible promise between the original parties. It must be in writing and there must be an intent that it run, which, at common law, required the parties to expressly mention "assigns" if it related to something not then in existence.

2. Requirements for Running at Law
   In order for a covenant to run with the land at law, it must touch and concern land, i.e., relate to the property rather than to its owner personally. A covenant to pay money may be treated as touching and concerning land where it is payment for the performance of an act which touches and concerns land. Some jurisdictions require merely that the burden of the covenant touch where the burden is to run, and that merely the benefit of the covenant touch where the benefit is to run. Other jurisdictions require that both the burden and benefit touch in order for the burden to run.

   Most jurisdictions require that the covenantor and covenantee be in privity of estate (horizontal privity). This may be limited to landlord-tenant relationships, or to persons sharing interests in the same property, but many jurisdictions find privity between a grantor and a grantee.

Neighbors may create covenants running with the land only where there is no requirement of horizontal privity.

Some states also require that the entire estate of the covenantor pass to her successor (vertical privity) in order for the burden of the covenant to run.

3. Equitable Requirements
For a covenant to run with the land as an equitable servitude, it is generally only required that the particular burden or benefit involved touch and concern land. Horizontal and vertical privity are not required. However, equity requires that the party to be burdened by a covenant has had notice of it.

C. Subdivisions
1. Standing
The subdivider has standing to enforce covenants made by grantees in their deeds to individual lots, by virtue of being the original promisee. The homeowners' association generally has standing to enforce those covenants by virtue of having succeeded to the title to some of the common (benefited) land. Individual owners may enforce covenants in deeds of their neighbors made before they took title on the theory that those covenants benefited the subdivider's retained land and then ran through them. These owners may enforce covenants made by later purchasers from the subdivider if they can show that reciprocal burdens were implied from their own covenants, or that they are third party beneficiaries of the later covenants, or that the subdivider made promises to them (the owners) to restrict all retained land, whose burdens then ran and bound the later purchasers.

If the covenants were properly drawn originally, the fact that they are not mentioned in later deeds in the chain of title is irrelevant, since they will run with the land in any event, so long as new grantees can be charged with notice.

2. Common Plan
If some parcels in the subdivision are not uniformly restricted, a court may hold that other grantees cannot be charged with notice of the restriction, or that a theory of implied reciprocal servitudes or third beneficiary will not be allowed, or that the burden of a covenant is invalid because it is unfair to burden the owner of a parcel who does not have the benefit of enforcing it against others.

D. Termination and Nonenforcement
1.   Legal Defenses
     A covenant endures only for so long as is provided for in the original
     document or permitted by statute. It is also destroyed by merger of the
     benefited and burdened parcels, or release, or abandonment by the
     appropriate parties, or by prescription.

2.   Equitable Defenses
     Courts of equity will not enforce a covenant where changed conditions
     make the benefit no longer substantial enough to justify the burden.
     Acquiescence and laches are also defenses.

3.   Governmental Action
     Where government acquires property burdened by a restrictive covenant, it
     generally takes free of the covenant and must compensate the holders of
     the lost benefit as well as the holder of the burdened title. There is a
     division of authority as to whether or not property disposed of by the
     government at a tax sale goes free of burdens previously imposed upon it.

PART TWO: CONVEYANCING

VII. BROKERS
A. Licensing
Brokers are persons licensed to negotiate sales, leases, financing and related
real property transactions. Without a license, no person may claim
compensation for performing the above services, except for a finder's fee where
no more is done than introducing the parties to one another. Persons working
under a broker are usually called salespersons and must also be licensed.

B. Listings
A listing agreement is the employment contract between the broker and the
principal (usually the seller), whereby the broker is authorized to solicit offers
to purchase the seller's property on his behalf in return for a fee if she is
successful in doing so. The listing agreement may be required to be in
writing. Listing agreements are:

1. **Open**—where the broker earns a commission only if she is the procuring
cause of a satisfactory offer;

2. **Exclusive Agency**—where a commission is earned even if the offer is
presented by some other broker;

3. **Exclusive Right to Sell**—where a commission is earned even if the offer
is obtained by some other broker or by the seller himself.

C. Ready, Willing and Able Purchaser

A broker generally earns a commission when she is the procuring cause of a ready, willing and able purchaser, i.e. one who makes an offer which matches what the seller has asked for or which is acceptable to the seller and is either unconditional or where conditions are subsequently satisfied. Entitlement to a commission may be postponed or made dependant upon close of sale either by provisions in the listing contract or by state law.

D. Duties

A broker has obligations pursuant to:

(1) *Contract.* She must perform any obligations which she has undertaken by virtue of the terms of her listing contract.

(2) *Agency.* She must show loyalty, integrity and good faith as an agent to her principal;

(3) *Malpractice.* She must meet the standards of due care expected of a professional in this field;

(4) *Licensing.* She must comply with the duties imposed upon her by virtue of her license.

E. Agency

A listing from the seller makes the broker his agent and may also make another broker cooperating under a multiple listing arrangement a subagent of the seller rather than an agent of the buyer, especially where both receive their commissions from the seller. A broker often works under a dual agency arrangement, representing both seller and buyer in the same transaction.

VIII. CONTRACT OF SALE
A. Enforcible Contract

A binding contract for the sale of land requires an intent to be bound and consideration. If one party is required to be "satisfied" with some provision of the contract, it may be illusory. The contract must be in writing and must describe the property, the price, and the parties, although the purchaser may indicate that title is to be taken by a "nominee." Part performance, consisting of the purchaser taking possession and (sometimes) paying part of the price or making improvements, may excuse the lack of the writing. A court will imply a reasonable time for performance if one is not specified in the contract.

B. Marketable Title

A purchaser is entitled to a marketable title, i.e., one which is free from any reasonable doubt as to validity and the existence of any encumbrances or defects. If the vendor owns less than he has contracted to convey, or if there are irregularities in his chain of title, or if the property is subject to an encumbrance, it is unmarketable. Land use ordinances and physical defects in the property do not affect title, and monetary encumbrances may be removed by utilizing a part of the purchaser's funds to satisfy them. If title is unmarketable at the time for closing, the purchaser may withdraw or may sometimes be granted specific performance with an abatement of the purchase price.

C. Equitable Conversion

Once a binding, specifically enforceable contract has been executed, the purchaser becomes the equitable owner of the property and the vendor holds legal title only as security for payment. Following this doctrine, many states hold that the purchaser thereafter takes the risk of innocent destruction of the premises. Other courts imply a provision in the contract that the purchaser will receive the property in the condition it was in when the contract was executed, thereby allocating the risk of loss to the vendor (or sometimes until the purchaser takes possession). The parties may independently insure themselves against risk of loss or may contract between themselves as to how the risk should be allocated.

D. Performance

The vendor performs by tendering a valid deed; the purchaser performs by paying the price. Once the contract has been performed, its provisions end and are replaced by provisions in the deed. However, the purchaser may have subsequent rights against the vendor by virtue of fraud or warranty doctrines.

E. Breach

Unless time is made of the essence, both parties have a reasonable time after the closing date in order to complete their performance. If either party fails to perform the contract, the other may terminate or sue for specific performance or damages.

IX. CONVEYANCES
A. Formal Requirements Of Deeds
1. Writing and Contents

In order to be effective, a deed must be signed by the grantor and must contain words indicating an intent to transfer title to the property. It must identify the grantee and adequately describe the property.

Parol evidence may resolve ambiguities in the description, and when there are internal inconsistencies, monuments prevail over courses and distances, which prevail over names and quantities. It is generally assumed that reference to a boundary with width is to its center. Boundary lines may change where a waterway is involved as the course of the waterway changes. Condominium boundaries include altitude as well as surface location and exclude the physical walls and floors, which are part of the common project rather than the unit conveyed.

Where neighbors relocate a common boundary orally, their agreement is upheld if it was acquiesced in and was the result of uncertainty or disagreement, but not where it arose from mistake or conscious intent to change or set the line.

It is not required that the grantee sign the deed, or that the signatures be notarized, or that the deed be recorded, or that there be consideration.

2.   Types of Deeds
A deed which contains no title covenants is a quitclaim deed. A warranty deed does contain such covenants. A grant deed contains some but not all of the possible covenants of title.

B.   Delivery
A deed passes title only when it is delivered i.e., when the grantor has manifested an intent that a completed legal act has occurred. If the grantor intends instead that title pass only in the future, there is no delivery (except where the deed transfers a future interest in the land and it is delivered with an unconditional present intent). In two party transactions, an attempted conditional delivery of a deed means either that there is no delivery or that title passes absolutely and without the condition. A grantor may effectuate a future or conditional transfer of title by employing an escrow agent and unconditionally delivering the deed to the escrow agent with instructions to deliver it to the grantee at the later time; in that case the second delivery relates back to the first. Title does not pass where the deed is not delivered, and where title has passed, a redelivery of the same deed back to the grantor does not cause title to be transferred back.

X.   PRIORITIES
A.   Priority Disputes
The common law principle of "first in time, first in right" has been replaced by the recording doctrine of protecting a bona fide purchaser. The prior grantee of a deed or other instrument may lose priority to a subsequent grantee if she fails to record. This rule permits potential purchasers of land to rely upon the chain of title as shown in the records.

B.   Recording Systems
1.   Recordable Instruments
Any instrument affecting title may be recorded, i.e. copied into the official records and indexed according to the names of the grantor and grantee or according to the location of the property. These indexes permit a title searcher to trace the title from its current holder back to the original source (through the Grantee Index) and then determine whether any owner impaired the title while holding it (through the Grantor Index).

2. Recording Acts
    The two most common kinds of recording acts are notice statutes, which protect any subsequent taker who is without notice of an unrecorded instrument, and notice-race statutes, which protect any subsequent taker without notice who also records first. Race statutes and period of grace statutes no longer play any significant role.

3. Value
    Recording acts only protect subsequent takers who have given value in reliance upon the records. Donees, unsecured creditors, judgment creditors, and persons who have merely promised to pay are not protected. Those who pay value (for a deed or a mortgage) are protected so long as it is more than nominal consideration. Execution of a negotiable note and cancellation of a prior debt generally qualify as paying value. Where only part of the price has been paid, the payor is given pro tanto protection. The purchaser at an execution sale is protected as a purchaser for value, although the jurisdictions are divided when that person is also the judgment creditor.

4. Notice
    Subsequent purchasers who have notice of a prior unrecorded transaction are not protected against it. This includes actual knowledge as well as constructive notice from the records. Misindexed documents and wild documents (those not linked up to any instrument in the chain of title) are generally not held to give notice. The jurisdictions are divided as to whether instruments which are recorded after the owner has parted with title, or before he has acquired title, or which relate to other property owned by him, give notice. Courts impose a duty to inquire on any purchaser confronted with suspicious information and impute to him such knowledge as a reasonable inquiry would produce. Thus, a purchaser may have a duty to investigate defectively recorded instruments, unrecorded instruments which are mentioned in recorded instruments, and rights of persons in possession of property (unless their possession is consistent with the record title, and they are not tenants).

XI. TITLE ASSURANCE
A. Title Covenants
1. Types of Deed
    A quitclaim deed contains no covenants of title. A grant deed may, by statute, have certain limited covenants of title implied in it. A warranty deed contains some or all of the six conventional covenants of title.

2. The Six Covenants
    The present covenants of title are covenant of seisin, covenant of good right to convey, and covenant against encumbrances. These assert that the grantor does have a title to transfer which is free of all

encumbrances, except those expressly or impliedly excluded. The future covenants are covenant of quiet enjoyment, covenant of warranty, and covenant of further assurances.

3.   Breach of Covenant
     The present covenants are breached at the moment the conveyance is made, if ever. The future covenants are breached only when the grantee is injured. Future covenants run with the land and may be enforced against the covenantor by a remote grantee. The measure of damages depends upon the covenant breached and may equal the amount paid for the property or the cost of removal or depreciation of market value caused by an encumbrance. An after-acquired title by the covenantor is held to inure to the benefit of the grantee.

B.   Title Insurance

A title insurance policy guarantees that its insured owns the title described in the policy, subject only to those defects described in the policy. The policy generally excludes claims against the title which exist because the insured was not a bona fide purchaser or which could have been ascertained from a physical inspection of the property, including boundaries. The policy does insure against the "off-record" risks of incompetency, forgery, and non-delivery as to any document in the chain of title. Where a title insurance company is liable, it may compensate the insured for the loss or may acquire the outstanding claim against the title or resist it in court.

XII. MORTGAGES

A mortgage is a security arrangement whereby the obligor agrees that if he fails to perform the obligation he has undertaken, the obligee may utilize the property which has been given as security.

A.   Documentation

The mortgage instrument is secondary to some other document (i.e., a promissory note) evidencing the primary obligation, for which the mortgage is given as security. It was originally drafted as the grant of a fee simple subject to condition subsequent (payment) to the mortgagee. It often appears now as a deed of trust or as some other financing arrangement.

B.   Foreclosure

Courts of equity permit the mortgagor to perform late, in order to avoid a forfeiture of his property. The mortgagee is entitled to go to court to establish a time limit for late performance and to have the security sold (or, previously, given to her directly) to satisfy the obligation. Any surplus from a foreclosure sale goes to the mortgagor; conversely the mortgagor may owe a deficiency judgment if the sale does not produce enough. If the rents have also been pledged, they may also be applied to the debt.

C.   Junior Mortgages
A junior mortgage is foreclosed and sold subject to the senior mortgage and is eliminated by a senior foreclosure sale. The junior mortgagee receives any surplus from the senior sale in preference to the mortgagor.

D.   Transfers
Property subject to a mortgage is transferred subject to that mortgage. The transferee may also assume the mortgage, thereby undertaking personal liability on the underlying obligation. A transfer of the note by the mortgagee carries the mortgage with it.

PART THREE: RIGHTS RELATING TO LAND

XIII. MISCELLANEOUS DOCTRINES RESPECTING LAND
A.   Water
   1.   Stream Water
      A riparian owner has an absolute right to draw off stream or lake water when there is no effect upon the flow or it is used solely for domestic purposes. If the flow is affected and the use is nondomestic, the natural flow doctrine permits downstream users to enjoin the diversion automatically, whereas the reasonable use doctrine balances the intended uses of both riparians in deciding this issue. The prior appropriation doctrine, in western states, grants permits to take water depending upon the time of application and the intended use.

   2.   Surface Water
      The common enemy rule permits landowners to create dams or channels in order to keep or get unwanted surface water off their land. The civil law rule prohibits lower owners from damming and upper owners from cutting channels, requiring both to let the water follow in its natural drainage path.

   3.   Ground Water
      The eastern rule is that overlying landowners own underground water absolutely. The western rule limits this by principles of reasonable use or correlative rights.

B.   Support
   1.   Lateral Support
      Neighbors whose excavations cause land to subside are liable regardless of negligence unless they can show that the land subsided only because of the additional weight of buildings erected on it. If there is liability, the jurisdictions are divided over whether or not this requires compensation for improvements on the land.

2.   Subjacent Support
     There is absolute liability for injury to land and buildings caused by the removal of support from excavation or other work conducted directly below the surface of the land.

3.   Modifications
     Landowners may agree that one will furnish additional support to another's building or, conversely, that no duty of support is owed. Some jurisdictions require excavators to shore up neighboring buildings.

C.   Freedom From Interference

1.   Trespass
     A trespass is an unprivileged intrusion upon land; it is actionable because it interferes with an owner's right to exclusive possession. Even without harm there is liability for at least nominal damages.

2.   Nuisance
     A nuisance is an unreasonable interference with the use and enjoyment of land. There is liability only where harm results. Determination of whether a nuisance exists requires a weighing of the utility of the acts of both parties, a comparison of the harm caused against the cost of correction, and a consideration of the nature of the locale.

D.   Airspace

1.   Rights
     Title and right to develop air space may be severed from surface rights. Generally the owner of the surface has the right to develop overhead.

2.   Invasions
     Commercial air flights in navigable air space are not actionable by property owners below. Under certain circumstances an overflight may create liability in trespass if it is too low, or in nuisance if it creates too much disturbance, or it may constitute a taking of property if the government is involved.

E.   Fixtures
Personal property becomes part of real property when it is affixed to land with an intention that it become a permanent part of land and it is adapted to the land. Where the same person owns both the land and the personalty, conversion to a fixture may be significant upon death, mortgaging, property taxation, or condemnation in eminent domain. Where the chattel is owned by someone other than the owner, this may lead to the transfer of title from one to the other.

F. Waste
The holder of a present possessory interest in land of less than a fee simple absolute owes a duty to holders of future interests and to concurrent owners not to do unreasonable harm to their interests, either by affirmative steps which damage the property or by the failure to make normal repairs to protect it from substantial deterioration.

XIV. LAND USE
A. Authority to Regulate
Land use is generally regulated by cities or counties pursuant to authorization from the state. Direct voter regulation through the initiative or referendum process is sometimes permitted.

B. Forms of Regulation
1. Planning
Land use regulation is frequently preceded by a plan developed by the local planning board. The plan consists of the community's goals and purposes, with regard to the physical development of the territory.

2. Zoning
A zoning ordinance sets forth the applicable restrictions for each zone; a zoning map designates the zoning category applicable to each parcel of land. Zoning divides property into use and height districts; it also regulates the size of lots and buildings by way of minimum floor space, minimum lot size, floor to area ratio, open space, and setback requirements. Cluster zoning permits the owner of several parcels to violate bulk requirements as to individual lots so long as the standards are satisfied by the aggregate project; planned unit development does the same with regard to use as well as density. A floating zone is one described in an ordinance but which is applied to a parcel of land only after application by an owner. A holding zone is intended to temporarily prohibit intensive use of the land while the community plans for the future.

Most zoning ordinances are cumulative, i.e., higher uses are permitted in lower classifications. They also generally include provisions for conditional uses or special exceptions—activities which may fit in many zone categories, but only after discretionary review and imposition of special conditions. They generally permit preexisting uses to continue as nonconforming uses, but may prohibit resumption after discontinuance, or enlargement, or may amortize such uses by permitting them to continue for only a limited number of years. Variances are given to property owners who would otherwise suffer unnecessary hardship because of special circumstances affecting their land. The legislative body of the locale may modify a zoning ordinance as to any particular parcel by amending the ordinance; contract or conditional rezoning involves such activity pursuant to a special agreement with the owner.

3. Subdivision Regulation

A community may require compliance with its demands before it will permit a subdivider to record a map of the subdivision. Such requirements originally included dedication of streets and construction of offsite improvements, but lately have been expanded to include dedication of land or payment of an in-lieu fee for parks, schools, etc.

4. Other Forms of Regulation

A community may control or manage growth by a moratorium or by limiting building permits based upon a point or quota system. It may preserve historic buildings or districts by prohibiting construction, reconstruction, or demolition of structures. It may regulate the size and placement of billboards, although its right to ban them totally is not entirely resolved. Also not fully resolved is the power of a community to delegate architectural approval to a design review board. Local agencies are generally required by federal or state environmental protection act to consider and to mitigate adverse environmental impacts created by projects for which their approval is required.

C. Judicial Review

1. Scope of Review

Legislative land use regulation is upheld if it bears a rational relationship to a permissible state objective; administrative activity requires substantial evidence to support it. Some courts reject the formal distinction between legislative and administrative action in favor of a test looking at the size of the parcel and the nature of the restriction or permit involved.

2. Judicial Standard

Courts may invalidate a land use regulation because it is not authorized by the state enabling act, involves an improper delegation of legislative power, is arbitrary, or was enacted or administered by improper procedures.

Constitutional doctrine may invalidate an ordinance when it violates the First Amendment (by overregulating signs, movie theatres, churches, etc. or intruding too far into family living arrangements). The Just Compensation clause of the Fifth Amendment may lead to invalidation where a regulation is so oppressive as to constitute a taking of the entire value of an owner's property. Equal Protection principles may be involved (either directly or by way of the general welfare requirement) to invalidate land use systems which exclude lower and middle income persons from residing in the community.

3.   Remedies
     A justly aggrieved property owner is usually denied any monetary
     recovery from the community and is instead limited to the remedy of
     invalidation.   In certain special situations, especially exclusionary zoning
     cases, site-specific relief may be ordered.

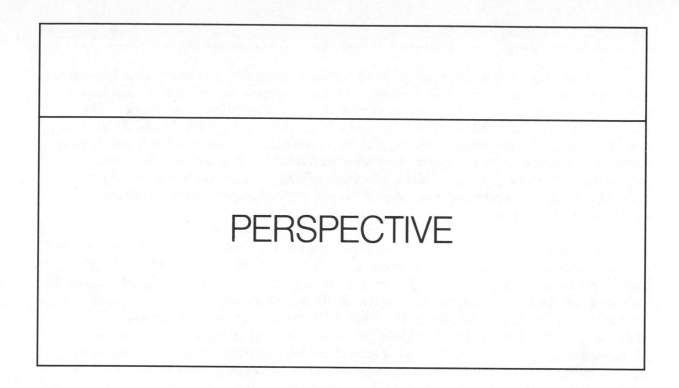

PERSPECTIVE

REAL PROPERTY

Real Property is a hard course. Probably, most law professors indulge the conceit that theirs is the hardest course in law school, but in the case of Property we seem to have the students on our side; the course usually wins unpopularity contests hands down. The casebook method most glaringly exposes its limitations here, because there is just not enough time to analyze all the cases, learn all the rules, cover all the history, apply all the concepts to real situations, and evaluate the results (socially, economically, jurisprudentially, or whatever). I know, from my own teaching and from talking to my colleagues in the field that all of us skip some cases, let some rules go unmentioned, omit some history, and permit many doctrines to pass by without applying or challenging them. (Of course, that never stops us from expecting our students to be competent in all of these respects on the exams.)

PROPERTY BOOKS

For years I have advised my students to utilize some of the existing outlines floating about. I would gladly recommend more scholarly texts to them if any of those grand old books had been kept current, but, sadly, that has not been the case. Tiffany, Burby, et al no longer fit a modern Property course; the American

Law of Property is also now out of date (besides being far too expensive for anyone except a law library); and the Restatement concentrates on all the wrong topics and is too often out of step with what the bar and the courts are doing. The student outlines constitute almost the only texts staying current in the field, but too often they demonstrate their origins by concentrating too much on what their authors happened to learn from their own individual professors in their own particular Property courses. (Since the first edition of this book was written, a new hornbook has appeared and should be studied whenever more extensive coverage is desired.)

So I have written this outline. It does not conform to just the course I teach; it includes many doctrines which I never mention in my class but I know do get talked about in other schools. It attempts to state all of the rules which might be required wherever the course is taught. It differs from my Nutshell on Real Property in that it constitutes a far more exhaustive survey of the field. But there is a cost. Unlike the Nutshell, precious little space is devoted to explaining or attempting to furnish a rational foundation for many concepts or to analyzing or criticizing them. There are very few citations to cases or law reviews. The text is filled with weasel-words, such as "some courts hold" or "the rule is modified by statute in some jurisdictions."

Consequently, do not expect to be able to pass a Property exam just by reading this book. To accomplish that you will have to read your casebook, brief the cases, go to class (and participate and take notes), and bandy the issues about in your study group. If some particular point still eludes or troubles you, you will have to go to someone or something more scholarly than the oversimplifications contained here.

Notwithstanding, I think that a book like this can still be helpful, as long as it is properly and cautiously used. It can be worthwhile in assisting you in organizing matters after you have finished covering some topic in class. You can use it to double check that you have all of the rules straight and in their proper order in your own summary. (But don't trust the book whenever your professors say the rule is the other way or the topic is to be organized differently. They grade your exams; I don't.)

PROPERTY PROFESSORS

Another reason why Property is so difficult—and one which cannot be eliminated by any textbook—is that the field consists of so many different (and arguably unrelated) topics. No two Property professors agree as to what should be left in or out of the course, or how it should be taught. Consequently you should, as quickly as possible, figure out the approach being followed by your own instructor and prepare yourself accordingly.

Some professors see Property as little more than a collection of disparate rules, held together only by the fact that they all relate to land. Adverse possession is adverse possession and has little to do with landlord and tenant or zoning. If your course is conducted in this atomistic fashion, then the biggest mistake you can make is to get the rules right but put them in the wrong universes. The rules governing a purchaser's right to marketable title look awfully much like those controlling a grantee's remedies under title covenants in the deed or under a policy of title insurance, except that they aren't exactly the same and they do operate differently. A right rule given in the wrong context on an exam is a wrong answer.

Other professors see Property as linked together by history, believing that the best way to understand how the rules work is to know how they came about in the first place. Names and dates become more important. Your answers on exams should also then go more deeply into the background of a rule as a vehicle for determining how it ought to apply in the hypothetical posed.

More recently, economics has appeared as an organizing principle for the field. Questions of efficiency (and equity) tend to pervade discussion of the utility of the rules. You may not have to understand what "Pareto optimality" is, but you should be able to make at least a primitive cost-benefit analysis of the application of a rule in a given context.

Finally, many professors hold some particular value or values especially dearly. If class discussion tends to frequently revert to, e.g., "protecting the environment," "housing the poor" or even "deconstructing the text" or "telling stories" then it is only common sense to look out for such issues on an exam (or get the issues or slogans into the answers anyway).

MY APPROACH

For me, all of the above approaches are appealing. Land is a wonderfully interesting and unique thing, and is hardly surprising that we have so many special rules about it. It has played different roles in our society at different times, depending on which of its characteristics was most important to people at the time. Originally, the fact that it was a durable and stable asset led to its being prized as a way for preserving the wealth already acquired. Rich people owned land and wanted to make sure that when they died their families were protected and their fortunes weren't squandered. It is hardly surprising that a society so concerned would develop an elaborate system of estates to account for all tastes. On the other hand, it is also not surprising that the rapid tempo of modern times, the dwindling of concern about the future and the broadening of legal interest to cover the less well-off have tended to reduce the significance of this approach to law. Also there is the fact that the old rules of estates did get pretty settled and do work rather well, so that computers can write wills on their own now.   These parts of Property today make sense only from an historical approach.

With the population booms and industrialization of this century, the adaptability of land has become more important than its durability.   Land is now a commodity which people develop and market.   Big segments of the population make their living as contractors, developers, brokers, landlords, speculators, etc.   The very rich still make their money in oil or banking, but most of the rest of us hope to make our modest killings in real estate—even if it is only the single family house we have owned throughout the inflation.   All this might be better understood "capitalistically" rather than historically, with a concentration on the transactional elements of real estate—buying, selling, building, leasing, and borrowing.

Finally, and only recently, the scarcity and vulnerability of land have become of real concern to many people.   Land is a vanishing resource which must be protected, rather than a commodity which can be abused at will.   The environmentalists worry about dwindling irreplaceable assets;   the agronomists bemoan the disappearance of prime agricultural land;   the preservationists want to save historic structures and places;   housing advocates worry about how and where the poor will live;   and city planners wonder how to conserve the sometimes nostalgic amenities of urban life.   Land use, the environment and economics have gradually insinuated their way into all of our Property courses and we are forced to think about what our real values are: can we make the pie bigger, cut it up more fairly, and—at the same time—preserve it for our children to savor?

THIS BOOK

In addition to the basic text, there are several other components of this book.   The Capsule Outline is for a last minute review, so you can be sure that you haven't forgotten anything really important and that all the rules are in the right places.   The Glossary is to spare you from running to a law dictionary when you come across the sundry technical and unfamiliar words real estate lawyers thrive on;   I also suggest that you use it as another form of review.   The Review Questions at the end of each chapter are for you to see if you can apply the rules in the chapters to situations which are different from the examples given in the text;   the true-false format is unimportant and you can change them into little essay questions if you prefer.   The Multistate Questions at the end of the book are to give you an opportunity to convert your knowledge into the peculiar form which the bar examiners admire;   they are also an attempt by me to juxtapose various topics of this book under individual questions to help you understand the interrelationships involved.   The full-length essay questions accompanying them are also designed to force you to tie the course together in more complicated contexts.

(A note on the cases mentioned in this text.   Only where a doctrine is inextricably related to a case—e.g., the Rule in Shelley's Case—have I referred to the case.

Even then I have given only the year and not the full citation, on the assumption that any such case will be more fully cited in your casebook.)

GRATITUDE

Finally, I want to express my appreciation to Christine Tour-Sarkíssian for putting the first edition of this book together, and to James F. Donaghue and Kelly Ann McMeekin for doing the same with this second edition.

*

PART ONE

INTERESTS IN LAND

Analysis

ADVERSE POSSESSION

Analysis

One who is in actual, open and notorious, continuous, exclusive, uninterrupted, and hostile possession of another's land for the requisite period of time will acquire title to that land by virtue of the running of the statute of limitations against the owner's cause of action in ejectment.

A. BACKGROUND

Questions of adverse possession arise when a person in possession of real property turns out either to lack good title to it or to have a title to the property which is defective or insufficient. Because of the problems in the possessor's title, there will be some other person who has "record title." The doctrine of adverse possession may be employed in these cases to allow the possessor to prevail against the record title holder. It is misleading to think of an adverse possessor as a squatter out to steal another's land; in most cases he is an innocent person with an honorable claim to the land. (In this section, masculine pronouns refer to the adverse possessor and feminine pronouns designate the holder of record title. In the following examples, Oona is the owner, and Paul is the possessor. All possessions are nonconsensual.)

Examples: (1) Paul took possession of property under a deed from Oona, the owner, which was defectively executed. Because of the defect, record title remains in Oona. However, if Paul continues in possession long enough, he may acquire title (and thereby effectively cure the defect) by adverse possession. Adverse possession in this case spares him the necessity of having to independently cure the defect in the deed.

(2) Paul purchases lot 1 but moves, by mistake, onto lot 2 and spends considerable money erecting a residence on it. If he resides on lot 2 long enough, he may acquire title to it (and thereby save his residence) by adverse possession.

(3) Paul, owner of lot 1, has mistakenly built his fence so as to encroach one foot onto Oona's property and has built valuable improvements on the property up to the fence. He may, after enough time, acquire title by adverse possession to the strip which he has improved but did not own.

(4) Paul has no title or right to the property but he comes on it and resides there, hoping to get away with this. If he continues it long enough, he may acquire title by adverse possession. This "squatter" case is probably the least common of the adverse possession situations.

B. EJECTMENT AND THE STATUTE OF LIMITATIONS

1. STATUS OF A WRONGFUL POSSESSOR
A person in wrongful possession of land owned by another has the following rights and liabilities:

a. The owner may bring ejectment against him (see below);

b. No other person who is not an owner, may bring ejectment against him ("the plaintiff must prevail on the strength of his own title, not upon a weakness in the defendant's title");

c. He may bring ejectment against any other person who subsequently intrudes upon his possession ("possession is 9/10ths of the law").

2. EJECTMENT
An owner of land has a cause of action in ejectment against anyone wrongly possessing her land. A plaintiff in ejectment must not only show that the defendant is a wrongful possessor but must also prove that she has a right to possession. If the plaintiff prevails, the defendant will be removed from possession and her own possession will be restored.

3. STATUTE OF LIMITATIONS
As with all causes of action, ejectment is subject to a statute of limitations. The cause of action for ejectment commences when the defendant takes wrongful possession, and it expires upon the completion of the appropriate statute of limitations. Once the statute has run, the owner loses her right to eject the possessor. Since no one else has a superior possessory claim, the possessor is now immune from any ejectment action and will be treated as an owner against the world. Although technically all that has happened is that the former owner's cause of action in ejectment is barred by the statute of limitations, the effect is as if the adverse possessor obtained a decree of quiet title against the former owner. He is thereafter functionally treated as owner, even though he lacks paper title. (Who would you buy from? Although there is no recorded title in his name, the principle of constructive notice requires that purchasers investigate the claims of those in possession.) His right of possession is superior to all the world. There is no one who may lawfully eject him, while he, on the other hand, may bring ejectment against anyone who takes possession of the property without his permission. (Note that the term adverse possession refers both to the period during which the statute of limitations remains open and to the period following the running of the statute. Adverse possessor similarly refers to a possessor during the running of the statute and to a possessor who has perfected his adverse possession by the running of the statute of limitations. Effective or successful indicates that the period of the statute of limitations has been completed, and the adverse possession has been accomplished.)

Example: Paul moved onto land which was vacant but which he did not own. He is subject to an ejectment action by Oona, the true owner of the land, but no other persons can sue to remove him merely by saying he is not the owner. (His lack of title does not entitle any stranger to oust him or take possession from him.) Conversely, if any stranger does dispossess Paul, He may bring an ejection action against the stranger, since Paul, as a prior possessor, has a better "title" to the property than does the stranger. Once Oona's cause of action in ejectment expires, she joins the rest of the world in an inability to eject Paul from the property.

C.   DURATION

An adverse possession must endure for the entire period of the statute of limitations, which varies by jurisdiction from five to twenty-five years. In some states, payment of taxes or taking under official deed or color of title by the possessor may shorten the time period required. (Color of title is discussed below.)

1.   CHARACTERISTICS OF THE DURATION
a.   Continuous
An adverse possession must be continuous, i.e., it must be maintained as regularly as circumstances demand. If the wrongful possession was so sporadic as to amount merely to occasional disconnected trespasses rather than to an actual continuous possession, no title by adverse possession arises. However, continuous does not mean constant; regular though limited activity may be sufficient. Behavior appropriate for an average owner of this type of property is usually deemed continuous.

Examples: (1) Every several months Paul camps overnight on Oona's property. Even though he has done so for over thirty years, the activity is too irregular and infrequent to give him a title by adverse possession.

(2) Paul spends eight months of every year residing on the mountain property, leaving it only when winter snows force him to lower elevations. Despite these absences, his possession may be regarded as sufficiently continuous to constitute an adverse possession, since it is an appropriate and normal usage in the environment.

1)   Abandonment
A possession is not continuous where the occupant abandons the property, even if he subsequently returns and repossesses it. If the possessor leaves the property without an intent to return, the statute

of limitations stops running; if he does later return, the statutory period starts afresh and does not continue from its previous point.

2) Prescriptive Easements
It is possible for continuous but limited use of the property to create a prescriptive easement even though not amounting to an adverse possession. Limited use of the property may fail to qualify as adverse possession where a court concludes that it does not constitute an ordinary use of the property; nevertheless, the fact that such wrongful activity has occurred for a long enough time may entitle the person to claim a prescriptive easement to continue those particular acts. Utilization of such a theory may also excuse the user from the need to comply with some other elements required by the doctrine of adverse possession.

Example: Paul grazed his cattle on Oona's property for the month of May every year. This was regarded as insufficient to give him title to it because the land was capable of considerably greater use, but it may entitle him to a prescriptive easement to graze in May every year thereafter. He may also be excused from showing that he paid taxes on the property in the past, even though this would be required were he to claim as an adverse possessor.

b. Uninterrupted
An adverse possession must be uninterrupted. There can be no other person (including the owner) holding possession as against the adverse possessor during the statutory period.

1) Interruptions by Third Persons
If a third person dispossesses the former possessor, then the record owner acquires a (new) cause of action in ejectment against that person (and subject to a new statutory limitations period), but no longer has a cause of action against the former possessor; the clock will resume running in favor of the former possessor only when and if he successfully recovers back his possession from the subsequent intruder.

Examples: (1) During the period a stranger took possession of the property for six months without consent of Paul and then voluntarily left. Paul's adverse possession has been interrupted, and in order to perfect his claim now, his time period must start all over again after he reenters.

(2) During the period Paul rented the property to a tenant for six months. His possession is uninterrupted because his tenant possessed under him, not against him.

During the period, Paul was ousted by a stranger but successfully sued the stranger and recovered possession. His possession was probably not interrupted since at all times he has acted like an owner, i.e., suing to get back his property. It may even be possible, under the circumstances, for him to include the stranger's time of possession for his own credit, much as in the previous example.

2) Interruptions by the Owner
    An owner may interrupt an adverse possession either by an entry or by litigation.

    a) Entry
        An open and notorious entry and retaking of possession by the owner constitutes an interruption of the exclusive possession of the adverse possessor and stops the running of the statute of limitations. (It is not required that the owner occupy exclusively, or continuously, since her claim is based upon her title, not upon a perfected adverse possession.) *Possession by the owner that is not hostile to the adverse possessor does not constitute an interruption of it.* (Exclusiveness and hostility are discussed below.) Continuous and uninterrupted are often used interchangeably by courts; the text interchanges them as required to give a sensible meaning.

        Examples: (1) Paul and Oona mistakenly lived in each others' house, and both frequently visited each other. Their respective claims of adverse possession would not be defeated by the visits between them, since such entries were permissive and did not interrupt the possessor rights each claimed. (I.e., if Oona were asked to explain what she were doing next door, she would attribute her presence there to Paul's invitation, not to any claim of right she had.)

        (2) Oona delivered a deed to the property to Paul, who then leased it back to her and she stayed in possession of the property under her lease. Her deed was not properly signed and, therefore, was invalid. Paul may, however, qualify as an adverse possessor against Oona if she continued as a tenant

for a long enough time. Her possession under the lease was under Paul, not against him. Therefore it did not interrupt his possession but in fact constitutes the very basis of it.

b) Litigation
An ejectment action, brought to completion, will interrupt an adverse possession (as of the date of its filing). However, acts short of that do not work an interruption, (such as posting a no-trespassing sign, asking the possessor to leave, or filing a complaint without following it up).

2. COMBINING POSSESSORY PERIODS: TACKING AND PRIVITY
An adverse possessor may include the possession of previous possessors and add these to his own time period if they were in privity with him. The linking together of two or more time periods is characterized as tacking. Each such period must, of course, meet all of the general qualifications of adverse possession (e.g., open, notorious, etc.).

a. Privity
There is privity between successive possessors when the possession of the second is derived from or explained by that of the first, rather than being hostile to or independent of it.

Examples: (1) The property was possessed by Paul's mother until she died. She purported to devise the property to him and he then took possession. He may tack the time of her possession onto his own time and claim the combined number of years, if either period alone is inadequate.

(2) Paul purchased the property from his predecessor possessor and thereupon took possession. He may tack his predecessor's possession onto his own. It does not matter that the deed was ineffective to pass any real title (the predecessor was not an owner), since it is privity of possession, not title, which is being considered. (For the same reason, it is irrelevant that the will was ineffective to pass any real title in the previous example.)

(3) The property was possessed by a stranger who was then dispossessed by Paul. The prior possession may not be tacked on since there was no privity between the two possessors. Here, the statute stopped running once the first possessor left and a new period started as to Paul when he entered. Paul may be subject to an action in ejectment by either the

previous possessor or by the record owner, both actions being subject to the statute of limitations.

b.   Boundary Strips

If it is a boundary strip which is being claimed by adverse possession, there may be privity between the successive parties even though their deeds all describe the basic plot and do not include the strip, so long as all parties have actually possessed the strip and intended to convey it, along with the basic parcel, by the deeds.

Example: Paul's predecessor erected a fence 10 feet north of the true lot line and possessed up to it for a number of years. He then conveyed his entire lot to Paul, copying the description of boundary lines contained in his own deed, and Paul possessed up to the fence for several years. Paul may tack the two possessions together even though the deed to him does not include the 10 foot strip.

3.   FACTORS WHICH EXTEND THE REQUIRED TIME
a.   Future Interests

An adverse possession is effective only when a cause of action in ejectment has become barred. Since holders of future interests generally cannot sue in ejectment until their interests become possessory, no adverse possession can even commence against them until that time.

Examples: (1) Oona died, leaving the property to her aunt for life and then to her daughter, i.e., aunt has a life estate, and daughter has a future interest—a remainder. Thereafter, during the aunt's life, Paul entered and remained on the property for the statutory period of time. This gave him title to a life estate (measured by the aunt's life) but not the fee simple. Until the aunt dies, the daughter has no right to possess, cannot bring ejectment against Paul, and is therefore not barred by the statute of limitations. Adverse possession is effective against the daughter only when the statute of limitations runs as against her own claim to possession, which will require the full statutory period after the aunt's death.

(2) Oona leased her property to a tenant for 14 years. One year later, Paul entered. Under a 10 year statute of limitations, he will acquire adverse possession of the leasehold in 10 years, but he will only thereby acquire the remainder of the tenant's leasehold estate (i.e., three more years). He will not become a successful adverse possessor as against Oona unless he continues to possess the property for at least 10 years after the leasehold expires. (Expiration of the

leasehold might be accelerated if the lease entitled Oona to receive periodic rent, rent was not paid, and Oona terminated the leasehold as a result. In that case adverse possession would commence against Oona as of the date of termination of the leasehold.)

b. Acts by Owner After Possession Commences
Acts unrelated to the possession which are undertaken by an owner after an adverse possession has commenced do not extend the statutory period.

> ***Example:*** After Paul had entered, Oona leased out the property (or sold it, or died). The time period required of Paul is not thereby extended. Oona's tenant (or grantee, or heir) must sue him within the time left under the statute of limitations, starting from his original wrongful entry. (What has really been transferred from Oona is her cause of action in ejectment with its remaining time period.)

c. Disabilities
If the owner is under a disability at the time the adverse possession commences, the period is extended. The typical disabilities which prolong the time to sue are insanity, minority, and imprisonment. Some statutes allow the owner the full, original time period after the disability ends; others provide some shorter, additional period for suit following termination of the disability.

> ***Examples:*** (1) Oona was insane (or a minor or in prison) when Paul entered the property and she did not recover her sanity (or gain majority or freedom from incarceration) until three years later. The time needed to acquire adverse possession may be extended three years on the ground that the statute did not begin to run until the disability ended.
>
> (2) Oona was both insane and a minor when Paul entered. The statute of limitations will start running only when she both recovers her sanity and comes of age. When there is double preexisting disability, both aspects must be removed before the time starts to run.
>
> (3) Oona became insane after Paul entered. The time period is not extended; subsequent disabilities do not affect the statute.

D. POSSESSION

There must be real possession by the adverse possessor. Nonpossessory activities (such as would not subject the defendant to liability in ejectment) will never ripen into an adverse possession. A series of characteristics is required of any possession claimed to be adverse.

1. OPEN AND NOTORIOUS

The possessor must act in a sufficiently public way towards the property such as to warn any reasonably diligent owner, checking her property, that someone else is there. Recordation is not required. If the possessor is in open and notorious possession of the property, lack of actual knowledge by the owner of that fact is no defense.

a. Effect on Possessor

The above rule protects the typical adverse possessor who is unaware that he does not own the property he possesses, so long as his possession of it is sufficiently overt. He is not required to notify the owner of his claim when he does not know in the first place that his title is defective and that someone else is really the owner.

b. Effect on Owner

The above rule compels an owner of property to make periodic inspections of her property, on pain of losing it to an adverse possessor. *A search of the records is not enough, since adverse possession does not depend upon recordation.* Presumably, an adverse possession which is open and notorious will be noticed by any owner taking the trouble to visit her land. This rule may be subject to an exception for small encroachments, which only a survey would reveal. However, the effect of such an exception is to eliminate the security existing owners (and new purchasers) have in knowing that what they see is what they own, if enough time has passed.

2. ACTUAL

An adverse possessor must actually possess the property. This does not mean constant presence but it does require some activity on the land and it is not satisfied by mere claims to it made from afar. Ordinary activities upon land generally constitute an actual possession.

Examples: (1) For over 30 years, Oona's neighbor, Paul, has (wrongly) asserted that the driveway to her garage is on his property; however, he has never made any use of the driveway or even stepped on it during this time. Any claim of adverse possession by him will fail, since his statements are no substitute for actual possession.

(2) For over 30 years, Paul has farmed the five acre parcel adjacent to his house, believing that it was his. This may be enough to give him adverse possession of that parcel, even though he has never lived on it, constructed any improvements upon it, or enclosed it. Farming may be an appropriate possessory activity under the circumstances.

a.   The Extent of Possession
Absent color of title (discussed below), an adverse possessor obtains title only to that property actually possessed by him.

Example: Paul entered onto an entirely unoccupied 40 acre tract; he built a house and improvements on one acre, cleared five more acres for farming, and enclosed an additional 10 acres for grazing his livestock; he only occasionally walked over the remaining 24 acres. Under the circumstances he had actual possession of only 16 acres and will acquire title to only that much (assuming that a trier of fact finds that improving, cultivating, and enclosing are all appropriate possessory acts under the circumstances).

b.   Constructive Possession
An adverse possessor who enters under a color of title may acquire adverse possession to the entire tract described in his document even though he may have actually possessed only a part of the property described in it.

1)   Color of Title
A document which purports to convey title to property but fails to actually do so constitutes a color of title to the property described therein. A void deed is a typical example of color of title. (If the deed were valid, the grantee would be an owner rather than an adverse possessor.)

Example: The same as the previous example (with Paul living, farming, and grazing only a part of the tract), except that he did so under a void deed to the entire 40 acres. If the 40 acres were owned by one person and constituted a single, physically discrete tract, there is constructive adverse possession of the entire parcel. If the 40 acres consist of two parcels divided by a stream, possession of one side of the stream might not amount to possession of the other side.

2)   Against Remote Owners
There is no constructive possession to any part of the property owned by a third party unless some part of that person's property is also actually adversely possessed.

Example: The same as the previous example, except that four of the unused 24 acres are owned by a third party. Here, Paul may claim actual possession of (the same) 16 acres and constructive possession of 20 more acres, but the four acres owned separately are outside his claim. It would require actual possession of some part of those four acres to support a claim of constructive possession of the balance. (The owner of the four acres has never had a cause of action in ejectment against Paul, and therefore the statute of limitations has not run.)

c.   Special Possessory Acts
In some jurisdictions, special acts of possession may be required in certain cases, e.g., in California, if there is no color of title, an adverse possessor must enclose, improve or cultivate the land.

1)   Taxes
Many jurisdictions require an adverse possessor to pay the property taxes due on the land during the possessory period, or provide that a longer period of possession is needed where such taxes have not been paid.

3.   EXCLUSIVE
An adverse possessor must have permitted no one else to possess the property adversely to him, i.e., without his permission. A person who does not attempt to exclude others is not regarded as a possessor of property. Exclusivity is thus one way of determining that the occupant was truly a possessor of the property and not just a casual trespasser.

Examples: (1) During the period of claimed adverse possession, strangers frequently possessed parts of the property without Paul's consent and he did not try to remove them. Paul will not succeed in his claim of adverse possession, since his possession was not exclusive.

(2) During the period of claimed adverse possession, Paul had many visitors, including overnight guests. Despite the presence of these other persons, his possession has still been exclusive since none of them were there without his consent. They were in possession under him rather than against him.

(3) During the period of claimed adverse possession, Paul and his wife were the only persons to possess the property, believing that they had purchased it from X. Together, they have been in exclusive possession, and will hold title together as tenants in common (most likely).

4.   ADVERSE; HOSTILE
The possession must not be one resulting from the owner's permission; it must be such as will warn the owner of an actionable claim and entitle her to begin ejectment against the possessor. The basic meaning of adverse is nonpermissive; it does not refer to the subjective mental states of owner or possessor and does not imply that there must be animosity between them. A person who occupies another's property without consent is legally adverse and hostile to the owner in the sense that she may bring ejectment against him. However, a few jurisdictions do also include a subjective component.

Example: Because of a mix-up, Paul moved onto Oona's property, and Oona moved onto Paul's property, and both built houses on the lots they possessed. Each should be entitled to claim adverse possession against the other (after sufficient time) despite the fact that both were unaware of the mistake and maintained cordial relations throughout the entire time period (even if invited into the other's house).

a.   Permissive Possession
One holding possession by virtue of the permission (actual or constructive) of the owner is not adverse to her. Where an owner has no cause of action, there is no running of the statute of limitations against her.

1)   Tenants
A tenant possesses land by virtue of the permission of the landlord. *Possession by a tenant is not adverse to the landlord.* A tenant possessing under a forty year lease will not thereby gain title to the property by adverse possession.

2)   Joint Tenants and Tenants in Common
All co-owners of property are entitled to possess the entire parcel. (They have "unity of possession," i.e., undivided rights of possession to the whole.) Thus, no one cotenant may object to the possession of another cotenant. Therefore, *the possession of any one cotenant is not adverse to the other cotenant, since she could not bring ejectment against the possessor.* Co-ownership is covered in Chapter III.

3)   Ouster
A possession begun permissively may become adverse if the possessor asserts a right to possess independent of/or against the owner and makes the owner aware of this change.

Examples: (1) Paul, tenant under a lease for the past 25 years notified Oona that he no longer regarded her as his landlord and would not pay any further rent.   Until then Paul's possession had been permissive rather than adverse to Oona and no statute had run.   But after he repudiated his tenancy, he became adverse to her.   She must bring ejectment against him within the appropriate time or lose her title.

(2) Paul and Oona are tenants in common (or joint tenants), but Oona has resided in another city for the past 25 years.   Paul wrote Oona telling her that she was no longer welcome to come on the property.   Paul has now ousted Oona, creating a cause of action for ejectment.   Prior to the letter, the sole possession of Paul was not actionable since he was, as a co-owner, entitled to possess all or part of the property.   (Oona had a similar possessory right, but her failure to exercise it had no effect on either Paul's possessory right or on her own possessory right in the future.)   Once Paul excluded Oona from the property, he interfered with her possessory right, and she must bring an ejectment action against him or risk losing her ownership if she does not.

4)   Notice of Ouster
It is generally required that the owner have notice of the ouster before it will be effective to start the running of the statute of limitations.   Since the fact of possession in these cases is not, by itself, sufficient to warn the owner of an adverse claim, some knowledge by her over and above the openness and notoriety of the possession of itself is required.

b.   **State of Mind**
Most courts require no particular state of mind by an adverse possessor; they treat adverse possession as an objective condition.   But some require that the adverse possessor know the property is not his, and a few others require, instead, that he believe that he is the owner.   These jurisdictions give a subjective significance to the requirement of hostility.

1) Boundary Disputes
The issue of hostility as objective or subjective is most frequently raised in boundary dispute cases where one neighbor's fence has encroached on the other's property.

Examples: (1) Paul's fence has encroached for 30 years on Oona's property, and Paul has known it. The majority hold that he has gained title by adverse possession of the encroaching strip despite his wrongful state of mind, because Oona has always had the opportunity to bring ejectment. But a minority hold that "title cannot be acquired by larceny."

(2) Paul's fence has encroached for 30 years on Oona's property, but Paul always believed that the fence was on the true line. The majority hold that he has gained title by adverse possession because Oona still could have brought ejectment despite his innocent intent. But a minority hold that his mistake robs his possession of the requisite hostility since he presumably "did not intend to claim what he did not own."

E. EFFECT

1. TITLE AND IMMUNITY
By virtue of the operation of the statute of limitations against the owner, an adverse possessor acquires a new, independent title to the property. It is not a derivative title, such as he would have if the owner had conveyed the property to him. It is a new title, created by the fact that no one any longer has standing to eject him. This title relates back in time to his original entry and thus also insulates him from any liability for recent trespasses, which would otherwise not be barred by the statute.

a. Marketability
The title obtained by an adverse possessor may not be marketable as that word is used in vendor-purchaser situations, since it is not discoverable from the records, and may subject a subsequent purchaser to litigation at a later time. The adverse possessor may be required to obtain and record a quiet title decree before he is able to tender a marketable title to a prospective purchaser. Marketable title is discussed in Chapter VIII.

Example: After Paul had been in open, notorious, continuous, etc., possession for over 30 years, he signed a contract to sell the property to Betty. Betty made a title search, discovered that Paul was not the record owner and notified him of her intent to withdraw from the contract. Paul offered to obtain affidavits from the neighbors as to the nature and duration of his adverse possession. However, he probably cannot compel Betty to purchase, even with this documentation, since there is no way to guarantee that if Oona does later make a claim, these papers will be effective against her. She is not bound by litigation between Paul and Betty, in which she was not a party, and she may have various defenses to the adverse possession, e.g., a disability extending the statute of limitations.

2. NONPOSSESSORY INTERESTS

Adverse possession does not defeat nonpossessory interests of third parties to the property unless the possession is actually adverse to those interests. The holder of a nonpossessory interest in land has no cause of action until some actual interference occurs; thus, an adverse possession does not, by itself, necessarily generate a cause of action in such a case.

Example: Third persons hold right of way easements and covenants imposing building heights limitations on the property. If Paul did not stop these persons from using the rights-of-way or did not build above the height limit during his possessory period, his title by adverse possession is subject to their easements and covenants.

3. GOVERNMENT CLAIMS

Adverse possession is not effective against governmental entities, with regard either to claims of title or to claims against nonpossessory governmental interests. The public's rights cannot be impaired by the failure of officials to act in a timely fashion.

Examples: (1) Paul possessed a parcel of land in the city park for a long enough time to qualify as an adverse possessor. Even though all of the requirements of adverse possession may have been met, he will not acquire any title, since public land is involved. (Lazy or corrupt officials cannot give away the government's land.)

(2) Paul successfully adversely possessed Oona's property and erected a structure which exceeded the height limits imposed on it by both restrictive covenants and the local zoning ordinance. Although he may acquire title free and clear of all restrictive covenants affecting the property (if he was adverse to them), he does not hold it free of the zoning restrictions upon use of the land. Zoning is covered in Chapter XIV.

F. REVIEW QUESTIONS

1. T or F Paul was in possession of land until Rachel ousted him. In Paul's action for ejectment against Rachel, she raised the defense that Paul has no valid title to the land because it was owned by Oona. The defense is good.

2. T or F Paul owned lot 1 and adversely possessed a 10 foot strip encroaching onto lot 2 (believing that the strip was part of his property). He then conveyed his property to Sam by a deed which only described lot 1, but Paul and Sam both believed that the strip was included in the description. Sam may tack on Paul's former possession to his own to accumulate the years necessary to satisfy the statute of limitations.

3. T or F Paul entered onto Oona's property in 1970 and commenced adverse possession. In 1975, Oona conveyed her property to Sue. Under a 10 year statute of limitations, Sue has until 1985 to sue.

4. T or F Paul adversely possessed Oona's property for 5 years. Then Rachel obtained a judgment against Paul and conducted an execution sale of this land, purchased it herself, and took possession. If Rachel remains in possession herself for 6 years, she will have perfected adverse possession as against Oona under a 10 year statute of limitations.

5. T or F Paul adversely possessed Oona's property for 30 years, which was long enough to give him title to it by adverse possession. The next year, Paul left the property. Oona may reclaim the property.

6. T or F Paul adversely possessed Oona's property for 10 years, which was enough under a 10 year statute of limitations to give him title to it by adverse possession. Nevertheless, in the 11th year, Oona sued for damages for trespass by Paul for his activities in his 10th year of possession. Oona prevails.

*

II

ESTATES IN LAND

Analysis

A. PRESENT ESTATES

1. PRESENT ESTATES VS FUTURE INTERESTS
A person may have an interest in land which gives her an immediate right to possess the land, or may instead have some form of ownership right which is postponed until a later time. In this second situation, the law treats the person as having a future interest in land: the interest is owned in the present, but will not be enjoyed until the future. *A present estate, on the other hand, is subject to immediate enjoyment.* (Feminine pronouns are used in this chapter to indicate the first grantee, or person who gets; masculine pronouns indicate the grantor, or person who gives, and subsequent grantees, i.e., those who get later. Assume the title is transferred through a deed.)

> *Example:* "Owner gives to Ann for life and then to Bob." Ann got a present estate in land; she may enter upon and use the property immediately. Bob gets a future interest; he does (presently) own an interest in this property, but he will not enjoy it until a later time.

2. TRADITIONAL VS NOVEL ESTATES IN LAND
The common law permitted only a limited number of types of estates in land to be created. Attempts by parties to create interests in property which did not fall within one of the permissible categories were rejected by the courts. Those which are described in this chapter were basically the only allowable forms of estate at common law.

3. FREEHOLD VS NONFREEHOLD ESTATES
The common law distinguished between freehold estates, which had no ascertainable termination date, and nonfreehold estates, whose termination date could be calculated. *The holder of a freehold estate was said to have seisin and was the one who owed the important feudal services to the lord. A nonfreeholder was one who had possession of the land but not seisin; the seisin in such a case was in the person under whom the nonfreeholder held.*

4. THE FREEHOLD ESTATES
All of the present estates in land (freehold and nonfreehold) may be classified according to their duration, i.e., when and how they end. They are listed below in order of greater to lesser duration. All of the freehold estates have in common the lack of any ascertainable termination date, i.e. it is not calculable in advance precisely when they will end.

  a. The Fee Simple
  This estate has the greatest potential duration of any form of interest in the common law system. It is inheritable by heirs of the owner, and therefore will endure so long as the then current owner dies with heirs; consequently it is potentially infinite.

b.   The Fee Tail
This was the next most enduring common law estate. It was inheritable by issue of the then current owner, but not by collateral heirs; children would take, but not parents, nephews, aunts, etc. Because of this restricted form of inheritability, its duration was potentially shorter than that of the fee simple.

1)   Modern Status
Most jurisdictions have abolished or modified the fee tail estate. In some, a grant attempting to create a fee tail is treated as creating a fee simple instead; in others, the restriction to issue is honored only for the first generation and not thereafter, i.e., it is treated as involving a "definite" rather than "indefinite" failure of issue. Because of its contemporary insignificance, the fee tail will receive only limited treatment in this chapter.

c.   The Life Estate
This estate is not inheritable, and therefore endures only so long as the holder of estate lives. Its duration is obviously smaller than that of the fee estates. It arises either as a result of the wording of the grant (a conventional life estate) or by virtue of the operation of law in certain instances (a legal life estate—described later).

d.   Creating Language
At common law, no estate was inheritable unless the conveyance was to the grantee "and his heirs"; a grant without reference to heirs, created merely a (noninheritable) life estate rather than a fee.

1)   Words of Inheritance
At common law the phrase "and his heirs" was treated as consisting of words of limitation rather than words of purchase; the grant was not construed as giving anything to the heirs (they were not "purchasers," taking by the deed). Rather, the words were taken to signify that the estate was not to end upon the death of the grantee, but was to be inheritable. The words described the lack of any limitation upon the duration of the estate.

Examples: (1) Fee Simple—"To Ann and her heirs." (Assuming females could take.)

(2) Fee Tail—"To Ann and the heirs of her body." The words of limitation here indicate that inheritability is limited to issue.

(3) Fee Tail Special—"To Ann and the heirs of her body by her husband Bob." Inheritability is further restricted here to children of a particular marriage.

(4) Fee Tail Male (or Female)—"To Ann and the male heirs of her body."

(5) Life Estate—"To Ann." The absence of words of limitation meant that, at common law, Ann took a noninheritable estate. Today, however, most jurisdictions hold that an estate equal to the duration of that held by the grantor is deemed intended despite the absence of words of inheritance, unless a life estate is either expressly specified (e.g., "To Ann for life") or else clearly intended (e.g., "To Ann and then on her death to Bob").

(6) Life Estate Per Autre Vie—"To Ann for the life of Bob." Ann's life estate will end when Bob dies; Bob, not Ann, is the measuring life. This estate also arises when a life tenant conveys her entire interest to a third person, who then holds it for so long as she, his grantor, lives.

5. THE NONFREEHOLD ESTATES

Nonfreehold estates all have theoretically ascertainable termination dates and are distinguished according to how they are intended to terminate. They consist of:

a. The Tenancy for a Term.

b. The Periodic Tenancy.

c. The Tenancy at Will.

These estates are covered in the chapter on Landlord and Tenant.

6. ABSOLUTE VS DEFEASIBLE ESTATES

All of the foregoing estates have been described in their absolute form, i.e. subject to termination only upon a naturally occuring event (death, death without heir, death without issue, end of the term). However, an estate may be conditioned so as to terminate sooner upon the happening of some other event, over and above death or completion of the term. When so limited, an estate is referred to as defeasible rather than absolute. A defeasible estate should not be considered as "smaller" than an absolute one; rather it should be treated as "qualified," i.e., subject to qualifications not present in an absolute estate.

a. Determinable Estates

Any one of the previously described estates may be qualified so as to end automatically and to revert to the grantor if some specified event occurs or fails to occur. A determinable estate is thus subject not only to the natural termination of any freehold or nonfreehold estate (death, expiration of the term), but also to an independent qualification which may result in premature termination.

1) **Creating Words**
Generally, courts hold that a determinable estate has been created when the phrases "as long as . . ." or "until . . ." appear in the grant. The grant should make plain that the estate is to end automatically if the contingency occurs. It is also good drafting to provide explicitly that the property is to then automatically revert to the grantor.

> *Example:* "To Ann and her heirs, so long as liquor is never sold upon the premises . . . and if so, then back to me or my heirs." Ann's fee simple determinable estate will end automatically if she ever sells liquor (even though she is alive). After Ann dies, the estate will be held by her heirs subject to the same limitation (unless the restriction were worded to apply only to Ann).

2) **Applicable to All Estates**
Any freehold or nonfreehold estate may be made determinable. When an estate lesser than a fee simple is made as determinable, it is subject to termination either naturally (through death or expiration of the term) or abruptly (through occurrence of the terminating event).

> *Examples:* (1) "To Ann for life or until I return from abroad . . .." Ann had a determinable life estate; it will end either when she dies or when the grantor returns, whichever is sooner.
>
> (2) "To Ann for 5 years, so long as she waters the lawn every day . . .." Ann has a determinable term of years, which will end either by the passage of five years or by her failure to water the lawn.

b. **Estate Subject to Executory Limitation**
When an estate is made subject to automatic termination, but is then to pass to a third party rather than revert to the grantor, it is sometimes labelled as subject to an executory limitation rather than as determinable.

> *Example:* "To Ann and her heirs, but if liquor is ever sold upon the premises then to Bob and his heirs." Termination is still automatic, but the estate will go from Ann to Bob (or from Ann's heirs to Bob's heirs) rather than revert to the grantor or his heirs.

c.   Estate Subject to Condition Subsequent
Any estate may be made subject to elective rather than automatic termination upon the occurrence of a stated condition. Such an estate is labelled as one subject to a condition subsequent. A condition subsequent is one which, if it occurs (or fails to occur, if so worded), brings about the destruction of an existing interest.

1)   Creating Words
In order to create an estate subject to a condition subsequent, the grant must contain language which:

(1) Includes words of condition, such as "but if . . ." or "on condition that . . ." or "provided that . . ."; and

(2) Includes a provision giving the grantor the power to terminate the estate when the condition occurs, if he so elects.

Examples: (1) "To Ann and her heirs, on condition that liquor is never sold on the premises or else I or my heirs may reenter and terminate her estate." Ann has a fee simple subject to condition subsequent.

(2) "To Ann for life, but if I return from abroad alive, then I may take back my estate." Ann has a life estate subject to condition subsequent.

(3) "To Ann for five years provided that she pays the rent when due and, if she fails to do so, then the landlord may terminate her leasehold estate." Ann has a term of years subject to condition subsequent.

2)   Constructional Preferences
Courts seek to avoid interpretations of grants which lead to the forfeiture of interests. Thus they will, where possible, construe restrictive language as creating an estate which is subject to condition subsequent rather than determinable, (or even more preferably, consisting only of a covenant or a mere nonbinding statement of purpose).

7.   TRANSFERABILITY
Unless prohibited by language in the grant, each of the estates described above is fully transferable. However, a person can not give more than he has (subject to the operation of the recording laws). If the grantor held a fee simple subject to condition, the grantee will only acquire a fee simple subject to the same condition, regardless of the language of the grant.

B. FUTURE INTERESTS

A future interest is an interest in land which does not entitle its holder to take possession of the land now, but provides that he will or may do so in the future. It is generally not referred to as an estate because it is at present nonpossessory. But it is a present property interest, which its owner may convey or devise to other persons before it ever becomes possessory.

1. TYPES

Future interests are classified according to the kind of present estate which underlies them and according to whether they are held by the grantor or by a third person. There are five recognized future interests:

a. *Possibility of Reverter:* An interest retained by the grantor following his conveyance of a determinable estate;

b. *Power of Termination:* An interest retained by a grantor following his conveyance of an estate subject to condition subsequent;

c. *Executory Interest:* An interest granted to a third person following his conveyance of an estate subject to an executory interest (also known as executory limitation);

d. *Remainder:* An interest granted to a third person by a grantor following his conveyance of a lesser present estate to a second person.

e. *Reversion:* An interest retained by the grantor following his conveyance of a lesser present estate.

a. The Possibility of Reverter

This is an interest retained by a grantor whenever the grantee has been given a determinable estate. Upon occurrence of the determining event, this interest vests automatically in the grantor.

> ***Example:*** Owen, holding property in fee simple, granted it "To Ann and her heirs for so long as liquor is not sold on the premises . . .." Ann has a fee simple determinable and Owen has a possibility of reverter. The creation of the determinable estate in Ann automatically creates a possibility of reverter in Owen. If Ann or her heirs ever sell liquor, title will automatically revert to Owen or his heirs.

1) Loss by Adverse Possession

The holder of a possibility of reverter faces the risk that title may come to him without his knowledge, since no action by him is required to produce the retransfer. If the grantee remains in possession of the land for a long enough time after the event creating the reversion, she may reacquire title by adverse possession (gaining a fee simple absolute). Thus, a grantor may prefer to create an estate subject to condition subsequent in order to eliminate this danger.

2) Transferability
Today, the possibility of reverter is fully alienable, devisable and descendable, i.e., transferable by deed, will, or nontestamentary succession. At common law, it was descendable but was not alienable or devisable. *A possibility of reverter is an interest which may only be created in the grantor; thereafter it may be transferred to a third person, but it could not be originally created in favor of a third person at common law.*

b. Power of Termination

This is an interest retained by a grantor when the grantee has been given an estate subject to a condition subsequent. If the condition subsequent occurs, the grantor may elect to bring about a forfeiture of the previous estate and a retransfer of the title. This interest is also known as a right of reentry or a right of entry.

Example: Owen, holding a fee simple, granted "To Ann and her heirs, but if any of them ever sell liquor on the premises then I or my heirs may reenter and terminate their estate." Ann has a fee simple subject to condition subsequent; Owen has a power of termination. Unlike the possibility of reverter, it is required that the grant specify the grantor's power to terminate the estate; furthermore the preliminary phrase "but if" itself requires some further elaboration of the consequences in order to be intelligible.

1) Elective
The power of termination requires action by its holder to bring about the termination of the preceding possessory estate; it does not operate automatically. It, therefore, is not in as great jeopardy of loss from the statute of limitations, which does not begin to run until an election to forfeit has been made. However, it is subject to a defense of waiver, estoppel or laches where the circumstances justify it.

2) Similarities Between Possibility of Reverter and Power of Termination
Both the possibility of reverter and the power of termination cut short prior estates. Both are interests created only in a grantor, although the possibility of reverter is fully transferable to third persons thereafter and the power of termination is transferable in some jurisdictions.

c. **Executory Interest**
This is an interest created in a third person when the grantor has created a defeasible estate in the grantee. *It is an interest which, if the equivalent had been retained by the grantor, would have been called a possibility of reverter or power of termination, but it is called an executory interest because it is created in a third person.* (The distinction between possibility of reverter and power of termination is not made with regard to executory interests; an executory interest vests title in the holder automatically.) Today, it is fully transferable.

Examples: (1) "To Ann and her heirs, so long as liquor is never sold on the premises and if it is, then to Bob and his heirs." Ann has a fee simple (subject to an executory limitation) and Bob has an executory interest in fee simple absolute. Once he takes, if he takes, he will hold in fee simple absolute.

(2) "To Ann and her heirs, but if liquor is ever sold on the premises then to Bob and his heirs." Ann has a fee simple (subject to an executory limitation) and Bob has an executory interest in fee simple absolute.

1) Shifting vs Springing Executory Interests
The examples previously given are shifting executory interests, i.e., they "shift" the title from one person to another, thereby cutting short the first estate. Another kind of executory interest is the springing interest, which creates a future interest in a third person not supported by any present estate in a grantee; it "springs" up out of the grantor's estate some time in the future.

Examples: (1) "To Ann and her heirs one year from today." Ann has a springing executory interest in fee simple absolute. The grantor retains title for the next year and then it springs up over to Ann.

(2) "To Ann for life and then, one year after her death, to Bob and his heirs." Bob has a springing interest because title will revert to the grantor upon Ann's death and then, one year later, spring up to Bob.

2) Barred at Common Law
Originally the common law prohibited executory interests. The maxim "no livery of seisin in futuro" meant that springing executory interests were impermissible, and the maxim "no condition in a stranger" described the rejection of shifting executory interests. However, these interests were recognized in equity (when created as

uses) and they became valid legal interests in land (for the most part) after the enactment of the Statute of Uses in 1536.

d.   Remainder
This is a future interest created in a third person which is intended to take after the natural termination of a preceding estate. It must be created as part of the same grant which created a prior possessory estate, and the preceding estate must be smaller than a fee simple.

Example: "To Ann for life and then to Bob and his heirs." Ann has a life estate and Bob has a remainder in fee simple absolute. Once Ann dies, Bob will have an estate in fee simple absolute.

1)   Remainder vs Executory Interest
Both the remainder and the executory interest are future interests created in favor of third parties, but a remainder does not cut short a prior estate. A remainder takes only when the prior estate naturally terminates (on the death of Ann in the above example). An executory limitation may follow a (defeasible) fee simple. It is impossible to create a remainder after a fee simple absolute, because it has no natural termination. (Upon death without heirs, the property escheats to the state.) A defeasible estate is always followed by either an executory interest in a third person, or by a possibility of reverter or power of termination in the grantor. An estate smaller than a fee simple (a fee tail, a life estate, or, today, an estate for years) is always followed by a remainder in a third person or by a reversion (not yet discussed) in the grantor.

Examples: (1) "To Ann and her heirs, but if she dies without having married, then to Bob and his heirs." Ann's estate is a fee simple (because of the phrase "and her heirs" in the grant). Therefore, Bob's future interest cannot be that of a remainder. He has an executory interest, and Ann's estate is more properly described as a fee simple subject to an executory limitation.

(2) "To Ann for life and then to Bob and his heirs, but if Ann ever sells liquor upon the premises, then to Bob and his heirs." Ann has a life estate subject to a condition subsequent (or executory limitation); Bob has both a remainder and an executory interest. He will take either upon Ann's death (by way of his remainder, following the natural termination of her life estate), or upon her selling liquor (by way of his executory interest, cutting short her defeasible estate).

2)   Successive Remainders
A grant may create more than one remainder interest. Only one present possessory estate may be created but there may be a series of remainders, one following the other.

Example: "To Ann for life, then to Bob for life, and then to Cal and his heirs." Ann has a (present possessory) life estate. Bob has a remainder of a life estate; he will take upon the natural termination of Ann's life estate and then he will hold a possessory life estate for so long as he lives. Cal has a remainder in fee simple absolute which will take upon the expiration of the two preceding life estates. (Bob's life estate may expire before it ever vests in possession, if Bob dies before Ann, but it is nevertheless a valid remainder interest of a life estate.)

3)   Vested vs Contingent Remainders
When a remainder is given to an ascertained person and is subject to no condition precedent (other than the natural termination of prior interests), it is vested; otherwise it is contingent. A contingent remainder, therefore, is one which has either been given to an unascertained person or else has been made subject to some condition precedent (other than the termination of the prior interests), or both. A vested remainder is always ready to take, regardless of when (and how) the preceding estates end, whereas a contingent remainder is not. Once the contingency has occurred or the taker is ascertained, the remainder becomes vested.

Examples: (1) "To Ann for life and then, if Bob has married before Ann dies, to Bob and his heirs." Ann has a life estate; Bob has a contingent remainder in fee simple absolute. Ann's life estate is not affected by the contingency relating to Bob; her estate ends on her death, neither enlarged nor reduced by Bob's contingency. Bob has a remainder in fee simple absolute, because when and if he does take, his estate will be absolute and subject to no conditions. But in order for him to take he must first have married; the presence of this condition precedent means that his remainder in fee simple absolute is contingent. Once he marries, his future interest becomes a vested remainder.

(2) "To Ann for life and then to Bob's widow and her heirs." Bob's widow is unascertained while he is alive. It may or may not be his present wife, depending upon whether she remains married to him and survives his

death. Ann has a life estate, and Bob's widow has a
contingent remainder in fee simple absolute.

a) Contingent Remainder vs Executory Interest
A contingent remainder involves a condition precedent relating
solely to it and not involving the prior estate. A (shifting)
executory interest involves a condition subsequent relating to the
prior estate; when the condition subsequent occurs, it is the prior
estate which is cut short. When the condition precedent in a
contingent remainder does occur, it means it is merely that the
remainder is then ready to take whenever the prior estate
naturally ends. *A condition precedent is one which must occur in
order for a future interest to be eligible to take; a condition
subsequent is one which destroys the interest which is subject to it.*
Do not confuse who is involved in the condition with who is
affected by it.

> *Example:* "To Ann and her heirs, but if Bob marries, then to
> Bob and his heirs. Ann is affected by the condition
> which relates to Bob. This is a condition subsequent.

4) Indefeasible vs Defeasible Remainders
A remainder may be made subject to a condition subsequent, so that
it will be eliminated if the stated event occurs. It then is defeasible
(or subject to divestment). If not so subject, it is indefeasible (or
indefeasibly vested).

> *Example:* "To Ann for life and then to Bob and his heirs, but
> if Bob or his heirs ever sell liquor on the land, then
> to Cal and his heirs." Ann has a life estate. Bob
> has a vested remainder in fee simple, but it is subject
> to divestment; it is not a contingent remainder
> because Bob is ascertained and there is no condition
> precedent. If Bob held a present possessory estate
> subject to the same restrictions, it would be a fee
> simple subject to a condition subsequent or an
> executory limitation. Cal has an executory interest in
> fee simple absolute, which may cut short (divest) Bob's
> remainder.

a) Contingent vs Defeasible
*A remainder is contingent when it is subject to a condition
precedent, which must occur in order for it to take. A remainder is
defeasible (or subject to divestment) when it is subject to a
condition subsequent which may terminate it if that condition occurs.*

Example: "To Ann for life and then to Bob and his heirs if he is 21 before Ann dies, but if Bob ever thereafter sells liquor on the premises, then to Cal and his heirs." Bob has a contingent remainder subject to divestment; it is contingent because it is subject to the condition precedent of his majority before Ann's death, and it is subject to divestment because of the condition subsequent relating to liquor. Ann has a life estate and Cal has an executory interest in fee simple absolute.

5) Partial Divestment

Where a remainder interest given to one person may later have to be shared with others, it is characterized as subject to partial divestment or subject to open. As new persons enter the class of eligibility the share of the former members of the class is correspondingly reduced.

Example: "To Ann for life and then equally to all of Bob's children and their heirs." If Bob has one son now, that child's vested remainder in fee simple may be reduced as other children are born to Bob and claim their fractional shares. (Once Ann dies and the remainder becomes possessory, the class closes and no later children of Bob will be admitted.)

6) Preferences

Courts prefer to construe grants as creating vested rather than contingent remainders. But a contingent remainder is constructionally preferred to an executory interest, and where a future interest is capable of taking either way, it will be treated as a contingent remainder rather than an executory interest.

Examples: (1) "To Ann for life and on her death to her children; the share of any child who has failed to survive her shall pass to the children of that child." A court may prefer to treat the remainder to Ann's children as being vested, subject to divestment by their grandchildren if they do not survive, rather than as a contingent remainder. (Survival is thus treated as a condition subsequent rather than a condition precedent.)

(2) "To Ann for life and then to Bob and his heirs if he is married when Ann dies, or to Cal and his heirs if Bob is not married when Ann dies." A court may prefer to treat Bob's and Cal's interests as alternative contingent remainders, rather than as a remainder in Bob subject to divestment by an executory interest in Cal.

7) Transferability
Vested remainders have always been transferable. At common law, contingent remainders were generally not alienable, although they were devisable and descendible; they are generally alienable today except where the remainder is in an unascertained person so that there is no person capable of conveying it.

e. **Reversion**
This is a future interest retained by the grantor when he gives away a smaller estate than he holds. Any time the estates granted to others do not equal the size of the estate held by the grantor, there is a reversion retained by him. A reversion, like a remainder, takes upon the natural termination of the prior interest.

Examples: (1) Owen, holding a fee simple, granted "To Ann for life." Owen has a reversion in fee simple absolute following Ann's life estate. His reversion arises automatically, and without the need for express language, by virtue of his conveying a smaller estate (a life estate) than he had (a fee simple).

(2) Owen, holding a life estate, granted "To Ann for her life." Owen has a reversion of a life estate, since Ann's life estate is smaller than his life estate. (Hers will end when either party dies; his will end only on his own death and will survive her death, if that occurs first.)

(3) Owen, holding a fee simple, granted "To Ann for life and then to Bob for life." The two life estates do not add up to a fee simple and, therefore, Owen has a reversion in fee simple following Ann's present life estate and Bob's remainder of a life estate.

(4) Owen, holding a fee simple, granted "To Ann for life and then to Bob and his heirs if he is married before Ann dies." Ann's life estate and Bob's contingent remainder in fee simple do not equal Owen's fee simple; therefore, Owen has a reversion in fee simple.

1) Always Vested
A reversion is always a vested interest, although it may be subject to divestment.

Example: The same facts as in the last previous example except that Bob does marry before Ann's death. Bob's timely marriage converts his contingent remainder into a vested remainder. The combination of Ann's life estate and

Bob's vested remainder in fee simple now equals Owen's original fee simple, and Owen now has no reversion. It may be said that the marriage divested Owen of his reversion.

2) Reversion vs Remainder
Both remainders and reversions arise when the granted possessory estates are smaller than what the grantor had, but *a remainder is always created in a third person and a reversion is always retained by the grantor. (A remainder may be considered as an interest created in a third person which would have been a reversion had it been retained by the grantor.)* The distinction depends upon the person who holds the interest at the time of its creation, not later. A reversion later transferred by the grantor to a third person continues to be a reversion rather than a remainder, and vice versa.

3) Reversion vs Possibility of Reverter and Power of Termination
All of these interests are retained by a grantor, but *the reversion arises because estates of a lesser quantity have been conveyed, whereas the possibility of reverter and power of termination arise when the estates granted to others are of a lesser quality, (i.e., are defeasible).* It is possible for the grantor to retain both a reversion and a possibility of reverter or power of termination. A reversion does not cut short prior estates as do the other two interests.

> ***Example:*** "To Ann for 10 years, but if she fails to pay the rent when due, then I may reenter and terminate her estate." Ann has a term of years subject to a condition subsequent. The grantor has a reversion and a power of termination: he will take either at the end of 10 years (by way of his reversion) or sooner if Ann fails to pay rent and he elects to act (by way of his power of termination). (At common law, the grantor would be said to have a fee simple subject to a term of years rather than a reversion, because Ann did not have seisin; today, however, his interest is called a reversion.)

4) Reversion vs Executory Interest
Both are future interests, but *executory interests are always held by third persons and always cut short prior estates. Neither characteristic is applicable to reversions.*

5) Transferability
A reversion is alienable and devisable.

2. DESTRUCTIBILITY OF INTERESTS
a. Contingent Remainders
At common law, if the condition precedent to a contingent remainder had not occurred by the time that the previous estates had terminated, then the contingent remainder was destroyed. A contingent remainder was thus required to become vested in interest, (i.e., become a vested remainder) on or before the time when it had to vest in possession; if this did not occur, the contingent remainder ceased to exist and could not be revived by a later occurrence of the contingency. This rule has been generally abolished today, but the text and the examples assume its validity for purposes of explanation.

> ***Example:*** Owen, holding a fee simple, granted "To Ann for life and then to Bob and his heirs upon his marriage." If Bob has not married by the time Ann dies his contingent remainder will be destroyed and the title will return to Owen by way of reversion. Bob's contingent remainder must become a vested remainder (by a marriage) no later than when it will vest in possession, (i.e. become a possessory fee simple upon Ann's death). Once title has reverted to Owen, a later marriage by Bob will not cause it to go from Owen to Bob. That would be an impermissible springing interest at common law (or else an impermissible gap in the seisin if title did not revert to Owen in the interim).

1) Premature Termination of Prior Estates
A contingent remainder is required to be vested not only when preceding estates naturally terminate but also when their termination occurs prematurely:

a) Forfeiture
At common law, an estate was terminated whenever its holder breached the oath of fealty to the lord, or committed treason or some other high felony.

b) Merger
Whenever two consecutive vested estates come into the hands of the same person, the lesser is merged into the greater and thereby ends. At common law, contingent remainders which depended upon that lesser estate would then be destroyed if they had not yet become vested.

> ***Example:*** Owen, holding a fee simple, granted "To Ann for life and then to Bob and his heirs upon his marriage." Ann later conveyed her life estate back to Owen. Now, Owen holds both a life estate and a reversion in

fee simple. If these two interests were separated by a vested remainder or executory interest, they would remain separate. However, when two interests are separated only by a contingent remainder, that is not sufficient to prohibit their merger. A merger occurs and the lesser is lost to the greater; thus the life estate merges into the reversion and is ended, even though Ann is still alive. If Bob has not married when this happens, his contingent remainder is not ready to vest and is destroyed. If he has married, then his vested remainder prevents a merger and he will take upon Ann's death.

c) Exception
Merger does not occur when all of the interests are created in the same document. Otherwise the grantor's obvious intent to create a contingent remainder would be immediately frustrated. Merger occurred in the above example because the two estates were subsequently held by the same person by virtue of a later transfer. However, at common law, even when both interests were created in the same document, a later transfer of them to a third person would lead to a merger.

b. Other Future Interests

1) Vested Remainder, Reversion, Possibility of Reverter, Power of Termination
These interests are held to be not subject to any condition precedent. Thus, they are never in danger of being destroyed by virtue of nonreadiness to take when prior estates terminate. *All of these interests are considered as vested rather than contingent and are therefore not subject to destruction.*

2) Executory Interest
The common law did not require that any condition precedent affecting an executory interest have already occurred by the time that the interest was to take effect. *An executory interest would take whenever the circumstances permitted, even though the precedent estate had previously terminated.* Since executory interests arose as equitable uses, where seisin was not involved, the difficulties presented by a gap in the seisin were irrelevant; when they were made into legal interests by the Statute of Uses they carried with them their indestructibility.

3) Equitable Contingent Remainders
The Statute of Uses "executed" certain equitable interests into legal interests. Thus transfers which had previously created equitable

interests (bargain and sale, covenant to stand seized) thereafter led to the creation of the equivalent legal interest. But, a contingent remainder, whether always legal or converted from equitable to legal remained destructible. It did not take on indestructibility merely because of its equitable origin or nature. Only a contingent remainder which remained continually equitable (as in the case of a trust), where seisin was not involved, took on an indestructible aspect.

Examples: (1) After the Statute of Uses (1536), Owen bargained and sold "To Ann for life and then to Bob and his heirs if Bob is married when Ann dies." Ann died before Bob married. Bob no longer has any estate. The bargain and sale resulted in an equitable life estate in Ann and an equitable contingent remainder in Bob. The Statute of Uses converted both equitable estates into legal estates. This meant that Bob had a legal contingent remainder. But, contingent remainders were destructible, even after the Statute, and thus his estate was destroyed for failing to vest in time.

(2) After the Statute of Uses, Owen, holding a fee simple, granted "To Ann for life and then one day later to Bob's heirs." Bob's heirs have an executory interest. (The one day gap means that the future interest will spring out of the grantor's reversion since it cannot take immediately upon the natural termination of the prior estate.) It does not matter whether Bob is still alive when Ann dies; his heirs will take whenever he perishes. Title would revert to Owen during any interim.

c. Executory Interest or Contingent Remainder?
At common law, an interest which could possibly take as either a contingent remainder or as an executory interest was treated as a contingent remainder and was therefore destructible. If the condition had not occurred by the time of termination of the prior estate, the future interest was destroyed rather than kept alive to take as an executory interest later on.

Examples: (1) Owen, holding a fee simple, granted "To Ann for life and then to Bob and his heirs upon his marriage." Since Bob could take by way of remainder (if he married before Ann's death), his future interest will be so treated. Therefore, if he has not married by then, it is destroyed. Because his interest could take as a remainder, it will not be treated as an executory interest, which would survive an early death of Ann. If Owen had said "To Ann for life, and then one day later, to Bob and his heirs upon his marriage," that could only be taken as an executory interest and it would be indestructible.

(2) Owen, holding a fee simple, granted "To Ann for life and then to Bob and his heirs if he is married when Ann dies, or to Cal and his heirs if Bob is not married when Ann dies." Ann later conveyed her life estate back to Owen before Bob married. If the future interests involved were treated as vested remainder in Bob subject to divestment (if he failed to marry in time) and executory interest in Cal (divesting Bob for lack of a timely marriage), then both would survive and would prevent any merger of Owen's life estate and reversion. But they are instead treated as alternative contingent remainders and are both destroyed; Bob's contingent remainder is destroyed because he is not yet married and the preceding life estate has ended; Cal's contingent remainder is destroyed because he takes only if "Bob is not married when Ann dies," which has not yet happened, and the preceding estates have all terminated.

C. RULE AGAINST PERPETUITIES

1. THE RULE
"No interest is good unless it must vest, if at all, not later than 21 years after some life in being at the creation of the interest." The rule against perpetuities *makes certain nonvested future interests invalid if there is any possibility that the vesting might occur beyond a date in the future more than 21 years after the expiration of a life now in existence. An interest which may vest or fail to vest too remotely in the future is held to be immediately invalid.* The wording given is that of the common law rule; it is often modified by statute today.

Examples: (1) Owen grants "To Ann and her heirs, as soon as the property is zoned residential." Ann's springing executory interest could conceivably vest in possession more than 21 years after everyone now living has perished. Therefore, it is invalid.

(2) Owen grants "To Ann for life and then to her first child who graduates from college." The grant creates a life estate in Ann and a contingent remainder in one of her children. It is possible that this contingency will not be lifted until too far in the future. Ann may, at a later time, have a child who might be the first to complete college and yet not do so until more than 21 years after Ann and all of her other now living children are dead. Thus this contingent remainder could possibly vest (become a vested remainder) more than 21 years after all lives in being are ended.

2. APPLICABLE INTERESTS
The rule only applies to nonvested interests. Those future interests which the law treats as presently vested are, therefore, not subject to it. It is required that they become vested in interest, not necessarily vested in possession.

a. Vested Interests
Exempt from the rule are vested remainders, reversions, possibilities of reverter and powers of termination.

> ***Example:*** Owen grants "To Ann and her heirs, so long as liquor is never sold on the premises." Owen's possibility of reverter is not subject to the rule even though it may not take until far in the future, if at all.

b. Nonvested Interests
Subject to the rule are contingent remainders, executory interests and remainders subject to open. Options are also subject to the rule.

c. How Interests Vest
1) Contingent Remainders
A contingent remainder vests within the meaning of the rule when it becomes a vested remainder. Thus, a contingent remainder must be certain either to become a vested remainder or to fail within 21 years of all lives in being in order for it to survive application of the rule against perpetuities.

> ***Example:*** "To Ann for life and then to her children for their lives and then to Bob and his heirs if he is still living, or to the Red Cross if he is not." The Red Cross has a contingent remainder which will either become a vested remainder (if Bob dies before all of Ann's children) or fail (if Bob outlives Ann's children) in less than 21 years after the end of all lives in being (since it will occur the death of Bob's, who is a life in being).

2) Executory Interests
An executory interest vests by becoming possessory. Thus, an executory interest must be certain to take possession or to fail within the measuring period in order for it to survive the rule.

> ***Examples:*** (1) "To Ann and her heirs, but if liquor is ever sold upon the premises, then to Bob and his heirs." The sale of liquor could first occur more than 21 years after the death of Ann and Bob, which is too remote. That possibility makes this executory interest invalid.

(2) "To Ann and her heirs, but if Ann herself ever sells liquor on the land then to Bob and his heirs." Bob's executory interest can take only within Ann's lifetime (since the grant restriction doesn't apply to her heirs). Because there is no possibility that Bob's interest may vest or fail outside of the time period, it is valid.

(3) "To the Board of Education, but if the property is not used as a school at any time within the next 20 years, then to Ann." The presence of the saving clause ("within the next 20 years") protects the gift to Ann.

3) Remainders Subject to Open (Class Gifts)

If a remainder interest is given to a class of persons, it is deemed vested only when the class is closed and all conditions precedent for every member of the class have been satisfied. *The entire class gift is void if the interest of one member might possibly violate the rule.* However, some jurisdictions protect these gifts by a "rule of convenience" which treats a class as closed at distribution to any member of it is entitled to demand his share.

Example: "To Ann for life and then to her surviving children when they reach the age of 25." Ann could have another child, who would not turn 25 until more than 21 years after the death of all other parties. That possibility invalidates the gift to all children even those living, unless the rule of convenience is applied to save it and there is one child who is 25 when she dies.

d. **Charities**

An exception to the rule is created when both the present and the future interests are given to charities. The future interest is valid in that case even though the time of vesting is otherwise too remote.

Example: "To the United Crusade, but if the property is ever used for religious purposes, then to the Red Cross." This remote executory interest in the Red Cross is valid because both takers are charities. The gift would be invalid if either were not.

3. **MEASURING LIVES**

Any life may be used as the measuring life so long as it is then in being. Different results, therefore, may follow between inter vivos grants and wills.

Example: Owen's will provided, "To my grandchildren when they reach 21." Because the grant is contained in a will it is valid, since Owen could not have any more children after his death (when his will took effect) and so no grandchild could possibly take more than 21 years after the death of all his living children. But, if this provision were contained in an inter vivos trust document, the grandchildren's remainder interest would be invalid since it is possible that Owen might yet have another child (who, being now unborn cannot be used as a measuring life) and whose own children might not turn 21 until more than 21 years after all of Owen's now living children and Owen himself (the lives in being) are dead.

4. IMPROBABILITY

An interest is void if it can conceivably vest or fail too remotely in the future; it does not matter how improbable such an event is.

Examples: (1) *Fertile Octogenarian.* "To Ann for life, then to her children for their lives and then to her grandchildren." Ann is 80 years old and absolutely infertile. But, the contingent remainder to her grandchildren is invalid because the rule regards it as possible that she may yet have another child who will outlive her and all of her now living children by more than 21 years, thus postponing the closing of the class of grandchildren too long.

(2) *Unborn Widow.* "To Bob for life, then to his widow for life and then to her heirs." Bob is 80 years old and married. The rule treats it as possible that he may yet divorce and then remarry a person now unborn, whose death more than 21 years after his death (he is the only life in being here) will postpone too remotely the vesting of the contingent remainder in her heirs.

a. Wait and See Approach

Some jurisdictions now reject invalidity in improbable cases. Either by statute or court decision, they follow a rule which validates any interest which actually vests within the allotted time, even though it could conceivably have taken longer.

5. EFFECTS OF VIOLATION OF THE RULE

If an interest is held to violate the rule, it is stricken from the document. The rest of the gift remains as if the invalid provision had never existed. This may create a new reversionary interest in the grantor or else may enlarge some preceding estate in a grantee. In the following examples, Owen held in fee simple.

Examples: (1) Owen grants "To Ann for life, remainder to Ann's children and their heirs when they reach 25." The clause referring to the children is stricken. Ann has a life estate, and Owen has a reversion in fee simple (because there is no longer a remainder).

(2) Owen grants "To the Board of Education, so long as the property is used as a school, and then to Ann and her heirs." The Board has a fee simple determinable. The gift to Ann is stricken, and Owen has a possibility of reverter.

(3) Owen grants "To the Board of Education, but if the property is ever not used as a school, then to Ann and her heirs." "Then to Ann and her heirs" is stricken, and because the condition subsequent (not using the property for a school) depends upon the presence of a provision for someone to take after the condition, it also fails. Thus, the Board's estate becomes one in fee simple absolute.

a. Infectious Invalidity
If a court determines that the invalid interest was essential to the grantor's plan it may strike down the entire gift, and not merely the invalid part.

D. THE RULE IN SHELLEY'S CASE

1. THE RULE
If, in a single document, a freehold estate is given to a person and a remainder (in fee simple or fee tail) is given to her heirs, this remainder becomes a remainder in the ancestor rather than in her heirs. The rule shifts ownership of certain remainder interests from the heirs to the ancestor. (Most jurisdictions have abolished the rule today, but here we treat it as operative.)

Example: "To Ann for life and then to her heirs." The grant creates a remainder in Ann's heirs. The rule, however, changes that into a remainder interest in Ann, their ancestor.

2. CONSEQUENCES OF THE RULE
The rule acquires considerably more impact by virtue of two consequences which often follow the shift of title of the remainder from heirs to ancestor:

a. Contingent Into Vested
A remainder to the heirs of a living person is always contingent, since the remaindermen are unascertained. *Once the remainder is shifted to the ancestor, it may become vested.*

Examples: (1) "To Ann for life and then to her heirs." The grant created a remainder in the heirs but the rule moves it to the ancestor. As written, it created a contingent remainder in unascertained persons; now it creates a vested remainder in an ascertained person, Ann. She has a life estate and a vested remainder in fee simple.

(2) "To Ann for life and then, if she never drinks liquor, to her heirs." The rule still shifts the remainder to Ann from her heirs, but it remains a contingent remainder in her, since it is subject to a condition precedent, which the rule does not affect.

b. **Merger**

When two adjacent interests exist in the same person they will merge. Furthermore, a merger will occur even when they are separated by a contingent remainder, thereby destroying the contingent remainder, unless all interests were created in the same document. *The shift of title produced by the rule may lead to such a merger.*

Examples: (1) "To Ann for life and then to her heirs." The rule changes the contingent remainder in the heirs into a vested remainder in Ann. Those two interests now merge to give Ann a fee simple.

(2) "To Ann for life, then to Bob for life if he is 21, and then to Ann's heirs." The grant gives Ann a life estate and her heirs a contingent remainder; it becomes a life estate and vested remainder in Ann, separated by a contingent remainder in Bob. Because these were created in the same document, there is no merger or destruction of Bob's interest. But, if Ann conveys both her interests to a third person, merger and destruction of Bob's contingent remainder will occur.

3. **REQUIREMENTS OF THE RULE**

The rule only operates where the interests are of the right sort. Otherwise, the grant is left unaltered.

a. **Freehold in the Ancestor**

The ancestor must have been given a freehold interest in land—a life estate or a fee tail. It need not be a present possessory estate; it may be a remainder interest, vested or contingent.

Example: "To Ann for life, then to Bob for life, and then to Bob's heirs." The rule changes the remainder in Bob's heirs into one in Bob, which then merges with his remainder life estate.

The grant becomes life estate in Ann, vested remainder in fee simple in Bob.

b. Remainder in the Heirs

The interest given to the heirs must be a remainder; the rule does not apply if it is an executory interest. (The remainder will inevitably be contingent because of the nonascertainability of heirs, but it may also be subject to other conditions precedent.)

Example: "To Ann for life and then, one day after her death, to her heirs." The grant creates a springing executory interest in Ann's heirs and is unaffected by the rule.

c. Same Quality

The two interests must be both legal or both equitable. The rule does not apply when one interest is legal and the other equitable.

Example: "To Ann for her life, and then, in trust to her heirs." The equitable remainder in the heirs is not altered, since the life estate in Ann is legal and therefore of a different quality.

d. Heirs vs Children

The rule applies only when the grantor uses the word "heirs" and in its technical sense.

Examples: (1) "To Ann for life and then to her children." The rule does not apply.

(2) "To Ann for life and then to her son Bob." The rule does not apply (even though Bob may be Ann's sole heir).

4. RULE OF LAW

At common law, the rule was applied to any grant which met its conditions even though the grantor may have expressly stated his intent that it not apply. It was not a rule of construction, which would only seek to enforce the grantor's intent.

E. THE DOCTRINE OF WORTHIER TITLE

The common law prohibited a person from transferring a future interest to his own heirs, requiring instead that they take by descent upon his death, a "worthier" way of acquiring title. (The Rule in Shelley's Case applied to a grantee's heirs; this doctrine affected the heirs of the grantor.) The doctrine applied differently to inter vivos and testamentary transfers.

1. INTER VIVOS DOCTRINE
An inter vivos gift of a future interest to the heirs of the grantor is void.

Example: Owen, holding in fee simple, granted "To Ann for life and then to my heirs." The remainder to Owen's heirs is invalid; only the grant of the life estate to Ann is good.

a. Consequences
Once a remainder interest has been invalidated, it is necessarily replaced with a reversion in the grantor. The grantor's heirs will inherit the same interest (but only if the grantor dies without having acted to eliminate his reversion).

Examples: (1) Owen, holding a fee simple, granted "To Ann for life and then to my heirs." The gift to the heirs is void and Owen has a reversion in fee simple absolute. But he may convey to someone else, divesting his heirs entirely. Furthermore, his creditors may reach that interest.

(2) Owen, holding a fee simple, granted, "To Ann, in trust for me for my life and thereafter for my heirs." Revocation of a trust can be accomplished only if the holders of all beneficial interests agree. But here, Owen may revoke the trust himself because the doctrine gives him a reversion, by virtue of destroying the remainder.

b. Rule of Law
Like the Rule in Shelley's Case, this was a rule of law and not a rule of construction. It was not defeated by language in the grant indicating that the grantor did not want it to apply.

c. Heirs
Like the Rule in Shelley's Case, the doctrine applied only when "heirs" was used and in a technical sense. A grant to the children of the grantor did not come within the rule.

d. Modern Status
Most jurisdictions continue to follow this doctrine, but it is now only a rule of construction and may be rebutted by evidence of contrary intent.

2. TESTAMENTARY DOCTRINE
A testamentary devise of a freehold estate of the same quality and quantity to a person as he would otherwise take by descent if the testator had died intestate is void. Instead, the heir takes by descent rather than devise.

a.   Modern Status
This doctrine has been generally abolished.

F.   RESTRAINTS ON ALIENATION

A restraint on alienation is a provision in a grant restricting the grantee's power to convey the property to others.   Whether any particular restraint will or will not be permitted depends upon the estate restrained, the kind of restraint, and the extent of the restraint.

1.   THE ESTATE RESTRAINED
As a general rule any direct restraint imposed upon a fee simple is invalid; only estates less than fees may be subject to restraints upon alienation.

Example: Owen grants "To Ann and her heirs, but the property may never be conveyed."   The restriction is repugnant to the fee simple granted to Ann, and is therefore invalid and ineffective.

a.   Concurrent Estates
Restrictions limiting the power of joint tenants or tenants in common to seek partition are usually upheld.   Such provisions appear in the deeds or by-laws of most condominiums and cooperatives.

b.   Lesser Estates
Restraints on alienation of nonfreehold estates are commonly upheld.   The no-assignment clause in a lease is a common example.   Such restrictions are also usually upheld when applied to life estates or future interests.

2.   THE KIND OF RESTRAINT
Restraints on alienation may be written in different ways.   The most common are:

(1) *Disabling.*   Where the grant provides that any attempt to convey the property is automatically void.

(2) *Forfeiture.*   Where the grant provides that the grantor may terminate the estate if a conveyance is made.

(3) *Promissory.*   Where the grantee merely covenants not to convey the property.

Disabling restraints on alienation are always void, even when less than a freehold estate is involved.   Forfeiture restraints are automatically invalid only where a fee is involved; if lesser estates are involved they may be upheld. Promissory restraints may or may not be valid depending upon the other variables. The due on sale clause in a mortgage (which involves an installment loan immediately due on transfer of the property) was viewed by some state courts as constituting a restraint on alienation because it made it harder for the owner to sell the property, whereas other courts held that a loan provision regarding timing of payments did not amount to a restraint on alienation. (See Mortgages.)

3. THE EXTENT OF THE RESTRAINT

A restraint may be total or partial. A partial restraint restricts the grantee only in some particular respect:

a. As to Time

A restraint may only limit the grantee for a limited period of time. While a disabling restraint is always void, a forfeiture or promissory restraint may be valid if it is limited in time. In some jurisdictions, it must both be limited as to time and must not involve a fee simple.

b. As to Persons

A restraint may only prohibit the grantee from conveying to certain persons. Forfeiture and promissory restraints may be valid when partial as to potential grantees. However, when racial categories are employed, the restraint is held invalid on Equal Protection grounds.

c. Preemptive Rights

The inclusion of a right of first refusal in a grant constitutes a partial restraint on alienation (e.g., "To Ann but if she decides to sell the property she shall first offer it for sale to the grantor"). A restraint of this sort is generally valid.

G. COMMON LAW MARITAL ESTATES

At common law, spouses were not regarded as an heir qualified to take by intestate succession. But by virtue of a lawful marriage, each spouse was entitled to a life estate in certain properties of the other. Because these interests were not created by deeds from one to the other, they were characterized as legal rather than conventional life estates.

1. WIFE'S INTEREST: DOWER

A wife was entitled to a life estate in $\frac{1}{3}$ of all property of which her husband had been seised sometime during the marriage.

a. Prerequisites

1) Wife's Status

For the wife to take dower, she must have been married to her husband at the time of his death. A wife lost all dower claims once a final divorce was obtained. A pending divorce proceeding at the time of his death did not disqualify her.

2) Husband's Property
The husband must have been seised of the property sometime during the marriage and it must have been property which was inheritable by his wife's issue (whether or not there were any). Thus, the following interests in the husband were not subject to dower:

a) Term of Years
Since there is no seisin in a nonfreehold estate, the wife had no dower interest in any such tenancy held by the husband.

b) Life Estate
This interest does involve seisin, but it is not inheritable, terminating as it does upon the husband's death (even in the case of a life estate per autre vie). Thus, there is no dower.

c) Fee Tail Special
If the terms of a fee tail limited it to issue of a previous spouse, then there was no dower. Dower did attach to a fee tail general, where the issue of this spouse would qualify, whether there were such issue or not.

d) Defeasible Fee
If an estate was qualified (e.g., determinable, or subject to a condition subsequent or executory limitation), then any dower interest in it might be defeated by occurrence of the stated condition. However, it is sometimes held that the future interest is postponed to the dower right, especially where the event relates to death of the husband.

e) Joint Tenancy
Since the survivorship principle of joint tenancy prevails over common law intestate succession, the wife's dower interest in property held by her husband in joint tenancy with another person occurs only if her husband is not the first joint tenant to die.

f) Future Interests
Future interests do not involve seisin (which is always in the person holding a present possessory freehold estate); therefore there is no dower claim in them.

g) **Freeholds Previously Conveyed**
Dower attaches only to estates held by the husband sometime during the marriage. If he was seised of a freehold estate but conveyed it away prior to his marriage, there is no dower in it. On the other hand, a wife's dower claims are not impaired by any conveyance of such property during the marriage the transferred property remains subject to her interest.

h) **Trusts and Naked Titles**
There is no dower in a purely equitable interest, since seisin is not involved. There is also no dower in a bare legal title held for the use of someone else. Thus, if title is transferred to X in trust for Y, there are no dower rights in either X's or Y's widows.

b. Interest Prior to Death: Dower Inchoate
During the marriage and before her husband's death, the wife's interest is not a legal estate in land. However, it is protected against fraudulent conveyances by her husband, and her interest is not alienable or subject to seizure by creditors.

c. Interest After Death: Dower Consummate
Upon the death of her husband, the wife has a $\frac{1}{3}$ life estate interest in every eligible parcel of land ever owned by her husband. If the husband has not satisfactorily provided for his wife in his will or if she is dissatisfied with the assignment of property proposed by the heirs, she may have the court set aside a $\frac{1}{3}$ share to her for life.

d. Modern Status
Many states have abolished dower entirely, and most others have modified it significantly from what it was at common law. In most jurisdictions, the widow is either allowed to reject what her husband has provided in his will for her and to take instead, as a "statutory share," a fee simple interest (rather than a life estate) in $\frac{1}{3}$ of all the property owned by her husband on death, both real and personal, or else is protected by community property or marital property laws.

2. HUSBAND'S INTEREST: CURTESY
A husband had, at common law, a much greater interest in his wife's lands than she had in his. He had an interest in all, not merely $\frac{1}{3}$ of her property. The nature of his right depended upon the status of the relationship:

a. Before Children: Jure Uxoris
As soon as he married, the husband acquired a life estate in all property of which his wife was seised. It became a life estate measured by two lives and terminated upon the death of either. The husband's jure uxoris

interest was much greater than his wife's right of dower inchoate. He had a legal life estate, and was entitled to occupy the property and dispose of its rents and profits.

b. After Children: Curtesy Initiate
Once issue were born alive and the wife survived childbirth, the husband acquired a life estate in his own right in all of his wife's freehold estates. The former, smaller life estate by jure uxoris merged into this larger interest in him, and his wife's interest was converted into a reversion. The husband had curtesy in all estates of the wife, whether legal or equitable, so long as they were inheritable by issue of the marriage.

c. After Death: Curtesy Consummate
So long as issue had been born alive, whether they survived thereafter or not, the husband continued his life estate interest in all of his wife's freehold property upon her death. The property was his until he died.

d. Modern Status
Jure uxoris is everywhere abolished, having been destroyed by the Married Women's Property Acts of the 19th century which gave wives control over their own property. All states which have abolished dower have also abolished curtesy, and it has also been eliminated in some states which have retained dower in one form or another. Generally, it has been replaced by the statutory share concept or by community property or marital property principles.

H. REVIEW QUESTIONS

1. T or F A grant to Ann and her heirs, "so long as the land is used for church purposes," gives Ann a fee simple subject to condition subsequent.

2. T or F Owen had a life estate. He conveyed "to Ann for my life." Owen now has a reversion.

3. T or F A grant "to Ann for life and then to Bob for life if Bob is married before Ann dies," gives Bob a contingent remainder of a life estate.

4. T or F Owen had a fee simple. He conveyed "to Ann for life." He then conveyed his entire remaining interest to Bob and his heirs. Bob has a remainder.

5. T or F A grant from Owen "to Ann for 10 years and then to Bob if Bob is married before the end of the 10 year period," is void as to Bob at common law.

6. T or F   A grant from Owen "to Ann for life and then to Bob and his heirs if Bob is 21 before Ann dies, or to Cal and his heirs if Bob is not 21 before Ann dies," leaves nothing in Owen.

7. T or F   Owen had a fee simple. He conveyed "to Ann for life, then to Bob for life if he is 21 when Ann dies, and then to Cal and his heirs." Ann and Cal both conveyed their interests to Don before Bob was 21. Don has a fee simple absolute.

8. T or F   After the Statute of Uses, Owen conveyed legal title to "Ann for life and then to Bob and his heirs if he is married when Ann dies." Ann died before Bob married. Bob's estate is destroyed.

9. T or F   A grant from Owen "to Ann for 21 years, then to my oldest descendent then living for his or her life, then to his or her oldest child then living," violates the rule against perpetuities.

10. T or F   A grant "to Ann for life, then to Bob for life, then to Bob's heirs," gives Bob a vested remainder in fee simple absolute.

11. T or F   A grant "to Hubert and his heirs for so long as the property is used for church purposes," gives Hubert an estate in which his present wife may claim dower on his death.

*

III

CONCURRENT OWNERSHIP

Analysis

Any of the estates described in Chapter II may be held by more than one person. If two or more persons share the ownership of some estate in land they are referred to as concurrent owners and their relations to each other and the outside world are subject to the rules set forth in this chapter. (Note that the division of a fee simple into present estates and future interests does not fall under the topic of concurrent ownership. In such cases ownership of the fee is divided but each of the parties holds an interest separate and independent of the others, and no concurrent ownership is involved.)

A. TYPES

1. JOINT TENANCY

This estate was the preferred form of concurrent ownership at common law. The courts presumed that it was intended unless the grantor expressly designated some other kind of concurrent ownership.

a. Survivorship

The principal characteristic of an estate in joint tenancy is survivorship—the right of the surviving joint tenant to take the share of the other joint tenant upon his or her demise. This right of survivorship prevails over the claims of heirs of the decedent (if she died intestate) or her legatees (if she left a will). While alive, each joint tenant is regarded as owning the entire estate, subject only to the equal claim of the other. The common law expression was that each was seised "per my et per tout"—by share (moeity) and by the whole. Upon the death of one, the other's complete interest is freed from that restriction. The survivor is not treated as inheriting from the decedent, but merely as coming into his own.

> *Example:* Ann and Bob were joint tenants. Ann died, leaving a will in favor of Cal (or died intestate, leaving Cal as her heir). Bob prevails over Cal, under the doctrine of survivorship, and now owns the entire estate.

1) Natural Persons
The fact that a corporation does not die, making application of the principle of survivorship impossible, means that it can never hold property in joint tenancy.

2) Third Party Claims
Many courts hold that claims of third parties to the property, which depend upon the survival of one of the joint tenants, fail if that joint tenant dies first.

> *Example:* Ann and Bob are joint tenants, and Ann's share of the property is subject to judgment and mortgage liens held

by her creditors. If Ann dies, Bob will take the property by survivorship free of the claims of her creditors, since the property on which they held claims has vanished. On the other hand, if Bob dies first, Ann's creditors may reach the entire estate, not just her half, in satisfaction of their claims. (While Ann and Bob are both alive, her creditors may reach her one half of the property.)

3) Multiple Ownership
A joint tenancy may be shared by more than two persons. The principles of survivorship apply regardless of how many joint tenants there are.

> ***Example:*** Ann, Bob and Cal are joint tenants. If Ann dies, Bob and Cal will take her interest by survivorship and continue as joint tenants, each holding one-half rather than one-third. If Bob dies thereafter, Cal will become sole owner by virtue of survivorship.

b. Eligible Property
Any interest in land may be the subject of a joint tenancy, so long as it is capable of being subject to the principle of survivorship. Joint tenancy can be created in a present estate or in a future interest; it is not necessary that the estate be inheritable by the survivor's heirs.

> ***Examples:*** (1) "To Ann and Bob for their joint lives as joint tenants and then to Cal and his heirs." Ann and Bob have a joint tenancy in a life estate. On the death of one, the survivor will be sole life tenant; on the death of the second, Cal's remainder takes. (In the examples henceforth, "and his heirs" will be omitted in accordance with modern usage.)
>
> (2) "To Ann for life and then to Bob and Cal as joint tenants." Bob and Cal have a joint tenancy in a remainder interest.

1) Fractional Ownership
It is not necessary that an entire fee simple be shared in order for a joint tenancy to exist; lesser interests may also be jointly owned.

> ***Example:*** "One-third to Ann and Bob as joint tenants, and two-thirds to Cal" makes Ann and Bob joint tenants as to their one-third. On Ann's death, Bob alone will own that one-third of the property. Cal owns two-thirds throughout, and is not affected by the deaths of Ann or Bob.

2) Personal Property
Joint tenancy may apply to personal as well as to real property. It is common for two parties to hold a savings account or safe deposit box in joint tenancy, in order to entitle the other to take by way of survivorship.

c.   Creation
In order for a joint tenancy to be created at common law, it was necessary that four unities exist:

1) Unity of Time
All joint tenants must take their interests at the same time.

> ***Examples:*** (1) Owen conveyed a one-half interest to Ann last month and the other one-half interest to Bob last week. No matter what Owen said in his deeds, Ann and Bob are not joint tenants because they have not taken at the same time.
>
> (2) Ann conveyed to herself and Bob as joint tenants. They are not joint tenants, because the conveyance from Ann to herself was meaningless and she merely continued her original ownership (as to one-half). Therefore, she and Bob did not acquire ownership at the same time. To achieve the result desired Ann must convey the entire estate to a third person (a strawman) who will then convey to her and Bob so that they will take a new title at the same time. Some statutes today dispense with the strawman requirement and permit an owner to convey directly to herself and another as joint tenants.

2) Unity of Title
All parties must take by the same instrument in order to qualify as joint tenants. Separate deeds to two persons, even though delivered to them simultaneously and naming them as joint tenants will not achieve that result.

3) Unity of Interest
All of the joint tenants must hold equal interests, both as to size and duration. Any difference between their interests defeats the creation of a joint tenancy.

> ***Examples:*** (1) "One-third to Ann and two-thirds to Bob as joint tenants." There is no joint tenancy, despite what the

grant says, because the parties do not have equal interests.

(2) "One-half to Ann for life and one-half to Bob in fee simple, in joint tenancy." There is no joint tenancy since the parties have estates of different duration.

4) Unity of Possession
Each joint tenant must have the same basic right to possess the entire property. This requirement is not unique to joint tenancy, since it describes the possessory rights in any cotenancy. It is rather a fundamental characteristic of concurrent ownership; parties whose possessory rights are geographically divided are neighbors rather than co-owners. Each co-owner of property is entitled to possess the entire property, subject only to the equal possessory rights of all the other co-owners. Conversely, no co-owner is entitled to exclude any other co-owner from any part of the property, and such a wrongful exclusion creates a cause of action in ejectment.

a) Subsequent Agreements
Nothing prohibits parties who are already joint tenants from making agreements between themselves as to rights of possession. Their joint tenancy will continue even though one has been allowed to take or control exclusive possession.

5) Express Language
The common law preference for joint tenancy meant that one would be found to exist whenever the four unities were present. Now, however, the preference is against this estate. *Thus, in order to create an estate in joint tenancy today it is also necessary for the grantor to expressly recite such an intent.* Typically, such a deed will recite "to . . . in joint tenancy, and not as tenants in common, together with the right of survivorship." In some jurisdictions, the omission of any part of this language will defeat the joint tenancy.

Example: "To Ann and Bob and then to the survivor of them." A court might hold that this grant creates a joint life estate with a contingent remainder to the survivor rather than a joint tenancy. (This would have a significantly different effect in terms of the power of either party to sever the estate.)

d. **Severance**
A joint tenancy may be severed, i.e., converted into a tenancy in common, thereby losing the characteristic of survivorship.

1)   By Inter Vivos Deed

A joint tenant is free to convey away her interest; the signature or
consent (or even knowledge) of the other joint tenant is not required.
Since there is no unity of time or title between a new grantee and
the other original owner, they will be tenants in common rather than
joint tenants. The joint tenancy has been severed.

Examples: (1) Ann, a joint tenant with Bob, conveyed her interest to
Cal. Bob and Cal are tenants in common.

(2) Ann, a joint tenant with Bob and Cal, conveyed her
one-third interest to Dee. Dee is a tenant in common as
to one-third of the property with Bob and Cal. Bob and
Cal hold the other two-thirds as joint tenants between
themselves and will take each other's interests by
survivorship. But there is no principle of survivorship
affecting Bob or Cal on Dee's death or entitling Dee to
take either of their shares when they die.

2)   Contract to Convey
A binding contract to convey executed by one joint tenant may sever
the joint tenancy under the doctrine of equitable conversion (which
treats the contract purchaser as equitable owner). A binding contract
to convey executed by both joint tenants may also be held to work a
severance, making the parties tenants in common as to the proceeds
to be received from the sale; alternatively, their right to the proceeds
may be treated as continuing in joint tenancy. Equitable conversion
is covered in Ch. VIII.

3)   Lien or Mortgage
A lien given to a third party upon the interest of one joint tenant is
generally not held to sever the joint tenancy. Thus in jurisdictions
which treat a mortgage as a lien, the execution of a mortgage by one
joint tenant does not sever the joint tenancy. A severance may be
held to occur in those jurisdiction's where a mortgage is treated as a
conveyance of title to the mortgagee rather than merely a lien. (If
there is no severance, the mortgage may be destroyed if the
mortgaging joint tenant dies first, and the other then takes the entire
title by survivorship.) In any jurisdiction, a foreclosure and sale by
the mortgagee produces a severance and makes the foreclosure
purchaser a tenant in common as to the interest sold. Mortgages are
covered in Chapter XII.

4) Lease

A lease executed by one joint tenant is generally not treated as severing the joint tenancy. However, the leasehold may end if the leasing joint tenant dies first. In some jurisdictions, the lease is treated as suspending the joint tenancy for its duration, so that the leasehold is not terminated by such a death. Leases are covered in Ch. IV.

5) Murder

In some jurisdictions, the murder of one joint tenant by the other severs the joint tenancy so as to prevent the murderer from taking by survivorship. (Alternatively, it is sometimes held that the surviving murderer holds the property in constructive trust for the victim's heirs.) Murder is not covered in this book.

6) Testamentary Disposition

Provisions in a will do not sever a joint tenancy. If the joint tenancy has not been previously severed, the principle of survivorship applies upon the death of the first joint tenant, and overrides any attempted testamentary disposition.

e. **Modern Changes**

The differences between common law and contemporary treatment of the joint tenancy may be summarized as follows:

1) Reverse Presumption

The common law preferred joint tenancies and construed ambiguous grants to create them; joint tenancy is today disfavored and must be expressly designated.

2) Strawman

At common law, an owner could not create a joint tenancy in himself and another without going through a strawman; a direct conveyance is often permitted today.

3) Abolition

Some jurisdictions have abolished joint tenancy completely. A grant purporting to create one may be held to create a tenancy in common (or a joint tenancy without survivorship, which is the same thing) or a joint life estate with a contingent remainder in the survivor (which is an unseverable joint tenancy).

2. TENANCY IN COMMON

A tenancy in common arises whenever no other form of concurrent ownership has been explicitly designated, or when the grant specifies such a tenancy.

Example: "To Ann and Bob," without more, creates a tenancy in common today, since the grantor has failed to indicate that a joint tenancy or some other way of sharing ownership is intended. "To Ann and Bob as tenants in common" also creates such an estate.

a. No Survivorship
The principle of survivorship does not apply to tenancy in common. When a tenant in common dies, his or her share passes according to the terms of any will or by the rules of intestacy to heirs if there is no will. The other tenant in common takes only as a legatee or heir if such is the case.

Example: Ann, a tenant in common with Bob, died, leaving all her property to Cal. Cal becomes a tenant in common with Bob. Bob would take only if Ann named him in her will or if he were her heir.

b. No Unity of Time or Title
There is no requirement that tenants in common have unity of time or title.

Example: Owen granted a one-half interest to Ann last month, and granted a one-half interest to Bob last week. Ann and Bob are tenants in common even though they took at different times and by different instruments.

c. No Unity of Interest
Tenants in common are not required to have equal interests in the property.

Example: "One-third to Ann and two-thirds to Bob." Ann and Bob are tenants in common, owning disproportionate shares.

1) Presumption of Equality
Where the grant is silent, there is a presumption that the parties hold equal interests. This presumption may be rebutted by showing a contrary intent or an unequal payment of the purchase price.

d. Unity of Possession
All co-owners, of whatever sort, have unity of possession. Their interests are undivided; there is no one certain part of the land which any one of them can claim exclusively. Each cotenant is entitled to possess the entire premises, subject only to the equal rights of the other to do the same.

e. No Severance
Severance describes the conversion of a joint tenancy into a tenancy in common. A tenancy in common, being already the weakest form of concurrent ownership, is not subject to severance. Partition is the word to

describe the actual division of any one concurrent estate into two separate (divided) estates. This is discussed below.

f. Tenancy in Coparcenary
A precursor to the tenancy in common was the tenancy in coparcenary. Generally, property was inherited by the eldest son of the owner (primogeniture), but if there were no male heirs, then all the daughters took equally, i.e., as coparceners; this also applied to male heirs in the County of Kent. Under their rules of gavelkind tenure, coparceners all held equal shares, but without survivorship. Today, since primogeniture no longer exists, the estate has been superceded by the tenancy in common.

g. Creditors' Claims
Creditors of either party may reach their share of the property through authorized collection procedures. A creditor who so acquires such property becomes a tenant in common with the remaining original co-owner. Since tenancy in common lacks the feature of survivorship, creditors are not affected by the death of either owner; the claims remain attached to the original interest and are neither destroyed nor enlarged by the death.

3. TENANCY BY THE ENTIRETY
This estate is like a modified joint tenancy between spouses. It no longer exists in most jurisdictions, and has never existed in community property states.

a. Survivorship
The principle of survivorship applies to a tenancy by the entirety. Upon the death of either spouse, the other takes the entire estate free of all claims of heirs and legatees.

b. Requirements
In addition to the four unities needed for a joint tenancy, a tenancy by the entirety requires that the two grantees be validly married (unity of person—a fifth unity).

1) Express Language
At common law, a tenancy by the entirety was created whenever the grant was made to both spouses and the other four unities were present; there was no requirement that the grantor recite an intent to create such an estate. Today, because of the presumption in favor of tenancy in common, it is necessary in some jurisdictions to include such a statement of intent in the deed.

c. Severance

Unlike a joint tenancy, a tenancy by the entirety cannot be severed by the deed of one of the spouses to a third person. A conveyance by one spouse may be effective to transfer that interest but it will remain subject to the survivorship rights of the other spouse. This makes it relatively impossible for creditors of one spouse to reach property so held.

d. Termination

A tenancy by the entirety is not subject to partition but it may be ended in one of three ways:

1) *Death.* Whereby the survivor takes the entire estate;

2) *Divorce.* Which converts the estate into a tenancy in common or a joint tenancy in different states;

3) *Mutual Agreement.* In the form of cross-deeds by the parties.

4. COMMUNITY PROPERTY

This form of coownership, held by spouses, is derived from the civil law and exists in most western states.

a. Requirements

Property is community property if it is acquired during the marriage. It is not required that the deed specify that community property is intended, although the specification of some other form of concurrent ownership may defeat the general presumption of community property. In some jurisdictions, assets received by gift rather than purchase are treated as the separate property of the receiving spouse rather than as community property. Assets which the parties bring to the marriage, as well as what those assets are converted to afterwards, are separate property.

b. Termination

Originally, the husband (because he was held to have management and control of the community property) could unilaterally convey the entire title to a third person; today, the signatures of both spouses are generally required, and a deed signed by only one spouse may transfer no interest at all to the property. Severance and partition are not applicable to community property; it is instead subject to a division between the spouses in a divorce action or by agreement or conveyances executed between them.

c. Survivorship and Inheritance

The principle of survivorship does not apply to community property. Each spouse may devise one-half of the property; however, when a spouse dies intestate, the other spouse will inherit that interest, in preference to other heirs.

5. CONDOMINIUMS, CO–OPS AND TIME SHARES
a. Types
1) Condominiums
Condominium ownership gives an individual fee title to the space inside a unit (apartment) of the building, together with ownership in common with all other unit owners of the common features of the building (walls, halls, etc.). Thus, there is concurrent ownership of the building itself but separate ownership of the individual units.

2) Cooperative Apartments
In a cooperative apartment, title to a building is held by a corporation; an individual acquires the right to occupy a separate apartment by purchasing stock from the corporation, which usually carries with it a lease to a unit ("proprietary lease"). Thus, there is no real concurrent ownership of realty involved here except that several people will own stock (which is personalty rather than realty) in the same corporation.

3) Time Shares
In some arrangements of this kind, an individual has divided, separate ownership of her unit only for a certain time period each year (e.g., the month of May) and holds a remainder interest for the rest of the year in common with the other owners of the same unit and also concurrent ownership of the common facilities of the building with all other owners of the building. (There are other forms of timesharing arrangements, such as a lease or license rather than ownership for the interval.)

b. Consequences of Shared Ownership
1) Partition
Generally, the bylaws of a condominium association (to which all owners may be required to belong) prohibit partition except under special circumstances, such as physical destruction of the building or favorable vote of a supermajority of the members. Since cooperative ownership does not entail separate titles in individuals, partition is an inappropriate mechanism.

2) Boundaries
Generally, the condominium deeds declare that the walls of the unit constitute its boundary even though the settling of the building may cause these walls to deviate somewhat from the original lines shown on the condominium map. (Otherwise, unit owners might be guilty of trespassing on their neighbor's property if the building tilted at all.)

In a cooperative building, any description would be contained in the lease.

3) Financing
    a) Condominium
        Each unit owner is able to separately mortgage her unit, and the default of any neighbors upon their own mortgages has no impact upon the other owners. Unit owners remain liable collectively, however, for all obligations relating to the common parts.

    b) Cooperative
        Since all assets are owned collectively in a cooperative, there may be no individual financing of units. The entire unit may be subject to a blanket mortgage. Thus, a default by any one member of the cooperative must be cured by the collective action of the others. Taxes and assessments are also jointly, rather than individually, imposed.

4) Preemptive Rights
    Cooperative and condominium ownership may give the community organization a right of first refusal to purchase the unit when the owner indicates an intent to sell it at a certain price. The association is allowed a short time to match the offer which the owner has agreed to accept. Such preemptive rights also exist in other tenancy in common arrangements, though less frequently. When co-owners are involved, they generally involve attacks based on the rules regarding restraints on alienation. This can violate the rule against perpetuities unless drafted so as not to last too long.

5) Tenancy in Partnership
    The Uniform Partnership Act provides that a partner is co-owner with all other partners of all partnership property held as tenants in partnership. The partnership is treated as an entity which can hold title in its own name. The partners have interests in the partnership, not the property.

B. POSSESSION AND INCOME

The principle of unity of possession, common to all types of concurrent ownership, means that all co-owners are fully entitled to possess the entire premises. They have undivided interests and no one co-owner may mark off part of the space and claim it for exclusive use. The parties are free to enter into agreements allocating possessory rights. If they cannot agree as to how possession is to be shared, their only remedy may be to have the property partitioned, so that their concurrent ownership ceases.

1. **OUSTER**
    No one co-owner may exclude any of the others from all or part of the premises. Such an exclusion constitutes an ouster, entitling the dispossessed party to bring an action in ejectment. Unless and until such an ouster occurs, the sole possession by one of the co-owners is not actionable and may not be complained of by the others; their remedy is to move in themselves if they object to the sole possession. Ouster in adverse possession is covered in Chapter I.

    a. **Exclusive Lease**
        While any cotenant has the power to lease out her interest in the property, she cannot validly execute a lease or deed giving her lessee or grantee the right to exclusively possess all or some part of the property. Such exclusive possession would work an ouster of the other co-owners. The same is true for grant of an easement by one cotenant to a third party, since it would . . . convert the other tenants' possessory rights into those of a servient tenant.

2. **RENT LIABILITY**
    Most jurisdictions hold that one co-owner in sole possession is not liable for rent to the other co-owners, since he does not need their consent to be there. Some jurisdictions hold the tenant in sole possession liable for a fraction of the fair rental value of the premises. Some permit a rent liability to be asserted as an offset by the nonpossessors when the possessor seeks to recover contribution for expenses incurred in maintaining the property.

3. **DEPLETION**
    A tenant in sole possession who removes minerals from the property is required to account to the others for a share of the profits.

4. **WASTE**
    A tenant in sole possession who damages the property is liable to the other co-owners for the harm done. Both waste and depletion reduce the value of the entire estate, and are thus treated differently than mere possession by one cotenant.

5. **RENTS FROM THIRD PARTIES**
    Conceptually, a lease executed by one co-owner should not create any liability to the other co-owners, since it merely transfers that lessor's possessory right to the tenant, and does not exclude the other co-owners from possession. However, the Statute of Anne (1704) required a co-owner who received rents from third parties to share them with the other co-owners on the assumption that she is renting out the entire premises as their agent. Where community property is involved, the rent received is itself community property.

C. EXPENDITURES

1. **DOWN PAYMENTS**
   Where the parties make unequal contributions towards the down payment on property, it can be treated several ways. (The same applies when the entire price is paid at the time of acquisition.) Deferred payments are subject to different treatment.

   a. **Proportional Ownership**
      If title is taken as tenancy in common, (which permits unequal ownership interests), a court may allocate ownership according to the respective contributions of the parties. In a community property jurisdiction, acquisition of an asset during the marriage may be held to be the separate property of the spouse who used his or her separate funds to pay for it.

      Example: Ann and Bob purchased property as tenants in common, paying all cash. Ann contributed $60,000 and Bob contributed $40,000. A court could, given these facts, hold that Ann owned 60% of the property and Bob owned 40%. If this were a community property jurisdiction, the parties were married, and Ann put up the entire price herself from her separate (noncommunity) funds, a court could hold that the property belonged to her rather than to the community.

   b. **Gift or Loan**
      If title is taken as joint tenancy, the unity of interest requirement prohibits an unequal allocation of title. *Any excess contribution at the outset is therefore treated as a gift or a loan from one party to the other.* The presumption of equality of interests in tenancy in common may also lead to this result unless it can be shown that the parties intended to divide title according to their contributions. The presumption in favor of community property in western states may lead to the treatment of payment from separate funds as a gift to the community unless there is an agreement to the contrary.

      Example: Ann and Bob purchased property for $100,000 as joint tenants, but Ann paid the entire price herself. Unity of title requires that Bob hold a one half interest in the property despite his lack of contribution. Ann is treated as either having made a gift to Bob or as having loaned him $50,000. (If the transaction is treated as a loan, then on any resale of the property, Ann should recover an additional $50,000 from the resale price—perhaps plus interest—but Bob will be entitled to keep one half of the appreciation in value of the property.) If the parties were married, and this was a community property state, and Ann's payment came from her separate funds, and they took title as community property, her excess contribution could be treated as a gift from her to the community or perhaps as a loan from her to the community if the evidence supported such a transaction.

2. MORTGAGE AND TAX PAYMENTS

Once property has been acquired, certain payments must be made to keep from losing it. *When required mortgage or tax payments are made by one co-owner, there is no reason to assume that a gift was intended and there is a right to recover a share of it from the others.* This may be done through a direct action for contribution, or may be included as an element in an accounting or partition action between the parties. In community property jurisdictions, a tracing of the source of payments may be necessary in order to determine what percentage of the property is community and what percentage is separate.

a. Personal Liability

If the nonpaying co-owner was not personally liable for the obligation (but would have suffered loss of the property by a default), then the paying co-owner may not obtain a personal judgment for contribution, but is limited to obtaining a lien upon the other's interest in the property for reimbursement.

Example: Ann paid the back property taxes on the property in order to save it from being taken away from her and Bob. Property taxes are not a personal liability to the individual owner, so Bob was free to not pay them had he so desired. Consequently, Ann cannot recover a personal judgment against him for half the taxes. However, since his half of the property was saved by virtue of her expenditure, it is subject to a lien in her favor for that amount.

b. Offset by Rental Value

Where a required payment is made by a co-owner in sole possession who then seeks contribution from the other co-owners, they may be able to claim an offset for the value of his sole possession, even though they would have no affirmative right to charge him for it. If he has been collecting rents from third parties, he may deduct his expenses before sharing the balance with the other owners.

Example: Ann, who lived alone on the property, paid the mortgage and taxes herself. If Bob or his interest in the property is held responsible for some share of those expenditures, he may be able to offset that liability by the value to Ann of her exclusive possession of the property, even though he would not ordinarily be able to charge her a rent for that occupation. If Ann has rented out the property to Tina and received rent from her, she may deduct her proper expenditures before dividing up the income with Bob.

c. Redemption
A co-owner who reacquires the property at a mortgage foreclosure sale or tax sale is treated as regaining the title for the benefit of all the owners. The others may elect to reacquire their shares from him by reimbursing him for their share of what he paid.

3. REPAIRS
No co-owner can be compelled by the other to repair property, if he or she would prefer to permit it to stay dilapidated. Thus, a co-owner who does elect to make repairs cannot sue for contribution and obtain a money judgment against the other. *However, the cost of the repairs will be credited in favor of the repairer in a partition or an accounting action (and will be offset against any duty to share rents or profits).* In community property jurisdictions, the use of one spouse's separate funds to repair community property (or vice versa) may be treated either as a gift or a loan to the other or as an investment in the property.

4. IMPROVEMENTS
One co-owner cannot be compelled by the other to improve the property. If one voluntarily elects to expend funds for improvements, there is no right to demand contribuiton or to claim the expenditure in an accounting between the parties (unless the improvement has generated increased rents or profits). *A credit is given to the improver in any partition action, however.* In community property jurisdictions, the expenditure of separate funds to improve community property (or vice versa) may be treated as either a gift or a loan to the other or an investment in the property.

D. PARTITION

Partition is the division of a concurrently held estate into separate estates owned individually by the former common owners. It should not be confused with severance, which does not end the concurrent ownership relationship.

1. METHODS
Partition may be accomplished by voluntary act of all the parties or by court action sought by one of them.

a. Voluntary
Co-owners are free to divide the property as they mutually agree (subject to applicable zoning and subdivision laws concerning lot size). They may

accomplish this by cross deeds, conveying different parts of the land to each. Alternatively, they may sell the property to a third person and divide the proceeds.

b.   Judicial
Any joint tenant or tenant in common may bring an action to have the property partitioned. This does not require the assent of the others, and, in fact, this action is usually brought when the parties cannot agree about the property.

1)   In Kind
Where the property is capable of physical division, a court may do so, and allot to each of the co-owners a separate (divided), geographic segment of the parcel. Partition in kind is clearly inappropriate when the property consists of a single house on a single lot.

a)   Improvements
If one of the co-owners has improved some part of divisible property, it is appropriate in a partition action to award that improved part to the improver.

b)   Owelty
Where partition in kind cannot lead to perfect equality of shares, it may still be done and the party receiving the greater share of the land may be required to make a cash payment (owelty) to the other in order to equalize the distribution.

2)   By Sale
Where the property is not capable of physical division, a court may order that it be sold and the proceeds divided among the co-owners according to their respective interests.

a)   Credits
A co-owner who has repaired or improved the property may receive a greater share of the sale proceeds according to the increase in value this has produced. Compensation is usually measured according to the increase in value of the estate, rather than by the cost of the work done.

2.   INABILITY TO PARTITION
There are two situations where concurrently owned property may not be partitioned.

a.   Covenants
Co-owners may covenant between themselves not to partition the property. Such covenants are generally not treated as illegal restraints on alienation

and are held to run with the land. Most condominium projects include covenants by the individual unit owners not to partition except upon destruction of the project; in some cases, statutes prohibit partition, eliminating the need for condominium covenants against partitioning.

b. Marital Property

Tenancy by the entirety and community property are not subject to judicial partition. In community property jurisdictions, all such property is subject to the control of the divorce court and is awarded to the individual spouses according to the state's domestic relations law. Where tenancy by the entirety is involved, a divorce converts the estate into a joint tenancy or tenancy in common, which is then subject to an independent action for partition if either party elects to bring one.

E. TRANSFERS

This issue has been mainly covered in other contexts already. It is summarized here primarily for cross reference purposes.

1. LIFETIME TRANSFERS

a. Tenancy in Common

A tenant in common has the power to convey his or her interest in the property. The signature or assent of the other tenants in common is not required. The effect of the conveyance is to make the grantee a new tenant in common with the existing owners.

b. Joint Tenancy

A joint tenant has the same power to convey as does a tenant in common. Transfer of a joint tenancy interest severs the joint tenancy (as to that share) and makes the grantee a tenant in common.

c. Tenancy by the Entirety

Neither tenant by the entirety may transfer an interest in the property. Only the entire estate may be transferred by the joint act of both tenants.

d. Community Property

When the husband had management and control of the community, it was possible for him to convey the estate to a third person by his act alone. Today, the signature of both spouses is usually required for any transfer to be effective, although a bona fide purchaser of community property which stood of record in the name of only one party may be protected when taking a conveyance from that party.

2. **DEATH TRANSFERS**
   a. **Intestate Succession**
      1) Tenancy in Common
         The separate interest of each tenant in common passes to her heirs upon death. The other cotenant takes only if he qualifies as an heir.

      2) Joint Tenancy and Tenancy by the Entireties
         The principle of survivorship passes all of the title of the first dying tenant to the survivor, in preference to inheritance by the heirs.

      3) Community Property
         Generally, the surviving spouse takes all of the community property when the other dies intestate.

   b. **Testamentary Transfers**
      1) Tenancy in Common
         A tenant in common may dispose of her half interest of the property by will.

      2) Joint Tenancy and Tenancy by the Entirety
         The principle of survivorship defeats the contrary disposition in any will left by the first dying tenant.

      3) Community Property
         A spouse usually has testamentary power over one-half of the community property. It passes to the surviving spouse only when he dies intestate or else names the surviving spouse as legatee.

F. REVIEW QUESTIONS

1. T or F A conveyance from Ann "to Ann and Bob as joint tenants," creates a joint tenancy between Ann and Bob.

2. T or F A conveyance to Ann, Bob and Cal, giving Ann one-half, and Bob and Cal each one-fourth, all in joint tenancy, makes the three of them joint tenants.

3. T or F A conveyance "to Ann and Bob," without more being said creates a joint tenancy.

4. T or F If Ann, Bob and Cal are joint tenants, and Ann dies and then Bob dies, Cal takes all of the property.

5. T or F If Ann, Bob and Cal are joint tenants, and Cal conveys to Don, and then Ann dies, Don becomes owner of one-half the property.

6. T or F   A lease of the property must be executed by both of the two tenants in common to be valid.

7. T or F   A cotenant in possession may recover for all expenditures made on the property.

8. T or F   If a person owning a house marries, the house becomes community property in those states which have community property systems.

IV

LANDLORD AND TENANT

A. LEASEHOLD ESTATES

A tenancy is an estate in land created by a conveyance from the landlord (lessor) to the tenant (lessee). A lease is the usual document used to create this estate. A lease may be viewed as conveying the property to the tenant for a time (always of shorter duration than the Landlord's ownership interest). Much of landlord-tenant law may be understood historically by recognizing that the lease was originally regarded as a conveyance from Landlord to Tenant rather than as a contract between Landlord and Tenant.

1. NONFREEHOLDS

Freehold estates are described in Chapter II. Technically, they are distinct from nonfreehold estates because they involve seisin, which does not characterize nonfreehold estates; at common law the tenant of a nonfreehold had possession but not seisin. *Nonfreehold estates have a termination date which is known or may be calculated in advance.* Thus, a tenancy is typically for some set period of time, whereas a freehold ends on death or death without issue or heirs, all uncertain future events. (Life tenancies are not covered in this chapter.)

2. LANDLORD'S AND TENANT'S INTERESTS

By executing a lease, a landlord carves an estate out of her fee simple and conveys it to the tenant. Thereafter, she has only a future interest (today called a reversion) in the property, along with whatever contractual rights and obligations are created by the lease. The tenant has a present possessory estate in the property together with his contractual rights and obligations. At common law, the tenant's interest was regarded as personalty rather than realty (a "chattel real"). This could affect out of state probates. (In this chapter feminine pronouns refer to the landlord; masculine pronouns designate the tenant.)

3. COMPARED TO LESSER INTERESTS

The holder of any present possessory estate, whether freehold or nonfreehold, has the right to exclusive possession of the spacial location he "owns"; this is inherent in the notion of possession. Except as otherwise limited by his lease, a tenant has the same possessory rights (during his tenure) as does an owner; he may act as he pleases on the land, he may exclude all others, and he owes the general tort duties of care to others. Thus, it may be important to determine whether a person currently on the premises is a tenant or is there in some other capacity (although the resolution of the ultimate issue—e.g., liability for personal injuries—may depend on more than this classification feature). Related forms of presence are listed below, with mention of some factors courts often use to determine the nature of the occupancy.

a. Dominant Tenants (Easements)

The holder of an affirmative easement (or profit) has a privilege of entering land to perform some specified act, e.g., to walk across it (an easement of right of way). But he is not a possessor; he cannot exclude others and he cannot engage in other acts not enumerated in his grant. (If his easement is for a finite time period, it may be appropriate to say that he has leased an easement, but he is still a dominant tenant rather than a tenant as used in this section of the book.)

b. Licensees

Many persons are permitted to enter lands for brief periods for limited purposes, e.g., those delivering goods, making repairs, visiting, or attending a performance. Since their continued presence is usually at the will of the possessor, they are generally referred to as licensees. They are not possessors, since they cannot exclude others; it is true that their rights are contingent, but that is irrelevant, since a tenant at will (described later) has possession even though it may be revoked at any time by his landlord.

c. Lodgers, Guests, Concessionaires, etc.

One occupying a hotel room usually does not have possession of it; management retains the right to enter for, e.g., cleaning. Employees who are permitted to "bunk" or sleep on the premises are similarly regarded. Concessionaires in department stores generally do not have possession of the space allocated to them for their sales. The grounds for making these distinctions are primarily factual, e.g.: length of stay, sharing of common facilities, relation to other services, relocatability of space involved.

B. TYPES OF TENANCIES

There are four tenancies, although one of them (tenancy at will) rarely arises in a landlord-tenant context and another (tenancy at sufferance) should not properly be considered as a tenancy at all. The two major tenancies are the tenancy for a term and the periodic tenancy. *As with the freehold estates, the basis of distinguishing tenancies from one another is by their duration or, correlatively, their method of termination.*

1. TENANCY FOR A TERM

This estate has a fixed term and ends automatically and without notice at the completion of that term. It is also known as a tenancy (or estate) for years.

a. Specification of the Term

The term is usually stated in the lease as some fixed period of time, e.g., one year, six months, three weeks. Technical problems arise when the term is set according to some future event, e.g., "until the end of the war" because this could be considered as creating a freehold estate (possibly a fee simple determinable) or, where the event is within the control of a party, which could create a tenancy at will instead.

1) Commencement of the Term
    The lease will usually provide when the term begins. Until that date, the parties may be regarded as having a contract for a lease rather than a lease, and contract rather than property law principles may apply. Where the term is to commence at some uncertain time in the future (e.g., completion of construction), the rule against perpetuities may be violated. (See Chapter II.)

b. Duration of the Term
The common law imposed no upper or lower limit on the duration of such tenancies. An estate for years could exist even though the term was for only two weeks, so long as there was a definite duration, after which the estate automatically ended. Many statutes today limit leases to 50 or 99 years on doctrines more or less similar to the policy of the rule against perpetuities.

c. Creation
A tenancy for a term is usually created by a written lease, although a writing is required only if the term is long enough to come within the statute of frauds—one year in most states. In determining duration, most jurisdictions include the time covered in any option to renew contained in the lease.

d. Automatic Termination
A term of years ends automatically at the close of the last day of the term. Neither party needs to give notice to the other. Since termination is automatic, notice would in fact be unavailing, as neither party can unilaterally extend or abbreviate the term. Only by mutual agreement can the parties lengthen or shorten the original term.

2. PERIODIC TENANCY
This estate has a fixed period, but that period is continuously and automatically renewed unless proper and timely steps to terminate it are taken. Its termination feature is therefore the reverse of the tenancy for a term, which ends automatically unless special steps are taken to continue it. It is also known as a tenancy (or estate) from period to period, e.g. from month to month.

a. Creation
There are a number of ways in which a periodic tenancy can arise:

1) Express Agreement
A periodic tenancy is created whenever the leasing document explicitly so provides. A "rental agreement," which sets forth a periodic rent and provides for termination only upon appropriate notice by one of the parties, creates a periodic tenancy.

a) Statute of Frauds
A writing is required for a periodic tenancy only when the basic period itself is long enough to come within the statute. Potential renewals of short terms usually do not bring the tenancy within the statute.

2) Implication
Whenever one person possesses property with the consent of the owner and pays rent to her, a periodic tenancy arises even though the parties have made no formal agreement to that effect.

a) Invalid Lease
If a lease for a term is invalid for any reason (e.g., failure to comply with the Statute of Frauds), but the tenant enters under it and pays rent to the landlord, a periodic tenancy arises. This substitute periodic estate may, in fact, last longer than the original term estate, since it does not automatically terminate on the intended expiration date of the term.

b) Holdover
When a tenant for years remains in possession after the expiration of the term and continues to pay rent to the landlord, a periodic tenancy may arise and replace the previous term estate.
Thereafter, as a result, the tenant may (or will have to) stay in possession until effective steps to terminate the periodic tenancy are taken.

b. **Length of the Period**
There is no required length of period. It may be a tenancy from year to year, month to month, week to week, etc. If the document fails to specify the length of the period, it is taken to be the basis by which the tenant pays rent or by which rent is estimated. Thus a rent of $1200 per year, payable at $100 per month, may be construed to create either a tenancy from year to year (how the rent was estimated) or from month to month (how it was paid). The difference is significant in determining how to terminate the estate.

c. Termination

A periodic tenancy is terminated by one party giving timely notice to the other of an intent to terminate. Otherwise the periodic tenancy renews automatically for the next period.

1) **Time Required for Notice**

At common law, notice had to be given at least one period in advance (up to 6 months). Thus, a tenancy from month to month required at least one month's notice for effective termination. The notice requirement is often modified by statute today and lease agreements frequently specially provide for the kind of notice necessary to terminate.

2) **Effective Date of the Notice**

At common law, a periodic tenancy could only be terminated upon an anniversary date. Thus, notice of termination was effective only when it purported to terminate as of the end of a period. If a tenancy from month to month began on the fifth day of each month, it could only be terminated as of the end of the fourth day of a future month. Today, statutes sometimes provide that a periodic tenancy may be terminated as of any date, after proper notice, without requiring that termination coincide with an anniversary date.

3) **Consequence of Ineffective Notice**

At common law, an improper notice of termination was entirely ineffective. A notice which attempted to terminate as of a premature termination date was often held entirely inoperative even as of the next valid potential termination date. This rule is less rigorously applied today.

Examples: (1) Tom was a tenant from month to month, paying rent on the fifth of each month. Laura, his landlord, sent him a notice of intention to terminate his tenancy as of September 5th; however, she did not send it to him until August 10th. The notice is invalid to terminate the tenancy on September 5th because it was not sent far enough in advance (30 days for a month to month tenancy). The notice may also be ineffective to terminate the tenancy on September 10th (thirty days) or on October 5th (the next anniversary date) or at any time thereafter. Laura may be required to start over and send Tom a new notice which states a proper date, in order to validly terminate this tenancy.

(2) Tom, a periodic tenant, quit the premises and sent Laura a letter advising her that he had left. The letter

is ineffective to terminate the tenancy. It could not work to terminate the tenancy as of the date it was sent (too soon), nor could it terminate it as of any later date, (because no such date was given). His tenancy may continue to renew until he sends a proper notice of termination.

4)   Effect of Nontermination
When a periodic tenancy renews, all of the terms and conditions also renew and continue to apply. The tenant owes the same rent as before. There is no uniformity among jurisdictions as to how rent or other provisions may be changed between periods. Some permit a landlord to state in her notice that the rent will increase if the tenant elects to stay on for the next period; others do not allow this.

4.   TENANCY AT WILL
This estate lasts until either party elects to terminate it, either expressly or impliedly. It lacks the predetermined termination date of a tenancy for a term, and it is not automatically renewed regularly as is a periodic tenancy.

a.   Creation
A tenancy at will may be created by express agreement of the parties, i.e., by a leasing arrangement which is made terminable at the will of either party. (But if a regular rent is charged, it will probably be treated as a periodic tenancy.) Alternatively, it can arise by implication when one enters on land with the consent of the owner but with no agreement or payment of any rent. One who enters under a void deed is a tenant at will; a tenant who enters under a void lease is also a tenant at will—at least until some rent is paid, at which point he becomes a periodic tenant (measured by the period covered by the rent).

1)   Where Terminability Is Not Mutual
If the agreement permits only one party to terminate at will, there may not be a tenancy at will. The old rule read mutuality into the arrangement and made it a tenancy at will, but many courts now treat it as a defeasible estate, instead.

b.   Termination
1)   By Notice
A tenancy at will is terminated by notice given by either party. The common law imposed no requirement of advance notice but some statutes do add such a restriction.

2) By Implication
A tenancy at will is terminated by the death of either party or by a transfer of either party's interest to a third party. These events are also referred to as terminations by operation of law.

4. TENANCY AT SUFFERANCE
This label describes the status of a tenant who has held over after the expiration of his tenancy (of whatever sort) and against whom the landlord has not yet taken action. It arises from inaction by the landlord rather than by the mutual consent of the parties. The term is used to indicate that the tenant is not (yet) a trespasser, having originally entered onto the premises rightfully, even though he may now be there wrongfully. This is covered in the section on holdovers, below.

C. POSSESSION

Since a lease transfers a present possessory estate to the tenant, the right of possession belongs to the tenant. As possessor, the tenant may engage in any activity he wants, subject to restrictive covenants in the lease and the law of waste. The tenant's right to possess does not require that he physically occupy the property unless this is required either explicitly or implicitly (e.g., by a percentage rent provision) in the lease. The tenant's possession also includes implied easements in the common areas, which are regarded as being under the possession and control of the landlord. Once possession of the premises has been transferred to the tenant, the landlord has only a limited right to enter them.

1. RIGHT TO POSSESSION AT COMMENCEMENT
The tenant has the legal right of possession as of the day his leasehold estate commences. If the landlord has made it impossible for him to enter at that time, he may terminate the lease and/or recover damages. A breach by the landlord occurs if she:

(1) fails to have any possessory right herself to the property (e.g., was not the owner);

(2) personally prevents the tenant from entering and taking possession (e.g., possesses it herself, and doesn't leave);

(3) has given another party a prior right of possession (e.g., has signed an earlier lease with someone who is now in possession under it).

a. Possession Withheld by a Stranger
When the tenant is unable to take possession of the property because a third party is in possession, but without the consent of the landlord, the courts are divided as to the tenant's rights.

1) Legal Possession

Some courts hold that a landlord is required only to deliver legal possession to the tenant, i.e. the right to possession, and is not, responsible for interference by third persons. The tenant has the same remedies available against the wrongdoer as would the landlord, and therefore he must go against the possessor rather than sue his landlord for damages or termination. This view is sometimes known as the American Rule, although it may be followed by only a minority of state courts.

2) Actual Possession
Other courts hold that the landlord is obliged to put the tenant into actual possession at the commencement of the lease. If that is impossible because of wrongful possession of a third person, the tenant may terminate the lease and/or sue the landlord for damages, even though she was not herself at fault, on the ground that she as landlord was better able to remove the wrongful occupier (usually the former tenant) than is the new incoming tenant. This is sometimes referred to as the English Rule although a majority of American courts adhere to it.

3) Language in the Lease
The lease itself may recite whether legal or actual possession is being given to the tenant. In some jurisdictions, a waiver by the tenant of the right to actual possession is invalid.

2. RIGHT TO POSSESSION FOR THE DURATION OF THE TERM
A landlord may not interfere with the tenant's possession at any time during his term. This obligation is imposed upon the landlord by virtue of having executed a lease. *She is said to have impliedly covenanted in it that the tenant shall have the quiet enjoyment of the premises for the life of the lease.*

a. Extent of Protection
A landlord does not warrant that the tenant shall be free from all possessory intrusions during the leasehold; she is not an insurer of the tenant's actual possession. But she does warrant that the tenant shall not be disturbed by her, by persons acting under her, or by persons holding a title superior to her, i.e., those with a paramount title.

1) Paramount Title
A lease impliedly represents that the landlord's right to transfer possession to the tenant for the entire duration of his term is not subject to any legal impediment. If third persons actually interfere with the tenant's possession by virtue of a lawful claim, there is an

"eviction by paramount title" entitling the tenant to relief against the landlord.   The following situations are illustrative:

a)   *No Title*.   Where the landlord had no claim to the property at all, the true owner appears and dispossesses the tenant;

b)   *Mortgage*.   Where the landlord's title is subject to a mortgage and the mortgagee forecloses because of nonpayment by the landlord;

c) *Insufficient Estate*.   Where the landlord has only a life estate or joint tenancy interest in the property and dies before the leasehold term is completed (assuming, in the case of joint tenancy, that the court does not hold that the execution of a lease by only one joint tenant severs or suspends the joint tenancy).

d)   *Preexisting Tenancy*.   Where the landlord has previously leased the premises to another tenant whose term has not yet ended.

2)   Strangers
The implied covenant of quiet enjoyment does not protect the tenant against possessory intrusions by parties who have no connection with the landlord and no legal claim to the property.   The tenant's remedies here are against the intruders.

> *Example:*   Because of a severe housing shortage, a group of people seeking shelter take over Tom's apartment while he is vacationing and refuse to leave when he returns.   He has no remedy against Laura in this case, but must himself act to remove the squatters.

3)   Eminent Domain
The government may elect to acquire property for its own use, and may do so without the owner's consent (so long as the acquisition is in the public interest and just compensation is paid).   When the government elects to take the entire fee, it acquires both the tenant's leasehold and the landlord's reversion.   Although this does not constitute a breach of the covenant of quiet enjoyment (since the landlord is not responsible for what the government elects to do), it nevertheless terminates the obligation to pay rent, since the leasehold is terminated.

a)   Allocation of the Condemnation Award
The government is required to pay just compensation for property acquired by condemnation.   The value is determined independently of the lease (otherwise private parties could control

the size of the condemnation award by entering into exaggerated lease agreements just prior to governmental takings). The award belongs to the persons whose property has been taken, which includes both landlord and tenant. The value of the tenant's leasehold is often equal to his rent burden, meaning that he receives no compensation when that is the case. However, if his leasehold was worth more than his rent liability, then he is entitled to a share of the award to compensate him for this lost "bonus value".

> *Example:* Tom's lease entitled him to possession for another year at a monthly rent of $1000; however, because of increased neighborhood attractiveness, the premises had a current fair rental value of $1200 per month. This means that Tom's lease had a bonus value of $200 per month, and he might have sublet it for a $200 monthly profit or sold (assigned) his remaining one year for the present value of $12 \times \$200 = \$2400$ (an assignee would be willing to pay Tom the present value of this $2400 in order to rent the premises for $200 per month less than they were worth). The condemnation award should be similarly treated; Tom should receive from it the present value of his $200 monthly bonus value.

b) Temporary Takings
   Where the government takes the property only temporarily (i.e., for a shorter period than the balance of the tenant's term), the lease is not terminated and the tenant's rent liability is not suspended. The government has taken only property of the tenant in this case, not the landlord, and the award belongs entirely to the tenant.

c) Partial Takings
   Where the government takes only a part of the property (e.g., an easement or physical strip), most courts hold that the tenant's rent liability is unaffected. Therefore, his share of the condemnation award includes not only the bonus value of this part of the premises, but also a capital sum which can be amortized over the balance of the leasehold to cover the rent burden of that part taken.

> *Example:* The government acquires a strip of property for street widening purposes. Tom's rent was $1000 per month (which was also the fair rental value of the premises), the strip had a fair rental value of $150 per month,

and the lease had one year to run. From the government's award, Tom should receive the present value of $150 a month for the next 12 months, which will cover his "excess" rent liability during that period. Laura will receive the balance of the award. If the rental value of the premises had increased over the rent reserved, then Tom's award should be increased to cover the loss of that bonus value as well.

b. Eviction Necessary
The mere existence of an adverse claim to the property does not constitute a breach of the implied covenant of quiet enjoyment. There must first be an "eviction."

Example: During the course of the lease, Tom learns that Laura's title is subject to a prior mortgage. But unless and until Laura defaults on it and the mortgagee actually forecloses and dispossesses Tom, there has been no breach by Laura of the implied covenant of quiet enjoyment. Until the eviction, Tom is "estopped to deny" Laura's title.

1) Partial Eviction
A landlord is guilty of a breach of the covenant of quiet enjoyment if she evicts a tenant from all or part of the premises. If an eviction is by paramount title, the tenant's remedies may differ depending upon whether the eviction is total or partial. Remedies are discussed below.

c. Remedies
At common law, *covenants in leases were treated as independent* (i.e., the nonperformance of a covenant by one party did not justify a refusal by the other to perform any covenants applicable to him). However, a major exception which arose to the doctrine of independent covenants was that the tenant's duty to pay rent was dependent on the landlord's duty to furnish him quiet enjoyment; this doctrine arose when rent consisted of a share of the crops, which the tenant could obviously not pay after he was ousted from possession.

1) Rent Excused
Where the landlord breaches the covenant of quiet enjoyment and causes an eviction of the tenant from the premises, the tenant is no longer obliged to pay rent. Some courts hold that a tenant who has been partially evicted by the landlord may remain on the premises without paying any rent, on the ground that a landlord may not "apportion his wrong." If the eviction is caused by a paramount title

and is only partial, rent liability may be only reduced rather than totally eliminated.

2) Destruction

At common law, the landlord did not warrant the continued existence of the premises. *The tenant's obligation to pay rent was not terminated merely because the premises were destroyed, unless destruction was caused by the landlord.* Many jurisdictions, however, now follow the civil law rule that destruction of a material part of the premises does entitle the tenant to terminate the lease. Lease provisions frequently cover this matter.

3) Frustration

If the premises have been leased to the tenant for some particular purpose which, because of subsequent legal or other developments, becomes impossible, the tenant may be entitled to terminate the lease under a frustration theory even though there is no covenant or warranty in the lease to that effect. It is generally required that the intended use be known to the landlord (or that the tenant be limited to that use by the lease), that the use be totally frustrated, and that the frustrating development have been unforseeable.

4) Damages

The tenant may be also entitled to recover damages from the landlord for any breach of the covenant of quiet enjoyment. This may include moving costs, increased rent paid elsewhere or loss of rental value in the premises (if the tenant has not completely quit).

3. ABANDONMENT

A tenant has no general duty to remain in actual possession during the term of his lease and a landlord has no remedy against a nonpossessing tenant who continues to pay the rent and perform the other covenants of the lease. But where a tenant both leaves the premises and stops paying rent, the landlord has a number of options.

a. Recover Rent

The common law permitted a landlord to ignore the tenant's abandonment, make no attempt to relet the premises, and continue to claim the rent as it fell due each period. The tenant, could not, by his unilateral departure, bring about a termination of the lease.

1) No Duty to Mitigate

Under this common law rule, a landlord had no duty to mitigate any loss caused by an abandoning tenant. She could allow the premises to stay vacant and recover the entire amount of the rent from the tenant as it fell due. Many jurisdictions now either directly impose an obligation to mitigate (i.e., attempt to rerent the premises), or do so indirectly, by limiting the landlord's recovery to damages rather than rents, as discussed below.

2) Time to Sue
A landlord may sue for rent only as it falls due and not before. Thus, where the lease calls for monthly payments of rent, the landlord may file suit each month for that rent, or may permit the months to accumulate (up to the limit of the statute of limitations) and then sue for all of the back unpaid rent. A landlord is generally not allowed to sue for rent not yet due merely because the tenant has abandoned and defaulted.

a) Rent Acceleration Clauses
The lease may provide that the entire balance of the rent becomes due immediately after any default by the tenant. If the clause is not declared invalid as a penalty, the landlord may then be able to claim the remainder of the rent for the term once the tenant abandons.

b. **Accept a Surrender**
At the opposite extreme, the landlord may treat the tenant's abandonment and nonpayment of rent as an offer to surrender the leasehold back to her and she may accept this offer by retaking possession herself. After such a reconveyance, the leasehold merges into the landlord's reversion.

1) No Writing Necessary
Courts treat this as a surrender by "operation of law," in order to avoid the requirement of the statute of frauds that a conveyance of a leasehold estate from tenant to landlord must be in writing.

2) Termination of Rent and Lease
Once the leasehold is ended by surrender there is no longer any rent liability owed by the tenant, and the landlord is free to relet the premises.

3) Contrary Lease Clause
A lease may provide that the tenant remains liable for rent despite a termination of his estate. Such a provision is often held invalid or is very strictly construed because it charges the tenant for possession of an estate no longer available to him.

c. **Relet the Premises**
A remedy midway between holding a tenant for the entire term and completely terminating his estate permits the landlord to relet abandoned premises as the tenant's agent and then recover from him the difference

between the rent originally set in his lease and the rent she is able to collect from the new occupant.

1) Availability
    Some jurisdictions require that the lease expressly include this remedy in order for the landlord to employ it. Others require the landlord to first notify the tenant of an intent to so act or require that the tenant consent to it. It is generally treated as a question of fact (or intent) whether the landlord's reentry has been as an agent of the tenant to mitigate a loss or on her own behalf in order to accept a surrender.

    a) Prohibited Acts
        If the landlord extensively remodels the premises, or enters into a new leasing agreement significantly different or longer from that original lease, a court may refuse to treat the reletting as for the tenant's account and will instead declare that there has been a surrender by operation of law. On the other hand, it is appropriate for the landlord to enter abandoned premises in order to check their condition and to secure them against vandalism and other dangers. Some jurisdictions permit the landlord to send a notice to the tenant to make certain that the tenant has abandoned before she enters.

2) Recovery of Difference
    Exercise of this remedy does not terminate the tenant's original rent liability although it is reduced by the amount collected from the new tenant. The landlord may sue the tenant for the difference each period, or permit it to accumulate. Various accounting issues may arise in these situations.

    Example: When Tom abandoned, his lease had one year remaining at a rent of $1000 per month. Laura spent a month repairing the premises (at a cost of $2000) and looking for a new tenant, before she was able to lease them to Newt for three years at a rent of $1200 per month. A determination of Tom's liability, if any, should consider the lost month, the repairs made by Laura, and the longer term of Newt's lease as possible offsets against the higher rent she is receiving.

d. **Damages**
    Either the lease may provide or the jurisdiction may require that a landlord will recover damages instead of rent, or as an additional entitlement from an abandoning tenant.

1) Difference Value

A landlord may recover damages following a tenant's abandonment, measured by the difference between the rent that the tenant would have paid and the fair rental value of the premises over the balance of the term. This is the benefit of the bargain to the landlord.

Example: If the rent reserved in Tom's lease was $1000 per month and the premises had a fair rental value of $750 when he abandoned, then Laura's damages equal $250 times the number of months remaining in Tom's lease.

2) When Recoverable

Unlike rent, a landlord may recover damages as soon as the breach occurs. Thus, she may sue for her entire damages immediately after the tenant abandons. Because the award covers losses which would not arise until the future, the loss for the each future month must be discounted down to present value (along with the addition of interest for the loss for those months which have already passed by the time the award is made).

4. HOLDING OVER

A tenant's possessory right last only as long as the tenancy endures. Thus, a tenant is expected to have removed himself and his belongings by or before the end of the lease term. A tenant who does not quit the premises at the proper time stays on wrongfully. The term "tenant at sufferance" is used to designate such a person.

Examples: (1) Tom, a tenant for a term, did not vacate the premises on June 30, the day his one-year lease expired. He is, on July 1, a tenant at sufferance.

(2) Tom, a tenant from month to month, gave proper notice of termination to Laura (or vice versa) to take effect on March 15. But Tom did not leave on that day; he is, on March 16, a tenant at sufferance.

(3) Tom remained on the premises after having failed to pay the rent and having received a notice from Laura to quit the premises for nonpayment of rent. He became a tenant at sufferance once this notice period expired.

a. Landlord's Elections

Once a tenant fails to leave when his tenancy ends, he becomes subject to an election of remedies by the landlord:

1) Eviction
The landlord may take steps to force the tenant to leave the premises.
Once the landlord signifies her intent to not permit the tenant to
stay, he becomes a trespasser on the premises, and may be removed.

   a) Self-Help
      An English statute in 1381 made it a crime for a landlord to
      recover possession of the premises by force, even when the tenant
      was wrongfully maintaining possession. However, such a "forcible
      entry" was held to constitute only a criminal, nor a civil, wrong,
      and the tenant could not sue the landlord for trespass. Today,
      many courts make the landlord liable to the tenant in tort for
      even a peaceable entry, thus compelling the landlord to use the
      judicial process to evict the tenant. Other courts permit the
      landlord to make a peaceable entry, but may treat, e.g., picking
      the lock, as constituting the use of force. In some jurisdictions,
      shutting off the utilities in order to evict the tenant is penalized
      as a kind of constructive forcible entry on the landlord's part.
      Clauses in the lease may permit the landlord to use forms of self-
      help otherwise prohibited, but such clauses are often held to
      violate public policy. In no jurisdiction is the landlord permitted
      to use force against the tenant personally to recover possession.

      (1) *Forcible Detainer.* Some jurisdictions penalize forcible
         detainers as well as forcible entries. Thus, a landlord who
         obtains possession peaceably (i.e., while the tenant is out),
         but then uses force or threats to keep the tenant out
         (perhaps changing the lock), may be liable to the tenant for
         tort damages.

   b) Ejectment
      A tenant no longer entitled to possession is guilty of ejectment
      when he refuses to leave. Ejectment is the traditional cause of
      action brought against wrongful possessors of land, and it restores
      the plaintiff to possession and awards her damages from the
      dispossession. It is covered more fully in Chapter I.

   c) Summary Dispossess
      *Statutes in all jurisdictions provide a speedy judicial proceeding for
      the removal of a tenant wrongfully refusing to leave.* Such
      summary dispossess, or unlawful detainer statutes vary in detail
      from state to state. The common features of such proceedings
      are described below:

      (1) *Preliminary Notice.* A notice to perform (pay rent), or to
         quit, or to perform or quit may be required where the

tenant's estate has not terminated but the tenant has defaulted in his performance of some obligation required in the lease. If the tenancy has already terminated with the tenant holding over, then no such notice should be required, although some jurisdictions still require the landlord to send a notice to quit to the tenant in these circumstances.

(2) *Summons*. Most jurisdictions provide for a shorter summons period than is generally applicable to other causes of action, e.g., 3 to 5 days.

(3) *Pleadings*. In general, a tenant is not allowed to plead affirmative defenses or cross-complain, which would delay the accelerated nature of this proceeding. Theoretically, only the landlord's right to possession is at issue. However, courts have permitted several affirmative defenses to be raised despite their dilatory effect upon the process, e.g., the implied warranty of habitability, retaliatory eviction.

(4) *Trial*. These matters are usually entitled to priority on the trial calendar.

(5) *Relief*. A judgment in favor of the landlord leads to prompt restoration or possession. Some states permit damages or rent for the wrongful withholding; others consign that to a separate action.

(6) *Appeal Bond*. The tenant may be required to post an extra large bond if he desires to appeal a judgment ordering him to quit the premises.

d) Damages
A tenant who remains in possession after his term has ended and after the landlord has indicated her nonconsent to his remaining is liable for damages measured by the use value of the land. "Rent" is inappropriate, since a tenancy is no longer involved. In some jurisdictions statutes provide for a doubling or trebling of damages against a holdover tenant, especially if the holding over is wanton or malicious.

2) Involuntary Renewal
A landlord may, alternatively, compel the holdover tenant to remain on as a tenant. The tenant's consent is generally not required.

a) Tenancy Created
The new tenancy which arises when a landlord compels a holdover to stay is generally treated as a periodic tenancy, regardless of the nature of the original tenancy. Thus a tenant, who is made to stay for one additional month because of his failure to quit at the end of the previous month, may find himself held for the following month as well unless he gives the proper notice of termination required of periodic tenants.

> *Example:* Tom failed to quit on the last day of his term. Laura elected to make him stay for another period. Tom is now a periodic tenant, whose new tenancy will not terminate at the end of the next period, even if he does quit at that time, unless he or Laura gives proper notice of termination.

b) Length of the Period
At common law, the previous length of time employed by the parties for estimating rent was used to set the length of the period of the new tenancy created by the landlord's election after the tenant held over. Thus, if the original lease set an amount for a yearly rent (even though it might be made payable monthly) the new tenancy could be treated as a tenancy from year to year. Many statutes now prescribe that the period for paying rent determines the duration of the new period, regardless of how it was estimated in the lease.

c) Same Terms
Once a holdover tenant is made into a periodic tenant, all of the covenants and provisions of the original leasing agreement apply and he owes rent at the previous rate.

d) Partial and Involuntary Holdovers
Some courts refuse to permit the landlord to compel a tenant to stay where his holding over was involuntary (e.g., due to illness or a moving company strike) or only partial (e.g., a few boxes left on the premises).

b. Method of Making Election
Written or oral notice by the landlord is effective to manifest her election against a holdover tenant. *Once she accepts rent from the tenant, she is deemed to have elected (consented) that he stay, and a periodic tenancy arises.* If she delays too long, even if no rent is paid she may lose her power to elect by virtue of laches.

D. RENT

Any person possessing the property of another is deemed to owe rent unless that obligation has been waived by the owner. Waiver can be explicit or implied from the circumstances (e.g., employee housing). Usually, there is a lease provision establishing a specific rent liability.

1. RENT CONTROL

Generally, the amount of rent charged is a matter of private contract between landlord and tenant. Where a tenancy for a term has been created, the rent is set for the entire term and be renegotiated only at the end of the term (for the next term). Where a periodic tenancy exists, the same rent carries over for each new period, unless proper advance notice of a new rental charge has been given. Most states hold that a tenant who continues in possession for the next period, after having received proper notice of a rent increase, has impliedly assented to it. Where there is no agreement between the parties as to rent, the tenant is deemed to owe the reasonable rental value of the premises, unless a waiver is indicated.

a. Form of Payment

The rent charged may also include other expenditures to be made by the tenant on behalf of the landlord, e.g., property taxes and insurance premiums and other assessments (a "net lease"). There may be provisions for periodic recalculations according to changes in the consumer price index or other indicators (a "cost of living" or "escalator" clause). Additional rent may flow from the success of the tenant's business on the premises (a "percentage lease"). An agreement by the tenant to make improvements on the property and not to remove them (as trade fixtures) at the end of his term may also be viewed as a form of additional rent.

b. Rent Control Ordinances

Cities in several states (including New York, Massachusetts, New Jersey and California) have enacted local rent control ordinances limiting the amount residential landlords may charge their tenants. Courts generally uphold these restrictions against claims of unconstitutional interference with contract on the ground that they are justified when an emergency (a shortage of apartments) exist; they have also been upheld against antitrust and similar charges. By virtue of existing at a local level, generalizations are hard to provide. Some common features are listed below.

1) Original Rent

When a rent control ordinance is first enacted, it may freeze all rents at the existing level. More commonly, it "rolls back" rents to the level they were at some earlier date (before landlords became aware of the possibility of controls and raised their rents in anticipation of controls). This rent becomes the base rent for the unit regulated.

2) Adjustments

A rent control board generally is authorized to promulgate general cost of living increases periodically for all regulated units and to grant individual increases on petition by a landlord. Increases are usually granted where the landlord shows that she cannot otherwise receive a proper return on her investment (to avoid a lawsuit by her claiming the ordinance unconstitutionally "takes" her property without just compensation), or where her expenses have increased. The tenant may resist an increase by showing that the increased expenditures were unnecessary or may seek a decrease by showing that the landlord is no longer providing essential services or is failing to make repairs.

3) Protected Premises

Many ordinances exempt single family and two family housing from their restrictions, including only larger apartment buildings. Some exclude luxury rentals.

4) Vacancy Decontrol

Some ordinances permit the landlord to set a market rent once the tenant has vacated. Others permit a larger, but still restricted increase, when the tenant leaves. There are frequent disagreements whether a unit has become vacant when it passes from one tenant to another by virtue of death; intrafamily transfers generally do not trigger rent increases, but leave open transfers arising from, e.g., the divorce of the parties or the death of a gay lover.

5) Conversion and Demolition

Many ordinances restrict the right of landlords of residential buildings to demolish or convert them to condominiums or cooperatives, thereby worsening the shortage of apartments. The landlord may be required to provide relocation housing for the tenants, to offer the tenants "insider" prices on the condominium units being sold, or to permit the tenants to continue as renters even though the building is converted. There may also be quotas or other kinds of restrictions on the right to convert the building.

2. TIME OF PAYMENT

At common law, rent was due at the end of each period. Most leases now require it to be paid at the beginning of the period.

a. Nonapportionment

At common law, rent was not apportionable. It did not accrue each day as the period progressed but instead accrued all at once on the final day of the period. Thus, if some event occurred to relieve the tenant of liability before the last day of the period, no rent whatsoever was due for that period.

b. Acceleration

The lease may provide for the acceleration of all of the unpaid balance of the rent for the rest of the term upon a breach by the tenant. However, such a provision may be held unenforceable as a penalty or forfeiture.

3. RIGHT TO RENTS

The common law doctrine, that covenants in leases were independent, prohibited a landlord from dispossessing the tenant for nonpayment of rent. Despite such a default, the landlord was still obliged to honor the covenant of quiet enjoyment and not disturb the tenant's possession.

a. Distraint

A landlord's common law remedy against a tenant who did not pay rent was seizure of his chattels. This remedy is now generally held to be unconstitutional as depriving a tenant of property without notice or hearing if any state action is involved.

b. Termination

Today a landlord is generally permitted to terminate the leasehold of a defaulting tenant. This remedy may either be provided by statute or by inclusion of a condition subsequent in the lease, giving the landlord a power of termination for nonpayment of rent. This is exercised by the summary dispossess procedures described previously.

4. ADVANCE RENTAL PAYMENTS

Where the lease requires the tenant to pay money to the landlord in advance, his right to recover it back at the end of the term (or sooner) may depend upon its characterization. (In some jurisdictions there is a public policy requirement that all unused advance rental payments be refunded to the tenant at the end of the term regardless of how they are characterized in the lease.) Many states also regulate the amount which residential landlords may collect through these devices, and also impose upon them the duty to transfer such funds to new owners when the building is sold.

a. Security Deposit

This may be retained by the landlord at the end of the term lease only to the extent necessary to cover an actual loss sustained by her which the deposit was intended to secure, usually unpaid rent, physical damage or cleaning. During the term, the landlord holds the funds in pledge for the tenant, and may be required to credit the tenant with interest earned on the funds.

b. Advance Rent
The landlord must apply such payments towards that period (usually at the end of the term) which the payment was intended to cover. These funds may be kept by landlord even when she has entered the premises after abandonment by the tenant (see Section C.3. above) and terminated the lease and tenants future rent liability.

c. Bonus
If the tenant has given money to the landlord in order to induce her to execute the lease in the first place ("as consideration for the execution of the lease"), it belongs to her absolutely and need not be returned or applied to the rent or against other losses, if allowed by local law.

E. CONDITION OF THE PREMISES

This section covers the rights and liabilities of the parties arising out of conditions of disrepair of the premises.

1. COMMON LAW BACKGROUND
The common law treated a lease as a conveyance (sale) of the premises from landlord to tenant for a time. The rules of liability for defects were analogous to those applicable to vendor and purchaser in the case of sale of a fee.

a. Landlord's Nonliability
At common law, a landlord had no duty to put or keep the premises in good repair for the tenant, or to make the premises suitable for the tenant's intended use. She was subject only to a duty not to commit fraud, i.e., not to misrepresent the condition of the premises or to conceal material defects from the tenant.

1) Existing Defects
The doctrine of *caveat emptor* assumed that the tenant would inspect the premises prior to renting them. He took the premises "as is" except for those defects actively concealed by the landlord. He could not thereafter complain to the landlord about any preexisting defect which he later discovered.

2) Subsequent Defects
The fact that the tenant had possession of the premises throughout the term was held to eliminate any duty on the part of the landlord to maintain them in repair for that time. A leasing of property

implied no warranty by the landlord that the premises would remain in good condition for the tenant.

3) Exceptions

The landlord was held to have an obligation to make the premises fit for the tenant where the premises were furnished and the tenant was renting them for a short time only, on the ground that it was inappropriate to assume that the tenant had made a complete inspection under those circumstances. A similar duty existed, for the same reasons, where the lease was executed before construction of the premises was completed. (The important related topic of constructive eviction is discussed later.)

b. **Tenant's Liability**

A tenant in possession is the holder of a present possessory estate; the landlord holds a future interest in the same premises. *The tenant, therefore, owed to the landlord a common law duty not to commit waste on the premises, i.e., a duty to keep the premises windtight and watertight, by making minor repairs so as to avoid larger losses later, and also a duty to repair any damage he himself caused.* Waste is covered in Chapter XIII.

c. **Mutual Nonliability**

If the premises are damaged or destroyed by outside causes (e.g., acts of the elements or of strangers), neither party may have any duty to the other to repair or rebuild. A landlord has no general duty of repair, and, if the injury does not qualify as waste, the tenant has no special duty to repair it. Each may suffer some loss from the injury but neither can compel the other to correct it.

d. **Termination**

Where there is no duty to repair, neither party may terminate the lease for failure of the other to make a repair. *Thus at common law, a tenant could not quit paying the rent because his premises were destroyed, nor could his landlord terminate his estate if he refused to repair or rebuild the destroyed premises.* Statutes now commonly provide for the termination of residential leases upon a destruction of the premises, and most commercial leases cover, in great detail, the rights of the parties upon destruction of the premises.

e. **Repair Covenants**

1) By the Tenant

A covenant by a tenant to repair or to keep the premises in good repair extends his duty beyond that of avoiding waste and may require him to repair damage resulting from any cause. Some courts read the covenant as including obligations to make structural repairs or to rebuild premises which have been completely destroyed, unless these are expressly excluded.

2) **By the Landlord**
A repair covenant by a landlord eliminates her basic nonresponsibility and may require her to make the covered repairs within a reasonable time after receiving notice from the tenant. It usually does not require her to inspect the premises during the term to search for disrepairs.

f. Inadequacy of the Common Law Rules Today
The above doctrines made some sense in an earlier agrarian economy where the tenant was the sole and long-term possessor of isolated property, usually possessing sufficient skills to make all necessary repairs. They have little or no validity when applied to the modern urban, short-term apartment dweller who cannot examine the interior structure of the building prior to renting, and who sensibly expects the landlord to keep up the premises. The contemporary tenant is better viewed as a consumer of housing services rather than as holder of a leasehold estate in real property.

2. CONSTRUCTIVE EVICTION
The most significant early judicial departure from the common law rules came through the doctrine of constructive eviction. This doctrine permitted the tenant to quit the premises in certain cases of disrepair.

a. Relationship to Actual Eviction
Courts had already created one exception to the doctrine of independent covenants by permitting a tenant to terminate his lease and his rent liability if he had been actually evicted by the landlord. *The doctrine of constructive eviction gave the tenant this same right to quit when the landlord made it impossible for him to enjoy the premise as intended in the lease, even though she did not actually evict him. The landlord was held to have a duty not to interfere with the tenant's quiet enjoyment of the premises by virtue of an implied covenant to that effect in the lease.*

Example: If Laura enters and physically dispossesses Tom from his apartment, then he has been actually evicted and need no longer pay rent. If she instead destroys the common stairway so that he cannot get to his apartment without extreme danger, she may have constructively evicted him. There may also be a constructive eviction if she rips out his bathroom fixtures.

b. Change of Remedy, Not Right

The doctrine of constructive eviction does not by itself alter the basic common law principle that a landlord has no duty to put or keep the premises in good repair for the tenant. But it does eliminate the inability of a common law tenant to quit when the landlord breached a duty to him. The common law doctrine of independent covenants limited his relief to an action for damages for the breach, but did not excuse him from his duty to continue paying the rent. Constructive eviction gave him such relief by virtue of making his duty to pay rent dependent upon the landlord's honoring her obligation of quiet enjoyment towards him.

c. Elements

A tenant is entitled to terminate his lease and claim a constructive eviction only when certain facts are shown to exist:

1) Fault by the Landlord

The landlord must be at fault, i.e., have breached some duty owed to the tenant. The doctrine of constructive eviction does not of itself impose any new duties upon the landlord; some independent ground of fault must be found.

   a) Covenant to Repair

   If the lease contains a covenant by the landlord to repair, her failure to make such repairs may constitute not only a breach of the repair covenant but also a breach of her implied covenant of quiet enjoyment, if the nonrepair is sufficiently serious as to disturb the tenant's quiet enjoyment. The tenant may then elect to terminate the lease rather than bring an action for damages against her. If there is no such covenant to repair, then a landlord's refusal to make repairs creates no basis for claiming a constructive eviction.

   b) Covenant to Supply Services

   If the lease contains a covenant by the landlord to supply utilities to the tenant, her failure to do so may entitle the tenant to quit for the same reason as above. In the absence of such a covenant, the doctrine of constructive eviction does not impose any duty to supply the services.

   c) Other Covenants

   The doctrine of constructive eviction is not limited to matters concerning the physical condition of the premises. Breach of any covenant by the landlord may conceivably serve as a basis for claiming constructive eviction if it materially disturbs the tenant's quiet enjoyment, thereby breaching the implied covenant of quiet enjoyment.

Example: *Noncompetition Covenant:* Laura breached her covenant to Tom that she would not rent space in her shopping center to any merchant selling the same goods as Tom sold. Tom might claim a constructive eviction and terminate his lease as a result.

d) **Active Interference**
A landlord is subject to the same obligations as are imposed on the general public not to actively interfere with the tenant's possession and enjoyment of the premises. When a landlord engages in tortious activity which does interfere, the tenant may be able to claim a constructive eviction.

(1) *Acts of Third Parties.* A landlord does not insure that strangers will not interfere with the tenant's enjoyment of the premises. Her covenant of quiet enjoyment promises only that she herself and those acting under her will not do so.

Example: Tom's next door neighbor conducts a nuisance so that he cannot sleep at night. This does not entitle Tom to claim a constructive eviction by Laura (unless she is the neighbor).

(2) *Other Tenants.* Courts are divided as to whether a landlord is liable for disturbances caused by other tenants. Some declare her not responsible for the social and civil relations of her tenants; others do hold her responsible when she has the power to control the behavior, as when it violates lease provisions or occurs in common areas.

e) **Common Areas**
As possessor of the common areas, the landlord retains responsibility for them. Failure to maintain them in proper condition may constitute a constructive eviction if this affects the tenant's enjoyment of his own premises.

f) **Statutory and Judicially Imposed Duties**
(See implied warranty of habitability, Section 5).

2) **Material Interference**
Not every breach of covenant or delict by the landlord entitles the tenant to claim a constructive eviction. The interference must substantially interfere with his use and enjoyment of the premises in order to amount to breach of the implied covenant of quiet

enjoyment. Objective harm of a *nontemporary* nature is generally required.

3) Departure by the Tenant
In order to claim constructive eviction, a tenant must quit the premises promptly after the disturbance.

a) Excusable Delay

The tenant is not required to leave the premises the moment a breach occurs. He is allowed time to seek for new premises and to prepare for the move. Negotiations for corrections to be made or promises by the landlord to eliminate the problem will excuse an immediate exit.

d. **The Nature of the Relief**
1) Drastic Remedy
By requiring the tenant to quit the premises, the doctrine of constructive eviction is at odds with the general principle of mitigating damages. It forces the tenant to take extreme action: abandonment and termination of his lease. *This poses a serious risk since, if a court decides that he was wrong in quitting, he will remain liable for rent and/or damages as a tenant who has prematurely abandoned.* A few courts permit the tenant to seek declaratory relief to determine in advance if he is entitled to quit.

2) Damages
The doctrine of constructive eviction does not entitle the tenant to remain on the premises and recover damages. (Other theories doing so are discussed below.) His basic remedy is elimination of further rent liability by leaving.

a) Departure and Damages
A tenant who has quit and moved elsewhere because of a constructive eviction may be entitled to recover consequential damages i.e., moving expenses and increased rent paid for new premises.

3. **ILLEGAL LEASE**
A few courts hold that the leasing of seriously defective premises (i.e., in violation of the building code) constitutes an illegal contract. The tenant may terminate the lease, quit the premises, and eliminate any further rent liability.

a. **Comparison With Constructive Eviction**
The doctrine of illegal contract generally relates to defects which existed at the commencement of the lease whereas constructive eviction is usually

applied to subsequent defects. Both doctrines permit the tenant to quit
and thereby escape rent liability.

b. Rent Liability

If the tenant does quit under an illegal lease theory, he owes no further
rent. If he remains in possession, the landlord cannot charge the rent
reserved in the void lease, but the tenant is not entitled to remain on the
premises rent free. The landlord may evict him or may recover damages
from him if he remains in possession based on the reasonable rental value
of the premise or his rent liability may be determined by formulae taken
from the implied warranty of habitability (discussed below).

4. STATUTORY DUTIES

Many states now have special habitability statutes for residential premises.
These acts generally both impose repair obligations upon the landlord and
create new remedies for the tenant if the landlord fails to repair. In some
jurisdictions, the same results have come from judicial rather than legislative
action.

a. Repair and Deduct

Some statutes compel the landlord to put residential premises in a
tenantable or habitable condition at the outset and to maintain them that
way for the duration of the lease. A failure to make the statutory repairs
within a reasonable time entitles the tenant to make the repair himself
and to deduct the cost from the rent, up to some specified amount, e.g.,
one month's rent (per year).

b. Rent Withholding

Some statutes permit the tenant to withhold the rent and/or pay it into
an escrow account until the required repairs are made. The landlord is
denied access to the rent funds until she repairs. Once the repairs are
made, the funds belong to the landlord.

c. Receivership

Some statutes permit the tenant to have a receiver appointed by the court
to collect the rents and to utilize them to make the necessary repairs. In
this situation, the funds are not merely withheld from the landlord; they
are instead applied to make the repairs, as if the landlord were subject to
a mandatory injunction to improve the premises.

d. Retaliatory Eviction

Some statutes and court decisions prohibit the landlord from terminating a
tenancy or raising the rent in retaliation for the tenant's assertion of
rights to habitable premises.

e. **Invalidity of Waiver**

Some statutes and courts declare invalid any lease provision whereby a tenant purports to waive his rights to habitable premises.

5. IMPLIED WARRANTY OF HABITABILITY

This relatively new development in the field of tenant's rights has arisen primarily from court decisions. It has gradually spread from jurisdiction to jurisdiction and its contours are still being worked out.

a. **Background and History**

Although the principle of *caveat emptor* has traditionally applied to real estate conveyances (sales and lease), in certain other areas of law courts were holding that the seller of a product should be treated as having impliedly warranted that the product had certain desirable characteristics (e.g., that is was fit for its intended purpose or that it was free from certain defects). Such protection has long been afforded to buyers of personal property. It has also been applied for some time in certain specialized real estate transactions, as where a person purchases premises which are under construction or rents furnished premises for a short period. In 1970, the Federal Court of Appeals for the District of Columbia held, in *Javins v. First National Realty Corp.*, that *a landlord of urban residential property impliedly warrants that the premise will be habitable for the duration of the tenancy.* That decision has been followed in numerous other jurisdictions by both courts and legislatures. Usually, it applies to all residential premises, although some statutes limit the warranty to multifamily housing (apartments) and some court decisions limit it to urban housing situations.

b. **Standard of Habitability**

Habitability has generally been defined by the courts to mean substantial compliance with the applicable housing code or building code. A violation of a code requirement which materially affects the health or safety of the tenant is therefore a violation of the landlord's implied warranty of habitability. There are also indications that premises sufficiently dilapidated may violate the implied warranty even if there is not a technical code violation.

1) Code Enforcement

Building codes generally regulate new construction and do not force owners to modify their buildings as codes are revised. Housing codes, which cover only residential structures, impose ongoing duties upon owners. Enforcement of these codes is, as a matter of municipal law, vested in building officials, and private citizens generally cannot directly compel a property owner to bring her building into compliance.

2)   Compared to Personal Property Warranties
The fact that an ongoing duty of maintenance is involved in the implied warranty makes it considerably stronger than the warranty implied in personal property transactions, which is generally restricted to existing defects. Similarly, application to known (patent) defects as well as unknown (latent) defects also carries this warranty beyond the normal consumer protection rules for personal property.

c.   **Tenant's Remedy**
1)   Termination
A tenant faced with a violation of the implied warranty of habitability may elect to terminate the lease and quit the premises. In such a situation, there is little difference between this doctrine and that of constructive eviction, except that here a duty to repair is directly imposed on the landlord by the doctrine itself whereas constructive eviction requires an independent showing of such a duty on the landlord. The tenant may also be entitled to damages incurred in moving to replacement premises.

2)   Rent Reduction
The most important, and new, form of relief which this doctrine makes available to a tenant is the right to remain on the premises and pay a reduced rent under one of the following formulae:

a)   Reduced Market Value
The tenant is held liable for the actual market rental value of the premises rather than the rent reserved in the lease. (Technically, the landlord is liable to the tenant for the difference between the rent reserved in the lease and the fair rental value of the premises, which works out to charging the tenant fair rental value.)

b)   Deduction of Difference Value
The rent reserved in the lease is reduced by an amount equal to the difference between the rental value of the premises "as is" and the rental value which they would have had were they in the "warranted" condition.

c)   Proportional Reduction
The rent reserved in the lease is reduced by a percentage equal to the degree which the livability of the premises has been reduced by noncompliance with the warranty.

d)   Effectiveness of the Formulae
Where the premises come into violation of the implied warranty after the original leasing, all three formulas produce

approximately similar results. Where the premises are in known violation of the warranty at the time of the leasing, all of the formulas lead to surprising outcomes. This is illustrated in the following examples.

Examples: (1) Tom rented the premises for $1000 per month, and subsequently, the heat stopped working, thereby reducing the fair rental value to $600 per month. Tom is probably liable for only $600 per month thereafter under any of the formulas. Under formula a), this is the fair rental value. Under formula b), it may be assumed that the fair rental value of the premises "as warranted" is what Tom agreed to pay for them when they were in good condition, meaning that his rent is reduced by the difference between $600 (the as is value) and $1000 (the as warranted value); under formula c), if the fair rental value is now $600, the livability of the premises has apparently been reduced by 40%, and Tom's $1000 rent should be reduced similarly.

(2) Tom rented the premises when the heat was already not working. Under formula a), he should have no reduction since the amount he agreed to pay was presumably the fair rental value of these premises. (There should not be any difference between rent reserved and rental value in an arms length transaction where there is no fraudulent concealment of defects from the tenant.) Under formula b), the as warranted value would be higher than the rent reserved (since Tom would obviously have to pay more if the heat were working than he pays when it is not working); if the heated premises would rent for $1400, then the difference between the as warranted and the as is values is $400, which is then deducted from the $1000 Tom pays, meaning he pays $600 rent for premises worth $1000! (If Laura were "generous" enough to rent him the premises for $900—$100 below fair rental value—Tom could then reduce his rent to $500 under this theory.) Under formula c), Tom's enjoyment of the premises seems to be reduced by $4/14$ths and his rent should be correspondingly reduced to approximately $754.

3)   Defense to Eviction
Under this doctrine the tenant is permitted to defend against an
action brought by the landlord to evict him for nonpayment of rent
by showing a breach of the implied warranty of habitability. (This is
a significant departure from the previous prohibition in many
jurisdictions against the use of affirmative defenses in summary
proceedings brought by the landlord to recover possession; such
defenses were considered inconsistent with the intended speedy nature
of the eviction process and the tenant was required to raise them in
a separate proceeding.) During the litigation, the tenant may be
required to pay the rent into court each month until the matter is
resolved; following a successful outcome for the tenant, he is
thereafter required to pay only the reduced amount determined by the
formula and so long as he pays the reduced amount of rent
determined to be owed, he cannot be evicted.

6.   TORT LIABILITY

This section covers the potential tort liability of a landlord to tenants and
third persons for injuries caused by conditions of the premises and also the
potential liability of the tenant to third persons under the same circumstances.

a.   Basic Principles

1)   Tenant
*Under tort principles, a tenant is a possessor of land, who owes others
certain duties of care as to the condition of the premises.* The common
law determined the extent of the duty according to the visitor's status
as trespasser, invitee, licensee, etc. Today many jurisdictions treat
status as but one factor in determining whether the tenant has
exercised due care under all of the circumstances.

2)   Landlord
*At common law the landlord was generally not liable in tort for defective
premises.* With regard to preexisting defects, she was protected by
the doctrine of *caveat emptor*. With regard to subsequent defects, the
fact that the tenant was in possession eliminated any duty (or right)
for her to enter and repair. The same was true with regard to
injuries suffered by others; their rights were against the possessing
tenant rather than against the landlord.

a)   Exceptions
Courts have, over the years, created a number of exceptions to
the principle of landlord nonliability. These have become more
important than the original rule. They are covered in the
remainder of this section.

b.   Latent Defects
A landlord may be liable in tort for injuries caused by latent defects in the premises which were known to her and not disclosed to the tenant. This derives from the principle that a seller should not conceal material facts affecting value from the buyer.

1)   Knowledge
The fraud theory underlying this doctrine requires the landlord to have actual knowledge of the defect and the tenant to not know of it. That either party might have been able to discover it by a reasonable inspection is generally irrelevant. The landlord has a duty to speak the truth, not a duty to inspect, and contributory negligence on the part of a tenant is no defense to fraud. However, some courts have extended the doctrine in one or both of these directions.

2)   Nature of Duty
The duty is one of disclosure, not of repair. Once a landlord has disclosed the defect to the tenant, she is generally not liable for subsequent injuries resulting from it. However, failure to disclose makes her liable not only for the reduced value of the premises but also for injuries suffered by the tenant from the hidden defect.

3)   Injuries to Third Persons
a)   Landlord Liability
Third persons may recover for their personal injuries from the landlord for her failure to disclose a latent defect to the tenant. However, if the landlord has made the disclosure to the tenant, she has fully discharged her duty and third parties may not recover from her; she is not obliged to notify every guest of the tenant.

b)   Tenant Liability
As possessor of the premises, the tenant owes a duty of due care to his guests and others. He may become liable to them for their injuries due to the defect if he failed to repair it or failed to warn them of it. If the defect was unknown to the tenant as well, he could be liable if a court determined that due care required him to inspect prior to inviting others in. If the landlord had informed the tenant of the defect, her disclosure may serve both to insulate her from liability and to make the tenant liable to the guests for injuries.

c. Common Areas
The landlord is deemed to be in possession of the common areas; the tenants only have rights of use. Thus, the principles of possessor liability apply here to the landlord rather than the tenants.

1) Landlord's Duty

The duty of care owed to others is the same here as for any possessor of land. Depending on the circumstances, it may include an obligation to inspect, to warn, to repair, etc. Thus, a tenant injured by defective conditions in the common areas—whether preexisting or subsequently arising—may be able to recover from the landlord in tort.

2) Third Persons

Guests and other visitors may be able to recover from the landlord for defects in the common areas by showing a failure of due care. The tenant is not a possessor of the common areas and thus will not be liable for their injuries there.

3) Crimes

Many courts now hold that the landlord has some obligation to secure doors, windows, halls and other common areas from criminal intrusion. Tenants and visitors who suffer from criminal activity because of her failure to so act may therefore be able to recover from the landlord.

d. Negligent Repairs
Although a landlord has no general duty to make repairs, if she undertakes to do so and then performs negligently, she may be liable to tenants and guests, especially if the purported repair created an appearance of safety.

e. Contractual Repairs
If the lease requires the landlord to make repairs and she fails to make them, her liability is not limited to the cost of repairs but also includes injuries resulting from the disrepair. Generally, the tenant must have first given notice of the need for the repair.

1) Visitors

Few courts still allow the landlord to defend on privity of contract grounds against the claims of third persons injured by a condition which the landlord had covenanted to repair. However, if the landlord was never notified of the disrepair she may not be liable to the guests; if the tenant knew of the disrepair and failed to notify the landlord, the tenant may be the one liable to them. Even if the tenant did notify his landlord, he may also be liable (along with the landlord) to his guests for failing to show due care under the circumstances to them, e.g., by warning them away from the defective area.

f. Code Compliance
Local housing and building codes impose duties of repair on the landlord as owner of the property. These laws are often viewed as safety statutes or ordinances, intended to protect users of the property. *Thus, a landlord may be held liable in tort for injuries resulting from a failure to comply with such codes.*

1) Visitors
Third persons may also be held protected by these codes and may recover from the landlord for injuries due to violations. Although a housing or building code may not, of itself, impose duties upon the tenant, he may nevertheless be liable to his guests if he failed to exercise due care towards them, e.g., by not warning them.

g. Public Premises
A landlord is sometimes held liable for injuries suffered by members of the public on premises which the landlord knew were to be open to them immediately following their rental by the tenant.

h. Due Care by the Landlord
A few courts have rejected the principle that a landlord has no general duty of care. They treat lack of possession as but one factor in determining whether the landlord has exercised due care towards tenants and visitors under all of the circumstances.

1) Tenant's Misconduct
Some courts hold a landlord liable to third parties for failure to prevent the tenant from engaging in criminal or tortious activity which her lease entitled her to control.

i. Exculpatory Clauses
Some of the above rules may change where the tenant has agreed to make repairs or to indemnify the landlord or not to hold her liable for injuries suffered by him.

1) Effect on Third Parties
If the tenant has covenanted to repair or to indemnify the landlord, this may give third parties additional rights to recover against him for their injuries. But a landlord and tenant cannot agree between themselves that the landlord will not be liable in tort to other persons who have not entered into that agreement; injured third persons may still recover from the landlord if she is liable under one

or another of the above theories, despite any protective clauses in the lease.

2)   Effect on the Tenant
Many jurisdictions now hold that an exculpatory clause in favor of the landlord is void as against public policy and may not be used by her as a shield against any liability she would have under any of the above theories.

F. TRANSFERS BY THE PARTIES

1.   RIGHT TO TRANSFER
A leasehold interest in land, like any other possessory estate, is fully transferable. Thus, unless restrained by lease provision, a tenant may convey or lease his estate to others. Conversely, a landlord may freely transfer her reversionary interest to others.

a.   No-Assignment Clauses
Leases commonly provide that the tenant may not transfer his interest to others without the landlord's consent. These clauses are upheld because of the legitimate interest the landlord has in the identity of the person occupying her premises. However, since they do restrain alienation, such provisions are strictly construed. (Restraints on alienation are covered in Chapter II.) Thus, for example, a clause prohibiting assignments will not be read to prohibit subleases, or vice versa.

1)   Duty of Reasonableness
Most courts do not require a landlord to act reasonably with regard to granting or withholding her assent to a proposed transfer by the tenant where her consent is required; she may arbitrarily refuse to accept a new tenant even though he is fully qualified. However, there is a growing trend in favor of imposing a duty of reasonableness upon the landlord in this situation, or prohibit the landlord from using the clause as a device to raise rents. Additionally, many no-assignment clauses provide that the landlord's assent "shall not be unreasonably withheld." Furthermore, in those jurisdictions where a landlord is required to mitigate damages after a tenant's breach, this leads to the same result by virtue of limiting her loss to what could not be reasonably avoided.

2)   Waiver
A landlord who accepts rent after a transfer has been completed, knowing of that fact, is generally held to have waived her rights to object to the transfer.

a) Second Assignment
The Rule in Dumpor's Case (1603) provides that once a landlord consents to an assignment she loses the right to object to any subsequent assignment, on the ground that the clause is indivisible. Many courts still follow this doctrine, although it may generally be avoided by a clause in the lease providing that consent to one transfer does not constitute consent to further transfers, or by similar qualifying language in any document executed by the landlord assenting to the first transfer.

3) Remedies
A no-assignment clause is usually written so as to permit the landlord to terminate the tenancy if an improper transfer is attempted. If the covenant contains merely a promise not to transfer, then there may be only liability in damages for its breach. Clauses purporting to make the transfer itself void are generally held to be invalid. (See Chapter II.)

2. KINDS OF TRANSFERS
a. By the Tenant
1) Assignment
Transfers by the tenant of his entire estate in some or all of the leasehold premises constitutes an assignment. The transferee must take the entire balance of the leasehold interest for an assignment to occur. The assignee becomes the new tenant of the landlord and they are said to be in privity of estate.

a) Partial Assignment
If only a physical portion of the premises is transferred, there may still be an assignment, so long as the assignee takes that part for the entire balance of the term.

2) Sublease
If less than the entire leasehold estate is transferred to another person the transaction is treated as a sublease rather than an assignment. The subtenant is treated as holding of the tenant rather than the landlord, and there is no privity of estate between the subtenant and the landlord. Rather, the initial privity of estate between landlord and original tenant continues.
Example: Tom had one year remaining of his term of years. He transferred the premises to Slade for 11 months. Slade became Tom's subtenant rather than Tom's assignee; Tom remained Laura's tenant.

a) Contingent Reversion
  Some jurisdictions find a sublease even when the entire balance of the term has been transferred if the original tenant retains a power to terminate the transfer for failure of the transferee to pay the rent or to perform some other obligation. Other courts reject this and treat the transfer as an assignment because such a "contingent reversionary interest" was not an estate at common law.

b) Intent
  Other jurisdictions distinguish between assignment and sublease based upon the intent of the parties rather than upon technical feudal considerations. For these courts, how the parties labeled the transaction, whether the transferee is paying the same or a different rent, and whether it is paid to the landlord or to the original tenant are more important than the duration of the transferee's interest in determining whether the transaction creates an assignment or sublease.

b. By the Landlord

A landlord may transfer her reversion, either by lease or by sale. A lease to take effect upon the expiration of the present lease could be viewed as a lease of the landlord's reversion. A sale by the landlord of her reversion generally involves a transfer of the right to receive rents as well, but it is possible for the landlord to convey the reversion while retaining the right to receive the rents or, conversely, to assign the rents while retaining the reversion. Assignment of rents provisions are common financing arrangements, leaving title in the landlord, but giving the creditor the right to the rents.

3. EFFECT OF TRANSFERS

a. On the Tenant's Assignee

Since the assignee succeeds to the tenant's entire estate and is in privity of estate with the landlord, he becomes subject to the benefits and burdens of all covenants running with the land. (See Chapter V.) The assignee is entitled to enforce all covenants made by the landlord and is required to perform all covenants made by the tenant, including the covenant to pay rent.

1) The Effect of a Second Assignment
  An assignee is liable for the performance of all covenants running with the land for only so long as he holds the leasehold estate. Once he assigns that estate, he is no longer in privity of estate with the landlord. Thus, he is not liable for breaches by the next assignee. (This doctrine does not apply where the first assignee has also "assumed" the obligations of the lease; that is discussed below.)

b.   Upon the Tenant

Although a tenant who has assigned is no longer in privity of estate with his landlord, he has nevertheless made promises to the landlord from which he has not been released; i.e., his privity of contract with the landlord has not been terminated. *Thus he remains liable, as a surety, if the assignee fails to perform.* The landlord may sue the original tenant for the rent if the assignee fails to pay it. If the original tenant then pays the rent, he has an action over against the assignee, who is the party primarily liable for the rent by virtue of being in possession of the premises.

c.   Upon an Assuming Assignee

Where an assignee has assumed the obligations of the lease, i.e., promised his transferor that he will perform them, there arises a privity of contract between the assignee and the landlord, and the landlord is treated as a third party beneficiary of the assumption agreement. This privity of contract, like the privity of contract between landlord and original tenant, survives subsequent transfers of the leasehold estate, with the consequence that an assuming assignee is liable for breaches by a subsequent assignee just as the original tenant is.

1)   Release Required

A tenant or assuming assignee needs a release executed by the landlord in order to terminate the continuing liability created by their respective promises.

a)   Assent to Transfer No Substitute

Consent by the landlord to an assignment is not deemed to constitute an agreement to release the transferor from his existing contractual liability; an express release is usually required.

b)   Assumption Not a Release

The fact that an assignee has promised the tenant to perform all of the tenant's obligations does not discharge the tenant from those duties; one cannot assign away duties. The assumption adds to the landlord's rights (who may now sue either party); it does not subtract from them. Only an agreement by the landlord can release the tenant from his duties to her.

d.   Upon the Sublessor

1)   Against the Landlord

A sublease executed by a tenant has no effect upon the privity of estate or privity of contract which exists between him and his landlord. As tenant of the landlord, he remains liable for the performance of all of the lease covenants and continues able to enforce the landlord's covenants against her.

2) Against the Subtenant
Any covenants made by the subtenant to the tenant or vice versa may be enforced by the one against the other. Tenant and subtenant are in both privity of estate and privity of contract with regard to any promises they have made to each other. With regard to their rights and duties, they stand as landlord and tenant to one another.

e. **Upon the Subtenant**
A subtenant is liable to the tenant for breach of any covenant contained in the sublease. *He is not liable to the landlord for breach of any covenant in the main lease nor can he enforce against the landlord any of her covenants in that document.* Between landlord and subtenant there is neither privity of contract (unless the subtenant has assumed) nor privity of estate. *However, if the subtenant fails to perform the covenants of the main lease, and the tenant also fails to do so, the landlord may be able to terminate the leasehold, which will destroy the subleasehold as well.* The subtenant may not be legally liable to the landlord for the rent, but he risks losing his estate if the landlord is not paid.

1) Assuming Subtenant
If the subtenant promises the tenant that he will perform the obligations of the main lease, then the landlord may enforce this promise directly against the subtenant as a third party beneficiary. Such an assumption, however, does not work to release the tenant from liability to the landlord unless there is an agreement to that effect made directly by the landlord.

f. **Upon the Landlord's Transferee**
When the landlord sells the reversion, her buyer takes title subject to the burdens and benefits of any covenants in her existing leases which run with the land (e.g., the burden of the covenant to supply heat to the tenant and the benefit of the tenant's covenant to pay rent).

G. REVIEW QUESTIONS

1. T or F Tom held over after the expiration of his five-year lease and Laura accepted another year's rent from him. Tom thereby became a tenant from year to year.

2. T or F Tom was a tenant from year to year (January to January). In October the premises were completely destroyed by fire and Tom quit.

At common law, Tom's liability for rent ended in January of the next year.

3. T or F Tom was a tenant for a year. In the fourth month of his tenancy he defaulted in the rent and Laura had him judicially evicted. Laura may also recover the rent due for the balance of the term.

4. T or F Tom was a tenant for a year. He abandoned in the fourth month of his tenancy. Laura may recover for the remaining eight months rent, but must wait until the end of the term.

5. T or F Tom was a tenant for a year. In the fourth month of his tenancy he was deprived of possession because of acts of third parties. Tom may refuse to pay rent until Laura restores him to possession.

6. T or F When Laura rented the premises to Tom they were infested with termites but neither party knew this. Later the termite infestation caused a wall to collapse, injuring Tom. Tom cannot recover from Laura for his injuries.

7. T or F In the middle of Tom's tenancy a hurricane destroyed the premises. Neither party can compel the other to rebuild.

8. T or F Tom rented premises from Laura and used them for a movie theatre. The local building authorities then informed Tom that he must install two extra washrooms on the premises (because of his theatre operation) or else they will make him shut down. Tom may terminate his tenancy if Laura refuses to pay the cost of the washrooms.

9. T or F Tom quit during the fourth month of his one year tenancy, claiming that he was constructively evicted due to Laura's failure to supply heat to his premises. The lease says nothing about heat. Laura may continue to hold Tom for the rent despite his departure.

10. T or F Laura covenanted to keep Tom's premises in good repair. Tom subsequently observed that the hot water faucet was loose and asked Laura to correct it. Laura failed to correct it and a guest of Tom was scalded while using the faucet. Laura's covenant gives Tom a defense, so that the guest may recover from Laura, but not Tom.

11. T or F Tom's lease provided that he would not assign his lease without Laura's consent and also provided that Laura would supply heat to the premises. Tom assigned his lease to Ann without Laura's consent. Ann may compel Laura to supply heat.

*

EASEMENTS

Analysis

A. DEFINITIONS

1. EASEMENT

An easement is a nonpossessory interest (use) in land; someone else other than the holder of the easement has possession of the land. The holder of an easement has some privilege to use the property or some right to control some aspect of its use, but is not thereby entitled to possess the property. An easement arises by some act of the parties and thereby differs from natural rights which arise by law (e.g., support, riparian rights, freedom from nuisance, etc.). Easements exist only where specifically created. It is a usufructuary rather than a possessory interest. It is both a restriction upon the rights and privileges of the possessor of property and also an incumbrance upon the title of the owner of the property. It is sometimes called an incorporeal hereditament (an inheritable nonpossessory interest).

2. SERVIENT; DOMINANT

A parcel of land subject to an easement is referred to as the servient tenement; the owner or possessor of that land is referred to as the servient tenant (indicated by masculine pronouns in this chapter). *A parcel of land benefitted by an easement is referred to as the dominant tenement, and its holder is the dominant tenant* (indicated by feminine pronouns in this chapter). There is always a servient tenement and servient tenant, but when an easement is in gross, there is no dominant tenement, only a dominant tenant.

3. APPURTENANT; IN GROSS

An easement is appurtenant when it benefits land. An easement is in gross when it benefits a person; in such a case there is no dominant tenement but there is always a servient tenement, i.e., the land burdened by the easement. It may not always be plain whether an easement is appurtenant or in gross. Technically, an easement must be intended to and must in fact benefit a person with regard to her possession of land in order to be appurtenant, but the rigor of this requirement is offset by a judicial preference for easements which are appurtenant rather than in gross (although no so for profits).

a. Not Adjacent

There is no requirement that the dominant tenement of an appurtenant easement be adjacent to the servient tenement. Appurtenant means that the easement benefits land rather than a person, not that the dominant and servient parcels are contiguous to each other.

4. PROFIT

When the use includes the right to remove some product of the soil (oil, gas, timber, etc.), the interest is referred to as a profit, or an easement with a profit. For most purposes, profits are subject to the same rules as easements. Only when a different principle applies to profits will they be specially mentioned here.

5.   LICENSE
When the use is revocable at the will of the servient tenant, it is referred to as a license.   Using the terminology of possessory estates, this is an easement at will, except that it is instead referred to as a license.   (In all other respects, the classification scheme for estates applies to the various durations of easements, e.g., easement for life, easement for years.)

6.   AFFIRMATIVE; NEGATIVE
An affirmative easement permits the dominant tenant to do acts affecting the servient land which would otherwise be unprivileged.   A negative easement gives the dominant tenant the right to prevent the servient tenant from doing acts affecting the servient land which would otherwise be privileged.

a.   Spurious
The right to compel a possessor to perform an act on the possessor's land is not an easement.   It is not an affirmative easement, because it does not entitle the holder to do any act herself on the land; it is not a negative easement, because it does not entitle the holder to restrain the commission of some act on the land.   To indicate that this interest only looks like an easement, it is sometimes referred to as a spurious easement; it is probably a covenant running with the land (discussed in the next chapter).

Examples: (1) Steve (the servient tenant) granted Dita (the dominant tenant) "the right to walk over my property to get from your house to the road."   Dita's easement is appurtenant, since the privilege of crossing Steve's property benefits her in her capacity as possessor of her house.   Her easement is affirmative: without the easement she would be committing an unprivileged act (a trespass) in crossing Steve's property. If Steve were to grant Dita the right to swim in his pool, regardless of where she lived, she would have an easement in gross.

(2) Steve granted Dita "the right to mine coal on my property for 10 years."   Dita has a profit in gross for a term of years. It is a profit because it involves removal of a product of the soil; it is in gross because it benefits Dita personally and not any land she owns; it is for a term of years because of the duration stated in the grant; it may be appurtenant if she is limited to using the coal to heat her neighboring house.

(3) Steve granted Dita "an easement of view over my property."   Dita has a negative easement: the right to stop Steve from building on his own land, which he would otherwise be free (privileged) to do.

(4) Steve said to Dita, "You may park your car on my property until I tell you to stop."   Dita has a license, a revocable nonpossessory interest in Steve's land.

(5) Steve sold Dita a ticket to see a play being performed in his theatre. This is regarded as a license rather than an easement, as a matter of public policy.

(6) Steve granted Dita "the right to occupy my apartment for the next five years, but for residential purposes only." Dita has a leasehold estate rather than an easement. The document gives her possession rather than mere use of the premises. Although her possessory right is somewhat restricted by the lease, it does not leave possession in Steve as would the grant of an easement.

7. HOHFELDIAN TERMINOLOGY

A set of concepts proposed by William Wesley Hohfeld in 1923 is frequently helpful in describing easements, especially the following four terms: A "right" is a legally enforceable claim by one person that another should do or not do a certain act (e.g., a right to be paid or a right to not be assaulted). Correlatively, the other person is under a "duty" to do or not do that specified act (e.g., a duty to pay or a duty not to assault). Where the second person is not under a duty, she has a "privilege" to do or not do that act, e.g., the first person has "no right" to make him do it or not do it.

Examples: (1) *Affirmative Easement.* Dita's right of way over Steve's property gives her a privilege to walk over it, and Steve has no right to complain. If Dita did not have an easement, she would be under a duty not to trespass on Steve's property, and he would have a right to tell her to keep off.

(2) *Negative Easement.* Dita's easement of view gives her a right to demand that Steve not build on his property so as to block her view, and Steve is under a corresponding duty not to build. If Dita had no such easement, she would have no right to demand that Steve not build, and he would be privileged to build as he wished.

B. CREATION

1. EXPRESS LANGUAGE—GRANT AND RESERVATION

A deed is the proper instrument for creating an easement as opposed to the old common law livery of seisin. If the deed is from servient to dominant tenement, the easement has been granted. An easement may also be created in a deed which conveys other property to the dominant tenant, in which case the easement is usually granted as appurtenant to the other property conveyed. The deed may also grant property and reserve an easement in that property in favor of the grantor. (Sometimes the grantor will "except" rather than "reserve" an easement, but the word except more technically refers to withholding title to a physical part of the land, e.g., "excepting the north ten feet" rather than "reserving an easement over the north ten feet".)

Example: Dita, who owned lots 1 and 2, conveyed lot 1 to Steve "together with a right of way over lot 2, but reserving the right to lay a sewer pipe from lot 2 across lot 1 to the public sewer." Both Steve and Dita have easements in each other's land. Steve has an easement by grant and Dita has an easement by reservation.

a. Reservation in Favor of Third Party

Many courts hold that an easement cannot be reserved in favor of a third party. It is required that the grantee first reserve it for herself and then transfer it to the third person.

b. Requirements
The creation of a easement must be in compliance with the general requirements for the creation or transfer of interests in land.

1) Creating Language
No special language is required to create an easement. Ambiguous wording may force a court to determine whether some kind of possessory estate with restrictions has been created instead (such as a lease for limited purposes). The rules of estates for determining duration are equally applicable to easements.

2) Writing
The statute of frauds requires that there be a writing, usually a deed properly executed and delivered by the grantor. An exception is generally made for easements of less than a year, an analogy to short term leases.

a) Signature by Grantee
At common law, the reservation of an easement by a grantor was viewed as the regrant of the easement from grantee to grantor, thus requiring the grantee's signature. (Only an "exception" from a deed was effective without the grantee's signature, but since exceptions refer to existing interests in land, easements are not "excepted" because they do not exist until there is a separation between one person's use and another's possession. One cannot have an easement in his own property.)

b) Effect of No Writing; Estoppel
The oral grant of an easement usually creates a license, because the interest remains revocable by the grantor. However, detrimental reliance by the grantee may, by virtue of the doctrine of estoppel,

make the license irrevocable, converting it into the equivalent of an easement (an "easement in equity).

Examples: (1) Steve orally told Dita that she could maintain a sewer pipe across his land; she then installed the pipe at considerable expense. The interest granted was initially a license because it was not written; but her reasonable reliance made it irrevocable and disables Steve from revocation. Consequently, it would now be called an easement or an irrevocable license.

(2) Steve wrote Dita a letter telling her she could walk across his property until he changed his mind; Dita then paved the walkway. This did not make her license irrevocable. The interest granted here was a license because of an expressed intent to make it revocable and not because of failure to comply with the statute of frauds. Thus, reliance is irrelevant and the instrument remains a license.

c. Restrictions

The parties are not free to create any form of nonpossessory interest they can imagine and label it an easement. Courts have traditionally resisted the creation of "novel interests" in land and refused to enforce new or different land arrangements. In some cases, this required legislative recognition of socially useful new forms of dealing with land (e.g., solar easements, historic preservation easements, etc.).

2. BY IMPLICATION

When a possessory interest in property is conveyed, a court may imply from the circumstances that the parties also intended to grant or reserve an easement as well, despite their failure to say so in the deed. *The determination that an implied easement exists is an inference that the original parties would have added language to the deed granting or reserving the easement had they thought about it.* The requirements discussed in this section are employed by courts to make certain that the inference is appropriate. (Examples are at the end of the section.)

a. Requirements

1) Severance of Commonly Owned Parcels
No easement will be implied except from a deed conveying some, but not all, of the grantor's land. This partial conveyance both satisfies the statute of frauds and furnishes the foundation for the implication that the parties intended to benefit one of the parcels at the expense of the other, since both parcels affected were subject to their control.

a) Subdivision of Land
As an alternative to conveying part and retaining part, the grantor may convey parts of his property to different grantees under circumstances which generate an implication that he intended that one grantee's land be benefitted or burdened by the other's. There is still a writing to satisfy the statute of frauds and a severance of one parcel into two with the parties having had control over both of them.

2) Prior Use
No easement will be implied unless the use existed prior to the severance. The implication of the intent to grant or reserve an easement is based upon the assumption that the parties intended to permit the preexisting use to continue, but they failed to express that intention in the deed. Thus, before the severance has occurred, one part of the property must have been being used for the benefit of another part (e.g., a path in the front used to get to a house in the back). This is referred to as a *quasi easement.* Uses which do not commence until after severance of parcels can never create an implied easement.

a) Apparent
It is generally required that the prior use be apparent or at least discoverable by a reasonable inspection; otherwise there is no basis for implying that the parties intended that it continue after the severence of parcels, e.g., a grantee who did not see the path could not be expected to have taken subject to it or to have benefitted by it. In cases where land is conveyed by reference to a recorded subdivision map, rights of way and other features shown on the map may be treated as easements implied in favor of the grantees despite the lack of express granting language in the deeds.

b) Continuous
It is also required that there be some permanent adaptation of the parcels to each other, in order to justify an inference that the parties intended the arrangement to continue in the future.

c) Necessary
Unless the easement furnishes a significant benefit to the claimed dominant tenant, a court will not imply its existence against the alleged servient tenant. If an easement by implied grant is involved, this may merely mean that its existence is reasonably beneficial to the grantee; if an implied reservation is claimed, however, many courts require strict necessity, consistent with the principle of construing grants against the grantor.

d)   Other Factors

The Restatement adds, as considerations: the price paid, the presence or absence of reciprocal benefits, and the language of the deed in deciding this issue.

e)   Ineligible Uses

From the nature of things, it is impossible to imply the creation of an easement in gross or a negative easement.

Examples: (1) Steve's lot had a house on the rear part of it with a walkway running from it across the front part of the lot to the street. He divided up his lot and sold the rear part to Dita. He may be held to have also impliedly granted her an easement over his retained front part.

(2) Steve's lot also contained a water tank to the west of the house, with pipes running from the tank under the house to the public water system; he did not convey this part of his property to Dita when he transferred the house to her. It will be difficult for him to prevail in his claim that he impliedly reserved an easement over her property for the water pipes if they were not visible to her or if he cannot show a high degree of need for the easement on his part.

(3) Steve's lot also contained a large yard behind the house which he kept vacant in order to enjoy the view from the rear windows of the house; he did not convey this rear part of the property to Dita when he conveyed the house to her. Dita cannot stop Steve from building on the land later, by claiming that he had impliedly granted a negative easement of view to her, since mere nonuse of one part of the property does not imply an intent that some other part is to be benefitted thereby. More would have to be shown.

(4) After the conveyance, Dita erected a hot tub on Steve's retained land to the rear of her house; Dita then sold her house to Enid. Enid cannot claim that an easement was impliedly created when Dita sold to her (even though the hot tub was visible). Steve's property was not involved in the conveyance and there was no severance of parcels such as is needed

to create an easement by implication. Dita and Enid could not have, even by express language, affected the status of Steve's parcel by virtue of a conveyance of a different parcel and without Steve's assent.

(5) After the conveyance, Steve conveyed his retained front part of the land to Ted. Ted will acquire title to that part subject to Dita's easement as to the walkway whether or not it was apparent to him when he purchased. The easement has already been created by virtue of the former severance and conveyance to Dita, and it need not be recreated in every transaction thereafter. Once Dita has acquired an easement by implication from Steve's deed to her, Steve's retained land is subject to that easement and, when transferred, is transferred subject to it. The rules discussed here relate to the creation of easements, not to their transfer.

3)   Necessity
When there is absolute necessity an easement will be implied, whether or not there was any prior use beforehand. If a conveyance operates to landlock a parcel of land, an easement of way will be implied in its favor even though none existed previously. This is implied out of public policy rather than the intent of the parties, and thus the requirements for easements by implication need not be met.

a)   Duration
Generally, an easement by necessity lasts only so long as the necessity exists. Once that is no longer the case, the easement ceases.

b)   From Plat
An easement of access over streets shown in the plat (map) of the subdivision will be implied if those streets were not dedicated to the public as public ways, on the assumption that the buyer purchased in reliance upon what appeared on the plat. Some courts limit the easement to only those streets necessary to give the owner access from her property to the nearest public way (the narrow or necessary rule); others give the owner easements in all the streets shown on the plat (the broad or unity rule); an intermediate (or beneficial or full enjoyment) rule gives the owner easements over all the streets whose use preserves the market value of the owner's lot. The same rule is also sometimes applied to parks and other public recreation areas shown on the plat.

3.   PRESCRIPTION

The doctrine of adverse possession is applied, by analogy, to long-continued use, creating in the user a prescriptive right to continue the use.   Thus, an unpermitted use which is open, notorious, continuous, hostile, uninterrupted, etc., may, after the statutory period, ripen into an easement.   Differences between the rules as applied to adverse possession and to prescriptive easements are discussed below.

a.   Adverse; Hostile

As with possessory claims, "adverse" generally means merely nonpermissive, and does not require any particular subjective animosity. However, consent by the possessor may have a more significant effect in defeating a claim of adverseness of use since, in some jurisdictions, an owner may post his property with signs stating that permission to use (or cross) the property is granted, thereby defeating claims of prescription.   In some states, use of unenclosed, unimproved land is presumed to be permissive.

1)   Negative Easement

A negative easement cannot be acquired prescriptively, since there is no adverseness involved.   The failure of an owner to do some act upon his land creates no right in others to insist that he continue to refrain from so acting thereafter.   (England, however, has an "ancient lights" doctrine, which does protect long existing views even though these are merely negative easements).

b.   Exclusive

It is not required that the adverse use be exclusive, since exclusiveness applies to possession, not use.   An adverse possessor must have been exclusive for the entire statutory period, but an adverse user need not prohibit others from making any use of the property, so long as their activities do not interfere with hers.

Example: Throughout the prescriptive period Dita wrongfully walked across Steve's property.   The fact that others may have also done so during that time does not defeat her claim of a prescriptive easement.

1)   Public Claims

The absence of a requirement of exclusivity means that the public may be able to acquire certain recreational rights in private land. This is discussed later.

c. Uninterrupted

For similar reasons, simultaneous use by the possessor does not necessarily interrupt a prescriptive use. An interruption occurs only when the possessor actually blocks the adverse use.

Example: If Steve also walked across the same path which Dita used, he did not interrupt her adverse use. Steve must have erected some kind of barrier or brought suit against her to stop the statutory period from running.

1) Lost Grant Theory

Under an old competing theory of prescriptive usage, a long continued use was treated as generating an inference that in the distant past the servient tenant (or predecessor) had granted an easement for that use to the dominant tenant (or predecessor) which was subsequently lost. A court which still takes this theory literally may treat protests by the owner of the property as rebutting the inference of such a grant and thereby defeating the claim of an easement. Elsewhere, ineffectual protests by the owner do not stop the running of the period, but in fact confirm adversity.

d. Continuous

Seasonal adverse use may be sufficient to acquire a prescriptive easement, so long as it is regular and more than occasional. Such limited use may generate an equivalent, limited prescriptive easement.

Example: If Dita grazed her cattle on Steve's land every spring, she may have acquired a prescriptive easement to graze every spring thereafter. If she drove her car over his property at 5 P.M. every day, she may have acquired a prescriptive easement to continue driving over it at that hour.

e. Taxes

In those jurisdictions which require that an adverse possessor have paid the taxes, this burden is not imposed upon prescriptive easements, since easements are generally not taxed separately.

f. Tacking

When a prescriptive appurtenant easement is involved, tacking generally occurs through transfers of the dominant tenement. Tacking for a prescriptive easement in gross is similar to that for adverse possession.

g. Public Prescription

England recognized rights of use in the public when such use had been continued for "time immemorial." This is not followed in the United States. However, some jurisdictions do employ a doctrine of implied dedication to the effect that a landowner who fails to prohibit the public from making use of his property for a long enough time has impliedly dedicated it to the public for their use. This may be limited, by decision or statute, to certain kinds of land (e.g., beach frontage or woods).

C. SCOPE AND VARIATIONS

Because an easement entitles its holder to assert only limited rights and privileges in property, courts are often called upon to determine the extent of those interests. They must, e.g., determine whether new or different activities by the dominant tenant are permissable and whether acts by the servient tenant, which may somewhat interfere with the dominant tenant, are to be allowed.

1. EXPRESS EASEMENTS

Where an easement has been created by an express grant or reservation, its language is the controlling determinant of what activities are allowed to its holder. Where the grant or reservation is explicit as to activities, neither party is entitled to act otherwise than as prescribed.

a. Where Silent

An easement may be explicit as to some features, but silent with regard to others. Courts generally fill in the gaps through use of a "rule of reason," assuming that the parties would have settled the matter reasonably with regard to both of their interests had they dealt with the matter—i.e., that the dominant tenant would have been permitted to act in a way which was reasonably beneficial to her so long as it was not unreasonably burdensome to the servient tenant.

Example: Steve granted Dita an easement of "right of way" over his property but his grant did not specify where it was to be. A court will nevertheless uphold the grant and determine its location (and width) according to whatever evidence it has before it. Once so determined, its location is fixed as if that had been specified in the grant.

1) Factors

Circumstances which may aid a court in determining whether some particular activity is reasonable are: whether it occurred prior to the creation of the easement, whether it occurred without objection after the creation of the easement, the purpose of the easement, and the consideration paid for it, if any.

Example: Steve granted Dita an easement of "right of way" over his property. Whether this means Dita may only walk over the property or may also drive her car over it depends upon whether Steve also drove over it, whether he objected, whether her garage fronted in the property, etc. If the grant said that Dita was only allowed to walk, then those considerations would be irrelevant.

2)   Development of the Dominant Tenement
Courts assume that the parties contemplated a normal development of the dominant tenement over time and thus intended to permit changes in use which corresponded to that development.

> *Example:*   Steve granted Dita an easement to drive across his land between 9 and 5 every day. Because of the clear language of the grant, it is clear that Dita may not drive across the land at night. But whether she may convert from a car to a truck is a question which must be resolved according to how a reasonable dominant and servient tenant would have handled the matter had they thought about it. One way would be to ask, e.g., how necessary is the truck to Dita and how troublesome is the truck to Steve. If the need for a truck arises out of the fact that Dita has put her formerly residential dominant tenement to a commercial use, the question might be resolved by asking whether commercial development of her property is reasonable in light of what is happening in the area generally.

b.   Enlargement of Dominant Tenement
Where an easement appurtenant is involved, the dominant estate cannot be enlarged geographically so as to extend the benefit of the easement to other land. The servient owner need not show any unreasonable increase in burden in order to prohibit such an enlargement.

c.   Enlargement by Prescription
An otherwise impermissable enlargement by the dominant tenant of the easement or the dominant parcel may become privileged if it is carried on long enough to satisfy the requirements of prescription without the servient tenant taking action to stop it.

2.   IMPLIED EASEMENTS
There is no express language to aid in construction where the very existence of the easement is itself implied, so *the same circumstances which a court employs to determine that the easement should be implied must also be used to determine its scope.* Principles of reasonableness again apply where there is no circumstantial evidence available to resolve the issue.

Example: When Steve sold his house and stable to Dita long ago, a path ran from the stable over his retained land to the public street. As a result, there arose an easement of right of way by implication and its scope was for Dita to ride her horse across the path to get to the street. Now that cars have generally replaced horses, and her stable has become a garage, Dita may be allowed to drive across the same path.

3. PRESCRIPTIVE EASEMENTS

The original adverse use which created the prescriptive easement is taken as a pattern for determining what new uses are to be allowed. It is assumed that the servient tenant who did not sue when the original adverse use occurred would also have tolerated similar uses but might have objected had they been significantly different.

Example: For a long enough time, Dita bicycled across Steve's property at 3 P.M. every day. Now she has started crossing at 4 P.M. and is using a motorcycle instead. She is probably allowed to cross at 4 P.M. since there is no reason to assume that this would have any more aroused Steve than did the trips at 3 P.M. But it cannot be assumed that he would have tolerated a motorcycle merely because he did not object to a bicycle. Therefore, a court could allow her only to bicycle across (at 3 P.M. or 4 P.M.). If Dita does in fact motorcycle long enough without being stopped by Steve, she may thereby prescriptively enlarge her easement so as to gain the right to continue this new use.

4. USE BY THE SERVIENT TENANT

Since the servient tenant retains possession of the servient property, he is entitled to use and enjoy the property, so long as it does not interfere with the dominant tenant's easement.

a. Creation of Easements in Others

What a servient owner may himself do on the property, he may permit others to do. *Thus, a servient tenant can give third parties similar or overlapping easements in the same property, so long as these do not unreasonably interfere with the first dominant tenant's rights and so long as the original easement had not been made "exclusive."*

Example: Steve may walk across Dita's right-of-way over his own property. Likewise, he may also permit others to walk there as well. However, he cannot park his car on the right-of-way or allow others to do so if this makes it impossible for Dita to cross.

b. Relocation

Where the location of the easement is described in the grant, the servient tenant is often prohibited from relocating it elsewhere on his property even though this might not unreasonably interfere with the dominant tenant's use.

5. REPAIRS

The dominant tenant has the obligation of keeping the easement in repair. The servient tenant has no such repair obligations towards the dominant tenant, but as the possessor of the property, he may be liable in tort for disrepairs on principles analogous to a tenant's liability to guests injured on the premises. (See Chapter IV.)

6. REMEDIES

Either party is entitled to enjoin unreasonable activity of the other relating to the easement. In extreme cases, abuses by the dominant tenant may lead to extinguishment of her easement entirely.

D. TRANSFER AND SUBDIVISION

The parties involved in creating an easement may be specific as to its transferability or as to the effect of transfers of the dominant and servient parcels. Where they have failed to so provide, the following rules apply.

1. BURDEN

The burden of an easement is not separable from the servient land. Transfers of the burden of an easement refer to transfers of the land subject to it.

a. Transfer

A conveyance or lease of the servient tenement transfers it subject to the easement, and the transferee becomes the new servient tenant.

b. Subdivision

A subdivision of the servient estate leaves each new parcel subject to the easement unless it was so located geographically as to apply to only some parts of the servient land, in which case the other parts are then no longer servient.

> *Example:* Steve's property is subject to a right of way easement which runs from east to west across the northern edge of his property. If he sells the property, his purchaser will take it subject to his easement, whether the deed refers to it or not because Steve cannot convey more than he has (i.e., a fee subject to an easement). If he divides his property into an east and west parcel, each will be subject to the easement. If

Steve subdivides his property into a north and south parcel, then the south parcel is free from the easement.

2. BENEFIT

Since the benefit of an easement can exist apart from land (when it is in gross), it is possible to speak of transferring the benefit apart from transferring the dominant tenement.

a. Easement Appurtenant

A transfer of the dominant tenement carries with it all incidental benefits, including easements appurtenant. The grantee of a dominant tenement automatically becomes the new dominant tenant. Any attempt by the grantor to hold back the benefit of the easement and keep it for herself will fail as an impermissible attempt to convert an easement appurtenant into an easement in gross without the consent of the servient tenant.

1) Subdivision

When the dominant tenement is subdivided, the benefit is divided among all of the new parcels, so long as it was not originally confined to one geographic part of the property and so long as this division does not create an unreasonable burden upon the servient tenement. If the easement was "exclusive", i.e. even the servient tenant was excluded from making such use of the property, the dominant tenant is then permitted to subdivide without restriction.

b. Easements or Profit in Gross

Common law prohibited the transfer or subdivision of an easement or profit in gross. A more modern view permits them to be transferred when they are commercial. In some jurisdictions, they may be subdivided only when they are quantifiable (e.g., the right to mine ten tons of coal a year or the right to make ten trips a day over a road), or when some royalty is being paid. (These features permit a court to assume that the subdivision does not lead to a greater burden on the servient tenant than he originally intended.)

Example: If Dita has a right of way over Steve's land appurtenant to her single family house, she may improve her property by replacing the house with an apartment building and give all of her tenants the right to use the way as well. Or, she may subdivide her property into several lots, or a condominium project, and give the purchaser of each lot the right to use the way. All of this is subject to the condition that the increased usage not unduly burden Steve.

E. TERMINATION

There are numerous ways by which an easement is terminated. They are listed below. (Examples at end of this section cover all forms of termination.)

1. NATURAL DURATION

If an easement is created for only a limited time (e.g., an easement for a term of years), it terminates once the time passes. As with possessory interests today, it is generally assumed that an easement appurtenant is intended to be in fee simple unless a shorter time period is indicated.

a. Easement in Gross

At common law, easements in gross were treated as enduring only for the life of the taker, but commercial easements in gross today are generally treated as fee simple interests.

b. Licenses

Revocable interests terminate whenever a revocation occurs. Thus, a license lasts only until it is revoked.

1) Irrevocable Licenses

A license which became irrevocable under estoppel principles described earlier may be subject to judicial termination once the court perceives that fairness of changed circumstances no longer requires that it continue.

c. Easements in Structures

An easement in a building is generally held to end when the servient building is destroyed. This does not apply if the building is voluntarily torn down, although economic obsolescence may be held sufficient to justify an intentional destruction of the building and the easement along with it.

d. Necessity

An easement of necessity is held to end once the necessity for it disappears.

2. MERGER

When a dominant tenant acquires the servient estate, or vice versa, the two interests are merged and the easement is terminated.

a. Temporary

Where there is only a temporary merger of the dominant and servient estates (e.g., a lease of one parcel to the other owner), the easement is not destroyed, but its existence is suspended for the duration of the merger.

b. Reseparation

Where there has been a complete merger and consequent extinguishment of the easement, reseparation of the parcels does not revive the easement, although it is possible that an implied easement may be held to be created if the circumstances are appropriate.

3. RELEASE AND ABANDONMENT

A dominant tenant may convey her easement to the servient tenant (by a release deed) and the easement will merge into the servient estate and be destroyed. The servient tenant then owns his estate free of any easement (i.e., it is no longer a servient estate).

a. Oral Release

An oral attempt by a dominant tenant to release an easement is ineffective; the statute of frauds requires a writing for the conveying of an interest in real property.

b. Abandonment

An oral statement of release by a dominant tenant, followed either by extended nonuse or by conduct which unequivocally demonstrates an intent to abandon an easement will terminate it. This "transfer by operation of law" is allowed as a useful exception to the statute of frauds.

c. Estoppel

An oral release by a dominant tenant followed by detrimental reliance by the servient tenant will terminate an easement.

4. PRESCRIPTION

If a servient tenant unreasonably interferes with an easement, the dominant tenant may sue. Her failure to assert this cause of action within the statutory period will lead to loss of the right to sue, and therefore loss of the easement.

5. FORFEITURE

Where a dominant tenant abuses an easement and the circumstances make it such that an injunction cannot solve the problem, a court may declare the easement terminated. Attempted conversion of an easement appurtenant to one in gross by the dominant may also lead to its destruction.

Examples: (1) Steve built a house directly blocking the right of way Dita has over his property. If she does nothing about it within the statutory time period, she will lose her easement to Steve by prescription.

(2) Dita stopped using her right of way over Steve's property for a period in excess of the statute of limitations. She has not lost her easement. Nonuse does not terminate an easement, and there is no loss by prescription here, since Steve has done nothing actionable.

(3) Dita told Steve that she was abandoning her right of way and then stopped using it for many years. Her continued nonuse may take her oral release out of the statute of frauds and terminate the easement.

(4) Dita told Steve that she was abandoning her right of way, and both of them plowed up their portions of the road. The easement has been terminated, first, by abandonment because Dita's acts have confirmed her oral statement, and second, by estoppel because Steve acted in reasonable reliance to his detriment on her statement. She cannot resume use of the road thereafter.

F. REVIEW QUESTIONS

1. T or F Dita and Steve owned adjacent lots. For the past year, without asking, Dita has driven across Steve's lot to get to a road, so that there is a well-worn path visible on his land from her garage to the street. Dita sold her lot to Ann, and no mention of an easement appeared in the deed. Ann claims an implied easement over Steve's land. Ann will prevail if she can prove that the easement was apparent, continuous and necessary.

2. T or F Dita and Steve owned adjacent lots. Dita regularly drove across Steve's lot to get to the road. After she had done so for two years she and Steve had a conversation where he told her that she could continue to cross and she thanked him for giving his permission. If the statutory period for prescriptive easements is ten years, Dita will obtain a prescriptive easement if she continues driving for eight more years after the conversation.

3. T or F Dita and Steve owned adjacent lots. Dita erected a building on her lot which was so heavy that if Steve made any excavation whatsoever on his lot her building would subside. After 25 years Steve has lost the right to excavate on his lot due to the creation in Dita of a prescriptive easement of support.

4. T or F Steve granted to Dita "an easement of right of way from your property over my property to the road." Dita then granted to Ann "the right to drive over the road which Steve has given me," but did

not convey her land to Ann. Ann may drive over Steve's property, if she owns adjacent land, but not otherwise.

5. T or F   Steve granted to Dita a right of way from her house over his property. Later Dita sold her house to Ann, but the deed did not mention an easement. Ann may use the right of way.

6. T or F   Steve granted to Dita the right to draw water from a stream crossing his property. Steve later granted a similar right to Ann. Dita can automatically stop Ann from drawing water from the stream.

7. T or F   Steve granted to Dita a right of way over his property and Dita paved a driveway from her garage over Steve's property to the road. Later Steve bought Dita's property, and then conveyed it to Ann. Although no mention of the driveway is contained in the deed, Ann may claim the right to drive over Steve's retained property.

*

VI

COVENANTS RUNNING WITH THE LAND

Analysis

A. *Nature*
   1. *Compared to Assignments*
   2. *Compared to Easements*
   3. *Compared to Conditions*
B. *Requirements*
   1. *General Prerequisites*
   2. *Requirements at Law*
   3. *Requirements in Equity*
C. *Subdivisions*
   1. *Standing to Enforce the Covenant*
   2. *Omitted Restrictions and Notice*
   3. *The Role of a Common Plan*
D. *Termination and Nonenforcement of Covenants*
   1. *Legal Defenses*
   2. *Equitable Defenses*
   3. *Effect of Governmental Action*

A. NATURE

A covenant running with the land is a promise which may be enforced not only by the original promisee (covenantee) against the original promisor (covenantor), but may also be enforced by or against the successors of either party, solely by virtue of them having succeeded to ownership of the appropriate land.

Example: Prudence promised Pete that she would maintain the fence between their parcels. If the promise is one which runs with the land in all respects, then Pete or the person who subsequently owns his property may enforce it against Prudence or the person who subsequently owns her property. (In this chapter, feminine pronouns designate the promisor; masculine pronouns refer to the promisee.)

1. COMPARED TO ASSIGNMENTS

Contract principles today permit the assignment of rights and the delegation of duties, although they did not do so when the doctrine of covenants running with the land was first created. These contract doctrines require, however, a subsequent act by one of the contracting parties transferring the right or duty. *When a covenant properly runs with the land, its benefit or burden is transferred automatically with the conveyance of the estate and without the need for any express assignment or delegation.*

Example: Prudence promised Pete to maintain their common fence. If the covenant were held not to run with the land, then Pete's successors could enforce it only if Pete actually assigned his contractual rights to them, and Prudence's successors would be bound by it only if they accepted a delegation of her contractual duties to them. If it were held to run with the land, then Pete's or Prudence's successors are bound automatically.

2. COMPARED TO EASEMENTS

Easements also frequently "run with the land." As far as the burden of an easement is concerned, a servient tenant can transfer no more than she has, i.e., a servient tenement; thus the burden of the easement is automatically transferred to every successor owner of the servient estate. If the easement is appurtenant, its benefit is automatically transferred along with any transfer of the dominant estate. (The benefit of an easement in gross does not run.) Technically, covenants are created by promissory language ("I promise . . ."), whereas easements arise from conveyancing terminology (" I grant . . ."), but linguistic form is not controlling, and a court might decide that an interest is a covenant or an easement independently of how the parties have characterized it.

a. Affirmative Covenants and Easements

An affirmative covenant constitutes an obligation by the covenantor to perform some act (either on her own land or on the covenantee's land). An affirmative easement entitles the dominant tenant to perform some act upon the servient land; it does not compel the servient tenant to act. An easement which purported to function in the manner of an affirmative covenant would be a "spurious easement," i.e. not an easement.

b. Negative Covenants and Easements

Negative covenants are not clearly distinguishable from negative easements, since both impose obligations upon the burdened party (the covenantor or the servient tenant) to refrain from engaging in otherwise privileged activity upon her own land. In many situations, a transaction may be treated as creating either a covenant running with the land or an easement. The range of easements was limited at common law and a particular obligation involved may sometimes be classified according to whether or not it fell within the traditional common law categories of easements.

Examples: (1) Prudence promised Pete to maintain her fence. This is an affirmative covenant. It is not an easement, because it imposes an affirmative obligation on Prudence with regard to her own land.

(2) Prudence promised Pete that she would not erect a fence between their properties. This could be a negative covenant or a negative easement. It is probably a negative covenant because the common law list of easements did not include promises not to erect a fence. However, if Pete obtained this arrangement in order to protect his view or his sunlight, it might be construed as an easement of view or of light and air.

3. COMPARED TO CONDITIONS

An owner of property may be restricted in some respect either by a condition imposed upon her title (a determinable estate or one subject to a condition subsequent) or by a covenant to the same effect. The primary determinant is the language employed, since the rules of estates require special language for the creation of conditions and do not permit the substitution of promissory phrases. The remedy for breach of a condition is loss of the estate, whereas contract remedies (damages or injunction) are appropriate for breach of covenant. The harshness of a forfeiture for breach of condition leads courts to prefer to treat ambiguous language as promissory rather than conditional. In either event, the restriction "runs" with the estate, since the holder of a qualified fee may not convey more than she has.

Example: Pete conveyed property to Prudence by a deed which recited "Grantee may not build a fence upon her property." A court will probably construe this as a covenant respecting Prudence's land (i.e., as if the deed said "Grantee promises not to build a fence") rather than as a condition upon her title (i.e., as if the deed said "so long as grantee does not build a fence" or "but if grantee does build a fence, then back to grantor") in order to avoid a forfeiture if a fence is built. In either event, the restriction may apply to successors of Prudence.

B. REQUIREMENTS

In order for a covenant to run with the land, a bewildering array of technical requirements may have to be met. There is no consistency of judicial opinion on the matter. The following discussion states the more common requirements, but there is probably a contrary or minority view with regard to every one of them.

1. GENERAL PREREQUISITES
a. Basic Enforceability
No covenant will run with the land unless it is also an enforceable promise as between the original parties. Thus, it must not violate any positive rules of contract or constitutional law.

Example: A covenant to the effect that the property will not be sold or leased to certain racial groups will not run with the land, because enforcement of it is held to violate the Equal Protection clause of the United States Constitution. Such covenants are not enforceable as between the original covenanting parties, and are also not enforceable, therefore, by or against successors. The same would be true for a covenant to commit a crime, or a gambling contract.

1) Statute of Frauds
Because a covenant which can run with the land concerns land, most courts hold it is subject to the statute of frauds and must be in writing and signed by the original promisor. A minority rule eliminates this requirement on the ground that the covenants themselves are not interests in land, but merely refer to land.

a) Acceptance by the Grantee
The signature of the promissor is not required when that person is also the grantee under a deed which contains the promise. Her acceptance of the deed is treated as manifesting her assent to the promise.

b) Implied Reciprocal Covenants
Some courts hold that, under certain circumstances, a covenant received by a covenantee implies a reciprocal covenant on his part back to his covenantor, even though it was not expressly stated in the document.

Example: Pete obtained a promise from his neighbor Prudence that she would not put her land to a commercial use. A court might imply a reciprocal obligation on Pete's part to keep his own land similarly restricted.

b. Intent
No covenant will run with the land unless the original parties actually intended that it do so.

1) Express Language
The common law required that the intention that a covenant run with the land be expressed through use of the word "assigns" if the covenant related to something not yet in existence (in esse). Where the covenant did refer to some existing thing, the intent that it run could be inferred from the general language. Today, most courts do not require special terminology in either situation.

Example: At common law, it would have been necessary to say, "Prudence covenants for herself and her assigns to erect and maintain a fence upon her property" in order for its burden to run, since the fence was not in existence at the time of the covenant. Today, most courts determine from the circumstances whether it was the intent of the parties that successors to Prudence be bound by the covenant, regardless of whether assigns were mentioned.

2. REQUIREMENTS AT LAW
Some jurisdictions distinguish between enforcement of covenants at law or in equity and impose different tests depending upon whether monetary or injunctive relief is sought. The legal rules are older, deriving from *Spencer's Case* (1583), whereas independent enforcement in equity did not occur until *Tulk v. Moxhay* (1848), 265 years later. The legal requirements are set forth below. (The equitable rules are discussed later).

a. Touch and Concern
The only covenants which may run with the land are those which relate to land, i.e., "real" covenants. This is expressed in the requirement that the covenant must touch and concern land.

1) Benefit and Burden
Every promise involves a burden imposed upon the promissor and a benefit gained by the promisee or a third person. These two aspects must be analyzed separately with regard to the issue of touching and concerning land.

a) Burden
The burden of a covenant generally touches and concerns land if it affects the covenantor in her capacity of owner or possessor of land rather than personally, i.e., if it is something she can perform only as owner or possessor.

(1) *Negative Covenant.* If the covenantor is, as a result of her covenant, prohibited from doing something upon her land in a manner which she would otherwise be free to do, then the burden of her covenant touches and concerns her land. If, instead, the prohibition applies to behavior not connected with the land, then it does not touch and concern her land.

Example: Prudence promised never to build a house on her property and never to smoke cigarettes. The burden of her first promise touches and concerns her land and affects her only as landowner. But the burden of her second promise relates to her own personal activity and does not touch and concern her land.

(2) *Affirmative Covenant.* If the activity which the covenantor agrees to undertake occurs upon her own land and compels her to act in a way an ordinary landowner would not be required to act, then the burden of her promise touches and concerns her land. If, instead, her promised activity may be conducted anywhere, whether or not she owns land, then it is personal and does not touch and concern land.

Example: Prudence promised to maintain a fence on her property and to go to church every Sunday. The first burden does touch and concern; the second does not.

b) Benefit
The benefit of a covenant touches and concerns land if it increases the covenantee's use or enjoyment of his land, i.e., if it is something he will enjoy only because he owns or possesses the land. Generally, this means that his land has become more valuable rather than his net worth.

Example: Prudence promised her neighbor Pete that she would: (1) not build a house on her property; (2) build a fence along her adjoining property line; (3) not smoke; and (4) go to church. The benefits of covenants 1 and 2 do touch and concern Pete's land, since his view and his privacy are improved, and his land is more valuable as a result. But covenants 3 and 4 do not increase Pete's enjoyment of his land or raise its value; they benefit only some personal interests he has and do not touch and concern land.

c) Money Covenants

A promise by one party to pay money to another is generally not related to land, since both its burden and benefit can be performed and enjoyed by nonlandowners. Nevertheless, where the payment can be treated as a substitute for some act which would touch and concern land, then the promise to pay may be held to touch and concern land.

(1) *Covenant to Insure.* A covenant to keep premises insured may be regarded as the equivalent of a covenant to keep those premises in good repair. Such a covenant would touch and concern land as to both the benefit and burden if the insurance proceeds had to be used to repair any damage to the property. If the covenantee could pocket the proceeds, the covenant would be considered personal.

(2) *Covenant to Pay Assessment.* A covenant to pay a periodic assessment to a neighborhood organization or homeowners' association for maintenance of common areas may be treated as the equivalent of a covenant to maintain the common areas, which does touch and concern land. (If the association is permitted to spend the money for unrelated purposes, the assessment may still "run" with the land if it has been made a lien upon the land, like a mortgage. But, this involves an entirely different theory.)

2) Burden vs Benefit

It is possible that a promise may contain a burden which touches and concerns land while its benefit does not do so, or vice versa.

Example: Non-competition Covenant—A promise by Prudence not to engage in business activity upon her land which would compete with the business activity of Pete on his land is generally treated as involving a burden which touches and concerns her land (by restricting the activities which she could otherwise perform there). But some courts hold that the benefit of this promise does not touch and concern Pete's land; it increases the commercial value of his business, but does not relate to his physical use or enjoyment of the property. In such jurisdictions, the burden touches but the benefit does not.

3) **Effect Where Part of Covenant Does Not Touch**
There are differing opinions as to the running of a covenant where only the burden or only the benefit touches and concerns land.

   a) **No Effect on Other Side**
   A liberal view requires only that the side involved touch and concern land in order to run; the other side need not. Thus, a burden which touches and concerns land does run even if the benefit of that covenant does not touch and concern land; likewise, a benefit will run so long as it touches and concerns land even though the burden of the same covenant does not.

   b) **Benefit Must Always Touch**
   A stricter view declares that the burden of a covenant will not run with land unless both it and the benefit of the covenant touch and concern land. The benefit must, of course, also touch if it itself is to run. There is no requirement, however, that the burden must touch in order for the benefit to run because the running of a benefit is less drastic than is the running of a burden.

   Example: Prudence covenanted not to compete with Pete. If the jurisdiction holds that the benefit of such a covenant does not touch and concern land, but takes a liberal view with regard to the above requirement, then the burden runs even though the benefit does not. Therefore, Pete may enforce the covenant against Prudence's successors but Pete's successors may not enforce it against Prudence or her successors. Under a strict view neither the burden nor benefit run, i.e., Pete may enforce it against Prudence, but his successors can not enforce it at all, nor may he enforce it against Prudence's successors.

b. **Privity of Estate (Horizontal Privity)**
Many states require that the original parties to the covenant be involved in a special relationship at the time the covenant is made. This is referred to as privity of estate or horizontal privity, but there are divergent views as to what relationships satisfy this requirement.

1) Leases
The most narrow version of the privity requirement limits privity to landlord-tenant situations. Privity here means tenure. Only covenants in leases can run under this standard.

2) Shared Interests
A slightly less restrictive view finds privity in the holding of simultaneous interests in land, in which case covenants between co-owners or covenants relating to easements will run.

3) Conveyances
The prevalent view is that there is also privity in a deed, so that covenants between a grantor and a grantee will run.

4) Privity Unnecessary
The most liberal view dispenses with horizontal privity entirely and permits neighbors to enter into enforceable running covenants. (Otherwise, they may be required to execute cross-deeds to one another and back merely in order to satisfy the privity requirement.)

Example: In a deed from Pete to Prudence, she covenanted not to build any structure over two stories on the land. Because the covenant was contained in a deed, it will be enforced in those states which find privity in grantor-grantee situations; it will also be enforced in those jurisdictions which do not require privity at all. But it will not be enforced in that minority of states which require either a tenurial or a mutually subsisting relationship between the covenanting parties.

5) Benefit
In some jurisdictions, horizontal privity is not required when it is a question of the benefit running with land. Privity is required only when the burden is to run.

c. **Succession to the Entire Estate (Vertical Privity)**
Some jurisdictions hold that the burden of a covenant runs only to persons who succeed to the entire estate of the covenantor. This is sometimes stated as a requirement of privity between covenantor and successor. However, "privity" is used in an entirely different sense here from its meaning in the covenantor-covenantee relationship (horizontal privity). In jurisdictions requiring vertical privity, the burden of a covenant does not bind a person who takes a lesser estate from the covenantor, e.g., a tenant of the covenantor.

Example: Prudence purchased 40 acres from Pete and promised in her deed to keep all the land in good repair. She then conveyed 20 acres to Alice, and leased the other 20 acres to Stella. A court could hold that the burden runs to bind Alice, who has succeeded to Prudence's entire fee estate as to a part of the property, but does not run to bind Stella who has taken a lesser estate than Prudence had (a leasehold rather than a fee). The same result could follow if Prudence had leased the 40 acres from Pete (and covenanted to him in her lease) and then assigned her lease as to 20 acres to Alice and sublet 20 acres to Stella.

1) Benefit
In some jurisdictions, no vertical privity requirement is imposed if it is only a question of the benefit running with land. Such privity is required only when the burden is to run.

3.   REQUIREMENTS IN EQUITY
The assistance of equity is required whenever the plaintiff desires injunctive rather than monetary relief. In those situations, courts may dispense with some or all of the legal requirements. Covenants enforced in courts of equity are referred to as equitable servitudes, i.e. the equitable equivalent of legal easements (servitudes) and the requirements applied here can often be better understood in terms of easements. These requirements are set forth below.

a.   Touch and Concern
It is always required—for easements and for covenants—that the aspect involved (burden or benefit) relate to land in order to be transferred with the land. (If the benefit of an easement is in gross it does not pass with the land.) *No burden of a covenant will run, at law or in equity, if it does not touch and concern land, nor will any benefit run if it does not touch and concern land.*

1)   Where Only One Side Touches
Where the burden of a covenant does not touch and concern land, the benefit may still run as an equitable servitude. A few courts, following the old English prohibition against easements in gross, hold that the burden of an equitable servitude will not run with the land where the benefit involved does not also touch and concern land. But most courts permit the burden to run even when the benefit does not touch.

b.   Horizontal Privity
By analogy to the rules for easements (which do not require privity between landowners for one to give the other an easement) there is no horizontal privity requirement for equitable servitudes. Thus, covenants

between neighbors may be enforced in equity by and against their successors.

c. Vertical Privity

Just as an easement burdens and benefits all subsequent possessors of the servient and dominant tenements, whether or not they have succeeded to the entire estates of their predecessors, so also do equitable servitudes run with the land, even to those who have not taken the entire interest in the property held by the original parties to the covenant. Thus, a tenant of either covenantor or covenantee is bound or benefitted in equity by the covenant.

d. Notice

These equitable easements are created by equity courts only when it is equitable to do so. It would be inequitable to impose the burden of a covenant upon a successor to the covenantor who was unaware of its existence when she purchased the land. *Therefore, the burden of an equitable servitude does not run when there is no notice.*

1) At Law

Technically, a covenant runs with the land at law whether or not the successor has notice of it. However, such covenants are subject to the recording acts of the jurisdictions, and a bona fide purchaser who takes title without notice of an unrecorded covenant will generally take free of it. Thus, even at law, notice is made relevant. Recording is covered in Ch. X.

C. SUBDIVISIONS

It is possible for the developer of a new subdivision to control its architectural layout and continued maintenance through the use of covenants in the deeds, rather than through the more conventional political devices of zoning and taxation. A condominium or cooperative apartment building may be similarly regulated. This section deals with the enforcement of such uniform covenants.

1. STANDING TO ENFORCE THE COVENANT
a. The Original Subdivider

The subdivider is usually the original promisee of all the covenants made by individual purchasers and is, therefore, initially a proper party to enforce the covenant. If he has sold off all of the land, the benefit of the various covenants may have "run past" him, and he may, therefore, lack enforcement power. (It is also often the case that the subdivider is no longer available to enforce the covenant, having sold out and moved on.)

b.   The Neighborhood Association
A developer is generally not interested in maintaining any connection with a subdivision once it has been completed, and the individual owners also prefer self-regulation free of developer control. Typically, the developer creates a homeowners' association and turns over to it the enforcement role with regard to covenants contained in the purchasers' deeds.

1)   Transfer of Common Land
One way to give the homeowners' association power to enforce is to have all deeds to recite that the restrictions imposed upon the lots is for the benefit of certain common land retained by the developer, and then to subsequently convey that common land to the homeowners' association, when formed. As a successor owner of the benefitted land, the association may enforce the covenants contained in the individual deeds.

Example: Pete inserted in all of the deeds to lots in his subdivision a covenant by each purchaser to pay for the annual maintenance of the subdivision swimming pool (then still owned by Pete). He subsequently conveyed the swimming pool to the homeowners' association, which thus entitled it to enforce the promises to pay.

c.   Other Neighbors
1)   Subsequent Owners
A covenant, contained in a deed to one purchaser in a subdivision (which burdens her property), may be enforced against her by other lot owners who took deeds from the developer at a later time, on the theory that the covenant in her deed benefitted all of the developer's retained land and ran with that land when it was conveyed to the subsequent purchasers. (Be careful not to confuse this situation with the two variations discussed immediately below.)

a)   Subsequent Grantees From Prior Grantees
The above theory does not apply to benefit later purchasers in the subdivision who took their deeds from individual owners in the subdivision who themselves had preceded the covenantor. Land previously conveyed away by the subdivider cannot be directly benefitted by a covenant later made to him; some other theory must be employed (which is discussed below).

Example: Pete conveyed lot 1 to Al, lot 2 to Prudence, and lot 3 to Bob, in that order; Al then conveyed his lot 1 to Carl. Bob may enforce a covenant made by Prudence to Pete in her deed, on the ground that it burdened lot 2 and benefitted Pete's retained lot 3 and that the benefit ran with lot 3 when Pete conveyed it to Bob. But since Pete did not own lot 1 when Prudence covenanted to him, lot 1 cannot be treated as a benefitted parcel, nor does it acquire any such benefit by a later conveyance from Al to Carl, which involved no promise by Prudence.

b) **Subsequently Acquired Land**

The above theory is usually limited to land owned by the subdivider at the time the covenant is made to him. Land which is subsequently added to the development is generally not treated as benefitted by the covenant, and the purchasers of those parcels cannot enforce it against the original covenantor.

Example: Pete conveyed lot 1 to Prudence by a deed which contained a covenant by her. Later, he acquired some adjacent land and conveyed lot 2 from this newly acquired land to Al. Since lot 2 was not owned by Pete when he received the promise from Prudence, it was not benefitted by her covenant, nor could a benefit be subsequently conferred upon it when Pete later acquired it or when he conveyed it to Al, if that was not Prudence's intent.

2) **Prior Owners**

Prior grantees have a more difficult time enforcing restrictions against subsequent grantees. Theories sometimes available to them are:

a) **Running of the Burden**

If the developer promised one purchaser that she would impose restrictions upon all the rest of her land as she sold it off to later buyers, then all of her retained land became subject to a burden for the benefit of the lot just conveyed. When her retained land is then conveyed the burden of her earlier covenant runs with it, whether or not the deeds to it contain the promised restriction.

Example: Prudence conveyed lot 1 to Pete, inserting a covenant in her deed to him that all other land in the development would be restricted to residential uses. She then conveyed lot 2 to Ann, (without imposing such a restriction). Pete or his successors may prohibit Ann from engaging in any commercial activity on her property on the ground that lot 2 became subject to the burden of Prudence's covenant when lot 1 was conveyed to Pete and that this burden ran with lot 2 when it was conveyed to Ann. (Ann may have a defense if she can show that she took without notice.)

b) Creation and Running of the Burden
In some jurisdictions a negative restriction contained in the deed of a prior grantee is held to imply a reciprocal burden upon the subdivider's retained land, and this implied reciprocal restriction may then run with the retained land and burden any subsequent grantee.

Example: Pete conveyed lot 1 to Prudence by a deed restricting her land to residential uses; later he conveyed lot 2 to Al by a deed which contained no such restriction. Prudence may be able to argue that when she made her covenant to Pete regarding lot 1, an implied reciprocal covenant from Pete to her was created burdening his lot 2 and that this burden then ran with lot 2 to Al. (Al may have a defense if he can show that he took without notice.)

c) Third Party Beneficiary
In some jurisdictions, a covenant inserted in a subsequent grantee's deed may be held to benefit prior grantees, as third party beneficiaries. Although the common law held that an easement could not be created in a third person, courts do permit a third party to receive the benefit of a covenant made between the covenantor and the covenantee. This theory may apply if there is express language in the deed designating other neighbors as beneficiaries or if such an intent can be inferred from the circumstances, including the existence of a general plan in the neighborhood.

Example: Pete conveyed lot 1 to Al and then conveyed lot 2 to Prudence. Prudence's deed contained a covenant by her to use her land solely for residential purposes. Al may be able to argue that Prudence and Pete intended that his lot receive the benefit of the covenant by Prudence and he may therefore enforce her promise as a third party beneficiary. His case is easier if Prudence's deed recites that her covenant is intended to benefit all other parcels in the development.

2. OMITTED RESTRICTIONS AND NOTICE

Once a covenant has been properly created, its burden and benefit run with the land even though subsequent deeds to either parcel fail to mention it. However, it will not be enforced as an equitable servitude against any party who takes the land without actual or constructive notice of it.

Examples: (1) Pete conveyed lot 1 to Prudence, who covenanted to keep the property residential; Prudence then conveyed that lot to Ann without including such a restriction in Ann's deed. Pete may enjoin Ann from breaching Prudence's covenant if Ann can be charged with notice of it. Here there is record notice of the restriction because it is contained in Ann's chain of title. It therefore does not matter that Ann made no such covenant herself; the burden of Prudence's covenant ran with the land.

(2) Prudence conveyed lot 1 to Pete and covenanted in that deed that she would keep all her retained land in the subdivision residential; then she conveyed lot 2 to Ann without including such a restriction in her deed. Pete may enjoin Ann from breaching the restriction if Ann can be charged with notice of it. There is record notice of the restriction here if Ann can be charged with a duty of searching out all conveyances made by her grantor Prudence even though they involve other land (since the restriction is contained in a deed to lot 1 rather than lot 2). Again, if the burden of Prudence's covenant runs, it does not matter that Ann made no such covenant herself. Notice is covered more fully in Chapter X.

3. THE ROLE OF A COMMON PLAN

In several instances, a court may seek to determine whether or not the subdivision is subject to common restrictions. The fact that some parcels are unrestricted or are subject to different restrictions may be important for the following reasons:

a. Notice

In some jurisdictions, the notice requirement discussed above may be satisfied by virtue of the existence of a common plan. There may be record notice if there has been recorded a plat or map showing the entire development and its uniform restrictions. There may be inquiry notice if the surrounding properties in the subdivision have all been uniformly developed.

b.   **Third Party Beneficiary or Implied Reciprocal Servitude**
In some jurisdictions, third party beneficiary or implied reciprocal servitude theories, entitling prior grantees to enforce later covenants, will apply only if there is a common plan.

c.   **Unrestricted Parcel**
In some jurisdictions, the lack of a common plan may bar all enforcement of a restriction if there are any unrestricted parcels in the subdivision. A court might reason that it would be unfair to restrict one lot when its owner cannot enforce it against other lots. The entire plan might then fail on a domino basis.

D.   TERMINATION AND NONENFORCEMENT OF COVENANTS

Covenants which were originally properly created so as to be valid as between the parties and to run with the land, may, by virtue of subsequent developments, become unenforceable.

1.   LEGAL DEFENSES
Most of the grounds for the termination of easements also apply to covenants. The discussion below concentrates on the differences between termination of the two types of interests.

a.   **Language in Instrument**
The creating document itself may limit the life of the covenant. A covenant may be given the same kind of durational qualification as is applied to easements, although there is no special category or label for a "covenant at will," equivalent to a license.

1)   Renewal Provisions
Many subdivision and condominium restrictions provide for renewal of the covenants by a certain vote of the homeowners after some fixed number of years, or provide for termination by vote under certain circumstances (e.g., destruction of a certain percentage of the project).

2)   Statutory Duration
Some statutes limit the time period over which a covenant may be enforced. This statutory limitation will override any inconsistent (i.e., longer) time period prescribed in the document creating the covenant.

b.   **Merger**
A merger of the benefitted and burdened estates under one ownership will terminate the covenant. But where numerous neighbors are able to enforce a restriction upon one parcel, the merger of only some of the

parcels may not eliminate the burden or benefit of the covenant entirely and it may remain enforceable by the others.

c. Release

The party benefitted by a covenant may release the one burdened by it. Again, however, this may accomplish nothing if other parties are also entitled to enforce the covenant and have not joined in the release.

d. Abandonment

A covenant may be abandoned under the same circumstances as for easements. In the subdivision context, this may occur in two ways:

1) Failure to Continue Plan

If the developer inserts covenants in his early deeds but fails to continue this policy as to later deeds, he may be deemed to have abandoned his scheme, and the lack of a proper general plan for the subdivision may lead to nonenforcement even as against those covenants which were properly drafted.

2) Abandonment by Owners

If violations of existing covenants become so widespread within a subdivision that there is no longer any general plan in effect, the restrictions may be deemed to have been abandoned.

e. Prescription

If a covenantor or her successors has refused to observe the restraints of a negative covenant or has openly and notoriously refused to perform the obligations of an affirmative covenant long enough, the covenant may be subject to a statute of limitations defense.

2. EQUITABLE DEFENSES

When injunctive relief is sought for the enforcement of a covenant, certain special defenses may be available to the defendant. The refusal of equity to act because of these grounds does not necessarily mean that damages will also be denied.

a. Changed Conditions

Courts will not compel obedience to a restriction which no longer serves the purpose for which it was created. If the neighborhood has so changed that enforcement will unfairly oppress the defendant without achieving any significant advantage for the plaintiff, an injunction may be refused.

Example: Prudence's lot is subject to a restriction that she not build any structure over 30 feet high on it in order to preserve Pete's view. However, highrise buildings have surrounded the rest of his lot and he has no view left anyway. A court might decide that conditions have so changed as to no longer warrant equitable enforcement of the covenant.

1) Domino Problem

Generally, the changed conditions must affect the entire development where subdivision restrictions are involved. If the change affects only some parcels, most courts will not lift the restrictions lest this have a domino effect which would ultimately destroy the entire project.

Example: A subdivision of many square blocks is uniformly subject to residential restrictions. The owners on one of the outside streets of the project seek to have the restrictions lifted because the properties on the other side of the street (not part of the subdivision) have turned commercial. But since the interior of the subdivision remains residential their request will probably be denied, since to allow them this privilege could lead to the ultimate commercialization of the entire subdivision.

2) Zoning

A more permissive zoning of an area subject to restrictive covenants does not of itself constitute a change of circumstances, since most zoning ordinances do not prohibit uses higher than those specified in the classification. But the fact that the local government has so zoned the area might be relevant evidence that a change of conditions has already occurred.

b. Unclean Hands

If the plaintiff seeking to enforce the covenant has already breached it himself, it is likely that a court will not permit him to enforce it against another. But the fact that he has breached some other unrelated covenant should be irrelevant.

c. Acquiescence

If the plaintiff has tolerated breaches by other owners of similarly burdened property, he may be prohibited from enforcing it against the next owner of similarly burdened property. This defense is not applicable if the previously tolerated breaches have not substantially affected his property, whereas the one in question would.

Example: Pete, an owner in a large subdivision, has done nothing about the fact that some other owners have violated the common restriction against television antennas on their roofs. But if he can show that those other violators are too distant to be visible from his house, he may still be able to enjoin his next door neighbor Prudence from doing so.

d. Laches

The general equitable defense of laches is available to any covenantor who would be substantially harmed by the delay of the covenantee in seeking to enforce the covenant.

3. EFFECT OF GOVERNMENTAL ACTION

The enforceability of a covenant may be affected by the fact that the government has intervened in the title of the burdened parcel.

a. Eminent Domain

Where the government takes property by condemnation for a public use, it will generally acquire it free of any burdens imposed on it by restrictive covenants. Most courts today treat the interests of parties benefitted by a restrictive covenant as property rights and require the government to compensate them for their loss, (as well as to compensate the burdened owner for the loss of her title to the property).

b. Tax Sale

Where the government takes title to land by virtue of the failure of its owner to pay the taxes due on it, courts are divided as to whether or not the person who purchases it at the government tax sale takes subject to the burdens of covenants or free of them.

E. REVIEW QUESTIONS

1. T or F Tom, a tenant, covenanted to Laura, his landlord, that he would keep the premises insured against fire. The covenant does not require that Laura use any insurance proceeds to rebuild, but it does say that the parties intend it to run with the land. Tom assigned his lease to Al, who refuses to carry insurance. Laura can enforce the covenant against Al.

2. T or F Pete conveyed one of the two lots he owned to Prudence. One month later Prudence covenanted with Pete that she would not build any structure on her lot over 50 feet high. Pete conveyed the lot he had retained to Al. Al can enforce the covenant at law against Prudence.

3. T or F Pete conveyed one of two lots he owned to Prudence, together with an easement of right of way in her favor over his retained lot. One month later Prudence covenanted to keep the right of way in paved condition. Pete then conveyed the lot he had retained to Al. Al can enforce the covenant at law against Prudence.

4. T or F Pete conveyed a lot he owned to Prudence with a covenant in the deed that Prudence would keep the common driveway clean.

Prudence rented her property to Al, and Pete rented his property to Barbara. Barbara can enforce the covenant at law against Al.

5. Pete conveyed lot 1 to Ann with a building restriction in the deed, then conveyed lot 2 to Bob without such a restriction, and then conveyed lot 3 to Carol with a building restriction similar to Ann's. (The restriction was imposed on the grantee in each case, not the grantor.)

T or F   a.   Ann can enforce the building restriction against Bob.

T or F   b.   Ann can enforce the building restriction against Carol.

T or F   c.   Bob can enforce the building restriction against Ann.

T or F   d.   Bob can enforce the building restriction against Carol.

T or F   e.   Carol can enforce the building restriction against Ann.

T or F   f.   Carol can enforce the building restriction against Bob.

PART TWO

CONVEYANCING

Analysis

VII

BROKERS

Most real estate sales transactions are initiated through the services of brokers, who bring the parties together and often negotiate the terms of the transaction.

A. PERSONS QUALIFIED TO ACT AS BROKERS

In order to function as a real estate broker, an individual (indicated by female pronouns in the text) must have obtained a license from the appropriate state agency. The consequences of performing brokerage services without possessing a license may include loss of the right to compensation and civil or criminal liability.

1. FINDERS EXCEPTION

Many jurisdictions permit a person to charge or collect a fee for introducing buyer and seller (or borrower and lender, etc.) to each other even though she is not licensed as a broker. However, her services must be limited to making introductions. Actively participating in the negotiations or closing the transaction will be deemed to be acting as a broker and may result in sanctions for lacking a license.

2. QUALIFYING AS A BROKER

In order to obtain a license, an applicant must generally have some minimum educational background (e.g., a college degree) and must successfully pass an examination administered by the state. There are also character and fitness qualifications, generally disabling persons with criminal records from obtaining licenses. The qualifications are often ongoing, meaning that already licensed brokers must comply with continuing education requirements and may lose their licenses if found to have committed acts involving moral turpitude or in violation of the licensing statutes.

a. Salespersons

A salesperson's license is inferior to a broker's license and is issued on easier standards (e.g., less educational background, or passage of an easier examination). However, a real estate salesperson is generally not entitled to operate under her own name, but must act under the authority of a supervising broker.

B. SERVICES

A real estate broker is customarily employed by the owner of property to find someone interested in purchasing his property. (Male pronouns designate the owner/vendor/seller and female pronouns designate the purchaser/buyer in this chapter.) Less frequently, a broker is employed to locate property for her principal to acquire, i.e. as broker for the buyer rather than the seller. Brokers are also retained by landlords and tenants seeking persons or properties available for rental. (In the following text, the assumption is that the broker has been employed by the seller to find a buyer for his property.)

1. LISTING AGREEMENTS

The employment contract between broker and seller is referred to as a listing agreement, whereby the seller "lists" his land for sale. *A listing agreement authorizes the broker to seek persons to make offers to purchase the property from the owner; it does not authorize the broker to sell the property on behalf of the owner.* The agreement usually includes provision for compensation (often referred to as a commission) to the broker if her services are successfully performed. The statute of frauds may require the agreement to be in writing, even though it is technically an employment contract rather than a contract for the sale of land.

a. Open Listing

Where the seller agrees to pay the broker a commission only if she is the "procuring cause" of the transaction, the listing is referred to as open. A broker with such a listing earns no commission for a sale generated by a different broker or by the seller himself.

b. Exclusive Right to Sell Listing

Where the seller agrees to pay the broker a commission for any sale of the property, whether or not the broker was its procuring cause, the listing is referred to as an "exclusive" or "exclusive right to sell" listing.

> *Example:* Van gave Brenda an exclusive right to sell listing and—before it had expired—he sold the property to Pearl, whose offer had been presented to him by Cora, another broker. By virtue of his exclusive listing with Brenda, Van owes a commission to her, even though she had nothing to do with the sale. (Van may also owe a second commission to Cora depending on what agreement they had, if any.)

c. Exclusive Agency Listing

Where the owner agrees to pay a commission for any sale generated by any broker, but reserves the right to find his own purchaser without commission liability, an exclusive agency listing exists. (The owner has agreed to have no other agents, but to leave himself free to act as a principal.)

2. RIGHT TO A COMMISSION

Listing agreements generally provide that the broker will earn a commission calculated as a percentage of the sales price.

a. Ready, Willing and Able Purchaser

Unless the agreement provides otherwise, most states hold that a broker earns her commission when she produces a ready, willing and able purchaser. *It is not necessary that a sale actually occur for the broker to be entitled to a commission under this standard.* This is illustrated in the following examples:

Examples: (1) *Perfect Offer.* If Van listed his property for sale at $100,000 and Brenda presented an offer to him from Pearl to pay that much in cash, and if it is determined that Pearl had such funds available to her, Pearl was a ready, willing and able purchaser and Brenda has earned her commission *whether or not Van accepted this offer.*

(2) *Lesser Offer.* The same facts except that Pearl offered $95,000 rather than $100,000. Under the circumstances, Brenda has not yet earned her commission. However, if Van accepts Pearl's offer, then Pearl has become ready, willing and able and Brenda is now entitled to a commission.

(3) *Conditional Offer.* The same facts as in # 1 except that Pearl's offer to purchase is conditional upon her obtaining a bank loan for $75,000. Pearl is not yet ready and willing, and Van owes nothing to Brenda if he rejects Pearl's offer. Even if he accepts the offer, he is not liable for a commission *unless and until Pearl qualifies for the loan.*

b. No Deal No Commission

In the above situations, closing of the deal was not a condition precedent to entitlement to a commission; the commission is earned even if the contract is not performed because of breach or mutual abandonment. Some jurisdictions hold, however, that the broker is not entitled to a commission unless the sale is actually consummated. This result is justified on the ground that it is what sellers expect when they sign listing agreements. (Often this rule is limited to residential listing). The same result can occur if the listing so provides.

1) Commission Payable at Close

Where the law entitles a broker to a commission as soon as a ready, willing and able purchaser has been procured, but the listing agreement provides that it will not be paid until the close of escrow, the court may be required to interpret the agreement to determine whether closing of escrow was an absolute condition precedent to payment or whether it merely established the time of payment. In the latter case, the broker earns her commission even if the deal does not close.

C. BROKER DUTIES

Brokers are held to increasingly high standards of conduct to their principals in real estate transactions. Numerous theories are applied to impose liability upon them.

1. CONTRACT

A listing agreement is a contract between broker and principal and usually imposes certain duties on the broker. (It could be written as a unilateral contract, merely providing that the broker earns a commission if she performs, but brokers prefer bilateral contracts in order to prevent revocation by sellers and thus assume promissory obligations in order to create such contracts.) A broker who fails to perform those duties may be subject to liability.

Example: Brenda's listing agreement provided that she would diligently search for buyers of Van's property, but she did nothing at all after she got the listing. Under the circumstances, Van may be entitled to revoke the listing, refuse to pay a commission to her for any sale made, or recover damages from her for injuries suffered from not having been able to sell his property.

2. AGENCY

A listing agreement generally creates an agency relationship between broker and principal. As agent, the broker owes the principal fiduciary obligations of loyalty, integrity and good faith, and may be liable for failing to attend to those duties.

Examples: Brenda, working under a listing from Van, told Pearl that she believed Van would accept a lower offer and encouraged Pearl to lower her offering price. Brenda may be liable to Van for putting Pearl's best interests above his.

Brenda, working under a listing from Van, made her own offer to purchase the property, not disclosing to Van that offer was from her. Even though the price and terms are fair, Van may later be able to set the sale aside on the ground that an agent may not transact with her principal without full disclosure because, inevitably, such a situation requires the agent to consider interests adverse to her principal.

a. Whose Agent

The broker is generally the agent of the person who has employed her and compensates her. In the conventional setting, this is the seller of the property (who signs the listing and pays the commission out of the sales proceeds he receives from the buyer). The broker may be the buyer's rather than the seller's agent where the buyer is the one who has initially retained her, even though her commission may come from the sales proceeds received by the seller.

1) Subagents

In many communities, brokers belong to a multiple listing service and submit their listings to the service for distribution to other members. Member brokers who receive listings from the service then contact their own prospects to interest them in purchasing the property. Thus there may be a "listing broker" and a "showing broker" involved in a sale, splitting the commission, and dealing separately with the principals. However, the brokers may not be, technically, agents of their respective principals. *The showing agent is more likely a subagent of the seller rather than an agent of the buyer,* since her authority was derived from the listing broker (the seller's agent) and her commission is paid by the seller (to the listing broker who then divided it with her). As a result, her fiduciary responsibilities may be owed to the seller rather than the buyer.

3. NEGLIGENCE

Brokers are professionals and expected to comply with professional standards of care. Thus, they may be liable for malpractice when their conduct falls below the standard of care customary in the community. Questions of whose agent the broker is, discussed above, may also be germane here, in terms of privity.

Example: Brenda failed to advise Van to check Pearl's credit rating or to advise Pearl to check Van's property for termites, and both parties suffered as a result. Brenda may be liable to Van for negligence if a jury decides that due care from a broker to her principal includes recommending he investigate the creditworthiness of the purchaser. But in order for Brenda to be liable to Pearl for negligence, a court would have to decide that Brenda owed a similar duty to Pearl, which might be difficult to establish in light of the fact that Brenda was not Pearl's agent.

4. PUBLIC DUTIES

Brokers may have their licenses restricted, suspended or revoked for engaging in conduct prohibited by their licensing statutes. Such breaches may also lead to the imposition of civil liability where harm has resulted to parties involved in the related real estate transaction. Some courts also hold that the fact that brokers are engaged in dealing with the public imposes upon them special duties (of care or honesty or fairness), and permit aggrieved parties to recover from them for breaches of such standards.

5. DISCLOSURE OF DEFECTS

At least one jurisdiction requires sellers of residential real property and their brokers to make a detailed written disclosure about the condition of the property to the purchaser. The disclosure statement is to be based upon a reasonably competent and diligent visual inspection of the accessible areas of the property.

Other jurisdictions require disclosure of defects and events that may affect a purchaser's decision to purchase a property (e.g., residence was scene of a murder).

*

VIII

CONTRACTS FOR THE SALE OF LAND (VENDOR–PURCHASER)

Analysis

E. *Performance*
1. *Performance by the Vendor*
2. *Performance by the Purchaser*
3. *Nonsurvival of Contract Terms*
F. *Breach*
1. *Remedies of the Purchaser*
2. *Remedies of the Vendor*

When the owner of an interest in land enters into a contract for the sale of that interest to another person, the body of law which regulates their relations during the life of the contract is referred to as vendor-purchaser law. The vendor-purchaser relationship endures until title to the property has been conveyed to the purchaser (at which time they become grantor-grantee) or until the contract is terminated for one reason or another. Thus, the rules discussed in this section regulate parties after they have executed a contract for the sale of land and before they have completed or terminated it. Throughout the chapter it will be assumed that a fee simple interest is being sold by a male vendor to a female purchaser.

A. ENFORCEABLE CONTRACT

In order for a vendor-purchaser relationship to exist there must be an enforceable contract between the parties. The general law of contracts is applicable to real estate arrangements.

1. INTENT TO BE BOUND
The parties must manifest an intent to be bound in order for a contractual relationship to exist. A statement by an owner to his broker agreeing to list his property for sale does not constitute an offer to sell it. (It is only an agency agreement, authorizing the broker to find a purchaser. See Brokers.) Thus when a purchaser does offer to buy, it is merely an offer which must be accepted by the owner in order for a contract to arise. The owner has the power to reject an offer to purchase even though it conforms perfectly to the terms set forth in his listing agreement with the broker. He may be required to pay the broker a commission under the listing agreement, but he is not required to sell to a potential purchaser until he actually accepts her offer.

2. CONSIDERATION
A vendor's promise to convey property must be supported by consideration; this is usually satisfied by the purchaser's promise to pay the vendor's price.

a. Illusory
If the purchaser's obligation to pay is made dependent upon her satisfaction with some feature of the property (e.g., zoning or approval of existing leases) or if the vendor's obligation to convey is made dependent upon his satisfaction with some aspect of the payment (e.g., the sufficiency of the purchaser's mortgage), a court may declare the contract illusory and therefore unenforceable. Many courts, however, enforce contracts which contain such satisfaction clauses, reading either an objective (reasonable person) or subjective (good faith) requirement into the provision. Additionally, a condition may be construed to also include a covenant; e.g., a clause providing that the purchaser's obligation to pay is subject to obtaining a mortgage is held to impose a duty on the purchaser to apply for the mortgage.

3. WRITING
The statute of frauds requires that a contract to convey real property be in writing and signed by the parties to be charged.

a. Description
The writing must describe the property to be conveyed. A full legal description is not necessary; an informal description (such as a street address) will suffice, so long as a court can properly determine what property is involved.

1) Items Included
A description of the land conveyed includes all improvements on it which have become part of the realty by virtue of the doctrine of fixtures. (See Fixtures in Chapter XIII.) Personal property which is not affixed is not transferred by the deed; if the parties desire to transfer such assets, a bill of sale referring to them should be executed.

Example: "123 Main Street" includes the house standing on that parcel, its doors and windows, as well as the nails holding them in. The description does not include the dishes, pots, or pans. Whether it includes the venetian blinds or wall-to-wall carpeting depends on whether they are held to be fixtures.

b. Parties

Both vendor and purchaser must be identified. The purchaser may indicate her intention to assign the right to purchase by designating that title will be taken by her or her "nominee," which is generally valid so long as she herself remains bound to perform the obligations required by the contract. Where the vendor has a fractional interest in the property, use of only his name or signature may not bind the other owners unless an agency relationship exists between them. The writing must, of course, be signed by the party to be charged.

c. Price
It is generally required that the contract specify the price to be paid, although some jurisdictions enforce contracts which simply call for a reasonable price. It is not required that the contract specify the method of payment, and if it is silent upon this matter a court will assume that the price is to be paid in all cash at the time that the property is conveyed.

d. Oral Modification

Many jurisdictions do not require that a subsequent modification or revocation of the contract be in writing. The statute of frauds is held to apply only to the initial creation of the contract, and subsequent changes may be by parol.

e. Part Performance

Courts of equity enforce oral contracts for the sale of land under an exception to the statute of frauds when they have been partly performed. There are a variety of views as to what constitutes sufficient part performance to take a case out of the statute.

1) Transfer of Possession

The most liberal view enforces an oral contract whenever the vendor has transferred possession of the property to the purchaser.

2) Possession Plus Payment

A more restrictive view requires that the purchaser have paid part of the price as well as have taken possession before her oral contract to purchase will be enforced.

3) Possession Plus Improvements

As an alternative to part payment, the purchaser who has been let into possession and has made improvements to the property may be permitted to enforce her oral contract.

4. TIME FOR PERFORMANCE

A contract need not specify a date for performance by the parties (generally referred to as the "closing" or "settlement"). If no such date is expressed, a court will imply that performance is to occur within a reasonable time.

a. Contract Dates

Where the contract provides that "time is of the essence," either party may withdraw if the other does not perform her obligations on time. However, if both parties are late in performing, a court may conclude that they have waived the clause; furthermore, in some jurisdictions, the sanction of the clause (inability to enforce the contract) applies only if the aggrieved party has given appropriate advance notice of a demand for timely performance. Where the contract does set a date for performance, law courts treat that as an essential provision and do not excuse belated performance by either side. Equity courts, however, excuse a delay which can be compensated for, unless the contract specifically recites that time is of the essence.

5.   INCIDENTAL PROVISIONS
a.   Payment Terms
Most contracts explicitly provide for how the purchaser is to pay the
price. Frequently, the offer to purchase is accompanied by a small deposit
to show that the purchaser is serious about wanting to buy. (For this
reason it is sometimes referred to as an "earnest money contract.") It is
also customary for the contract to provide for an increase in the down
payment within a few days after the vendor has accepted the offer. The
balance of the price is usually then required to be paid at closing,
commonly through use of funds borrowed from a bank (see Mortgages), or
borrowed from the vendor through use of a purchase money mortgage.
Alternatively, where an installment contract (also referred to as a
"contract for deed") is employed, the balance of the price is paid monthly
over many years and escrow does not close until the final payment is
made.

b.   Prorations
The due dates for many items of income and expense will probably not
coincide with the date set for the performing of the contract (e.g., tax
payments, mortgage payments, etc.). Adjustments made to the purchase
price to compensate for these differences are called prorations.

Example: The contract is to close on May 15. However, the $1200
property taxes for the entire year were paid by the vendor on
March 15 previously; to adjust for this, the amount owed by
the purchaser will be increased by $900 for the nine months
she will have of tax free possession. $1000 rent from a tenant
on the property covering the entire month was received by the
vendor on the first of the month; consequently, the amount
owed by the purchaser will be decreased by $500 to
compensate for the half-months rent she will not be receiving
from the tenant once the building is hers. (The adjustment
would go the other way if the taxes were paid after rather
than at the beginning of the year, and/or the rent was paid
after rather than at the beginning of the period.)

c.   Others
All of the rules in the following sections are generally subject to
modification by the parties. Thus, they may, if they care to do so,
provide otherwise for marketable title, risk of loss, remedies for breach,
etc.

B. MARKETABLE TITLE

There is implied in every contract for the sale of land a requirement that the vendor's title be marketable.

1. GENERAL MEANING

A title is held to be marketable when it is in fact a title to the entire estate covered in the contract and is not subject to any encumbrances or defects or to any reasonable doubts as to any of these matters. It is a title which an informed, prudent and reasonable purchaser would be willing to accept as performance of the contract.

a. Entire Estate

If the vendor has less than a fee simple absolute, or has only a fractional ownership interest in it (being a tenant in common, joint tenant, etc.), or owns a smaller geographic amount than what is described in the contract, his title is unmarketable, unless the contract itself only calls for the lesser interest actually held by him.

b. Good Chain of Title

If there are problems in the vendor's chain of title generating a reasonable uncertainty as to the complete passage of the title to him, a court may declare his title unmarketable. Some examples are:

1) **Name Misspellings**
   Where, earlier in the chain, title was granted to "John Smith" but later conveyed by "John Smythe," raising a doubt whether the person who received the title was the same one who subsequently purported to convey it. Where the discrepancy is between, e.g., "John A. Smith" and "John Adams Smith," it is not likely that a court will find a doubt justified.

2) **Boundary Discrepancies**
   Where the land is described in one deed as being 100 feet south of a marker and in a later deed as being 105 feet south of the marker.

3) **Defective Documents**
   Where some document in the chain was not properly notarized, or signed, even though it was acknowledged and/or recorded.

c. Unencumbered

A marketable title is one which is not subject to any encumbrance. Mortgages, back taxes, easements, covenants and leases are all encumbrances which render a title unmarketable, unless the purchaser has agreed to accept them.

1)   Monetary Burdens

The vendor is generally allowed to utilize the purchase price to satisfy mortgage and tax liens on his title in order to thereby convey a title free of those claims to the purchaser. This is usually accomplished by having the escrow agent take part of the funds deposited by the purchaser and pay them to the lien holders rather than the vendor, in order to satisfy and remove the liens from the title.

2)   Visible Easements

It is commonly assumed that a purchaser's offer to buy has been made with reference to visible easements of which she was aware. Thus, there is often an exception to the marketable title requirement for such visible easements, and a title subject to those may still be held marketable.

3)   Legal Restrictions

Zoning, subdivision and other land use regulations do not affect the marketability of title. A purchaser is not entitled to complain of a title merely because it is subject to such an ordinance. Some courts do treat official maps (which show the layout of present and future streets), as affecting the marketability of title. Existing violations of land use ordinances are also often treated as making title unmarketable.

4)   Physical Defects

Matters which relate only to the physical condition of the property do not thereby affect its title. Title may be marketable even though the structures are termite infested or built on improperly compacted fill. Building code violations may affect title if the city has instituted litigation or taken other action to abate the situation. Boundary encroachments (either by or against the property) do impair marketability.

5)   Off-Record Proof

A vendor's title might be good in fact by virtue of adverse possession operating in his favor to defeat any potential claims against him. Nevertheless, if this has not been established in court, his title may still be regarded as doubtful and, therefore, unmarketable.

Example: Pearl may reject Van's title on the ground that the records indicate that Van's brother may have some co-ownership claim under their father's will. The fact that Van has lived alone on the property for over 25 years does not absolutely settle that question in his favor since there may never have been an ouster, or the brother may have been in prison for a large part of that time, thereby tolling the statute of limitations.

2. IMPLIED IN THE CONTRACT

The statement that a marketable title is implied in every land sale contract means that the purchaser is entitled to insist upon a marketable title even though her contract does not expressly call for one. The language of the contract is relevant, not to see whether it calls for a marketable title, but to determine whether the implied requirement of such a title has been altered by express provisions to the contrary.

a. Excepting Individual Items

If some technical defect on title does not bother the purchaser, it is appropriate for the contract to recite that title will be accepted subject to that condition. The effect of such a recital is to eliminate the implied requirement of marketability as to that feature.

Example: Van's property is subject to a long-term profitable lease (which is in fact the reason why Pearl wishes to acquire his title). Their contract should recite that title will be accepted subject to the leasehold interest. This protects Pearl from Van's terminating that lease and protects Van from Pearl's withdrawing from the contract on the ground that his title is subject to a lease and therefore unmarketable.

b. Setting a Different Standard

If the contract calls for a title which is to conform to some other standard, e.g., "insurable," "deducible of record," "perfect," "satisfactory," a court must determine what sort of criterion is being employed and then measure the vendor's actual title against it. (Title insurance is covered in Ch. XI.) The fact that the contract provides for utilization of a quitclaim deed to transfer title is not regarded as altering the requirement that a marketable title be conveyed thereby.

3. CONSEQUENCES OF UNMARKETABILITY
a. Prior to Closing

A vendor has no obligation to have a marketable title prior to the date set in the contract for performance. His title must be marketable only at the time that he is obliged to tender a deed, and the purchaser may withdraw from the contract before that time only when it is absolutely plain that the vendor will never be able to obtain the title required. As stated, the vendor may use the funds received from the purchaser towards clearing his title so as to make it marketable by the settlement date.

b. **At Closing**
If the vendor's title is not marketable on closing day the purchaser may withdraw from the contract and/or seek judicial relief. Sometimes a vendor is allowed a reasonable time after the date set for closing to cure defects in his title if the contract does not make time of the essence and if he has not been given adequate notice of the purchaser's objections to the title.

1) Remedies
If a court holds that the vendor's title is not marketable, it may permit the purchaser to rescind her contract, award her damages, grant specific performance with an abatement of the price, or order the vendor to perfect his title. If the court holds title is marketable and the purchaser has refused to perform, it may award the vendor damages or specific performance. Specific performance, however, creates problems for the purchaser since the decree does not operate to quiet the title she receives as against the third parties whose claims against the title caused her to reject it in the first place.

c. **After Closing**
Once the vendor's deed is accepted by the purchaser, his obligation regarding marketable title is satisfied. If the title is in fact defective, the purchaser's only claims thereafter against the vendor must depend upon covenants in her deed, her rights under the contract having expired (unless the contract provides that its provisions are to survive the closing of escrow).

C. EQUITABLE CONVERSION

The fact that a court of equity will specifically enforce a binding contract for the sale of land, means that, in the eyes of equity, the purchaser is regarded as the (equitable) owner of the property from the moment the contract is executed and the vendor holds his legal title thereafter only as security for the payment of the price. The parties have been equitably converted from purchaser and vendor to owner and creditor.

1. ENFORCEABLE CONTRACT
The doctrine of equitable conversion does not apply unless the contract between the parties is one which could be specifically enforced. If, e.g., the vendor lacked a marketable title to his property, there would be no equitable conversion.

a. **Options**
Until an option to purchase is actually exercised, the doctrine of equitable conversion does not apply.

2. POSSESSION
The doctrine of equitable conversion affects title, not possession. A purchaser is not entitled to take possession of the property until legal title has been transferred to her unless the vendor permits her to enter prior thereto.

3. DEVOLUTION
By converting the vendor's title into a right to money, the nature of his asset is thereby changed from real into personal property. At common law, realty passed to heirs whereas personalty went to the next of kin, so that different relatives might take depending upon whether equitable conversion did or did not apply. (The same issue might be raised today if the vendor's will left his real and personal property to different persons.)

4. CREDITORS
After an equitable conversion, creditors of the vendor may be able to reach the balance of the price owed by the purchaser but not the title to the land. Creditors of the purchaser, on the other hand, may be able to reach the title.

D. RISK OF LOSS

Prior to the execution of any contract, all risk of loss from destruction of the premises not caused by either party is upon the vendor, as owner. After the contract has been consummated, and the purchaser is full owner, the risk of loss is solely hers. But there is disagreement as to who bears the risk of innocent loss during the contract period.

1. MAJORITY RULE
The doctrine of equitable conversion makes the purchaser equitable owner, and she must therefore bear the loss. She must pay the full price even when the premises have been totally destroyed prior to the close of escrow. (The vendor's title is marketable, even though his premises are not.) This is also known as the English Rule although it has now been repudiated by the English courts.

2. MINORITY RULE
There is an implied condition in the contract that the premises will be transferred to the purchaser in the condition they were in when the contract was first made. If they have been destroyed prior to the close of escrow, the purchaser is not obliged to pay the price. This is also known as the Massachusetts Rule.

3. UNIFORM VENDOR AND PURCHASER RISK ACT
The risk of loss is on the vendor unless the purchaser takes possession of the premises, in which event the risk shifts to the purchaser.

4.   SPECIAL AGREEMENT
None of the above rules apply when the parties have specifically provided for risk allocation in their sales contract.   Loss is determined according to the above doctrines only when the contract is silent on the matter.

5.   INSURANCE
Both parties have independent insurable interests in the property and may protect themselves separately against the risk of destruction.   The fact that one party may carry insurance does not mean that he or she will necessarily be the one to bear the loss as between them, although principles of unjust enrichment may be applied in order to avoid a windfall where one party is insured and the loss would otherwise fall on the other party.   Further, since the parties can agree among themselves as to risk allocation, a provision requiring one of them to carry the insurance may imply an agreement by the insuring party to assume that risk.

Where the vendor has carried insurance, the purchaser is often given the benefit of it through the doctrine of constructive trust.   Even where the insurance policy is treated as a personal indemnity contract for the vendor, the purchaser may be protected if the sales contract required the vendor to carry the policy or required the purchaser to pay the premiums.   Where the purchaser is the insured party courts are less likely to allow an uninsured vendor to benefit from it.

E.   PERFORMANCE

The contract is performed when the vendor delivers a proper deed to the purchaser conveying the requisite title and the purchaser pays the full price to the vendor. These are generally treated as concurrent conditions.   Neither party may thus demand performance by the other without simultaneously tendering his or her own performance.   When an installment contract is involved, payment by the purchaser is a condition precedent rather than concurrent, except for payment of the final installment.

1.   PERFORMANCE BY THE VENDOR
The contract usually requires the vendor to deliver a certain kind of deed conveying a certain kind of title to the purchaser.   Types and delivery of deeds are covered in Chapter IX.   The kind of title required has been covered in the section on marketable title above.   Unless time has been made of the essence, the vendor will generally be permitted to convey within a reasonable time after the date originally set for settlement.

2.   PERFORMANCE BY THE PURCHASER
The contract usually requires the purchaser to pay a set price to the vendor. If the price is not all cash, a mortgage may be involved (which is covered in Chapter XII).   Unless time has been made of the essence, the purchaser will

generally be permitted to pay within a reasonable time after the date originally set for closing.

3. NONSURVIVAL OF CONTRACT TERMS

Once title has passed and payment made, the contract has been completed and the rights of the parties are no longer governed by it. Their legal relations thereafter depend upon other doctrines. Two common post-contract doctrines are:

a. Fraud

If the vendor has made a material misrepresentation or has concealed a material fact from the purchaser, he will be liable for his fraud even after escrow has closed. Generally, a defrauded purchaser is entitled to rescind or to recover damages. The same is true where the purchaser has defrauded the vendor. Actions for fraud are inevitably filed after the contract has closed, since a discovery of the truth prior to then should lead to a refusal to perform by the innocent party.

b. Warranty

Many courts now impose a warranty of fitness or habitability upon certain vendors (e.g., mass producers of new housing). The subsequent discovery of a defect by the purchaser may subject the vendor to liability, despite the completion of the contract, so long as the action is filed within the relevant statute of limitations period. If the vendor's deed warrants title, there may be liability on that; this is covered in Chapter XI.

F. BREACH

1. REMEDIES OF THE PURCHASER

If the vendor fails or refuses to convey at the closing, the purchaser may withdraw from the contract, seek to have it specifically enforced, or sue for damages.

a. Termination

The purchaser may withdraw and terminate the contract immediately upon the closing date if time is of the essence and the vendor has not performed, or earlier, if the vendor has made it plain that he will not or can not perform. If the vendor's performance is delayed because of his need to clear title defects, the purchaser may be required to wait a reasonable time before cancelling. When the purchaser does so terminate, she is entitled to recover back all monies paid to the vendor. She may also have a purchaser's lien on the title for this restitutionary amount.

b.   Specific Performance

Because land is unique, the purchaser may obtain a decree of specific performance, which will order the vendor to convey title to her upon payment of the price, and will make whatever adjustments are necessary to compensate for the delay in performance. If the vendor's title is unmarketable, but the defects are merely technical or quantifiable, the purchaser may be granted specific performance with an abatement of part of the price.

c.   Damages

When the vendor has breached, the purchaser may sue to recover her deposit and her out of pocket expenses. Many jurisdictions also award her benefit of the bargain damages (equal to the difference between the market value of the property and the contract price). Others limit benefit of the bargain damages to cases of bad faith breach by the vendor and do not award them to the purchaser when the breach consists of the vendor's inability to tender marketable title. (Marketable title is thus treated as a condition but not a covenant when damages are so limited.)

2.   REMEDIES OF THE VENDOR

If the purchaser fails to pay the price, the vendor may seek specific performance, sue for damages, or withdraw from the contract.

a.   Specific Performance

A decree of specific performance orders the purchaser to pay the price to the vendor and requires the vendor to convey title to the purchaser. Mutuality is a major reason why specific performance is granted to a vendor, even though the relief obtained is purely monetary; however, damages may be regarded as inadequate for a vendor whose market has been "chilled" by the time consumed in preparing to convey to the purchaser and the subsequent loss of that deal. If the vendor's title is defective, he cannot compel specific performance, except sometimes where the defect is trivial and a small abatement of the price will fully compensate the purchaser for it.

b.   Damages

1)   Actual Damages

On breach by the purchaser, the vendor is entitled to withdraw from the contract and recover benefit of the bargain damages (i.e., the difference between the market value of the property and the contract price). While any subsequent resale price is not relevant (since the measure is not the difference between contract price and resale price, as is the case in many sales of personal property), some courts treat a profitable resale by the vendor as eliminating his right to general damages on the ground that any award at this stage would be a windfall and constitute a forfeiture to the purchaser. In addition to general damages, the vendor is also entitled to recover any out of pocket expenses he has incurred.

2) Liquidated Damages

A provision in the contract providing for the retention by the vendor of any deposit paid by the purchaser upon her default (or for the recovery of any other fixed amount) may be upheld as an enforceable liquidated damages provision, if the court determines that actual damages would be difficult to assess and that the amount selected represented a reasonable forecast by the parties, rather than an improper attempt to impose a penalty upon the purchaser. Some jurisdictions prohibit the use of such clauses and confine the vendor to his actual damages. Some jurisdictions uphold the clause only where it replaces actual damages and does permit the vendor to select actual or liquidated damages at his option; other jurisdictions hold that the inclusion of an enforceable liquidated damages clause automatically bars the vendor from recovering actual damages. Generally, specific performance remains available as a remedy despite the inclusion of a liquidated damages clause in the contract.

c. Termination

If the property has appreciated in value since the purchaser's breach so as to now exceed the contract price, the vendor may prefer to terminate the contract and resell the property elsewhere for a greater profit. He may be required, in such a case, to return the purchaser's deposit to her, less his out-of-pocket expenses.

G. REVIEW QUESTIONS

1. T or F   Van contracted to sell his property to Pearl. During the escrow period Pearl discovered that Van had previously given Ann an option to purchase the same property, and the option is still valid. Pearl may refuse to accept Van's deed as long as the option exists.

2. T or F   Van contracted to sell his property to Pearl. During the escrow period, Pearl discovered that there was a mortgage on the property. Pearl may withdraw from the contract because of the mortgage.

3. T or F   Van contracted to sell his property to Pearl. After escrow closed and Pearl had accepted Van's deed, she discovered that the property was subject to a recorded easement. She may rescind or cancel the deed and get her money back because the title was unmarketable.

4. T or F   Van contracted to sell his property to Pearl. Prior to the close of escrow, and before Pearl had taken possession, the property was damaged by fire. Under the Uniform Vendor and Purchaser Risk Act, Pearl may withdraw from the contract unless Van restores the property.

IX

CONVEYANCES (TRANSFER OF TITLE BY DEED)

Analysis

A conveyance is the transfer of title from one person to another. A deed is the usual instrument for conveying property. Title passes when a deed has been properly executed and delivered. The deed itself is not the title; it is merely the vehicle for transmission of the title. Thus, possessing a deed does not automatically equal holding a title. Technically, many of the rules described below also apply to the conveyance of leaseholds, but the discussion here speaks only of deeds to freehold estates.

A. FORMAL REQUIREMENTS

1. WRITING AND CONTENTS
The statute of frauds requires a writing for the transfer of any interest in land greater than a short term leasehold. A deed (which usually conveys a fee interest) must therefore be in writing.

a. Parties
The deed must identify the grantee. The person's name is not required so long as an adequate description is given (e.g., "To my only daughter") but a grant to a nonexistent or unascertained person is invalid. Some courts declare that a deed which leaves the name of the grantee blank is invalid, at least until the grantee fills it in (assuming that he has the authority to do so and assuming that the grantor does not die before it is filled in). The grantor should identify herself in the deed and should sign the document (or make an appropriate mark). The grantor in this chapter is indicated by female pronouns; the grantee by male pronouns.

1) Fraud
Although forgery of a grantor's signature always invalidates a deed, a signature which is fraudulently induced has a less certain effect. Where the fraud relates to the essence of the transaction (e.g., the grantee tells the grantor that she is only signing her autograph), the deed is automatically void. But where the fraud is collateral (e.g., the grantor signs based on the grantee's false promise to pay the price to her later), it is voidable, but not per se void. In that case, transfer to a subsequent bona fide purchaser may eliminate the grantor's power to invalidate the deed.

b. Granting Words
The deed must manifest an intent by the grantor to convey an interest in land to the grantee. Usually this is done by use of the word "grant" or "convey." No technical words are necessary. However, if the words used indicate a testamentary intent (e.g., "I leave to . . ."), the document may be construed to be a will rather than a deed.

c. Estate Granted

Unless the deed provides to the contrary, it is today presumed that a grantor has granted her entire interest in the property to the grantee. At common law, the failure to add "and his heirs" precluded the grantee from receiving a fee simple estate. See Chapter II.

1) Premises; Habendum

The above three provisions (i.e. parties, granting words, and estate granted) are often referred to as "the premises" of a deed. The premises will also contain reference to any consideration given, if such is mentioned. If the estate granted was less than a fee simple, the deed would contain a habendum clause ("to have and to hold") stating the limitation to the estate.

2) Ambiguous Estates

Careless drafting may not make it apparent whether a fee simple absolute possessory estate or some less interest was intended to be granted. Since a deed is not itself a contract, the question will only involve the grantor's intent, rather than the parties' mutual intent. Generally, a grantor is presumed to have intended to dispose of all that she had (rather than to divide her title into smaller interests), but restrictive language can rebut this presumption. Where possible, courts will treat restrictions as descriptive rather than limiting.

> ***Example:*** Grace's deed grants to Gene "a strip of land ten feet wide as a right of way." This could be construed as an easement or (more likely) as a fee simple in the strip subject to nonbinding restrictions.

d. Description of the Property

A deed must contain an adequate description of the property, one which furnishes some means of identifying the land to be conveyed.

1) Metes and Bounds

One way to describe the size, shape, and location of land is to begin with some known object (a "monument"), point in a certain direction from it (a "course"), indicate the distance that line is to follow, either in terms of measurement or by reference to a monument at the other end; this will provide one boundary or line. Then a new direction and length are given, to form the second boundary. The process is then repeated until the final line terminates at the same place where the first line originated, i.e., a parcel is completely enclosed.

a) Terminology

A monument can be a solid natural object (a tree, a boulder), an artificial object (a surveyor's stake or a fence), or what would otherwise normally be considered a line (a road, a creek, etc.). Distances can be stated in current measurements (feet, inches), or in the earlier precursors of a chain (66 feet), a rod ($\frac{1}{4}$th of a chain), or a link ($\frac{1}{100}$ of a chain). Angles are usually expressed in terms of degrees from the first direction toward the second direction (e.g., North 45 degrees East indicates a Northeast bearing line).

Example: "Beginning at the old oak tree near the bend in the creek, then going west for 200 feet to the center of Jones Road, then turning south along Jones Road for 200 feet to the creek, thence North 45 degrees East back to the point of the beginning" describes a triangle parcel of land between the tree, the road, and the creek.

2) The Federal Survey

Much of the United States has been mapped out by government surveys, with meridian lines (north-south) and base lines (east-west) affording reference points for the location of land parcels. Each state has one or more principle base and meridian lines. From these, additional lines are drawn every six miles. These are known as range (north-south) and township (east-west) lines. Their intersections form 36 square-mile townships, with each township divided into 36 square mile sections. These sections are numbered from 1 to 36, starting in the top right corner, going across to the top left corner, descending one square, and returning to the right side, then back again (much as Greek farmers once plowed their fields). Each section has 640 acres, and may be divided further into 160 acre quarter sections (northeast, northwest, etc.), and each quarter section may be again divided into 40 acre quarter-quarter sections, or smaller.

Example: "E $\frac{1}{2}$ of NW $\frac{1}{4}$ of SW $\frac{1}{4}$, Sec. 8, T 5 N, R 6 W, MDB & M, Cal." refers to a parcel of land in California (the description is best read in reverse order), located with reference to the Mount Diablo Base and Meridian (a mountain top east of San Francisco). The township is 30 miles north (T 5 N), and 36 miles west (R 6 W) of that point. Section 8 is one mile south of the northern end of the township and one mile east of the western end. The southwest quarter of that section is in the lower left; the northeast quarter-quarter is in the upper right of that part, and the east half is the left half of that, a 20 acre parcel.

3) Plat Maps

The development of raw land (acreage) into smaller parcels usually occurs through the subdivision process, described in Chapter XIV (Land Use). That development entails the subdivider preparing a street map (plat) of the proposed subdivision, showing both the streets to be laid out and the new parcels to be made available for sale. Once this map is approved by the local government and recorded, all sales of the parcels are made with reference to the recorded subdivision map (e.g., "Lot 23 of Block 15 of New Pines Subdivision, Official Records").

4) Ambiguous Descriptions

Extrinsic evidence may be utilized to resolve ambiguities in the description. Ambiguities can be patent or latent. An ambiguity is patent where it appears on the face of the deed by virtue of the use of inconsistent terms in the description; it is latent where the difficulty is discovered only when an attempt is made to actually locate the boundaries on the ground. Courts originally limited parol evidence to clarification of latent ambiguities only. Today, most permit any ambiguity to be so resolved.

5) Inconsistent Descriptions

Courts have developed a general hierarchy for selecting which description to prefer when there are inconsistencies in the deed: generally, references to monuments prevail over references to maps which prevail over references to courses or distances, which prevail over references to a name or quantity.

Example: If the deed refers to a certain tree as furnishing a corner of the tract, that call will prevail over a map which sets the corner elsewhere. But the map will prevail over an inconsistent description which says ". . . thence west for two hundred feet." And that description will prevail over an inconsistent reference to, e.g., "the Jones tract" or "being forty acres."

6) Boundaries Which Occupy Space

Where the deed refers to a street or stream or monument having width as a boundary, there is a rebuttable presumption that the reference is to its center unless the grantor is a public entity, or unless the grantor has indicated otherwise (e.g., "along the side of the road"), or does not own up to the middle. Where the grantor does not own adjoining land on the other side of the boundary, then it is presumed that the entire width of the boundary, has been conveyed to the grantee, so that the grantor does not retain a useless strip one-half of the width of the boundary.

a) Water Boundaries
Where a river or stream constitutes a boundary and the grantor owns the land beneath the water, the presumption in favor of using the middle is even stronger, in order to allow the grantee to make use of the waterway.

(1) *Accretion and Reliction/Avulsion.* Boundary lines between neighbors are held to change when the stream which separates them gradually adds land to one side (accretion) or removes it from the other (reliction) to conform to the new course of the waterway. Sudden, dramatic changes to the land caused by water (avulsion) do not change boundary lines.

7) Condominiums
Special problems are encountered in describing a condominium unit to be conveyed. The description must account for the fact that there are vertical as well as horizontal dimensions to the unit and the description must cover only the interior space between the walls, ceiling and floors, since the walls, etc. themselves are part of the common property rather than the individual units. It should also account for any settling of the building.

8) Changing Boundaries (Agreed Boundaries/Practical Location)

Under certain circumstances neighbors may, by their conduct, relocate the common boundary from where it is described in their deed, even though they have not executed a writing to that effect. The legal boundary between neighbors may be changed by execution of a deed from one to another. It may also be relocated through the doctrine of adverse possession, where one wrongfully occupies beyond her true line. Even where some of the elements of adverse possession are missing (e.g., duration, hostility, continuity, etc.), the related doctrine of agreed boundaries may produce the same effect.

a) The Mental State of the Parties
It is generally held that when the parties are uncertain or in disagreement as to their common boundary, an agreement between them as to a boundary to which they both acquiesce will be enforced against them and their successors even though it is not written.

b) Execution of the Agreement
Many jurisdictions require that the parties do more than merely verbally agree as to their mutual boundary. A writing is not required, but some possessory action may be required. A few

courts also require possession of the strip in question for a "long" time, in some cases equal to the period of adverse possession.

(1) *Acquiescence.* In some jurisdictions, the prolonged acquiescence of the parties to a particular line as their boundary eliminates the need for proof of an actual agreement between them.

(2) *Estoppel.* If neighbor A tells neighbor B that their mutual line is at a certain location, and thereby induces B to build up to that line, A may be estopped to subsequently assert that the line is incorrect. Courts are divided as to whether A must have known the statement was false or intended to deceive B.

(3) *Statements by the Common Grantor.* Courts also uphold an "incorrect" line when it was marked on the ground by the parties' common grantor, and both parcels were sold to them with reference to it, even though it differs from the boundary line contained in their deeds.

(4) *Running.* Once an agreed boundary has been established by acts of the parties, their successors are bound by it, even though there is nothing in the records to warn them of the fact that the written boundary lines are incorrect.

Examples: (1) Two neighbors, being uncertain as to where their true boundary was, agreed that the creek should be the boundary and both improved the lands on their respective sides of the creek for a number of years. The creek will now be treated as a legal boundary, even though a later survey reveals that the true line was 10 feet west (or east) of the creek.

(2) Two neighbors could not agree on their boundary: one thought it was ten feet west of the creek and the other believed that it was ten feet east of the creek. To settle their dispute they agreed on the creek as a boundary and farmed up to it on both sides for a number of years. The creek will now be the boundary even though a survey may later show that the line was really west of the creek.

(3) Two neighbors believed that the creek was their boundary, and each farmed up to it. Later it is discovered that the true boundary is west of the creek.

Many courts will not move the boundary to the creek, since the parties' behavior was based upon mistake rather than uncertainty or dispute. They will be relieved from the consequences of their mistake.

(4) Two neighbors knew that the true line between them was ten feet east of the creek but preferred to use the creek as their boundary. They orally so agreed and then farmed up to it. Their agreement is not enforceable here, since they have attempted to transfer a ten foot strip of land from one to the other without execution of a proper deed, as required by the statute of frauds.

e. Nonessential Elements
There are many features which commonly appear in deeds but which are not necessary to its validity. These include:

1) Grantee's Signature
    A deed is not a contract, and therefore mutual signatures are not required. It is generally required that the grantee accept the deed, but this is not the same as signing it.

2) Notarization; Witnesses
    The grantor's signature need not be acknowledged or witnessed for the deed to be valid. Notarization is generally required as a condition for recordation, but not in order to pass title.

3) Recordation
    A deed may validly pass title even though it is not recorded. Recordation is done to protect the grantee under the applicable recording act.

4) Prior Contract
    In most commercial transactions, a contract of sale precedes the execution of a deed, but in donative situations the grantor usually executes a deed without any prior arrangements.

5) Consideration
    Because a deed is not a contract, it is not required that there be consideration in order for it to be valid. Consideration is usually recited in a deed in order to qualify the grantee as a bona fide purchaser under the recording acts.

6) Seal
    A seal on a deed is no longer required.

2. TYPES OF DEEDS

Deeds are distinguished according to whether or not they contain representations by the grantor concerning the state of her title. A deed which includes no such representations is called a quitclaim deed; one which makes certain limited representations is called a statutory, grant, or bargain and sale deed; one with maximum protection for the grantee is called a warranty deed. The nature of these representations or title covenants is discussed in Chapter XI.

B. DELIVERY

A deed passes title only when it is delivered. A contract may take effect from the moment that it is signed, but this is not how a deed operates. Even after the grantor has signed it, it does not effect a conveyance of the title until delivery.

1. REQUIREMENTS

Delivery occurs when the grantor manifests an intent that a completed legal act has occurred. There is no ritualized physical act which always equals delivery, although the handing over of the deed to the grantee is generally good evidence that a delivery was intended. Delivery requires that the grantor have a present intent that the deed operate to transfer title; if she intends that the deed operate at some time in the future, there is no delivery. (In this respect, a deed is different from a will. A will is not intended to have any effect until after the testator dies, which is always some time in the future, as far as the testator is concerned.)

Examples: (1) Grace signed her deed, set it down, announced "I have now given my property to Gene," and walked out of the room, leaving it behind for Gene to take. The deed has been delivered because of the manifestation of Grace's intent to have title pass immediately. It does not matter that she did not personally hand the deed to Gene.

(2) Grace handed her deed to Gene saying "This deed will make you the owner of the property on your next birthday." The deed has not been delivered, because Grace had no present intent to make it operative; she intended that it become effective later.

a. Evidence and Presumptions

Since the fact of delivery is not one which can be determined from an examination of the deed itself, extrinsic evidence is always permitted on this issue, especially statements made by the grantor, either before or after the alleged delivery. There is a rebuttable presumption that a deed has been delivered if it is in the grantee's possession, has been recorded, or (sometimes) has been acknowledged. There is a rebuttable presumption that the deed has not been delivered if it is in the grantor's possession. The fact that a deed has been dated is not evidence that it has been delivered, but if there has been a delivery, there is a rebuttable presumption that it occurred on the date entered on the deed.

b.   Present Delivery of a Future Interest
Although the requirement of a present intent prohibits any future delivery to a grantee, this does not mean that a grantor may not create a future interest in land in favor of a grantee by a deed which is delivered in the present.   It is important to distinguish between permissible future interests in land and impermissible future deliveries of deeds.

Example: Grace executed a deed conveying to Gene an estate to take effect on his next birthday. (I.e., the deed recited "To Gene on his birthday next year". Technically, this created a springing executory interest, which would have been invalid prior to the Statute of Uses. See Chapter II.) She then handed the deed to him saying, "I now give you an interest in my property." This deed has been delivered and does convey a future interest to Gene. If on the other hand, the deed had purported to convey a present fee simple rather than a future interest, and Grace had handed it to Gene saying "I am giving you this deed to take effect on your next birthday," there would have been an ineffective delivery and title would not pass at this time.

c.   The Effect of the Passage of Time
What began as a future intent may become a present intent where the passage of time brings the deferred date or event into the present. If nothing has happened to alter the grantor's original intent, her awareness of the calendar will operate to convert her previously future intent into a present intent.

Examples: (1) Grace handed Gene a deed, saying "I am giving you this deed to take effect on your next birthday." The next year, Grace attended Gene's birthday party and said to him, "Well, now you are a property owner." Her deed has now been delivered. Although no delivery occurred when she first handed Gene the deed, it was delivered when she witnessed Gene's birthday without having first repudiated her previous acts. If she had, one day earlier, announced that she had changed her mind, there would have been no delivery, since there would not have been any time at which it could be said that she had intended a completed legal act (before the repudiation it was not completed because a future event remained necessary; after the repudiation, the intent was not to ever complete the delivery).

(2) Grace handed Gene a deed, saying "I am giving you this deed to take effect at my death." The deed has not been delivered and never will be. While alive, Grace's intent is always in the future, i.e., she rather than Gene is the owner. There is no time when it can be said that Grace intended that a completed legal act had occurred, since that would require a post mortem consciousness.

2. DELIVERY TO THE GRANTEE (TWO–PARTY TRANSACTIONS)
Most courts prohibit the conditional delivery of a deed directly to the grantee, pursuant to the rule requiring a present intent by the grantor. An attempted conditional delivery is treated either as no delivery, or as an absolute delivery with the condition then being stricken.

Examples: (1) Grace handed her deed to Gene saying "Here is the deed to my property, but you cannot live there until I die". If the court believed that Grace's intent was that Gene not be the owner until her death, then the deed was not delivered, since her intent was not present, as indicated in the previous example.

(2) Grace does the same as above, but now the court believes her intent was to make Gene the owner now. If it so concludes, the rule prohibiting conditions on a delivery comes into play, and gives Gene the fee simple immediately. He may enter at once and dispossess Grace without waiting for her to die.

a. Attempts to Effectuate the Grantor's Intent
The two above examples have in common the fact that they arise too late to do anything about it. Some courts attempt to honor the grantor's intent by treating the deed as if it contained the reservation of a life estate (or appropriate similar interest), thereby making the condition effective.

3. ESCROW (THREE–PARTY TRANSACTIONS)
A grantor may accomplish a future or conditional delivery of a deed by use of an escrow, i.e., a third party to whom the deed is delivered and who later delivers it to the grantee. If the first delivery (to the escrow officer) is unconditional, i.e., done without reservation of a right to revoke or recall the deed later, then a binding legal act on the part of the grantee has occurred and the escrow officer is authorized to make the second delivery to the grantee on the stated date or when the circumstances require, regardless of later changes of mind or the death of the grantor. Conditions may also be included with regard to the second delivery, so long as the first delivery (into escrow) is unconditional. It is not required that instructions to the escrow agent be in writing.

Examples: (1) Grace handed her deed to Ezra, saying "Give this to Gene on his next birthday (and I waive any right to recall the deed)."

Ezra may properly complete the delivery to Gene on his birthday, even though Grace may have died or attempted to cancel her instructions to Ezra. This is not an impermissible future delivery, such as discussed earlier, since Grace performed a binding legal act by handing the deed, irrevocably, to Ezra.

(2) Grace handed her deed to Ezra, saying "Give this deed to Gene if he marries Ann by next year (and I waive the right to recall it)." Ezra may deliver the deed if Gene marries in time. This is not an impermissible conditional delivery because Grace's delivery to Ezra was unconditional, i.e., she could no longer recall the deed.

a. Revocable Delivery

If the grantor reserves the right to recall the deed from the third party, then a true escrow has not been created, since no binding legal event has occurred. Instead, the third party is merely the grantor's agent, who may carry out her instructions only so long as his authorization continues and his principal and does not revoke. If his authorization does continue, he may make the second delivery and—at that time—title passes; the second, rather than the first, delivery is the significant event here.

1) Death of the Grantor

If the deed was given to the grantor's agent rather than to a true escrow, and the grantor dies before the stated condition occurs (or the condition was the grantor's death), then no delivery will occur. The agent's authority terminated on her principal's death, and once the principal is dead, she cannot have the required intent to make the second delivery effective.

2) Delivery to the Grantee's Agent

If the third party is merely the grantee's agent (i.e., one subject to control by the grantee), then again there has not been a true escrow created. Delivery to the agent of the grantee is delivery to the grantee. This is a two-party, not a three-party, transaction, and the rules governing those situations apply.

b. Relation Back

Where a valid escrow has been created, courts frequently declare that the second delivery relates back to the date of the first delivery whenever justice requires that this be done in order to protect the grantee. Relation back is often applied where the grantor dies, becomes incompetent or becomes subject to a dower claim after the first and before the second delivery; it is also applied to protect the grantee against creditors of the grantor who appear in the interim. Relation back is generally not applied as against a bona fide purchaser from the grantor who took without notice between the first and second delivery.

c. Agency

During the escrow, the escrow agent is regarded as the agent of both parties (i.e., she is not subject to any inconsistent subsequent instructions by either party, unless jointly given). After the close of escrow, she is regarded as the agent of each party, and is subject to their individual control.

> *Example:* After Grace had deposited her deed, and Gene had deposited his funds, the escrow agent absconded with everything. With regard to the funds, the loss falls on Grace or Gene depending on whether or not the escrow had closed. If it had not closed, then the funds were Gene's and he still owes Grace. If escrow had closed, the funds were Grace's. (With regard to the deed, no great loss has occurred, since the escrow agent cannot accomplish very much with a deed naming Gene as grantee.)

4. EFFECT OF A CONTRACT

A binding contract for the sale of property converts the purchaser into equitable owner of the property, and a court will order the vendor or escrow agent to deliver a deed to him notwithstanding any contrary intent concerning delivery by the vendor. The rules above are significant only in donative escrow situations. Where a commercial sale of property is involved and the parties have previously executed a contract to that effect, the rules of contract generally make delivery doctrines unimportant. Given the existence of a binding contract to convey, it is not important whether the grantor has waived or retained the right to recall the deed when she hands it to the escrow agent; she is bound to convey in any event. (Equitable conversion was covered in Ch. VIII.)

a. Commercial/Noncommercial Escrows

Some courts state that a commercial escrow is invalid in the absence of an enforceable contract of sale between the parties. Since noncommercial (donative) escrows do not require contracts, this requirement seems puzzling. It is probably best understood as a variation of the above rule: that the lack of a true escrow (i.e., the waiving of the right to recall) is unimportant when there is no valid underlying contract. Consequently, if there is no such contract and the grantor does not unreservedly hand the deed to the escrow agent, she is then free to revoke before escrow closes.

5. ACCEPTANCE

While it is technically required that the grantee accept a deed, acceptance is presumed in any case where the deed is beneficial. It is not required that he even know of the document. Where necessary, the grantee's acceptance will be deemed to relate back to the date of delivery.

6. EFFECT OF AN UNDELIVERED DEED

Generally, an undelivered deed passes no title whatsoever, either to the grantee or to any subsequent taker from him, even if it has been recorded. However, some courts protect an innocent bona fide purchaser where the grantor negligently permitted the grantee to take possession of the deed in the first place, or where she knew that the grantee possessed it or had recorded it and failed to take any steps to protect herself. (In these respects an undelivered deed is treated like a forged deed.)

7. THE ROLE OF A DELIVERED DEED

Once a deed is delivered, title passes to the grantee. Thereafter, the deed is merely a piece of paper. It has evidentiary value, but no continuing legal significance. Even if the grantee loses the deed, he remains the owner of the property.

a. Returning a Delivered Deed

If the parties desire to revest title in the grantor, a return of the deed will not perform that function since its language reads the other way. It is necessary for the grantee to execute and deliver a new deed, passing title back to the grantor and complying with all the formalities set forth above.

C. REVIEW QUESTIONS

1. T or F   On Grace's death, when her safe deposit box was opened, there was found a deed to Gene with the following note, "This deed is for Gene, so that he will be taken care of after I die." This is effective to transfer title to Gene.

2. T or F   Grace handed her deed to Ezra saying, "Deliver this deed to Gene when he is 21, and I waive the right to recall the deed." However, when Gene was only 19, Grace demanded that Ezra return the deed to her and he complied. On Gene's 21st birthday Gene may demand that Grace give him the deed.

3. T or F   Grace delivered her deed into escrow, but she did not own the property at that time. However, prior to the time when the escrow agent delivered the deed to Gene, Grace did acquire title to the property. Under the doctrine of relation back, the delivery to Gene relates back to Grace's earlier delivery into escrow, meaning that there was no title to be transferred.

X

PRIORITIES (THE RECORDING SYSTEM)

Analysis

A. PRIORITY DISPUTES

Priority issues concern the competing claims of two persons to the same interest in land, often arising from their having both taken the interests from the same grantor. Although textbook treatment of priorities generally deals only with deeds, any claims affecting title can be subject to priority conflicts.

Examples: (1) Owen conveyed the same property to both Ann and Bob by separate, inconsistent deeds. If Ann's deed prevails, she has priority over Bob in that she owns the property and he does not. (Feminine pronouns in this chapter refer to the person who first takes an instrument; masculine pronouns refer to the person who takes an instrument later.)

(2) Owen gave mortgages on his property to both Ann and Bob. If Ann's mortgage is prior, she holds a "first" mortgage on the property, and Bob holds a "second." The effect of holding a first or second mortgage on property is covered in Chapter XII.

(3) Owen gave a mortgage to Ann and a deed to the same property to Bob. If Ann has priority, Bob holds title subject to her mortgage; if Bob has priority, his title is not subject to her mortgage.

1. PRIORITY VS CONVEYANCE

This chapter does not deal with issues between a grantor and a grantee, but rather concerns the claims of competing grantees to the same title. A priority issue may be entirely resolved by showing that one of the grantees never properly received the instrument in the first place, which defeats that grantee's claims against both the other grantee and the grantor. In this chapter, however, proper execution and delivery of the operative instrument is always assumed.

a. Delivery and Forgery
It is generally only necessary for a deed to be delivered in order for it to pass title to the grantee; recordation is not necessary. Conversely, recordation can not validate an undelivered deed. The fact that a deed has been recorded raises a presumption that it has been delivered, but the presumption is rebuttable. The same is true for a deed where the grantor's signature has been forged; recordation cannot cure this defect.

2. COMMON LAW BACKGROUND

The common law system of priorities was "first in time, first in right," meaning that whoever took first prevailed over anyone who took later. The logic was that the grantor, having once conveyed to the first grantee, had nothing left to convey to the second grantee.

a. Bona Fide Purchaser Exception
The one exception to this principle at common law was that a subsequent taker of a legal interest prevailed over the prior holder of an equitable interest if he had taken in good faith, without notice of the equitable interest, and had paid valuable consideration for his interest. This bona fide purchaser exception became the foundation of modern recording law.

b. Policy
The reason behind the modern preference for a bona fide purchaser principle over a first in time rule is based upon the role of title searches in conveyancing. No purchaser desires to accept a title unless it is marketable, which means, among other things, that it has not been previously conveyed or encumbered. But the common law rule, protecting a prior grantee even as against a later grantee who had diligently searched the title and had not discovered the prior claim, meant that no potential purchaser could ever rely on a title search. In order to make searches reliable and titles stable, it was necessary to compel any person who acquired an interest in land to make it public so that others could discover it and, conversely, to penalize the person who failed to do so by permitting others to take priority over her. Thus, a recording system was needed.

B. RECORDING SYSTEMS

Most states do not have a system whereby a government office passes on the validity of title or executes certificates showing who is the true owner of an interest in land. Instead, each state provides a recording system: a library of official records and indexes to those records. Every document affecting title to land in the locale (usually the county) may be copied into the official records; risks are incurred by those who do not do so. The records are open to the public and the indexes tell searchers where documents may be found.

1. RECORDABLE DOCUMENTS
Any instrument affecting title may be recorded, i.e., copied into the records. This includes those documents which deal with voluntary transactions concerning titles, such as deeds, leases, easements, covenants, mortgages, and contracts for the sale of land. It also includes instruments which have, either directly or indirectly, some effect upon titles, such as judgment liens, tax liens, quiet title decrees, probate decrees, divorce decrees, and lis pendens. It is commonly required that an instrument be acknowledged or notarized before it may be accepted for recordation.

a. **Undocumented Claims**

Rights based upon an adverse possession, a prescriptive or implied easement, or a boundary agreement, do not arise from any written instrument and therefore are not subject to the recording law. The same is true for rights given by law, e.g., dower and curtesy. However, any judgment confirming or rejecting such a claim is recordable.

b. **Short Term Leases**

Most recording statutes do not require that short term leases (less than one to three years) be recorded. A short term tenant who fails to record her lease is thus not in danger of losing her claim as against a subsequent bona fide purchaser.

c. **Contracts and Options**

Some states do not permit contracts for the sale of land to be recorded (on the ground that title is not affected until a deed has been delivered); most states do permit recordation however, since equitable conversion does give the contract purchaser rights in the land itself which should be known to others. Options to purchase land present the same issues. However, since their connection is even more remote, they are less frequently capable of being recorded.

d. **Unacknowledged Documents**

Most states require that a document be notarized before the recorder may accept it for recording. Consequently, one party to a transaction may effectively prohibit recordation of the document by refusing to have her signature notarized. (Some documents specifically recite that they are not to be recorded, although it is difficult to provide for effective sanctions for breach of such a nonrecordation provision.)

2. INDEXES

Most states have Grantor-Grantee and Grantee-Grantor Indexes, which organize all documents in alphabetical fashion according to the names of the parties. Periodically, a new index is started; cumulative indexes are generally compiled every 10 years and usually consist of the last 10 annual indexes.

Example: If Owen conveyed his property to Ann in 1981 and she had it recorded, a copy of the deed will be entered into the Official Records and given a book and page number (e.g., Volume 250, Page 100), based upon when the Recorder received it; each document is entered serially as it comes in. The Recorder will also make an entry of the deed in the Grantor Index under Owen (on one of the "O" pages) and another entry under Ann (on an "A" page in the Grantee Index), and perhaps also an entry in a Tract Index, according to the street address or some other locator. All these references would direct the reader to Volume 250, Page

100. These entries would all be made in the 1981 Indexes; at the end of the decade they would be consolidated into the 1980–1990 Indexes, covering all documents copied into the official records during that 10 year period. There would be no mention of this particular deed in any of the 1970–1980 or the 1990–2000 Indexes, since it was not recorded during either of those decades.

a. Use of the Index (Searching a Title)
A typical title search begins with the name of the current owner of the property. That name is checked out in the Grantee Indexes (starting with the most recent and then going back in time) in order to locate the deed which conveyed title to that person. Then the name of the grantor under that deed (the previous owner) is checked out under the Grantee Indexes from that time on back to find out when title was given to him. Ultimately, a complete chain of title from the present owner back to the original source (usually the government) will be had from use of the Grantee Indexes. Then each name is searched in the Grantor Indexes (usually for the appropriate periods of ownership) to determine whether any owner suffered any encumbrances or made any conveyances during the period of his or her ownership. If the Grantee Indexes show a perfect and unbroken chain back to an indisputable title and the Grantor Indexes disclose no intervening claims against the title, the title will be regarded as marketable.

Example: Ann desired to search Owen's title:

(1) Starting in the present and going backwards in time, in the Grantee Indexes under "Owen," she learned that Owen acquired his title from Norma in 1966. (This deed was indexed in the 1960–70 Grantee Index under "Owen"; it was also indexed in the 1960–70 Grantor Index under "Norma," but Ann had no reason to look for such an entry.)

(2) Searching out "Norma" in the Grantee Indexes from 1966 backwards, she next learned that Norma took title from Michael in 1933 (indexed under "Norma" in the 1930–40 Grantee Index; also under "Michael" in the 1930–40 Grantor Index).

(3) Continuing the same process, Ann learned that Michael got the land from the United States Government in 1901, when it left the public domain (indexed in the 1900–10 Grantee Index under "Michael"; also in the 1900–10 Grantor Index under "United States").

(4) Turning to the Grantor Indexes, Ann started with "Michael" in 1901 and moved forward in time. (For convenience, the U.S. is omitted here.) She discovered that Michael gave a mortgage to Liza in 1905 (indexed as "Michael" in the 1900–10 Grantor Index, and as "Liza" in the 1900–10 Grantee Index). However, she found that it was paid off and cancelled in 1925 (the cancellation of the mortgage was indexed under "Liza" as Grantor and "Michael" as Grantee in the 1910–20 Indexes).

(5) Further search showed that a judgment in favor of Kurt was recorded against Norma in 1942 (indexed under "Norma" in the 1940–50 Grantor Index and under "Kurt" in the Grantee Index). A search of "Norma" in the Grantee Index and "Kurt" in the Grantor Index thereafter (moving towards the present) does not reveal that the judgment has ever been eliminated.

(6) Finally, the records show that Owen conveyed an easement in his property to Jill in 1975 (indexed under "Owen" as grantor and "Jill" as grantee), which also apparently has never been terminated.

(7) Ann now knows that Owen does have record title to the land, but that it is subject to a judgment lien and an easement, which may make it unmarketable.

b. Supplementary Indexes

Other sets of records may also be treated as part of the public records for recording act purposes, e.g., bankruptcy and probate court decrees affecting titles to land, actions of agencies acquiring land through eminent domain, and liens on land acquired by governmental agencies. If such records are treated as giving constructive notice of their contents, they are also made part of any record search by interested parties.

c. Tract Indexes

Some jurisdictions permit or require maintenance of tract indexes instead of, or in conjunction with, name indexes. A tract index is organized according to the location of the particular tract (or block), and all entries relating to that tract are entered upon the page dealing with that tract. Searches begin with the parcel identifier (e.g., block 100, parcel 30), rather than with the name of a party. Generally, this form of index reduces risk of error (although a document can still be inadvertently indexed under the wrong tract) and reduces the time required to make a search (since all documents will be found on one page). Private commercial title companies generally organize their records on tract principles rather than according to the official grantor-grantee system.

3. RECORDING ACTS

Recording statutes generally do not require that a deed or other document affecting title be recorded in order to effectively operate as between the parties; recording is not a condition of conveying. The statutes do provide (in effect) that: (1) any document affecting title may (should) be recorded; (2) by recording the document, constructive notice of its existence is given to the public; and (3) if the document is not recorded, the person claiming under it will lose priority as against certain other persons. The statutes differ as to the circumstances under which an unrecorded prior interest is defeated by a subsequent interest. They are described below.

a. Notice Acts

Such statutes declare that an unrecorded instrument is void as against any person who subsequently takes an interest in the same property without notice of that instrument.

b. Notice-Race Acts

Under these statutes the subsequent taker must not only take without notice but must also record his instrument before the hitherto unrecorded instrument is recorded. Thus, these acts protect any subsequent purchaser who takes without notice and records first.

c. Race Acts

These protect the party who records first, regardless of notice. Such statutes hardly exist today because of the perceived unfairness of protecting a subsequent purchaser with knowledge, merely because he has recorded first. They will not be extensively discussed.

d. Period-Of-Grace Acts

These give the first taker some additional amount of time to record before any sanction for nonrecordation is imposed. The speed of modern communication has eliminated the need for a period of grace and such acts have generally disappeared. They will not be discussed further.

Examples: (1) Owen conveyed to Ann, who did not record; Owen then conveyed the same property to Bob, who had no notice of Ann and who did record. At common law, Ann prevails over Bob because she took first. But under a notice act, Bob prevails because he took without notice of Ann's unrecorded deed; under a race act, he prevails because he recorded before she did; and under a notice-race act he prevails because he took without notice and recorded first.

(2) Owen conveyed to Ann who did not record; Owen then conveyed to Bob who did record, but Bob had actual knowledge of Ann. Under a notice act, Bob loses because he does not qualify as a taker without notice. Under a notice-race act, he also loses because, even though he recorded first, he had notice. Under a race act, Bob prevails despite his actual knowledge since he is only required to have been the first to record.

(3) Owen conveyed to Ann who did not record; Owen then conveyed to Bob, who was without notice of Ann, but Bob also failed to record. Under a notice act, Bob prevails because all that is required is that he take without notice. (His failure to record may jeopardize him vis-a-vis later other grantees from Owen if they take without notice of him, but it does not affect his contest with Ann.) Under a notice-race act, Bob loses because he has met only one of the two requirements necessary in order to prevail over a prior grantee—he has taken without notice but he has not recorded first. (However, if Bob now records before Ann does, he may yet prevail, under both notice-race and race acts.)

4. VALUE

Recording acts make unrecorded documents ineffective as against certain qualified persons. *To gain the protection of a recording statute as against a prior but unrecorded instrument, it is necessary for the subsequent taker to have given value for his instrument.* Recording systems protect the reliance of innocent purchasers; if value was not involved, the reliance was not detrimental and no great loss is incurred if the previous instrument is given priority.

a. Value Not Paid

The following types or person are held to have not paid value and, therefore, are not protected against prior unrecorded instruments:

1) Donee
One who takes by gift has done nothing by way of detrimental reliance and does not need recording act protection.

Examples: (1) Owen conveyed to Ann, who did not record; Owen then executed a gift deed to Bob, who did not know of Ann and who did record. Ann prevails, since Bob has not paid value, and therefore has not relied upon the records to his detriment.

(2) Owen executed a gift deed to Ann, who did not record: Owen then did the same with Bob, who did record. Ann prevails, since Bob has not paid value. Ann is not required to have paid value, since as first grantee she actually received a title and was not required to pay consideration for it. Value is required only of the second taker who is attempting to divest the first taker's actual title by virtue of the recording system.

(3) Owen conveyed to Ann, who did not record; Owen then conveyed to Bob, who paid value, took without notice of Ann, and did record; Bob then executed a gift deed to Carol. Carol prevails over Ann even though she did not pay value. Once Bob qualified as a protected person under the recording acts, title vested in him as against Ann. Bob then had a real title to convey to Carol, and it is not required that she qualify as a bona fide purchaser in order for the deed from him to her to be effective.

2) Unsecured Creditor

A general creditor who did not rely upon the records in extending credit is not protected by the recording acts. (It should be noted, however, that an unsecured creditor would have no special interest or claim upon the debtor's property anyway; that is what it means to be unsecured.)

Example: Bob extended credit to Owen, not knowing that Owen had previously conveyed his property to Ann by an unrecorded deed. As an unsecured creditor of Owen, Bob is not protected since he did not rely on the recording acts when he gave Owen credit.

3) Judgment Creditor

Recordation of a money judgment generally makes it a lien upon all real property of the judgment debtor in the county where the recordation is made. Thereafter the judgment debtor's property is subject to the judgment lien much as it would be subject to a mortgage lien for a like amount. However, most jurisdictions do not give the recording judgment creditor bona fide purchaser status as against unrecorded claims, since he did not obtain his judgment or make it a lien in detrimental reliance upon the records.

Examples: (1) Owen conveyed his property to Ann who did not record; Bob then obtained and recorded a money judgment against Owen based upon an automobile accident. Ann holds title to the property free of Bob's judgment lien, since he did not get himself hit by Owen's car or sue Owen because the records led him to believe that Owen still owned the property. (The small amount Bob paid to have his judgment recorded is not enough to qualify as the kind of detrimental reliance protected by the recording system.)

(2) Bob recorded a judgment against Owen, who then conveyed secretly to Ann. Ann takes the property subject to Bob's judgment lien, because Bob's judgment came first and does not require that he have detrimentally relied upon the records.

4) **Promissor**
A person who has merely promised to pay is generally not regarded as having paid value, since a court may release him from his promise.

Example: Owen conveyed his property to Ann, who did not record; he then conveyed it to Bob upon Bob's promise to pay for it later. Bob discovered Ann before he had paid Owen anything. Ann prevails. Bob can avoid harm to himself and to Ann by refusing to pay Owen. If Bob does go ahead and pay Owen, he may not be protected under the recording acts.

b. **Value Paid**
The following transactions are regarded as payment of value (and the second grantee is, therefore, protected):

1) **Payment of the Purchase Price**
This may be less than fair market value, but it must be more than a nominal amount. It should not be grossly inadequate when compared to the value of the property. (The chief reason why a deed generally recites that value has been paid to the grantor is to attempt to qualify the grantee as a bona fide purchaser for value under the recording act, should such status ever become necessary.) Value is not required to be given in money; love and affection do not qualify, but goods or services can constitute sufficient value.

a) **Payment to Owner's Successor**
So long as a person pays value to the one who appears to hold the record title, he may qualify as a bona fide purchaser for value under the recording act; it is not required that the payee be or ever have been a true owner.

Example: Owen conveyed to Ann who did not record; Owen then executed a gift deed to Bob, who did record; Bob conveyed to Carol who paid value for her deed and did record. Carol prevails as against Ann. As a result of Ann's failure to record her deed, Owen had a power to divest Ann by conveying to a bona fide purchaser for value; this power was transferred to Bob by Owen's deed and was exercised by Bob when he conveyed to Carol. By virtue of appearing on the records as owners of the property, Owen and Bob were able to create a better title in qualified third persons than they themselves had. The same result would follow if Bob had taken under Owen's will.

2) Negotiable Note

Even though a note is merely a promise to pay, where it is negotiable and has been transferred to a holder in due course, its maker is usually treated as having paid value for the property.

Example: Owen conveyed his property to Ann who did not record; he then conveyed it to Bob who gave him a negotiable promissory note for the price. If Bob's note has been sold to a holder in due course, he cannot avoid paying it. Therefore, he will be protected as against Ann by the recording acts.

3) Cancellation of Prior Debt

A conveyance made in cancellation or satisfaction of a preexisting obligation is generally considered as having been made for value, i.e. relinquishment of the former claim against the grantor.

4) Mortgages

A mortgagee loans money on the strength of a record search which tells him that he will receive a valid mortgage lien upon the debtor's property. His reliance is protected by the recording system. (He is a secured, rather than unsecured, creditor.)

Example: Bob accepted a mortgage as security for his loan to Owen without knowing of Owen's previously unrecorded deed to Ann. Bob is protected and will be given a mortgage lien upon Ann's property. (Ann's deed is valid as against Bob to the extent of giving her title, but Bob's lien is superior to her title. Thus, she holds title subject to his mortgage.)

a) Mortgage to Secure Prior Debt
If the mortgage is given to secure a preexisting debt, and no new consideration is given for it (such as an extension of time to pay), then the mortgagee has not detrimentally relied upon the records and is not protected.

5) Part Payment
When a second grantee has paid part of the price before learning of the first, he will be protected to an appropriate degree.

Example: Bob had paid ⅓ of the agreed-upon price to Owen when he learned of a prior unrecorded deed to Ann. He may be given ⅓ of the property (if it is divisible); or he may be given the entire property with the obligation to pay the balance of the price to Ann rather than Owen; or Ann may be given the property with the obligation to pay Bob back the amount which he actually paid to Owen.

6) Purchase at an Execution Sale
Although a judgment creditor is not protected by the recording acts, a sale under a judgment may pass a good title to an execution purchaser (one who purchases at a sheriff's sale conducted to satisfy a judgment). If the execution purchaser is a stranger to the judgment who bids and pays cash for the title, he prevails as against any prior unrecorded document. The sheriff has the power to convey to a bona fide purchaser despite the lack of a real title to sell, akin to the power of an heir or donee of the record owner to create a title in a bona fide purchaser.

a) Where Judgment Creditor Is the Execution Purchaser
Courts are divided as to whether a judgment creditor who bids at his own execution sale will prevail against a prior unrecorded instrument. Those which do protect the judgment creditor say that he has given up his judgment lien in exchange for the title, and has thereby paid value; furthermore, denying him recording act protection discourages the most promising bidder at the sale (to the detriment of the judgment debtor). Those which deny the judgment creditor protection say that his judgment can be restored to him if his title fails as against a prior claimant and he has therefore not given value.

5. NOTICE
A subsequent purchaser prevails over a prior unrecorded instrument only if he is without notice of it when he takes his own instrument. He will not prevail (except in a race jurisdiction) if he has knowledge or can be charged with notice of the prior claim.

a.   When Notice Matters

Notice received after a purchaser has paid consideration and taken title is irrelevant, since by then she has already detrimentally relied upon nondiscovery of the unrecorded instrument in purchasing the title. Generally, the protected reliance occurs when the price has been paid, although some courts require that the purchaser have taken title as well (this presents serious risks to installment purchasers whose contracts oblige them to make payments for many years before the seller is obliged to deliver a deed to the property).

b.   Actual Knowledge

If the subsequent purchaser was actually aware of the prior claim, regardless of how such knowledge was obtained, she will not prevail against it. Money paid by her after she knew of the rival claim is not a protected investment. She can avoid harm to herself and others by refusing to purchase once she learns of conflicting claims to the title—until the issue is resolved.

c.   Constructive Notice

A person is charged with constructive notice of whatever would be revealed by a proper search of the records. However, jurisdictions differ on what constitutes a "proper" search. All states require some title search and charge a subsequent taker with notice of most recorded and indexed documents. But there is judicial disagreement as to whether or not there is constructive notice in the following situations:

1)   Misindexed Documents

The recorder's office may wrongly index a recorded document, so that a searcher will not find it. Some courts read their recording acts to require only that the grantee deposit the deed with the recorder. They hold that an instrument is recorded once it has been so deposited, regardless of how it is thereafter indexed, even if it makes searching the records an impossible task. Other courts declare that a deed which cannot be located in the indexes has not been effectively recorded, thereby requiring the grantee to double check later on as to the correct indexing of her instrument.

Example: Owen conveyed to Ann, who deposited her deed at the recorder's office. The clerk inadvertently indexed it under the name "Ivan" rather than "Owen" in the Grantor-Grantee Index. Any subsequent purchaser from Owen, searching to see whether he had previously conveyed this property, would not come across this reference and would not discover the deed. A court could hold, therefore, that it had not been recorded within the meaning of the recording law.

2) "Wild" Documents

When a prior essential instrument in the chain of title has not been recorded, any later recorded instrument is "wild." The omission of a link in the chain of title means that a title search will not uncover any later instrument connected to it, even though the subsequent instrument itself has been properly recorded and indexed. Consequently, the "wild" instrument is generally held not to give notice.

Example: Owen conveyed to Ann who did not record; Ann then conveyed to Barbara, who did record. But it is unlikely that any searcher will ever discover Barbara's deed, for it is wild. It is indexed under the names of "Ann" (grantor) and "Barbara" (grantee), whereas the existing record chain of title ends with "Owen." Any person considering purchasing from Owen will search his name in the Indexes and will find neither the deed to Ann (since it was not recorded) nor the deed to Barbara (since it is not indexed with reference to Owen). For all practical purposes, Barbara's deed has not been recorded.

3) Late Recordation

An instrument which is not put onto the records until after the owner affected by it has already parted with title is considered by the majority to give notice, although it requires the title searcher to make a much longer search.

Example: Owen mortgaged to Ann who did not record; Owen then conveyed to Bob, who knew of Ann and recorded; Ann then recorded her mortgage; Bob then conveyed to Carol. A searcher normally checks out each name only during the period of actual ownership by that person. Here, the mortgage against Owen does not appear on the records until a time when Owen is no longer owner. It would take an extended search by Carol, checking each name all the way up to the present, to discover the mortgage. This is what the majority rule requires.

4) Early Recordation

An instrument which is recorded prior to the time that the person affected by it acquires title is held, by the majority, not to give notice, although an extensive title search could disclose the instrument.

Example: Ann gave Barbara a mortgage on property she (Ann) did not then own and Barbara recorded; Owen then conveyed the property to Ann and Ann recorded; Ann then conveyed to Carol. Carol will find Barbara's mortgage only if she checks Ann in the Indexes during the period prior to Ann's ownership. The majority rule does not require Carol to go this far.

5) **Deeds Out**
A deed by the same grantor to other land owned by him which affects the land in question is held, by the majority, to give notice to the grantee of this land, on the ground that the grantor's name provides a sufficient link. Other courts hold that the reference to a different parcel eliminates the basis for imputing notice to the grantee.

Example: Owen conveyed lot 1 to Ann, also granting to her in the same deed an easement over his retained lot 2, and she recorded; Owen then conveyed lot 2 to Bob. Bob will find this easement only if he checks the records for lot 1 as well as lot 2. The majority rule requires him to do so.

6) **Nonrecordable Documents**
Where the recorder has recorded a document which should not have been recorded (because it was not acknowledged or did not qualify for recordation under state law, e.g., a land contract), courts do not agree on whether it gives notice to subsequent purchasers. On the one hand, a searcher will have seen it (assuming it was properly indexed). But, on the other hand, some courts fear that holding that such a document gives notice eliminates any sanction against the recordation of documents which the state has said should not be recorded (although this can happen only when the recorder is negligent). Some courts resolve the issue by holding that such a document gives "inquiry notice." (Discussed below.)

7) **Years to Be Searched**
Theoretically, a search in the indexes should begin with the present day and go back in time to the beginning of the records. In some eastern states, this can require a search that covers several hundred years of documents. (The doctrine of adverse possession often eliminates ancient clouds on title, but is too dependent on factual evidence to satisfy the concerns of title searchers encountering old and inconsistent claims in the records.) Many states have Marketable Title Acts which are intended to make it possible for searchers to limit the number of years searches must cover.

a)   Elimination of Ancient Documents
Some statutes provide that documents clouding title, such as
mortgages, contracts to purchase land, rights of entry, or
unexercised options, or abandoned or dormant mineral rights,
which are over a certain age (e.g., 20 years old), may be ignored
by a title searcher, and its legal effect is nullified. Holders of
rights under such documents are required to rerecord a present
claim prior to the expiration date if they wish to have their
rights preserved. (This does not shorten the search period, since
the searcher must still go all the way back in time to look for
other documents not affected by this rule.)

b)   Marketable Record Title Acts
Some statutes provide for a "root" of title as of a certain number
of years ago (e.g., 40 years), entitling the searcher to treat the
last document recorded prior to that time as absolutely valid and
to search the records only for the time period following that
document. Under such statutes, the rule that recordation cannot
validate a forged or undelivered deed does not apply to the
document forming the root of title. This rule will not necessarily
shorten the period of search so long as any documents are
excepted from the rule (as is always the case with federal claims,
due to the Supremacy Clause), since the exception forces the
searcher to go back in time to look for excepted documents.

d.   **Inquiry Notice**
*Inquiry notice refers to the duty imposed upon a purchaser to make a search
outside of the records and imputes to him such knowledge as a reasonable
inquiry would produce.* It applies when a court determines that the
circumstances warranted an inquiry and that a reasonable search would
have revealed the fact in question.

1)   When Imposed
The duty to inquire arises in the following situations:

a)   Defective or Unrecordable Instruments
Some states require a purchaser to investigate the validity of any
defective or improperly recorded instrument, even though its
recordation may not in itself constitute constructive notice.

   Example: A deed which is not signed is not properly recordable.
If the Recorder does, however, accept it and copy it
into the records, it may still be held not to impart
constructive notice in some jurisdictions. However, a
court may hold that any person who actually sees it
in the records must go farther and investigate its

validity. Thus, if the deed was valid and this could be ascertained through a reasonable search, a subsequent purchaser will be charged with notice of that fact.

(1) *Curative Acts.* Some statutes provide that minor recording defects are to be disregarded after a short period of time (e.g., one or two years) following recordation. Under such statutes, a recorded but unnotarized document does give notice after that time period.

b) References to Other Instruments
Most states require a person to investigate references in recorded instruments to other instruments, even though those other instruments were not themselves recorded.

Example: Owen mortgaged to Ann who did not record, Owen then conveyed to Bob, who knew of Ann, by a deed which said "subject to Ann's mortgage" and Bob recorded; Bob then conveyed to Carol by deed which did not refer to the mortgage. A normal search by Carol will reveal the deed to Bob. The reference in it to the mortgage is suspicious, since the records do not contain any such mortgage. Therefore, Carol should ask Owen and Bob about it. If she knows who Ann is, or is able to locate her, she should ask her about the mortgage. If a reasonable inquiry would lead to the discovery of Ann's mortgage, then Carol will be charged with notice of it. (Carol is so charged, even though she may never check the records at all, since she will be charged with constructive notice of Owen's deed to Bob and of its contents. Carol does not profit, therefore, by avoiding the records.)

c) Possession
A person interested in acquiring an interest in property must not only search the records but must look at the property itself. There is a general duty to inquire of persons in possession of the property as to whether they claim any rights in it and a subsequent purchaser may be charged with notice of whatever facts such an inquiry would have produced.

(1) *Where Consistent With Record Title.* The duty to inquire generally does not arise when the possession is entirely consistent with what the records show.

(a) *Landlord-Tenant Exception.* However, most courts require a purchaser to inquire of tenants as to their rights, even when their possession is consistent with their recorded leases because it is so common for them to have collateral arrangements with their landlords which do not appear in the recorded leases.

2) What Sort of Inquiry
    Where an inquiry is required, and no such inquiry was made, or the one undertaken is challenged as inadequate (because it did not uncover the necessary information), it is a question of fact as to whether it was reasonably diligent. Generally, it must be more than a casual conversation with the person who was not likely to divulge the truth. The availability of alternate sources of information (other persons, other sets of records, public documents, including phone books, tax charges, and utility bills) also bears upon the adequacy of the search.

C. REVIEW QUESTIONS

1. T or F Owen conveyed his property to Ann, who did not record. Owen died leaving Bob as his heir. Bob conveyed the property to Carol who paid value, took without notice of Ann, and recorded. Carol prevails over Ann.

2. T or F Owen conveyed his property to Ann, who did not record. Owen conveyed the same property to Bob, who took without notice of Ann, paid value, and did not record. Ann then recorded. Ann prevails over Bob in both race and notice-race states, but not in notice states.

3. T or F Owen conveyed his property to Ann, who did not record. Owen then conveyed his property to Bob, who took without notice of Ann, paid value, and recorded. Bob then conveyed the property to Carol, who knew of Ann, did not pay value, and did not record. Ann prevails over Carol.

4. T or F Owen conveyed his property to Ann, who did not record. Owen conveyed the same property to Bob, who recorded but knew of Ann. Bob conveyed the property to Carol, who was without notice, paid value and recorded. Carol prevails over Ann.

5. T or F Owen conveyed his property to Ann, who did not record. Owen then borrowed $10,000 from Bob, giving Bob an unsecured promissory note. When the note fell due Owen was unable to pay, and Bob agreed to

accept the property in satisfaction of the note. Owen conveyed the property to Bob and Bob canceled the note. Bob prevails over Ann.

6. T or F   Owen conveyed his property to Ann, who did not record. Ann rented the property to Tom, who did not record his lease but did take possession. Owen then conveyed the same property to Bob who searched the records but did not view the land. Bob prevails over Ann and Tom under a statute which says that any unrecorded deed is void as to purchasers without notice.

*

XI

TITLE ASSURANCE

Analysis

A purchaser has a contract right to refuse to accept a deed which does not convey a marketable title. Once the deed has been accepted, there is no longer any contract right to marketable title. Any remedies he has thereafter arise, if at all, by virtue of assurances as to the title, either made by the grantor as title covenants in the deed or made by some third party in the form of title insurance. (In this chapter the grantor is indicated by feminine pronouns, the grantee by masculine pronouns.)

A. TITLE COVENANTS

It is common for the grantor to include in her deed to the grantee some representations or promises concerning the state of the title. The contract between vendor and purchaser often specifies the type of deed to be executed by the vendor with regard to these protections. Deeds are classified according to whether or not they contain such assurances.

1. TYPES OF DEEDS
a. Quitclaim
This is a deed which contains no representations whatsoever concerning the state of the grantor's title. *It purports to transfer to the grantee whatever title the grantor has, if any, but it does not represent that she does have any title to convey.*

1) No Implied Covenants
   The statute of frauds requires that any covenants of title be in writing. Thus, a quitclaim deed is held to contain no such covenants because none are expressed in it and none may be implied. A quitclaim is commonly used to buy up doubtful claims or by governmental officials who are unable to warrant the state of the title being transferred.

b. Statutory or Grant Deed
In some jurisdictions, statutes provide that there are implied from the word "grant" (or similar language) certain limited covenants, such as:

(1) That the grantor has not previously conveyed the estate she now purports to convey to the grantee;

(2) That the grantor has not personally permitted any encumbrances to be placed against the title.

These are often called "special" warranties because they do not cover acts of the grantor's predecessors, such as might be included in a general warranty deed. (It is also possible for a special warranty deed to be created by express language to that effect.)   A grant deed is sometimes referred to as a bargain and sale deed, or statutory deed.

c.   Warranty Deed
This is a deed which contains five or six express statements by the grantor concerning the state of the title.   These "usual" covenants are discussed in the next section.

2.   COVENANTS IN DEEDS
a.   Present Covenants
These are representations contained in a deed which concern the existing title held by the grantor and being transferred to the grantee.

1)   Covenant of Seisin
The grantor represents that she is seised of an estate of the quantity and quality which she purports to convey, i.e. she has both title and possession.

2)   Covenant of Good Right to Convey
The grantor represents that she is entitled to convey the property, i.e. that she has title (not necessarily possession) or is authorized to convey as agent of the owner.

3)   Covenant Against Encumbrances
The grantor represents that there are no encumbrances (easements, mortgages, etc.) against the title.   An encumbrance against the title does not affect the grantor's seisin or right to convey; thus this covenant affords different protection to the grantee.

a)   Preexisting Encumbrances
Unlike the special warranty discussed earlier, this covenant is "general," i.e., it protects against all encumbrances regardless of when they came into existence, even if the grantor was not personally responsible for their creation.

b)   Visible Encumbrances
Some courts treat a covenant against encumbrances as not including any easement which was visible at the time of conveying (e.g., a paved right of way over the property), on the assumption that the grantee must have seen it and intended to accept the title subject to it.

c)   Encumbrances Known to the Grantee
A few courts treat a covenant against encumbrances as not including any encumbrances actually known by the grantee (e.g., a mortgage disclosed on the preliminary title report), on the

assumption that the grantee intended to accept it. Most courts, however, do not equate knowledge by the grantee with willingness to accept such encumbrances and do not except them from coverage.

    d)   **Excepted and Assumed Covenants**
If the deed excepts some encumbrance from the grant (e.g., "subject to an easement") or recites that the grantee assumes the obligations inherent in the encumbrance (e.g., "grantee assumes the mortgage"), then the covenant against encumbrances in the deed is construed to not cover that item.

    e)   **Beneficial Encumbrances**
Some courts except from the coverage of a covenant against encumbrances any which actually benefit the land so encumbered (e.g., a power line easement serving the house from the street).

b.   **Future Covenants**
These are promises by the grantor to protect the grantee against some problem arising at a later time.

  4)   **Covenant of Quiet Enjoyment**
The grantor here covenants that the grantee shall be able to quietly enjoy the property as against lawful claims by any third parties.

  5)   **Covenant of Warranty**
The grantor here covenants to "warrant and defend" the grantee's title against the lawful or reasonable claims of any third parties.

    a)   **Special**
Covenants of quiet enjoyment and warranty are frequently written so as to be special rather than general, i.e. to protect against only certain specified title problems.

  6)   **Covenant of Further Assurances**
The grantor here covenants to do all acts which are reasonably necessary to protect or perfect the grantee's title if that becomes necessary. This covenant is common in a full warranty deed, although it is not always treated as required where the contract calls for the grantor to execute a deed containing the "usual" covenants.

3.   **BREACH OF COVENANT**
  a.   **When Breach Occurs**
    1)   Present Covenants
The present covenants are breached at the instant the conveyance is made, if the grantor lacks seisin, the right to convey, or a title free

of encumbrances. At that moment the grantee has a cause of action against the grantor for breach and the statute of limitations commences to run. It is not possible for the present covenants to be breached at any later time. Since the grantee may have not yet suffered any harm from the breach (nor even have known of it), a few jurisdictions add a requirement of damage for the cause of action to arise.

2) Future Covenants

The future covenants are breached only when the grantee suffers some interference with his use or enjoyment of the land. Some courts require that there be an actual eviction before the grantee may sue, but most permit a "constructive eviction," such as some lesser disturbance to him or even his purchase or compromise of the adverse claim. Future covenants may be subject to repeated breaches according to the nature of the problem.

b. Remote Grantees as Plaintiffs

1) Present Covenants

Since a present covenant is breached, if ever, at the moment the conveyance is made, there is no longer any covenant thereafter to be transferred to subsequent owners of the property. Some courts hold that a later conveyance by the grantee impliedly transfers his cause of action for any past breach to the new owner.

2) Future Covenants

Title covenants were the first covenants to "run with the land." (See Chapter VI.) Thus, a grantee may be able to sue a remote grantor/covenantor if a covenant is breached while he has title and if he is damaged as a result. Even after a breach, a future covenant survives and continues to run with the land. Most courts permit a future covenant to run to a remote grantee even though there may be a technical lack of privity of estate. For example, where the grantor had no title whatsoever to which the future covenant could attach and follow when the grantee thereafter conveyed to another. The fact that subsequent conveyances may have been by way of quitclaim deeds does not inhibit the running of these covenants.

> ***Example:*** Grace conveyed to Gene by a full warranty deed. However, she had no title to convey. Gene later conveyed to Hal, who was ultimately evicted from the property by the true owner. Gene may sue Grace for breach of the covenants of seisin or of right to convey, if the statute of limitations has not run on that cause of action (which arose when Grace conveyed); but he may not sue for breach of the covenant of quiet enjoyment, since he never

suffered from it. Hal may not sue Grace on the present covenants, since they did not run to him (unless Gene can be said to have impliedly assigned his causes of action for breach to Hal); but Hal may sue Grace on her covenant of quiet enjoyment, which did run to him. (Whether Hal may sue Gene depends on whether there were any covenants in his deed from Gene.)

c.   The Measure of Damages
Damages differ according to which covenant has been breached.

1)   Seisin, Right to Convey, Warranty, Quiet Enjoyment, and Further Assurances
Damages are generally the price paid for the property (or that part of it which has been lost) when these covenants are breached. The grantee may not recover for any appreciation in the value of the property after the conveyance, and a few courts limit him to nominal damages unless he has actually been ousted from the property. He also may not recover from the grantor for any improvements he has placed upon the property, although he may be able to recover for these from the true owner under a theory of unjust enrichment or an "innocent improver" statute.

2)   Encumbrances
Damages are the cost of its removal, if the encumbrance is monetary (e.g., a mortgage), or the reduction of market value caused by it if the encumbrance is nonmonetary (e.g., an easement).

3)   Remote Grantees
Some jurisdictions limit the remote grantee's recovery to the amount he has actually paid or the amount actually received by the remote grantor, whichever is smaller. Others permit the grantee to recover up to the full amount received by the grantor, even though that may exceed what this grantee paid.

d.   Estoppel by Deed—After-Acquired Title
Where a person purports to grant her property to another and thereafter acquires a title (or partial title) to it, that newly acquired interest is held to inure to the benefit of her grantee. The grantor is deemed to be estopped by her deed from asserting this after-acquired title against her grantee.

1)   Supporting Facts
Some courts apply this doctrine only when a full warranty deed is involved; other courts apply it whenever the deed contains a covenant of warranty even though the other title covenants are absent; still

other courts apply it to any deed which describes a particular estate in land, even though it contains no express title covenants. The doctrine is rarely invoked if the conveyance was by quitclaim deed. It is not required that the grantee have paid value for his conveyance.

The doctrine protects successors of the grantee as well as the grantee, but is subject to the effect of the recording acts (below).

Example: Grace gave Gene a mortgage upon property she did not then own; later she did acquire title to this property. Gene's mortgage immediately then attached to Grace's after-acquired title. If Grace had given Gene a deed to the entire fee simple, title would pass to him through Grace the moment Grace received a deed from the former owner. Her after-acquired title would "feed the estoppel."

2) Effect of Recording Acts

Although a subsequent purchaser can, by making an extensive search of the records for the time period prior to the grantor's acquisition of title, locate an instrument executed by her from which an estoppel by deed may be created, most courts do not require such a search to be made. The bona fide purchaser for value therefore prevails over a prior grantee claiming under a theory of estoppel by deed. This was covered in Chapter X.

B. TITLE INSURANCE

Title insurance is a guarantee, made by a third party who has examined the chain of title, that the title is what it is represented to be in the title insurance policy. Its chief advantage over title covenants is that it eliminates the dependance of the grantee on the continued presence and solvency of the grantor in the event that the title later turns out to be defective.

1. PRELIMINARY SEARCH

A title insurance company usually has its own set of land records and indexes, generally organized upon a tract basis. When a property is about to be sold, the company investigates the vendor's title and reports on it to the purchaser so that he or his attorney may determine whether to accept it (i.e., whether it is "marketable").

2. TITLE POLICY

If the preliminary title report is acceptable to the purchaser, then the title company issues a title insurance policy after escrow has closed, guaranteeing that the title is as described in the preliminary report (now vested in the purchaser rather than the vendor as a result of the conveyance).

a. Reported Defects

If the title company discovers some problem with the title (e.g., an easement), it discloses this fact to the purchaser in its preliminary report and in its title policy. The policy excludes liability under the policy for the existence of that defect. (Obviously, the title company cannot make existing defects in a title vanish; thus it does not insure against them.)

b. Guarantee of Accuracy

The title policy guarantees that the title insurer has made an accurate search of the records. If some defect later appears which the company should have discovered during its record search, then the company is liable for not reporting it as an exception. Basically, *the title policy insures that there are no defects in the title other than those disclosed in the policy.*

c. General Exceptions

A title policy does not insure against risks which the company cannot discover by a careful search of the records, e.g.:

1) **No Bona Fide Purchaser Status**
   If the insured fails to prevail as against an unrecorded claim only because he is not a bona fide purchaser under the recording acts (because he had actual notice of the claim or did not pay value), the policy generally provides that the title company is not liable. Otherwise it would have no protection against unrecorded claims which it could never locate.

2) **Possessory Rights**
   If the insured fails to prevail against an unrecorded claim because an inspection of the premises would have revealed it, the policy excepts liability. A title company will generally not make a physical inspection of the property and confines its exposure to risks of record. However, for an additional premium a title company may view the premises and issue a special endorsement based upon it. (This is commonly done when a construction loan is involved and there is a risk that mechanics' liens will prevail over the priority of the loan if construction began before the loan was made.)

3) **Boundaries**
   The policy generally does not insure the accuracy of the boundaries of the parcel (which cannot be determined from a search of the records and requires the employment of a surveyor). Again, for an additional fee, a title company may insure the accuracy of a survey.

4) Taxes and Assessments
The policy does not insure that the property is free of certain current taxes or assessments which, by law, may be valid liens even without or prior to the recordation of any instrument to that effect. Past due taxes and assessments usually appear of record and are therefore generally covered in a title policy.

d. **Off-Record Risks**
A title policy generally insures that every instrument in the chain was properly executed by a person competent to do so and was also properly delivered. This is a true insurance feature against the off-record risks of incompetency, forgery and nondelivery, since the company does not in fact know the truth of these matters.

e. **Subsequent Defects**
Title policy coverage reflects the state of the title as of the moment the policy is issued. It cannot cover subsequently arising defects, because those matters are beyond the insurer's control. Thus it is a "single premium" policy.

3. **TITLE COMPANY LIABILITY**
a. **Persons Protected**
A title company is liable to its insured for any harm suffered from the occurrence of an insured risk, so long as the insured continues to own the property or some interest in it. The policy does not run with the land to protect the next owner, who must purchase an independent title policy.

1) Lenders
Where a mortgage is involved, the lender usually requires a special policy be issued insuring that its mortgage is not only a valid lien on the title, but also insuring the ranking of the lien in terms of priority (i.e., the mortgage is a first rather than a second).

b. **Protection Afforded**

A title company will generally pay the litigation costs of any insured involved in a title dispute. The policy generally gives the company the option of resisting the claim, acquiring it (so as to make the title conform to what the policy represented it to be), or paying compensation to its insured to cover the loss (up to the policy limit).

Example: Gene obtained a preliminary title report after having contracted to purchase Grace's house. The report showed that title was vested in Grace subject to a long term lease and subject also to a mortgage. Gene informed the escrow agent (who was also the title company) that he would accept title subject to the lease but not subject to the mortgage (i.e., the escrow agent was to turn the money over to Grace only if a title free of the mortgage could be delivered to Gene). Since Grace had instructed the escrow agent to use part of the sales proceeds to satisfy the mortgage, escrow did close and a deed to Gene was delivered and recorded. Thereafter the title company issued its policy to Gene insuring that title was vested in him subject only to the lease. If it later turns out that the tenant under the lease has additional rights (e.g., an option to renew), the title company may not be liable, since this may fall under the exception for claims discoverable from a possessory investigation. But if a neighbor claims an easement over the property by virtue of some recorded instrument which the title company failed to discover, the company must either compensate Gene for his loss, purchase the easement from the neighbor, or challenge the neighbor's claim through litigation.

C. REVIEW QUESTIONS

1. T or F   After he had contracted to purchase Grace's property, Gene made a search of Grace's title and discovered that the property was subject to a recorded easement. He may nevertheless complete the escrow and accept a deed to the property since he will be protected by his policy of title insurance.

2. T or F   Mort borrowed money from Marie and gave her a note acknowledging the debt and a mortgage securing the note. Marie recorded the mortgage and obtained a policy of title insurance insuring its validity as a first lien on the property. If it turns out that Marie has only a second mortgage, she may recover from the title company.

3. T or F   After Gene had closed escrow and received a title policy insuring his title without exception, he discovered that the property was infested with termites and was built upon improperly compacted fill. He may recover against the title insurance company for failing to report these defects to him.

4. A title company is liable if any of the following restrictions against the owner's property were not mentioned in the title policy:

    T or F   a. The property is restricted to single family residence purposes by virtue of the local zoning ordinance.

T or F b. A right of way acquired by a neighbor from having walked across the property for longer than the statute of limitation.

T or F c. A mortgage on the property, given by a previous owner and not recorded but actually known to the insured at the time of purchase.

T or F d. A judgment lien against the insured by virtue of a judgment acquired against him and recorded after he had acquired title to the property and had purchased the title insurance policy.

*

XII

MORTGAGES

Analysis

A mortgage is a promise made by a property owner to a creditor that, if he does not perform some specified obligation, then the creditor may utilize the owner's property to satisfy the obligation. (In this chapter male pronouns refer to the mortgagor/debtor and female pronouns indicate the mortgagee/creditor.)

A. DOCUMENTATION

A mortgage transaction generally involves two documents. One document memorializes the basic obligation (usually a promise to pay, represented by a promissory note). The second document (the mortgage) provides that the obligee/ mortgagee may reach some property of the person signing this document (the mortgagor, who usually is the obligor under the first document) if the prime obligation (payment) is not performed. A mortgage is always security for some other obligation and is secondary to it. Jurisdictions differ as to whether the mortgage gives the mortgagee a title or a lien on the mortgagor's property.

1. MORTGAGE INSTRUMENTS
a. Condition Subsequent
At early common law, the mortgage was written as a deed conveying a fee simple from the debtor to the creditor subject to the condition subsequent of payment of the debt by a certain date ("law day"). If the debt was paid on time, title reverted to the mortgagor; if it was not, the mortgagee's defeasible title became absolute. (A straightforward document which purported to transfer title from the mortgagor to the mortgagee only when and if the mortgagor failed to pay the debt later would have created an illegal springing interest. See Chapter II.)

b. Mortgage and Deed of Trust
Generally, a mortgage loan involves execution of a mortgage ("I mortgage to you . . . ") or a deed of trust ("I convey in trust to a trustee for you as beneficiary . . . "). Sometimes one instrument is regarded as giving the creditor a lien upon the property and the other as giving her a title to it instead. For purposes of this chapter the two instruments are treated identically.

c. Alternative Security Instruments
Any document which makes property security for an obligation may be treated by a court as a mortgage, however it is worded. Thus a deed with an option to repurchase, a sale/leaseback, or a covenant not to convey property may be held to be a mortgage, if a court decides the document serves a security function. An installment sale of property, whereby the vendor retains legal title until the purchaser has paid in full, may also be deemed to constitute a mortgage. Once so characterized, the instrument then becomes subject to the general rules of mortgages discussed here.

B. FORECLOSURE

A mortgagee generally obtains relief under her mortgage by way of foreclosure. The development of this proceeding is described below.

1. EQUITY OF REDEMPTION
The common law fee simple subject to condition subsequent did not require the mortgagee to do anything in order to perfect her title on default by the mortgagor. Her estate enlarged into a fee simple absolute automatically once the time for payment had passed. However, at an early date courts of equity permitted the mortgagor to pay late, on the grounds that his deed was only a security agreement and that late payment would not harm the mortgagee and would save the mortgagor from a forfeiture of his property. *This right to pay the debt after it was due became an essential feature of every mortgage transaction (regardless of how the document was worded) and was known as the equity of redemption—a right enforceable in equity to redeem oneself from the consequences of a default.*

2. STRICT FORECLOSURE
In order to put a time limit on the mortgagor's ability to pay the debt late, it became necessary for the mortgagee—after the debt had come due and had not been paid—to go to a court of equity asking that a deadline for late payment be imposed. The equity court would then issue *a decree providing that if the mortgagor did not pay his overdue debt within a certain time, he would be "foreclosed" from ever being able to do so thereafter, and the property would thereupon belong to the mortgagee* free and clear of the mortgagor's power to recover it back by later paying the debt (i.e., free of the equity of redemption). This turnover of the property was referred to as strict foreclosure.

3. FORECLOSURE BY SALE
Later, courts began to decree that if the mortgagor failed to pay the debt within the additional time allotted, the property would be sold at a public auction, rather than go automatically to the mortgagee. The proceeds from this sale are used to discharge the indebtedness. This is the current procedure followed.

a. Surplus
The purpose of a foreclosure sale is to avoid the forfeiture which the mortgagor would suffer if the property has a value in excess of the debt it secured. In such a case, a public auction presumably produces a bid in excess of the mortgage debt and the surplus goes to the mortgagor.

b. Deficiency
Conversely, if the foreclosure sale fails to produce sufficient funds, the mortgagee may be able to obtain a deficiency judgment against the mortgagor for the balance due under the note. Deficiency judgments have been subject to extensive state regulation ever since the Great Depression.

Some states limit deficiency judgments to the difference between the mortgage value and the judicially determined value of the property, whenever that is higher than the amount bid; others provide for judicial establishment of a minimum price below which the property cannot be sold; others provide for a second right of redemption after the sale if a deficiency judgment was granted. Several jurisdictions bar deficiency judgments entirely in certain cases, e.g., if owner occupied residential property is involved, if the loan was purchase money, or if the foreclosure was nonjudicial.

4. NONJUDICIAL SALE

Many jurisdictions permit a mortgage instrument to give the mortgagee power to have the property sold at a public sale without the necessity of first suing in court. The methods of such sales vary from state to state and may be prescribed by statute or set by the mortgage documents. Generally, a waiting period is mandated before the mortgagee is permitted to sell the property. During this grace period, the mortgagor may be permitted to cure his default by paying only the amount in arrears regardless of the fact that the entire obligation (if there was an installment note) has probably been declared due by the mortgagee pursuant to the "acceleration" clause in the note. Such proceedings are occasionally attacked on due process grounds, but most courts hold that no "state action" is involved in such out of court proceedings so as to invite constitutional scrutiny.

5. POSSESSION AND RENTS

A mortgagor is generally entitled to retain possession of the property until a foreclosure sale has been completed. If the mortgage also pledges the rents and profits to the mortgagee she may be able to reach them prior to a sale by making a demand upon the tenants or by having a receiver appointed. Rents so collected are then applied towards discharge of the mortgage debt or to cover any deficiency generated at the foreclosure sale.

C. JUNIOR MORTGAGES

A land owner may impose more than one mortgage upon his property. Mortgages take priority according to the regular principles of recording law. (Notice, race, and notice-race rules apply to the recordation of mortgages.) A mortgage which is inferior to some other mortgage under the recording system is called a junior, or second (or third, etc.) mortgage.

1. JUNIOR FORECLOSURES

When a junior mortgagee forecloses, the property is sold subject to the senior mortgage (which remains a lien on the land). Thus, the high bid for the property should approximate the full market value of the land less the amount of the senior mortgage. If a third mortgage is foreclosed, the property is sold subject to the first and second mortgages.

2. SENIOR FORECLOSURES

A senior foreclosure sale transfers the property free and clear of the junior mortgages (and, of course, free and clear of the senior mortgage which is being satisfied by the sale). Thus a junior mortgage is wiped out by a senior sale, but the junior mortgagee is then entitled to claim any surplus resulting from the sale. The mortgagor receives any surplus from the sale only after all other lienors have been paid. The high bid at a senior sale should approximate the full market value of the property, free and clear of all liens.

Examples: (1) Assume property is worth $100,000 and is subject to first and second mortgages securing debts of $75,000 and $20,000 respectively. If the junior mortgagee forecloses and sells, a rational purchaser should only bid up to $25,000, since he will acquire a title subject to the first mortgage, (i.e., an asset worth $100,000, subject to a liability of $75,000). If $25,000 is paid, the junior mortgagee will receive $20,000 in satisfaction of her mortgage and the mortgagor will take $5,000 as surplus. The senior mortgagee will not be paid, but will still have a mortgage on the property.

(2) If, instead, under the same values, the senior mortgagee forecloses and sells, the high bid might be $100,000 (for a title free of all liens), which will be distributed first to the senior ($75,000), then to the junior ($20,000), and finally to the mortgagor ($5,000).

(3) If the property is worth only $90,000, there will be a shortage, rather than a surplus, which will fall on the junior. Regardless of who conducts the sale, the senior should ultimately end up with $75,000, and the junior with $15,000 and a deficiency judgment for $5,000 against the mortgagor, if one is allowable.

D. TRANSFERS

Both mortgagor and mortgagee may transfer their interests in the property.

1. MORTGAGOR

The fact that property is mortgaged does not prevent the mortgagor from conveying it, although the existence of the mortgage may mean that his title is not marketable unless it is paid off.

The inclusion of a clause in the note or mortgage accelerating the unpaid installment in the event of a transfer of the property (a due-on-sale clause) was held, in some jurisdictions, to constitute an impermissible restraint upon alienation; however, federal law now generally validates such clauses despite contrary state rules.

a. Effect on Grantee

A conveyance of mortgaged property is subject to the mortgage and the new owner has the practical obligation to continue paying the debt in order to avoid losing the property by foreclosure. However, a grantee is not personally liable for any deficiency judgment thereafter unless he actually assumed the mortgage obligation, promising the mortgagor that he would pay the note and thereby enabling the mortgagee to enforce this promise either as a third party beneficiary or under a theory of equitable subrogation. An assumption of the debt by the transferee does not release the transferor; both remain liable on the underlying obligation.

2. MORTGAGEE

A transfer of the note generally carries the mortgage along with it, whether that document is physically handed over or not. If the note is negotiable, the transferee may qualify as a holder in due course and take free of many defenses the mortgagor might otherwise have. (It is customary for the transferor to endorse the note, assign the mortgage and hand the document over to the transferee who should record the assignment of the mortgage and notify the mortgagor of the transfer.)

The federal government is heavily involved in the purchase and resale of residential mortgages (by way of "secondary market" operations) in order to assure a continued supply of mortgage funds into the housing market. By purchasing mortgages from conventional lending institutions and then selling them to investors with a payment guarantee, it enables mortgage lenders to have more funds available to make new loans to new borrowers. Instead of selling the mortgages themselves, the government can issue its own notes, backed by these mortgage pools, to the investors, in the form of "mortgage backed securities."

E. REVIEW QUESTIONS

1. **T or F** Mort's property is subject to a first mortgage held by Marie and a second mortgage held by Sid. If Mort defaults on his first mortgage and Marie commences foreclosure proceedings, Sid may intervene and cure the default on Marie's mortgage.

2. **T or F** Mort asked Marie to loan him $100,000 at 7% simple interest for three years. He offered to give her a note secured by a mortgage on

his $150,000 house. Marie declined to make the loan but agreed, instead, to purchase Mort's house for $100,000, giving him an option to repurchase it three years later for $121,000, and permitting Mort to stay in possession rent-free for the next three years. If Mort fails to exercise his option to repurchase promptly within the three years, he may be permitted to do so late.

3. T or F   Mort gave Marie a mortgage on two lots which he owned in order to secure a $100,000 debt to her. When he had reduced the debt by $50,000 he demanded that she release one of the lots from the mortgage. She may decline to do so.

4. T or F   Marie held a mortgage securing a $100,000 note from Mort. Later, he assaulted her, and she recovered a $25,000 judgment against him for personal injuries. She may refuse to release her mortgage on Mort's property until he pays both the note and the personal injury judgment.

5. T or F   Mort borrowed $100,000 from Marie and gave her a note secured by a mortgage on his property. Both documents provided that Mort waived his right to pay late and recited that Marie could have the property immediately and automatically upon default in payment by him. The provisions are valid.

6. Mort's property has a fair market value of $100,000. It is subject to a first mortgage held by Marie securing a note of $50,000 and a second mortgage held by Sid securing a note of $30,000.

   T or F   a. If Mort sells the property to Jean, a fair price for Jean to pay would be $20,000.

   T or F   b. If Marie forecloses and sells the property, a bidder should be willing to pay $70,000 at the sale, because the property will be sold subject to Sid's mortgage.

   T or F   c. If Marie forecloses and sells the property, a bidder should be willing to pay $80,000, because the purchaser will be acquiring Marie's and Sid's interests in the property, but not Mort's.

   T or F   d. If Sid forecloses and sells, a bidder should be willing to pay $100,000, the proceeds of which will be allocated $50,000 to Marie, $30,000 to Sid, and $20,000 to Mort.

   T or F   e. If Mort defaults on either mortgage, that mortgagee must obtain the consent of the other mortgagee in order to bring any foreclosure action.

*

PART THREE

RIGHTS RELATING TO LAND

Analysis

MISCELLANEOUS PROPERTY DOCTRINES

A. WATER

Different rules govern the rights of persons to take or dispose of water, depending upon whether the water flows in a stream, moves freely over the surface of land, or is underground.

1. STREAM WATER

This refers to water which flows in defined channels; similar rules apply to water contained in lakes. Although the text discusses only the rights of parties to take water from a stream the same principles apply to the discharge of water into a stream or lake, and to underground streams.

a. Riparian Rights

Land which is adjacent to a stream is called riparian (or littoral, if it is adjacent to a lake). At common law, nonriparian owners have no right to take water from a stream when that would affect the rights of riparians.

b. Absolute Rights

An owner of land adjacent to a stream or lake has an absolute right to draw off water in two situations:

1) No Effect on Flow
Where removal of the water has no effect upon the quantity, quality or velocity of the flow of the stream.

2) Domestic Uses
Where the water is removed for domestic uses on the riparian land, e.g., drinking, bathing, etc.

c. Correlative Rights

Two different doctrines regulate the right of a riparian to draw water from a stream for nondomestic purposes when the flow is thereby affected.

1) Natural Flow Doctrine
Every downstream riparian owner has an absolute right to have the stream come to him without alteration. Thus, any alteration of the flow entitles him to enjoin an upstream nondomestic use. This older rule is now a minority view. (In this section masculine pronouns refer to the downstream riparian owner or equivalent; feminine pronouns designate the upstream riparian owner or equivalent.)

2) Reasonable Use Doctrine
The rights of a downstream owner to the water is limited by principles of reasonableness, which require weighing the needs and intended uses of both the upstream and the downstream users. The balancing tests are much like those employed in nuisance cases.

Examples: (1) Ursula, the upstream riparian, appropriated stream water and put it to wasteful and unreasonable uses. However, her activities have no measurable effect on the quantity or velocity of the flow over the land of Don, the downstream riparian. Don has no cause of action against Ursula.

(2) Ursula appropriates water for drinking and bathing. Her activities reduce the flow of the stream over Don's land. Don has no cause of action against Ursula, since these uses of the water are domestic and reasonable and are, therefore, entirely privileged, although some reasonable use jurisdictions apply that standard even to domestic uses, giving it a higher ranking than other uses.

(3) Ursula appropriates water for commercial purposes. Her activity reduces the flow over Don's land. Under the minority "natural flow" theory, Don has a cause of action without the need to show more, since the flow was diminished. Under the majority "reasonable use" theory, Don must show that the reduced flow causes harm to his own reasonable use of the water, and he will not prevail if the court decides that he suffers no real harm or that his own use is not reasonable.

3)   Prior Appropriation System
The arid western states have generally replaced or supplemented riparian rights doctrines with an appropriation system. Under it, rights to take water are acquired by permit wherein priority of use in times of scarcity depends upon the date of application for the permit. Nonriparians may acquire permits to take water, which may be granted on conditions according to the uses intended to be made of the water. Under the Colorado doctrine, followed in the eight driest states, riparian rights are abolished entirely in favor of appropriation rights. Under the California doctrine, used in nine states, riparian rights and appropriative rights coexist.

Example: April, a nonriparian, applied to the local water board for a permit to draw off fifty gallons of water a day in summer in conjunction with her nearby mining operation. This permit would allow her to take the water even though there might not be enough left for later applicants, but her right to take water will be subject to the rights of prior appropriators, i.e., persons who have already received permits. If the jurisdiction follows the Colorado doctrine, Ursula and Dan have no rights as against April; if the jurisdiction follows the California doctrine, their riparian rights will receive some recognition and may possibly further limit April's rights to take water.

d.   Public Rights

Private rights to water may be further subject to public rights for recreational or related purposes on tidal or navigable bodies of water, under the public trust doctrine. The federal government, under the Commerce Clause of the United States Constitution, has a servitude over all navigable waterways in the country, which is superior to all private rights.

2.   UNDERGROUND WATER

Underground water percolating through the soil is often sought by the overlying owners for surface uses. Where the water is an underground stream with a defined channel, then stream rules apply, but the presumption here is that there is no stream. The major rules here deal with their right to drill wells and pump the water out.

a.   Absolute Ownership Rule

Diffuse underground water is owned by the overlying owner absolutely. No overlying owner may complain as to the activities of another overlying owner with regard to the common basin (or "aquifer"), except where the use is malicious. This rule, which originated in England, is generally applied only where water is plentiful.

b.   Reasonable Use Rule

The arid states limit activities of overlying owners by applying a principle of reasonable use. A relevant consideration in determining reasonableness is whether the water will return to recharge the aquifer.

1)   Correlative Rights Rule

In California, all overlying owners are treated as having equal rights to the water, and a court may apportion it among them.

c.   Appropriation

Many western states now apply their appropriation systems to underground as well as stream waters.

3.   SURFACE WATER

Surface water refers to water coming from rain, snow and streams which does not run in any well defined channel, but either spreads randomly over the ground or collects in ponds. Unlike stream and underground water, surface water is generally undesirable to landowners, who generally fight over attempts to get rid of it rather than attempts to keep it. (In those infrequent cases where the water is desired, the rule is that the first to capture it may keep it.) The rest of this section deals with owners' rights to rid themselves (or avoid receiving) surface waters. The jurisdictions are about equally divided between three major rules.

a. Natural Servitude Rule

This doctrine holds that each owner has a right to have water naturally flow away from her land and over her neighbors' land, and conversely, a duty to allow it to flow from her neighbors' land over hers. Thus, no owner is permitted to alter the contours of her land in order to cause water to leave her land or to keep it from coming onto her land. This is also known as the Civil Law Rule. It is subject to frequent exceptions of reasonableness, since otherwise it makes development of land extremely difficult. In some jurisdictions, it is limited to farm land, and even then it is subject to exceptions for good husbandry.

Example: Rain water lands on Ursula's land, and flows down onto Don's land, where it collects. If Don builds a dike to keep the water from flowing down onto his land, Ursula has a cause of action against him under the natural servitude rule. Similarly, if Don cuts a ditch in order to have the water flow over his land and onto his neighbor's land, his neighbor also has a cause of action. Exceptions to this rule may change these outcomes.

b. Common Enemy Rule

This doctrine allows each owner to take any non-malicious steps necessary to remove the water, or to keep it from coming onto her land. The rule furthers development, but is often made subject to principles of reasonableness, in order to allow neighbors to develop their lands as well.

Example: Under the same facts as above, Don may build a dike, or cut a channel, and neither Ursula nor Don's downhill neighbor may complain, unless the rule has been qualified by additional restrictions.

c. Reasonable Use Rule

This rule permits each owner to make cuts or build barriers in conjunction with the reasonable use of her land, so long as it does not unreasonably interfere with her neighbors' use of their land. This is an application of the principles of nuisance to water law. Its adherents contend that the exceptions to the Natural Servitude and Common Enemy Rules have in fact converted those rules into a reasonable use rule.

B. SUPPORT

Every parcel of land is physically supported by the land around it and below it. Removal of part of the surrounding land may cause the parcel in question to subside. When that surrounding land is owned by someone else, the owner of the parcel which has subsided may have a cause of action for loss of support.

1. LATERAL SUPPORT

Every parcel of land has a right of support from all adjoining parcels of land. Any neighbor whose excavation causes an owner's land to subside is liable to him. (In this section masculine pronouns refer to the owner of land which has subsided; feminine pronouns designate the adjoining owner who has caused the subsidence.)

a. Absolute

This right of support is absolute in the sense that liability for its removal is independent of negligence and is not justified by necessity.

Example: Owen's land subsided as a result of his neighbor Nora's excavation on her land. She is liable to him regardless of the fact that she used the most modern and careful excavation methods and that her land would be useless to her unless she could excavate upon it.

1) Natural Conditions

An owner is not obliged to keep neighboring lands artificially shored up. There is no liability, therefore, to a neighbor whose land subsides due to natural conditions upon one's own property.

Example: Owen's land subsided because a rainstorm caused a flood which washed away Nora's land and the support it formerly furnished to his land. He cannot recover from Nora for loss of support; she has no obligation to artificially shore up his land.

a) Water

Where support is lost due to the owner's removal of water, rather than soil, from her property, most courts do not hold her liable under support doctrines. This is treated as a matter of water law, rather than support law. Water law is covered in the prior section.

b) Artificial Support

An owner may replace the natural support her land furnished to her neighbors, and may replace it with a retaining wall or similar substitute. Thereafter, she is obliged to maintain the replacement support mechanism in satisfactory condition.

b. Improvements

Most courts do not extend the right of support to buildings or other improvements upon land. Thus if land subsides only because of the additional weight of the buildings on it, the neighboring excavator is not liable. The duty is one of support only to land in its natural condition. The owner must show that his land would have subsided even if buildings had not been erected on it (which he may be able to prove by demonstrating that the weight of the soil removed for the foundation equalled or exceeded the weight of the structures then added).

1) Measure of Damages

Courts are divided as to whether an excavator is liable for damage to buildings where the subsidence was not due to their extra weight (i.e., where the land would have subsided even if it had not been improved). Most courts do award damages for injury to the buildings, on the ground that this was a foreseeable consequence of the tortious conduct; a few deny recovery, on the ground that this gives preferential treatment to the person who first improves property. Where the excavator is guilty of negligence, there is always liability for damage to the buildings.

c. Persons Liable

1) Noncontiguous Neighbors

The duty of support is not necessarily limited to those neighbors having common boundaries with the owner; a remote neighbor may be liable if her excavation is the cause of the subsidence.

2) Predecessors

A neighbor is not liable for the excavations of her predecessors; liability does not run with the land. The predecessor excavator, however, may be liable, and the cause of action arises with the subsidence, not the date of excavation.

2. SUBJACENT SUPPORT

When mineral or other subsurface rights are severed from surface ownership, those who have a right to operate below the surface have an obligation to support the surface and its buildings.

a. Improvements

Many courts hold that the duty of subjacent support applies to both land and buildings. Other courts limit the duty to land in its natural condition. The duty does not extend to buildings subsequently erected on the surface.

3. MODIFICATION BY AGREEMENT

The right of support arises without need for an agreement. It is a natural right, differing from an easement in that no special facts (such as a deed or prescriptive use) need exist in order for it to appear. But it may be modified by consent of the parties.

a. Creation of Right

Neighbors may agree that one will furnish the other support for a building erected upon one of the parcels, i.e., to support the building as well as the land. Such an easement of support may be created by deed or by implication; it does not arise prescriptively.

b. Elimination of Right

Neighbors may agree that one has no duty to support the other's land at all. Such a release of support rights can occur by express language or by implication. It is not treated as excluding liability for negligent or malicious removal of support unless it explicitly so provides.

4. STATUTORY CHANGES

Some jurisdictions now require by statute that any person intending to excavate give notice to neighbors and, depending on the depth of the excavation or the foundations of the neighboring buildings, enter upon their properties and shore up their buildings (if allowed to do so) before commencing any excavation.

C. FREEDOM FROM INTERFERENCE

A person who owns or possesses land is entitled to have his possession and use and enjoyment of the property not interfered with by others. When the interference is by physical invasion there is liability in trespass; when the invasion is nontrespassory, liability is premised on nuisance.

1. TRESPASS

A trespass is any unprivileged, intentional physical intrusion upon land possessed by another.

a. Unnecessary Elements

Fault need not be shown in order to make out a case in trespass. Motive is irrelevant. If an unprivileged intrusion has occurred, its extent and duration are unimportant in determining if there is liability. Harm need not be shown when a trespass has been committed.

b. Intention

Trespass is an intentional tort. Therefore, if there is a complete lack of volition, there is no trespass. However, a negligent entry (e.g., where the entrant carelessly does not know where she is) is trespassing.

c. The Interest Protected

The right to exclusive possession is the interest which is protected from invasion by trespass. The plaintiff must show a present possessory interest in the property. Thus, an action in trespass is not available to protect holders of nonpossessory present interests (easements, covenants) or future interests (remainders, reversions, mortgages); these parties need some other form of action to protect their interests. On the other hand, a nonownership possessory interest, such as is had by a tenant or peaceable prior possessor is protected from trespassory invasion. Recently, shopping centers, although technically private property (because they are privately owned), have been treated as public places by some courts, thereby depriving their owners of the right to exclude "undesirable" members of the public (e.g., religious pamphleteers or political protesters). (In this section, masculine pronouns indicate the person injured by the trespass or nuisance, feminine pronouns designate the person committing the trespass or nuisance.)

Examples: (1) Paul has resided upon Oona's property without her consent but not long enough to acquire title by adverse possession. Tricia walked across the property. Paul, as possessor, may bring trespass against Tricia; lack of record title on his part is not a defense for Tricia.

(2) At the time of Tricia's entry in the previous example, the property was subject to an easement of right of way in favor of Dita. Although Tricia used the right of way, she did not interfere with Dita. Dita has no cause of action against Tricia. If Tricia had blocked the way, Dita would have a cause of action for unreasonable interference with her easement, but could not sue in trespass.

d. Nature of Trespass

Trespass is not limited to intrusions on the surface of land; it may occur overhead (an overhanging eave, a telephone wire, an airplane, a gun shot) or beneath the surface (a mine, a building foundation, a slant well). It need not involve an entry by a person, but may be committed through the activity of an inanimate object or animal so long as it results from an intentional act by the defendant.

e.   Privilege
When the entry is by consent of the possessor, it is privileged and therefore nontrespassory. Thus acts done under a lease, easement or license are nontrespassory. The refusal to leave, however, upon termination of the privilege may be trespassory.

1)   Public Need
Public policy may justify an otherwise unprivileged entry. A search warrant entitles a public official to enter land despite nonconsent of the possessor. Likewise, an owner of other property (e.g., a landlord or neighbor) may be entitled to enter in certain cases in order to protect her own property (e.g., to view waste or to stop a fire from spreading).

f.   Consequences
1)   Damages
A trespass creates liability in damages without proof of harm. If the trespass is a continuing one (but without permanent effect on the property) there may be repeated recoveries.

a)   Nominal
If no harm has occurred from the trespass the plaintiff may recover only nominal damages. This may be important when the litigation is employed in order to prevent the statute of limitations from running in favor of an adverse possession claim or in order to establish a title to the land in favor of the plaintiff and against the defendant ("trespass to try title").

b)   Compensatory
Actual damages may include not only physical harm to the land, but also personal injuries or lost profits, if these are forseeable.

c)   Punitive
Exemplary damages may be awarded if the trespass is shown to have been malicious.

2)   Injunction
Injunctive relief may be granted where there is a likelihood of continuing trespasses, where the harm may be irreparable, where damages will be difficult to calculate, or where the plaintiff holds a nonpossessory interest and has no standing to sue for damages for trespass.

3)   Adverse Possession
If the trespass amounts to a taking of possession (i.e., ejectment) and relief is not obtained within the statutory period of time, the trespasser may gain title to the property by adverse possession.

2.   NUISANCE

A nuisance (for purposes of this section) is a use of property which unreasonably interferes with the use and enjoyment of someone else's property. The most common kinds of nuisance are activities which inflict neighbors with dust or other pollutants, noise or vibration, insects, or affront their sensibilities (e.g., houses of prostitution, gambling, or funerals).

a.   Nuisance vs Trespass

A nuisance does not require a physical intrusion, as does a trespass, since trespass protects possession while nuisance protects use and enjoyment. But nuisance does require harm, which is not essential to trespass. Nuisance may be brought by the holder of any interest in land, whereas trespass is limited to injuries to possessors.

b.   Determination

Whether or not an activity constitutes a nuisance depends upon the harm it causes. Harm is the tort, not the effect of the tort. Therefore, fault need not be shown. If the interference with a neighbor's use and enjoyment is regarded as unreasonable, the activity will be considered a nuisance. *The unreasonable interference standard generally requires a court to engage in balancing the situations of the parties.* Some factors which may be employed are:

1)   Suitability
The relative appropriateness of the parties' activities to the locale;

Example: Nora proposes to open a slaughterhouse in a residential area. This will probably be declared a nuisance although it would be a perfectly proper use of land in an industrial neighborhood.

a)   Zoning
The fact that the defendant's activity is permitted by the applicable zoning ordinance does not automatically insulate it from nuisance liability, but it might constitute relevant evidence that some experts deem the activity suitable for the neighborhood.

b)   Priority of Use
A plaintiff is generally not defeated for having "come to the nuisance"; but the fact that the defendant's activity is already in

place when the plaintiff arrives may be relevant to the issue of suitability to the locale or to the relief granted.

2) Utility
The respective utility of the activities of the two parties;

Example: Nora's coal mine spreads dust over Owen's nearby house. A court could decide that the social utility of coal mining (in an energy-scarce era) is too great to allow it to be enjoined as a nuisance. But if the coal dust interfered with a critically vital national defense plant next door, the result might change.

3) Cost Avoidance
The comparative costs of avoiding harm (by corrective measures or by relocation) as between the two parties.

Example: Nora's sports stadium sheds great amounts of light upon Owen's neighboring house at night, making it hard for him to sleep. But a court might declare it not a nuisance because it is cheaper for Owen to buy darker blinds than for Nora to build a higher wall. (This same consideration might be employed, not to determine whether Nora is guilty of nuisance but whether she should pay damages instead of being enjoined.)

c. **Consequences**
1) Injunction
If the activity is found to constitute a nuisance, it will generally be enjoined. Courts frequently decide the injunction question by balancing the benefit an injunction will give to the plaintiff against the harm it will cause the defendant. This may involve some or all of the same factors as listed above. It is also possible for a court to grant the injunction, but to condition it upon payment by the plaintiff to the defendant for the loss thereby imposed on her; such a result means that the defendant does have a "right" (an entitlement) to engage in her activity, but that the court has given the plaintiff the right to compel her to sell it to him, unlike most other property rights, which can be purchased only if the seller is willing.

2) Damages

A court may declare that there is a nuisance but deny the plaintiff an injunction, and instead award damages to compensate for the reduced market value of the property. This has the effect of permitting the defendant to "purchase" a servitude over the plaintiff's land without the consent of the plaintiff, a form of private inverse condemnation.

3) Prescription
If the affected neighbor fails to act within the statutory time, the defendant's wrongful activity may ripen into a prescriptive easement.

d. Public Nuisance
A nuisance is public when its consequences affect the entire community rather than a limited group of neighbors. It is generally remedied by a civil or criminal action brought by public authorities.

1) Private Enforcement
If an individual property owner can show special harm (to person or property over and above what other members of the community suffer) he may bring a special action for injunctive or monetary relief.

D. AIRSPACE

Rights in land do not stop at its surface but extend some distance up towards the sky. At common law an owner was said to own to "the heavens above," but there was no occasion for serious analysis of this concept until modern technology led to high rise buildings and aircraft.

1. RIGHTS OF USE
Landowners are entitled to develop their property as high as they please (subject to height limitations imposed by local zoning). The loss of light and views caused by high rise development is generally not actionable by the neighbors unless they have somehow acquired special rights in that regard, and a tall building does not constitute a nuisance merely because of its height. (However, a high structure might be enjoinable as a "spite fence" if erected out of malice.)

a. Separated From the Surface
Rights to utilize airspace can be made distinct from surface rights, as in the following situations:

(1) An easement to run a utility line over the land of another;

(2) a leasehold interest in an apartment in an upper story of a tall building;

(3) ownership of a unit above the ground floor in a high rise condominium project;

Bernhardt–Property, 2d BLS—11

(4) a "transferable development right" granted to the owner by a local government to construct a larger or taller building elsewhere to compensate for restrictions on the right to build on the subject parcel.

2. INVASIONS IN AIRSPACE

A trespass is committed when one's possession is disturbed, whether it is on the ground or in the airspace above it. However, special considerations apply to overflying aircraft.

a. Trespass

Flights at high levels (as set by federal law) are not trespassory because the airlanes have become public highways. Technical private rights of possession at that height give way to the public's right of travel. Flights below the permissible levels may be trespassory, however.

b. Nuisance

Flights overhead or nearby (even if not directly overhead) may constitute a nuisance and may subject the operators or the airport to liability. Frequently an airport will seek to acquire a large apron of land around its perimeter in order to avoid liability for the noise which modern jet engines create. Public policy generally denies injunctive relief to neighboring property owners in such situations, limiting them to damages instead.

c. Taking

If the operator or airport is a governmental entity, adjacent property owners disturbed by its activities may be able to recover under constitutional provisions against the "taking" (in the Fifth Amendment) or "damaging" (in many state constitutions) of private property without just compensation. The property owners may claim that their property has been "inversely condemned" by the value-reducing activities of the airport or the aircraft.

E. FIXTURES

A fixture is a piece of property which was originally classified as personalty (a chattel) but is later treated as realty by virtue of its affixation to real property.

1. AFFIXATION

Conversion of personalty into realty occurs if three criteria are met:

a. Intention

If the chattel is intended (as inferred from the objective circumstances) by the annexor to become a permanent part of the land;

> *Example:* A house is treated as real property rather than as an aggregate of personal property items (nails, planks, etc.) because the objective intent of the builder is to make a permanent improvement to land, even though the structure may be just "resting" on the soil and not fastened down to it. Where a mobile home is involved, such objective intent may be lacking.

b. Annexation
If the chattel is actually annexed to land or to something appurtenant to land;

> *Example:* A toilet bowl, when bolted to the floor, ceases to be personalty and becomes realty because of the durable way in which it has been attached to the house.

c. Adaptation
If the chattel has been appropriated or specially adapted to the use or purpose of the land.

> *Example:* Wall-to-wall carpeting may become a fixture by virtue of having been specially cut to fit the house where it has been laid, even though it is held in place only by a few tacks.

2. EFFECTS
The consequences of a conversion from chattel to fixture differ, depending upon whether or not the annexor is also the owner of the land.

a. Common Ownership
Where both the chattel and the land to which it is affixed are owned by the annexor, frequent consequences are:

1) Subsequent Sale
A deed of the real property transfers title to all of the fixtures as well. Thus a deed describing the lot also transfers the house on the lot and its plumbing fixtures (but not the furniture).

2) Death
At common law, realty descended to the heir, whereas personalty passed to the next of kin. This same situation can arise today where a will devises all realty to one person and all personalty to another. In such a case, the fixtures go with the realty.

3) Mortgage

A real estate mortgage on the property covers all fixtures including (usually) those subsequently affixed. Thus, on foreclosure, the mortgagee may also sell the fixtures to satisfy the debt.

4) Taxation

Fixtures are taxed as real rather than as personal property.

5) Eminent Domain

When the real property is condemned, the condemnor must pay for all the real property, including the fixtures, whereas personalty need not be paid for and is to be instead removed by the owner.

b. **Divided Ownership**

Where the chattel is owned by someone other than the owner of the realty, common consequences (and problem areas) are:

1) Tenants

When a tenant affixes a chattel to the premises, it becomes part of the realty and title then passes to the landlord. Removal by the tenant thereafter might be waste.

a) Trade Fixture Exception

The law permits a tenant to remove chattels installed for the purposes of trade on or before the termination of the lease even though they have become fixtures. In some jurisdictions, the trade fixture exception has been broadened to include domestic and/or ornamental fixtures. The tenant may be required to repair any physical damage caused to the premises by removal of the fixtures.

2) Conditional Sellers

The failure of a conditional seller of a chattel to make a proper reservation of title as to it may result in loss of a security interest in it if it is so affixed as to become a fixture. The chattel seller must be particularly careful when the purchaser is only a tenant and/or when there is a mortgage on the realty. While a security interest in chattels is generally perfected through filing of a financing statement in the secretary of state's office (under the Uniform Commercial Code), that Act requires that security interests in fixtures be recorded in the (county) real estate records ("fixture filing") in order to have priority vis-a-vis other real estate interests.

3) Innocent Improvers

One who improves the property of another may lose title to the improvements if they become fixtures. Innocent improver statutes or the doctrine of adverse possession (if the improver has been in possession long enough) may afford protection in such situations.

F. WASTE

When title to land is divided into present and future interests, the holder of the present possessory interest is prohibited from using the land so as to cause unreasonable harm to the holder of the future interest.

1. PARTIES
The holder of any present possessory estate, i.e., a life tenant, tenant for years, or periodic tenant, is subject to the prohibitions against waste. The burdens differ somewhat as between holders of freehold estates (life tenants) and non-freehold estates (tenants for terms, etc.).

The holder of any future interest in land is protected by the law of waste. Holders of indefeasibly vested future interests (e.g., landlords, vested remaindermen, and reversioners) have greater remedies than holders of lesser interests, such as holders of contingent remainders, powers of termination, and possibilities of reverter. A mortgagee may be protected by the law of waste where the mortgage is treated as a conveyance of a title to the creditor (the "title" theory of mortgages).

The law of waste also protects nonpossessing holders of concurrent interests (e.g., the joint tenant or tenant in common), who has permitted the other to retain sole possession.

2. DEFINITIONS
The original definition of waste was any act which changed the appearance of the property (such that the holder of the future interest did not receive the land in the same condition as it was in when the prior possessor took possession). Modernly, waste has been split into three different categories:

a. Active Waste
This is harm done to the property as a result of acts done by the possessor. It is also called affirmative or voluntary waste. Originally, any act which significantly altered the physical condition of the land was regarded as waste, pursuant to the principle that the holder of the future interest was entitled to receive the land in the same condition as it then was. Four activities were treated as automatically constituting waste under this standard:

(1) Cutting Mature Trees, unless done to prepare the land for cultivation, or for fuel or repairs.

(2) Changing the Course of Husbandry, i.e., putting the land to a different agricultural use.

(3) Removing Minerals, except from mines already open.

(4) Demolishing or significantly altering existing structures, but not when they were erected by the tenant for the purposes of trade—a tenant is allowed to remove "trade fixtures" without liability for waste so long as this can be done without causing substantial harm to the premises. See Chapter XIII.

Subsequently, the doctrine of meliorating waste arose, which permitted the possessor to engage in such acts where their effect was to increase rather than decrease the value of the property. This principle now generally constitutes the revised definition of waste: acts which diminish the market value to the other interests in the property. (However, tenants—as opposed to life tenants—are often held to a more restrictive standard.)

b. Permissive Waste

This is harm resulting from the failure of the possessor to make normal repairs to the property in order to protect it from substantial deterioration (also called passive waste, e.g., failure to keep the premises windtight and watertight). The obligations imposed upon residential tenants are much affected by modern principles of habitability. (See Ch IV.)

1) Rebuilding v Repairing
There is no duty to rebuild structures destroyed by third persons or by acts of nature, although there may be a duty to protect them from further harm (e.g., boarding up the premises). In landlord-tenant situations, this situation is usually covered by repair covenants in the lease.

2) Financial Waste
The holder of the present estate is generally obliged to pay current carrying charges on the property, i.e., taxes and mortgage interest. Since the failure to do so may lead to forfeiture of the entire estate (through tax or foreclosure sales), nonpayment may be regarded as a form of waste, at least up to the amount of income the present estate produces for the possessor. Insurance premiums are not treated as required for the possessor. Consequently, a tenant who obtains insurance only for himself is not required to share the proceeds with the landlord following damage to the premises, but this rule is altered where both parties are named insureds or the lease requires the tenant to insure the landlord's interest as well.

3) Malicious Waste

Where the possessor unconscionably causes waste to the premises, she may be liable for treble damages, will not be protected by any "without impeachment for waste" clause in the lease or other applicable document, may suffer forfeiture of the possessory estate, and may be subject to action by holders of remote or unlikely future interests. This is also called wanton waste. Where the waste is not malicious, these consequences generally do not apply.

3. REMEDIES

The plaintiff may sue for damages, equal to either the cost of restoration, or the reduction in market value of the affected future interest. Where the waste is ongoing, equitable relief in the form of an injunction may issue. A court is unlikely to issue a mandatory injunction forcing the possessor to make repairs, although it may appoint a receiver to take charge of the property and make the repairs in the possessor's place; in some states, residential tenants may collectively petition a court to grant such relief to them when their premises are no longer habitable.

G. REVIEW QUESTIONS

Nora's property is adjacent to Owen's. She is privileged to undertake the following activities.

1. T or F She may excavate in order to build a house on her lot even though the excavation will cause Owen's house to subside, if she can show that his lot would have subsided even if he did not have a house on it.

2. T or F She may continue to burn leaves in her back yard even though the smoke interferes with Owen's use and enjoyment of his own land so long as she began her activity before he put up his house.

3. T or F She may walk across a corner of his property without liability for trespass so long as she believes that the boundary line is so located that she is walking on her own property rather than on his.

4. T or F She may divert water from the stream which flows across her property after it has passed over Owen's property which is upstream from her, even though she is taking the water for commercial use.

5. T or F She may string a power line wire from her house across Owen's lot to the public street without Owen's consent so long as the line never touches the surface of Owen's land.

6. T or F   She may rent part of Owen's property from him, and then build a shed on it, which she may remove at the end of her lease term, even though it has been bolted to the ground.

7. T or F   If she does remove the shed, as stated in the previous question, and thereby disfigures Owen's land, she is liable to him for waste.

XIV

LAND USE

Analysis

A. AUTHORITY TO REGULATE

Land use is subject to the police power of the states. The federal government does not engage in zoning or other direct forms of land use regulation (except on land which it owns) although it does indirectly influence state and local regulation through its allocation of money.

1. DIRECT STATE REGULATION

In only a few jurisdictions is land directly regulated at the state level. Hawaii has a statewide land use classification scheme, and a few other states have a permit process over and above local control which may apply to certain areas (those of "critical environmental concern" in Florida) or statewide (Vermont).

2. REGIONAL REGULATION

A state may create or authorize affected communities to create a regional agency to regulate development in the region because of the special environment and problems existing there, e.g., The (Lake) Tahoe Regional Planning Agency (which is the result of a bi-state compact between California and Nevada approved by Congress).

3. LOCAL REGULATION

The most prevalent form of land use regulation in the United States is at the county and local level, done pursuant to authorization by the state. Every state has some form of enabling act delegating power to regulate land to the local communities.

4. VOTER REGULATION

Some jurisdictions permit land use regulations to be enacted by voter initiative and reviewed by voter referendum. Others permit only the referendum, on the ground that the state enabling act requires a planning process as a preliminary step, which is lacking when the initiative is employed. The propriety of voter involvement may depend upon whether the land use regulation in issue is truly general legislation affecting all residents (such as a city-wide height limit), or a particularized treatment of a small amount of land (such as the rezoning of a single parcel) in which case due process considerations in favor of the landowner may lead to prohibition of zoning by ballot.

B. BASIC FORMS OF LAND USE REGULATION

1. PLANNING

Many states authorize the creation of local planning boards and often require that land use regulations be consistent with land use planning (or be "in accord with a comprehensive plan"). Consequently, there exists in many locales a Planning Commission (aided by a staff Planning Department), whose planning functions usually precede the enactment of land use regulations by the local legislative body. (Since land use regulation usually involves local practices, there is no consistent terminology for the various governmental entities involved; the Planning Commission, e.g., is referred to by different names in different places.)

a. General Plans

It is common for a local planning commission to be charged with drafting a comprehensive (or general or master) plan. Its generality may refer to its inclusion of numerous geographical parts of the community or to its inclusion of numerous aspects of land use concern (e.g., traffic, recreation, safety, etc.). A plan is generally a document stating the community's goals and policies relating to some aspect of the physical (rather than social) development of the locale. Such plans are often created as a result of staff reports by the planning department, hearings for purposes of obtaining public opinion, proposals by the planning commission, and enactments by the local legislative body, although the process varies from state to state as well as from community to community.

b. The Role of Planning

Despite the requirement of planning in most state enabling statutes, many courts do not require that a formal written plan exist as a prerequisite to valid land use regulation (including the Model Land Development Code of the American Law Institute); the planning requirement may be considered met so long as some forethought and/or general considerations are reflected in the legislation, showing that it was not the product of an impulsive response to a particular potential development. Other jurisdictions (notably California, Florida, and Oregon) require the drafting of complex master plans, including "mandatory" elements, such as housing, as a condition precedent to all land use regulation. Such plans may be subject to review by a statewide agency (e.g. the Land Conservation and Development Commission in Oregon) for consistency with statewide goals, and may also be the basis for a further "consistency" requirement that all land use regulation (subsequently enacted or perhaps even preexisting) be consistent with the comprehensive plan.

> *Example:* The community's general plan states that the northeastern part of the city should be kept as open space and low density use. However, the city's zoning ordinance permits heavy industrial uses there. In some jurisdictions, this inconsistency will lead to invalidation of the zoning ordinance.

2. ZONING

A zoning law usually consists of a zoning ordinance, specifying the regulations applicable to each zone, and a zoning map, indicating the zone characteristic of each parcel of land within the community. Zones (or districts) may be regulated as to use, height, and/or land coverage (bulk).   Within each district, the applicable restrictions should be uniform.

a.   Common Types of Zones
    1)   Use Districts
        Typical use districts are residential, commercial, industrial, and agricultural.   These districts may be further subdivided as to intensity of the permitted use.   Residential use districts are generally divided along a continuum from the single-family house down to the high-rise apartment building; commercial and industrial uses are often divided into light and heavy.   When an activity is regulated according to its external effects (e.g., noise, smoke), this sort of control is referred to as performance zoning.

        Example: In 1922, Euclid, Ohio was divided into 6 use districts: U–1 (single family dwellings and farming); U–2 (two-family dwellings); U–3 (apartments and hotels); U–4 (offices, retail stores and theatres); U–5 (warehouses and factories); U–6 (junk yards, cemeteries and garbage facilities).

        a)   Single Family Districts
           The most universal kind of residential zone is the single family district; it is also the most highly regarded.   However, it may be difficult to define.   The United States Supreme Court has upheld a single family district where family was defined to exclude any group of over two persons not related by blood or marriage.   (See *Village of Belle Terre v. Boraas* (1974).)   However, many state courts have held such form of classification invalid, either on constitutional privacy or associational grounds, or because they believe that such ordinances should be worded according to the physical nature of the structures rather than the personal relationship of the occupants.

    2)   Height Districts
        Building height regulation is one of the oldest forms of land use regulation.   A community may set different height limits for different parts of town.   These height limits may or may not coincide with use and bulk districts.

        Example: Euclid also had three height limit districts: H–1 (2½ stories or 35 feet); H–2 (4 stories or 50 feet); H–3 (80 feet).

    3)   Land Coverage
        Land coverage or bulk regulations take many forms.   The more common ones are listed below:

a)   Minimum Floor Space
      Example: Wayne Township, New Jersey, in 1949, required that
                  every one-story dwelling contain at least 768 square
                  feet and every two-story dwelling contain at least
                  1000 square feet of floor space. Lionshead Lake, Inc.
                  v. Wayne Township (1952), since held invalid in Home
                  Builders League Inc. v. Township of Berlin (1979).

b)   Minimum Lot Size
      Example: Easttown Township, Pennsylvania, in 1963, required a
                  minimum lot size of four acres per house. National
                  Land & Investment Co. v. Kohn (1965) held invalid.

c)   Floor-Area Ratio

      An FAR of 2 permits a building to contain twice as much floor
      space as there is lot area; thus if the lot is 1000 square feet the
      building may contain 2000 square feet of floor space (e.g., it may
      be built as a two-story building occupying the entire lot, or as a
      four-story building occupying one-half the lot). In San Francisco,
      FARs for residential buildings run from 1.8 to 4.8; the FAR of
      the Empire State Building in New York City is 25.

d)   Setback
      A front setback requires that every building be set back x feet
      from the lot line; a rear yard setback requires that every
      building leave open a rear yard of x feet (or x percent of the
      total space); a side yard setback requires that each building be
      set back x feet from its side lot line(s), so that all buildings are
      detached from each other.

e)   Open Space
      Most zoning ordinances prohibit a building from occupying the
      entire lot and require some minimum percentage of the land (up
      to 80% in some suburbs) to be preserved as open space.

f)   Cluster
      A cluster zoning ordinance permits the owner/developer of several
      parcels to comply with the density requirements listed above on
      an aggregate basis for the entire development, even though any
      given lot might be out of compliance. Thus, the buildings may
      be set close to one another (violating the setback ordinance for
      individual parcels) because sufficient open space has been
      preserved elsewhere in the development.

(1) *Planned Unit Development.* If the clustering principle is applied to use as well as density regulations, the ordinance or scheme is generally referred to as a planned unit development (PUD). Such an ordinance provides overall restrictions (e.g., not less than 80% residence and not more than 20% commercial in the entire development) but permits the developer to determine where each use will be sited in the project (as well as permitting a clustering of density features). (A community's power to regulate in this manner may be restricted by a state planned community enabling act.) Such ordinances frequently provide for developer application for appropriate PUD rezoning and simultaneous submission of site plans, followed by review of all aspects by a single agency. Unlike conventional anticipatory zoning, planning officials react to proposals made by the developer and engage in considerable bargaining over the project.

4) Floating Zones
A zoning ordinance may permit a certain type of use, but not include it within any of the districts actually shown on the zoning map. Such a use or zone "floats" until, upon application by a property owner, it is brought down and fastened onto some particular parcel. Thereafter, that parcel is subject to the new zoning. (Planned unit development is a use which often floats in this fashion.)

Example: Tarrytown, New York, in 1947, created a Residence B–B district for garden apartments of less than 3 stories on lots of over 10 acres, but no such district was ever mapped. The ordinance provided that such a district would be mapped whenever a qualified owner applied for such zoning. Rodgers v. Village of Tarrytown (1951).

5) Holding Zones
A community may be unprepared to comprehensively zone its entire territory at one time. In order to restrict development from occurring in an area before there has been an opportunity to plan and zone it, the planning board may temporarily zone the land for very low intensity uses. Such a holding zone (or other form of interim zoning) will be upheld if it is a bona fide effort by the community to give itself an opportunity to plan, but not when it is merely an attempt to preserve land as open space without having to pay for it.

b. **Common Characteristics**
Although not true of all zoning ordinances, most contain the following features in one form or another:

1)   Cumulative Uses
     Generally, uses are ranked on a hierarchy running from single family
     residential (as the "highest use") down to heavy industrial. Higher
     uses are usually permitted in lower use districts. When some or all
     higher uses are excluded from lower use zones, the zone is referred to
     as noncumulative or exclusive.

2)   Conditional Uses/Special Exceptions/Special Use
     A category midway between those uses prohibited in a zone and those
     permitted "as of right" consists of those *uses which may be allowed
     only after a special permit has been obtained following a discretionary
     review and the possible imposition of special conditions.* Activities such
     as hospitals, schools and churches are often permitted in most zones,
     but only after special consideration of the individual project (e.g.,
     impact upon the neighborhood, proximity of similar institutions) and
     the creation of special restrictions to ameliorate adverse effects (e.g.,
     landscaping, or noise and hour restrictions). A different agency from
     the planning commission (commonly called a board of adjustment)
     generally performs this function subject to standards set by the local
     legislative body.

3)   Nonconforming Uses
     When an already developed area is made subject to zoning, it is likely
     that some existing uses (such as billboards, gas stations, and
     junkyards) would no longer be allowable as new uses in the district.
     However, since such uses preceded the zoning it is customary for
     them to be allowed to continue as nonconforming uses. The structure
     rather than the use may be nonconforming, where new height or bulk
     regulations are enacted to cover already improved property. *Both
     local governments and courts are reluctant to order an owner to
     immediately discontinue an activity or to demolish a building which was
     lawful until the enactment of the new ordinance, because it may
     constitute a taking of property.*

     a)   Permissible Restrictions
          Because of the undesirability of nonconforming uses, a variety of
          restrictive techniques have been employed and are generally
          upheld:

          (1) *Resumption.* If the use is discontinued for a certain period
               of time or if the structure is destroyed, the owner may be
               denied permission to resume the use or rebuild the structure.

          (2) *Enlargement.* The owner may be denied permission to
               enlarge the structure or change the use of the property,
               except to convert it into a conforming use or structure.

(3) *Amortization.* The owner may be allowed only a certain number of years to continue the nonconforming features of the structure or activity. Courts generally uphold such amortization periods if they determine that the time involved is reasonable (i.e. 10 to 20 years).

c. Vested Rights

In order to acquire nonconforming use protection it is not always necessary that the structure have come fully into existence at the time that the new prohibitory regulation takes effect. If, for instance, construction is under way and the owner has a "vested right" to complete the project, the same protection may be afforded. *Generally, one obtains a vested right after having obtained a building permit and expended substantial funds in detrimental reliance on it before a new law has taken effect.*

d. Relief From the Zoning Ordinance
1) Variances

Most zoning ordinances allow the board of adjustment to grant a variance to a property owner when strict enforcement of the ordinance would cause unnecessary hardship because of the unique nature of the property. It is generally required that the board find that the grant of a variance will not adversely affect neighboring properties or the effectiveness of the zoning ordinance, and it may impose conditions upon the variance to mitigate its impact. The variance may deal either with a use restriction (e.g., permitting a grocery store in a residential zone) or a bulk restriction (e.g., waiving a height limit or setback requirement). Some jurisdictions do not permit use variances, and others (notably New York) require that greater hardship be established for a use variance than is needed for a bulk or area variance. It is common for conditions to be attached to the grant of the variance, e.g., landscaping or limitations in the intensity of the activity (number of hours open for business, number of cars, etc.).

a) Hardship

An owner must show more than that the property will have greater value in order to obtain a variance. He must show "unnecessary hardship," i.e., a deprivation to him of the privileges which all other owners have, because of the special nature (its topography or location) of his parcel. The hardship cannot be self-inflicted (e.g., selling off part of the parcel and then claiming that the part left is too small to comply with the minimum lot size). Courts disagree as to whether the purchase of property with notice of its restriction amounts to self-inflicted hardship.

2) Amendments (Rezoning)
An alternative form of relief available to a property owner is to *request the local legislative body to amend the zoning ordinance so as to rezone the parcel in question to a more desirable classification.* Rezoning is legislative, rather than administrative or quasi-judicial (unlike variances and special exceptions/conditional uses) and is done by the city or county council rather than by one of its land use agencies (the planning commission or board of adjustment).

a) Restrictions
Rezoning appears more subject to abuse than original zoning, and has consequently been subject to greater judicial scrutiny and legislative restriction.

(1) *Neighbor Protest.* Many statutes provide that rezoning of a parcel must be accomplished by a supermajority vote of the local legislative body (e.g. 75% rather than 51%) whenever a certain percentage (e.g. 20%) of the affected neighbors protest the change.

(2) *Mistake or Change of Condition.* Some courts require that the rezoning change be justified by showing that there was some mistake in the original zoning, or that conditions have changed since the zoning designation was first made.

(3) *Administrative Rather Than Legislative Act.* Led by the Oregon Supreme Court, some courts have held that rezoning of a single parcel of land is an administrative (or quasi-judicial) act despite its legislative appearance. This eliminates the deferential presumption of validity that true legislative zoning amendments have and subjects the enactment to much stricter judicial review. Fasano v. Board of County Commissioners (1973). Other courts have explicitly rejected this doctrine, and continue to treat rezoning as legislative, regardless of the size of the land rezoned.

(4) *Spot Zoning.* When the rezoning confers benefits on the affected parcel which are generally denied to other properties and a court can find no special circumstances to justify such preferential treatment, it may characterize the amendment as "spot zoning" and hold it invalid. Spot zoning is regarded by most observers as a short hand term for action which is arbitrary or not in accord with a comprehensive plan.

b)   Contract Rezoning
      If property is rezoned in return for the owner's promise to abide
      by special limitations or to grant certain benefits to the
      community (such as dedication of part of the land for street
      widening or recreation or imposition of special restrictions on the
      activity, such as short business hours) this arrangement is called
      contract (or conditional) zoning. Because it results in lack of
      uniform application of the zoning ordinance (since the restrictions
      or conditions imposed do not apply to other parcels similarly
      zoned), it is held invalid by a few courts.

c)   Holding Zones
      If the community is unprepared to comprehensively zone its
      entire territory at the start, it may effectively prohibit
      development in certain areas by zoning them for uses that are of
      such low density as to make it unprofitable for their owners to
      engage in any development whatsoever (e.g., single family
      residential with a minimum lot size of 10 acres).

      (1)   *Interim Zoning.* Where the community is seeking time to
            plan and needs to head off development for the time being
            in order to preserve its options, it may enact an interim
            zoning ordinance prohibiting development until the plan is
            devised. Legislation may permit such an ordinance to be
            enacted on an emergency basis, without prior notice, hearing,
            or planning, if there is first a supermajority vote and the
            ordinance has a short duration (e.g., one year).

      (2)   *Wait and See Zoning.* By making zoning overrestrictive, the
            community is generally able to require that all owners
            intending development obtain appropriate rezoning first. This
            technique can give the legislative body far more effective
            control over any project than does conventional zoning. It
            also permits the legislative body to require concessions from
            the owners which it could not demand under traditional as
            of right zoning-based uniform present standards.

3. SUBDIVISION REGULATION

*When a parcel of land is subdivided into smaller lots, and a map of that
subdivision is sought to be recorded, the local authority has the power—as a
condition of approving and recording the subdivision map—to require compliance
with demands it imposes upon the subdivider.* It may, for example, compel a
rearrangement of the proposed streets for better fire truck access. There may
also be regulation of the location of utilities and the siting of schools, parks,
etc.

a.   Compared to Zoning

A community's power to regulate the subdivision of land is not derived
from its power to zone and is generally separately authorized by a state
Subdivision Map Act or city planning enabling act.   It may be overseen
by the same agencies involved in the zoning process, but it lacks the
preset, definite standards which are supposed to characterize zoning.
Approval of a subdivision is more of a bargaining process between the
subdivider and the planning department.   Development of a tract of land
must generally comply both with the subdivision ordinance (as to street
layout, lot placement, etc.) and the zoning ordinance (as to segregation of
uses, control of density, etc.) and perhaps also the comprehensive plan.

1)   Mechanics
Approval and development of a subdivision typically proceeds
according to the following steps:

(a)   The developer submits a tentative or preliminary subdivision map,
showing how she proposes to subdivide and develop the property
(i.e. streets, public facilities, residences, etc.) to the appropriate
public agency.

(b)   The map is reviewed by all interested agencies, proposals are
made for changes to make the plan more acceptable to them, and
concessions are made by the developer to obtain the necessary
approvals.

(c)   When agreement is reached, following the above negotiations,
there is official approval of the tentative map.

(d)   The developer constructs the required public improvements (roads,
sewers, etc.) called for on the tentative map.

(e)   When those improvements are completed, the developer submits a
final subdivision map which, if consistent with the tentative map,
is approved and recorded.

(f)   The developer may now commence selling individual parcels in
the subdivision by deeds referring to their location on the
subdivision map.

If the subdivision is to consist of completed residences, the developer
will obtain building permits for them at some appropriate stage of the
process; such permits will be issued if they are consistent with both
the proposed subdivision map and with all existing zoning ordinances.
There may also exist between the developer and the government a

development agreement whereby the government agrees that the developer will not be affected by changes in the zoning laws which occur after the tentative map has been approved and before building permits have been issued or residences constructed.

b.   When Applicable

Subdivision regulation comes into play only if land is being divided into a subdivision, as defined by state law or local ordinance. This may depend upon the number of lots resulting from the division (under or over 5), the size of lots (e.g., more or less than 10 acres per parcel), and the purpose of the subdivision (e.g., residential or industrial).

c.   Exactions

A community generally requires the subdivider to construct roads, sewers and other offsite improvements in the subdivision as a condition for permitting a map to be recorded. It also usually requires dedication of the streets in the subdivision to it. As local governments face greater budgetary difficulties, they tend to impose more severe exactions upon subdividers, requiring them to dedicate land (or pay a fee in lieu of land) for parks, playgrounds, schools and other public services. In a few jurisdictions, these charges are impermissible unless they are "specifically and uniquely attributable" to needs created by the subdivision; but other courts uphold them so long as there is some reasonable relationship between the charge and the benefit to the subdivision. A demand for space for a park which serves citywide as well as subdivision needs might be rejected under the first test, but upheld under the second. The United States Supreme Court has ruled that a demand by the California Coastal Commission, that owners of beachfront property grant the public an easement of access over their property as a condition to rebuilding their house, constituted an impermissible taking of their property on the ground that there was no "nexus" between the demand (beachfront access) and the burden it sought to alleviate (blocking the view of the coast from the highway). Nollan v. California Coastal Commission (1987). If this standard is applied to subdivision exactions, it may be considerably stricter than the "reasonable relationship" standard described above.

d.   Sales

The regulation of sales by the subdivider to the public is not a matter of direct land use control and is rarely regulated by the local community. However, there is a significant body of state and federal regulation in this field, concerned primarily with consumer protection. Most laws are of the disclosure variety, requiring the subdivider to reveal to prospective purchasers the arrangements which have been made for roads, water, sewers, etc.

4. OTHER FORMS OF LAND USE REGULATION
a. Growth Management
In order to stop population growth from outstripping the community's ability to supply services, a local government may restrict the number of residential building permits issued. Under such a program, a property owner may not be allowed to build even though the applicable zoning and other conventional land use controls otherwise permit residential construction. The various mechanisms employed are:

1) Moratorium
The ordinance may entirely stop the issuance of residential building permits until some date in the future or the occurrence of some future event (e.g., the elimination of overcrowding in schools and overloading of water and sewage facilities, in Livermore, California).

2) Points
The ordinance may permit an owner to obtain a building permit only after having acquired a requisite number of points, in terms of services or amenities desired by the community (e.g., availability of sewage, drainage, parks, roads and firehouses; see Golden v. Planning Board of Ramapo (New York 1972)).

3) Quota
The ordinance may limit the issuance of building permits to a certain number per year (e.g., 500 allocated according to a point system, in Petaluma, California; see Construction Industry Ass'n v. City of Petaluma (1975)) or to certain geographic areas (e.g., areas designated as "urban development centers," in San Jose, California), or by some other method (e.g., 1 permit a year for every 10 acres owned by the applicant, in Raymond, New Hampshire).

b. Historic Preservation
A city may prohibit the owner of a landmark *building* from tearing it down or remodeling it. It could do so by purchasing a preservation easement in the building or its exterior, but it may also prohibit demolition or alteration of any building it has designated as noteworthy. Although such a technique may appear to discriminatorily single out certain buildings (thereby lacking the uniformity expected in zoning situations), it will nevertheless be upheld if it is part of a comprehensive plan. A city may also preserve an *entire district* as historic by appropriate zoning and design restrictions so as to regulate architecture within the district.

Examples: (1) In 1978, New York City prohibited the Pennsylvania Central Transportation Company from erecting a 55 story office building atop Grand Central Terminal so as to preserve

the Terminal as a landmark structure. Penn Central
Transportation Co. v. City of New York (1978).

(2) In 1936, New Orleans, Louisiana, enacted the Vieux Carre
Ordinance, by which a Commission regulates architecture
within the city's French Quarter and is charged with
preserving buildings there which have architectural and
historic value.

c. Sign Regulation

A community may regulate the size and placement of billboards. Courts
sometimes declare that aesthetic considerations cannot be the sole basis of
a regulation but may be included along with other purposes as a
justification. Sign ordinances are, therefore, sometimes upheld on other
than aesthetic grounds (e.g., in order to prevent crimes from occurring
behind billboards). Ordinances which entirely ban signs or billboards raise
First Amendment issues which have not been fully resolved by the courts.
The location of the sign (on-site or off-site), its content (e.g., commercial or
political), the nature of the restrictions (e.g., a ban or a size limitation),
and the alternative means of communication available are factors
commonly considered in such cases.

d. Architectural Control

A local ordinance may provide that no building permit (or renovation
permit, etc.) may be issued until there has been approval of the exterior
plans by a design review board (frequently composed of local architects
and persons in related professions). The validity of such ordinances has
not been completely resolved. Originally upheld as devices to protect
property values, aesthetic controls are now recognized as a legitimate form
of zoning control. They are frequently attacked on the ground that the
standards employed are too vague, that there is an improper delegation of
power to the design review board, that such control goes beyond the
proper purposes of land use regulation, or that it intrudes upon protected
speech.

e. Site Plan Review

In order to retain discretion to reject or modify projects despite their
conformity to all existing zoning standards, an ordinance may provide for
review of all aspects of the project, similar to subdivision review, and the
attendant power to demand changes as a condition for governmental
approval. Such a policy eliminates entirely the original notion of zoning
as establishing present standards uniformly applicable to all projects
within the zone, thereby entitling owners to build as of right when their
plans conformed to the existing rules, and replaces it with a system of
discretionary review and reaction to proposals generated by owners on an
ad hoc and negotiated basis.

f.   Environmental Review
The National Environmental Protection Act (NEPA) and similar state acts require all governmental agencies to consider the environmental consequences of their actions by way of preparation of an environmental impact statement (EIS) or report (EIR). Such a study typically identifies adverse environmental effects of a proposed project and considers any alternatives which would have less severe impact or measures which could mitigate against those effects. Generally, such a study is required for any project which requires governmental approval or permits, even though it is undertaken by private individuals. These statutes mandate consideration of the environmental impact of a project, but do not necessarily require the agency to refuse approval solely because of an adverse environmental effect.

g.   Performance Standards
Zoning may often accomplish its purpose of reducing the undesirable external effects of many activities by focussing upon the effects of the activities rather than upon the activities themselves, e.g., if the community is concerned with the smoke emitted from factories, it need not necessarily zone out factories but can zone according to their smoke emission, only permitting those with discharges below a certain standard to operate within the district. Performance standards are directed at noise, pollutants, smells, etc. and often overlap with conventional use and bulk zoning standards.

h.   Substantive Environmental Protection
Fragile, threatened, or endangered environmental resources are often subject to special regulation at the state or federal level. Generally, a special agency oversees and requires special permits for activities affecting the designated resource.

Examples: (1) Under the Federal Clean Air Act, the Environmental Protection Agency, and comparable state agencies, monitors emissions from sources such as factories and industrial operations in areas where ambient air is a concern. These agencies may also require control equipment be used to lower emissions from new or modified equipment, as well as retrofitted to existing equipment.

(2) Several Atlantic, Pacific, and Gulf Coast states have enacted statutes that authorize specific state agencies to map wetland areas and regulate their use and development. Generally, these statutes contain specific procedures for the permit process, restrictive standards for evaluation of permit applications, and penalties for violations. The United States

Army Corps of Engineers has similar responsibilities with regard to wetlands under the Federal Clean Water Act.

i. Eminent Domain

Where more direct or affirmative control of land use is desired, a community may utilize its eminent domain power to acquire title to property and then put it to the desired use. Zoning and related devices may generally prohibit a property owner from putting the property to uses objected to by the government, but rarely can compel the owner to put the property to the particular use most desired by the government; that can best be accomplished by the government acquiring title to the property so that it can dictate the particular use to which it will be put.

Example: If the city desires to have property in its crowded central area maintained as a park, it is unlikely that this can be accomplished through zoning, since such restrictive regulation would generally constitute a taking of the property so affected. Instead, the City may acquire the parcel through eminent domain proceedings and then operate it itself as an urban park. (See Fred F. French Investing Co. v. City of New York (1976).)

1) Acquisition and Compensation

Where the owner is unwilling to sell, the government may acquire title through judicial proceedings (sometimes referred to as condemnation actions) leading to transfer of title to the government and payment to the owner. The constitutional requirement of just compensation is generally satisfied by a judicial determination of the value of the property taken, which the government must pay (or else abandon the acquisition proceedings). The government is usually not required to pay the value of the property under the best possible use.

2) Public Use

The constitutional requirement is that property be taken only for public use. This standard is obviously satisfied when the land is taken for park purposes or for street widening or public utility needs. The courts have been so accepting of local legislative declarations of public use that this standard is now generally understood to mean public purpose rather than public use, i.e., eliminating the need for government itself to actually develop or maintain the acquired property.

Examples: (1) The District of Columbia engaged in an urban renewal project which led to its acquisition of all of the land in a slum neighborhood ("slum clearance") for redevelopment projects. The government action was upheld despite the facts that 1) some of the buildings taken were not themselves slums, and 2) after acquisition, the buildings were turned over to private individuals who agreed to develop the properties in accord with the redevelopment plan (i.e., "taking property from A to give to B"). See Berman v. Parker (1954).

(2) The state of Hawaii enacted a statute allowing a state agency to require large landowners to sell land to the tenant/occupants at prices set by the agency as part of a "land reform" measure. Although the Ninth Circuit Court of Appeals held that there was no public use involved, the Supreme Court held that the mechanism didn't violate the Fifth Amendment standard. Hawaii Housing Authority v. Midkiff (1984).

3) Inverse Condemnation
    Owners of property who believe that government has in fact taken their property through overly restrictive regulation may sue either to stop the activity or to recover compensation for what has happened. The latter proceeding is referred to as inverse condemnation, indicating that the condemnation action (for compensation) is occurring after, rather than before, the taking has occurred as in normal condemnation actions. Until recently, most states rejected owners' rights to recover compensation for improper regulation, limiting them to invalidation proceedings.

j. **Regulating Adult Businesses**
    Many communities regard adult movie theatres, book stores, and similar sexually oriented business activities as detrimental to their general welfare. However, because such activities involve constitutionally protected speech, outright prohibition is not possible. Instead, attempts are made to isolate and insulate these from other, especially residential, activities. Some communities regulate these activities by concentrating them into a single confined area; others do the exact opposite and prevent concentration by requiring that each activity be separated by some minimum distance from any similar activity. Both types of ordinances generally require that such activities be kept at some minimum distance from residential, church, and school districts (putting a "halo" around these protected activities).

    Example: Boston and Seattle have created "combat zones" confining all sexually oriented businesses to a single district in their downtowns. Detroit and Renton, on the other hand, require that each such business be separated by at least 1000 feet from any other such business.

k.   Impact Fees
Communities often impose fees upon new development, whether subdivision or construction, in order to offset the costs which the community will incur by servicing the development and its inhabitants. Such charges are frequently attacked on the ground that the services being funded are traditionally paid for by all residents through their taxes and that these charges are disguised special taxes, imposed on new but not old residents. Judicial reaction to such fees has been generally similar to the treatment of subdivision exactions, to which these charges are quite similar.

C.   JUDICIAL REVIEW OF REGULATIONS

1.   PARTIES
Property owners who object to the restrictions imposed upon them by regulations often sue to have them set aside. Developers often attack restrictions imposed upon owners on the ground that the restrictions will burden them if they acquire the property and/or will burden new buyers after the property is developed (frequently by raising the cost of housing, to the detriment of the poor). Neighbors who oppose the lifting of restriction (or the failure to impose them) on a parcel of land often sue to set aside whatever development permit the property owner has obtained from a government agency. More recently, various welfare organizations have begun to challenge regulations which make local housing or employment impossible or too expensive for their constituents. As plaintiffs, these organizations, along with developers, confront serious standing problems, especially in federal courts.

2.   SCOPE OF REVIEW
Most land use regulation is legislation done under the police power for the general welfare of the community. As such, it is subject to a presumption of validity and is upheld if the regulation bears a rational relationship to a permissible state objective.

a.   Administrative
When the official action involved is administrative or quasi-judicial rather than legislative, then courts generally inquire as to whether there is substantial evidence to support the action taken.

1)   Form or Substance
The traditional distinction between legislative and administrative land use activity turns upon the form of the action involved: zonings and rezonings are legislative because they are enacted by the local legislative body in legislative form, whereas variances and special exceptions are administrative because they are handled by a nonelected, appointed agency. Recently, some courts have questioned this approach and have held that a rezoning is administrative when

only a small parcel of land is involved. As such, the standard of review then becomes less deferential.

3. GROUNDS FOR ATTACK

Land use regulations are held invalid on a variety of grounds. There is no uniformity of standard, or even of characterization of the standard among the courts. Thus the matters discussed below could be classified in many other, different ways.

a. Unauthorized

Local land use regulation must generally be authorized by the state enabling act, delegating the requisite police power from the state to the community. New forms of local regulation are usually challenged on the ground that they are unauthorized if state law does not specifically provide for them. Noncumulative zoning, contract zoning, floating zones, planned unit development, growth management, historic preservation and architectural review have all been put to this test, and in some states have been held invalid for that reason.

b. Improper Delegation

A legislative body may delegate regulatory power to others only when it is accompanied by appropriate standards. Thus a design review ordinance, requiring review board approval of architectural plans without setting forth the basis for making such judgments, may be held invalid for this reason.

1) Neighbor Consent

An ordinance which prohibits certain activity from being conducted in a neighborhood unless a certain percentage of the neighbors approve may be held invalid on the ground that it improperly delegates legislative power to the neighbors.

c. Arbitrary

Wholly arbitrary ordinances are held invalid on the ground that they exceed the police power authority of the community or that they deny the affected parties (substantive) due process or equal protection of law. Arbitrary distinctions as to restrictions (e.g., prohibiting banks, but not savings and loans) or arbitrary boundaries (as to one side of the street rather than the other or the middle of the block) or arbitrary treatment of parcels (such as *spot zoning* a single parcel more favorably or more severely than all the surrounding parcels) are often invalidated by the courts.

Example: The United States Supreme Court invalidated a provision of the zoning ordinance of the City of Cleburne, TX, which required group homes for retarded persons to obtain a special use permit (also required for insane asylums, alcohol and drug centers, prisons and jails) on equal protection grounds because there was no rational basis for treating such facilities different from apartment, boarding, and fraternity houses and hospitals. (City of Cleburne v. Cleburne Living Center (1985).)

d. Improper Procedure

The imposition of any land use regulation must comply with appropriate standards of fairness in its enactment. Administrative regulations generally require significantly more notice and participation by affected persons than does general legislation, but even the latter may be set aside if parliamentary procedures were not properly followed or if there was bias or corruption on the part of the decision makers.

1) Interim Ordinances

The local government may be authorized to bypass the notice and hearing process for the enactment of emergency ordinances on a temporary basis. Such interim ordinances frequently require a supermajority vote and may exist only for a limited period of time (e.g., 12 or 18 months).

e. Speech and Association

Land use regulations may not intrude too far upon constitutionally protected rights of speech, association, and religion.

1) Speech

Activities which are considered to be engaged in speech, e.g., book stores, movie theatres, signs, etc. gain special protection under the First Amendment, and may not be arbitrarily excluded from a community through zoning ordinances. "Time, place, and manner" restrictions may validly be imposed (such as regulating the size of billboards or the hours of theatres), but such restrictions must be content neutral, and not primarily intended to suppress rather than regulate the speech in question. this creates special problems for sign ordinances distinguishing between e.g., commercial and non-commercial speech, or theatre ordinances distinguishing between adult and general movies.

2) Association

Single family zoning ordinances are held invalid by many state courts when they operate by defining the permitted uses in terms of the relationship between the occupants, rather than according to physical characteristics of the premises, e.g., by excluding groups of persons not related by blood or marriage rather than by excluding residences with separate entryways, utility meters, or bathrooms. Defining such zones in terms of social relationships is regarded as going beyond legitimate zoning purposes and intruding into the associational rights of persons desiring to live in the district.

3) Religion

The exclusion of churches from residential zones is sometimes regarded as unconstitutional under the First Amendment. Many courts do require that extra consideration be given to the claims of religious organizations for special treatment under the zoning rules. Where churches are given a protected status, it then becomes necessary to determine what ancillary church activities are also entitled to receive such protection (e.g., a parochial school, a pastor's residence, a community drop-in center, or a drug counselling or halfway house operated by the church).

f. **Taking**

Federal and state constitutions all provide that private property shall not be taken without just compensation. A land use regulation which operates so oppressively upon a particular parcel of land as to amount to a confiscation of its value and which does not provide for the payment of compensation to the owner may be deemed to have improperly "taken" the owner's property. No uniform analysis has yet appeared in the field of regulatory takings. Some commonly employed factors are:

1) Nature of the Act

It is easier to find a taking where the government has actually acquired title or possession or has physically damaged property than when it has merely reduced its value by severe regulation. However, the lack of any physical invasion does not mean that no taking has occurred.

2) Governmental Purpose

A taking is more likely to be found where no significant public benefit results from the regulation, since courts frequently balance the harm to the property owner against the benefit to the public. Some suggest that the government may depress property values in order to prevent a harm to the public but not in order to confer a benefit on the public, or that it may regulate among competing private interests but may not thereby acquire resources for itself. A related standard measures the nexus between the burden sought to be eliminated and the exaction demanded, and may find a taking when that connection is too weak; this was earlier discussed in connection with subdivision exactions.

3) Interest Affected

The owner must have a protected property interest before a taking can be claimed to have occurred from loss of it. This is sometimes referred to as a "vested right" or a "distinct investment-backed expectation." The owner of an undeveloped lot has no vested right to the continuance of its current zoning, whereas the owner of a completed building has nonconforming use protection against any immediate abatement after a change in the regulations.

4) Extent of Loss
Land use regulations causing losses of up to 90% of the value of property have been upheld against taking challenges, despite statements by the court that the extent of diminution is relevant. There are some judicial statements that a taking occurs only when the parcel is left with no economic value whatsoever. Courts are also more willing to tolerate a heavy loss when its duration is limited rather than permanent (as in a temporary moratorium).

5) Spreading the Loss
A loss which falls upon a single owner (as in spot zoning or landmark preservation) is more likely to be invalidated than one whose burdens are shared by a large segment of the community (e.g., single-family zoning of an entire neighborhood). A widespread burden implies an "average reciprocity of advantage" to each owner because of the similar burdens imposed on the others, which makes the restriction more justifiable.

6) Mitigation
A regulation may be saved from judicial invalidation by virtue of granting a variance to an owner who would otherwise be unfairly oppressed by it. Some ordinances provide for tax relief or some other form of compensation in order to ward off taking challenges.

   a) Transferable Development Rights
   A much discussed technique for both reducing the economic impact of a restriction in the owner (thereby making it less likely to work a taking, or alternatively being treated as compensation to the owner when a taking has occurred) is the TDR. In return for denying permission to develop the lot in question, the owner is given the right to utilize those unused development rights in some other area where they may be employed to create a larger than otherwise permitted structure. If the owner does not own property in the receiving district, they may sell the TDR to owners in that district. This technique has been employed in New York City as a device to save two small parks (unsuccessfully; see Fred F. French Investing Co. v. City of New York, (1976) and to prohibit construction over Grand Central Station (successfully; see Penn Central Transport Co. v. City of New York (1978). It is also used by communities to protect

environmentally sensitive areas, farm land, and to control growth management.

7) Relief
The traditional remedy against excessive regulation of land was invalidation of the restriction. However, in 1987 the United States Supreme Court ruled that the just compensation clause may require that the government pay damages to the injured landowner, as if the government had temporarily acquired the property during the period when its regulation denied the owner all use of the property. The landowner is thus entitled to bring an action for inverse condemnation, as described earlier, as well as or in lieu of a proceeding to declare the regulation invalid.

g. **Exclusionary**
Through a combination of large lot size and minimum floor space requirements, maximum bedroom restrictions, exclusion of apartments and mobile homes, and related devices, a community can so drive up the cost of housing as to effectively exclude middle and lower income persons from residing there. Since poorer residents impose greater burdens on municipal services and the municipal budget, there is often a strong desire, especially in the suburbs, to do so. However, as housing becomes more scarce and as more people flee from decaying cities into developing small towns in the outlying areas, these exclusionary techniques are becoming subject to increasingly critical judicial scrutiny.

1) Federal Courts
Decisions of the United States Supreme Court appear to hold that:

(a) housing is not a fundamental right;

(b) the right to travel is not infringed upon by land use regulations which make it difficult for certain persons to reside there;

(c) income is not a suspect classification;

(d) an Equal Protection case, in terms of race, requires a showing of discriminatory intent and not just discriminatory effect.

Thus it is fairly difficult to make out an effective exclusionary zoning case at the federal constitutional level. There are some indications that the Federal Fair Housing Act (Title VIII of the Civil Rights Act of 1968) may afford more generous relief to persons aggrieved by exclusionary zoning.

2)   State Courts
     Several state courts have not shown the same reluctance as the
     federal courts to intervene into local land use decisions which exclude
     the poor. In 1975, the New Jersey Supreme Court held that the
     general welfare requirement of the state constitution required a
     municipality to make a "variety and choice of housing" for rich and
     poor "realistically possible". Southern Burlington County NAACP v.
     Mt. Laurel Township (1975) (commonly referred to as Mt. Laurel I).
     Subsequently, that court held that townships located in state
     designated growth areas whose zoning restrictions are shown to limit
     construction of low and moderate income housing must not only
     eliminate those regulations which increase the cost of housing, but
     must also take steps to affirmatively provide or encourage the
     construction of such housing, by application for federal housing
     subsidies, and devices such as mandatory set-asides and density
     bonuses (described below). Southern Burlington County NAACP v. Mt.
     Laurel Township (1983) (Mt. Laurel II). The courts of New York and
     Pennsylvania have since authored opinions similar to Mt. Laurel, and
     the New Jersey legislature has enacted a statute providing for
     creation of a state Council of Affordable Housing to oversee these
     questions (combined with a moratorium on judicial action for six
     years), which has been upheld by the New Jersey Supreme Court.

     a)   Remedies
          Where a court finds the local zoning ordinances to be
          exclusionary, it may simply invalidate those which it determines
          are "undue cost generators", and leave the community to enact
          replacement measures. If it has reason to suspect that the
          community will only engage in further delaying tactics, it may
          appoint a special master to propose revisions in the zoning
          scheme which the court will then order adopted. If the action
          was brought by a party who wants to build housing in the
          community, but has been frustrated by the town's exclusionary
          devices, a builder's remedy can be granted, i.e., the town will be
          ordered to grant a building permit (or other appropriate license)
          to the plaintiff to permit her to construct her project. In
          Massachusetts, a state agency may overturn local rejection of a
          housing application and issue permits for its completion (known
          as the "anti-snob zoning" law).

     b)   Inclusionary Devices
          Communities which desire to fulfill what they perceive as their
          housing obligations to the poor may enact local ordinances
          designed to accomplish that. A density bonus ordinance provides
          that a developer who agrees to provide housing for low income
          persons may construct a larger building than would otherwise be

permitted under the local zoning ordinance (or be exempt from other similar rules). A mandatory set-aside ordinance requires that a certain percentage of every large scale housing development be set aside for below market rental or sale to applicants who meet prescribed income guidelines. Communities may be encouraged (or compelled) to employ such devices by virtue of state law, as is currently the case in California and Oregon. Conversely, mandatory set-asides have been held invalid in Virginia as taking developers' property without just compensation. (Board of Supervisors v. DeGroff Enterprises, Inc. (1973).)

D. REVIEW QUESTIONS

1. T or F The city intends to rezone a certain block of land from commercial to residential. Land on the block is currently undeveloped, but the effect of the rezoning will be to reduce the market value of the lots on the land by approximately 50%. If the city does attempt to so rezone the property, its action will be held invalid in court on the ground that it has improperly taken property of the owners without paying just compensation.

2. T or F In order to check runaway growth, the city recently passed an ordinance limiting the issuance of building permits for residential structures to 500 per year, to be granted to applicants in order of the date of application. This will be upheld in court as against the attack by an owner whose lot is zoned for residential use and whose construction plans comply with all other applicable building and zoning ordinances.

3. T or F A small town in a crowded metropolitan region is considering amending its ordinances so as to require a minimum lot size of 5 acres per house and a complete ban on apartment buildings. It may safely do so despite an area-wide housing shortage.

4. A property owner desires to build a house on his lot larger than is permitted under the local land use regulations. He should apply for:

T or F a. A subdivision permit.

T or F b. A variance.

T or F c. A conditional use permit.

T or F d. A writ of mandamus.

Bernhardt–Property, 2d BLS—12

T or F   e.   A rezoning application.

T or F   f.   A nonconforming use permit.

5. The city desires to zone a certain neighborhood as single family residential. Such an ordinance would be valid and could take effect immediately as to:

T or F   a.   A lot on which an office building is being constructed.

T or F   b.   A lot on which there now exists an office building.

T or F   c.   A lot which contains a single family residential structure which was being used for commercial purposes but is now abandoned.

6. Which, if any, of the following techniques would be absolutely unauthorized as a land use technique:

T or F   a.   A ban on billboards.

T or F   b.   A single family zoning ordinance limiting the number of unrelated persons who may reside in a residence.

T or F   c.   An ordinance prohibiting the conversion of apartment buildings to condominiums.

T or F   d.   An ordinance limiting the number of residential building permits which may be issued within a year.

T or F   e.   An ordinance imposing a city-wide height limit, enacted by initiative rather than by the city council.

APPENDIX A

ANSWERS TO REVIEW QUESTIONS

PART ONE: INTERESTS IN LAND

I. ADVERSE POSSESSION

1. *False.* Paul's prior possessory title is sufficient to enable him to retain possession against everyone but persons claiming a better title. Unless Rachel herself is the owner, Paul's lack of title is no defense.

2. *True.* There is privity of possession as to the strip even though the deed does not refer to it. (However, Sam has no color of title to the strip and therefore must prove actual possession of it, since there is no constructive possession.)

3. *False.* The period of adverse possession is not extended by subsequent transfers of the title to the property. What Oona sold to Sue was the right to bring ejectment against Paul within the next five years.

4. *True.* Even though the transfer from Paul to Rachel was involuntary there is nevertheless privity between them, since Rachel's right to possession is based upon Paul's former possession.

5. *False.* Once Paul had met all the requirements for adverse possession he was the owner. As such, his new title was not lost by failure to remain on the property. An owner continues to own whether or not he possesses property, unless someone else actually perfects adverse possession to it.

6. *False.* Successful adverse possession by Paul not only gave him a title, but also wiped out any liability based upon his wrongful possession during any part of the time, even those years not independently barred by the statute of limitations.

II. ESTATES IN LAND

1. *False.* Ann has a fee simple determinable. Ann's estate automatically ends when and if the property is not used for church purposes, whereas if she had a fee simple subject to condition subsequent the termination of her estate would be at the election of the person holding the future interest after it.

2. *False.* Owen has given his entire estate to Ann and under no circumstances will the property return to him.

3. *True.* Bob has a remainder interest which will take after the natural termination of Ann's estate. It is a contingent remainder because it is subject to the condition precedent that Bob be married at the time of Ann's death. It is a remainder of a life estate because, once Bob takes, he will have the property only for life and it will not descend to his heirs.

4. *False.* Bob has a reversion. A remainder is an interest created in a third party in the same document as a prior possessory estate. Bob's interest was not created in the document which created Ann's life estate. When Owen gave Ann her life estate he was left with a reversion. He later transferred that reversion to Bob, where it continued as a reversion.

5. *True.* Bob would have a contingent remainder supported by a term of years, which was impermissible. The seisin remains in Owen under this grant, since Ann has only a nonfreehold and Bob cannot take the seisin now, his estate being contingent. Thus if Bob could take it would necessitate the seisin passing out of Owen at a later time, which would violate the rule against springing interests.

6. *False.* The grant gave Bob and Cal alternative contingent remainders in fee simple, and it is always the case that the final estate in land must be vested, which contingent remainders are not. Thus Owen must have a reversion. This is more than a technical nicety. If Ann renounces or forfeits her estate before she dies, and if Bob is not yet 21, then neither Bob nor Cal can take: Bob cannot take because he is not 21, and Cal cannot take since it cannot be said that Bob will not be 21 before Ann dies (since she is not dead). Neither remainder is therefore ready to take, and consequently both are destroyed. The estate would thus vest in Owen by virtue of his reversion.

7. **True.** Don holds the present life estate of Ann and the vested remainder of Cal. Since these two vested estates are separated only by a contingent remainder they will merge when held by a third person and their merger will destroy intervening contingent remainders. Ann's life estate merges into Cal's remainder and is terminated; Bob's remainder is not ready to take and is destroyed.

8. **True.** The Statute of Uses executed only uses. This transaction led to the creation of legal estates in Ann and Bob, not equitable uses. Thus there is nothing for the statute to operate on. Bob's estate remains as a legal contingent remainder, subject to destructibility.

9. **True.** The final contingent remainder interest is bad, since it may not vest until the end of a life which may not have been in being when the interest was created. Owen's oldest descendant 21 years from now may be a person as yet unborn. The further gift to the unascertained child of that descendant on the descendant's death postpones the vesting of that contingent remainder beyond 21 years after a life or lives in being.

10. **True.** Under the Rule in Shelley's Case the remainder to Bob's heirs becomes a remainder in Bob. This converts it from a contingent to a vested remainder, since Bob is ascertained. His two estates then merge to give him a vested remainder in fee simple absolute. The rule does not require that the ancestor's estate be possessory.

11. **True.** Hubert has an estate in fee simple determinable. It is an estate inheritable by the issue of Hubert's wife, since they will qualify as heirs of Hubert on his death. Of course, if the terminating condition occurs the estate will end immediately, wiping out any dower interest his wife might otherwise have.

III. CONCURRENT OWNERSHIP

1. **False.** There is no unity of time or title between the parties, since Ann's title is older and derives from a different source than Bob's. (Ann

cannot convey to herself; she merely retains a half-interest.) Ann must convey to a strawman, who can then convey to Ann and Bob as joint tenants in order for her wishes to be fulfilled. This rule is much modified by statute now.

2. *False.* There is no unity of interest, since Ann has a larger share than Bob or Carl. The parties would be tenants in common. It might be possible to make Bob and Carl joint tenants as to a one-half interest in the land, with the other half being held by Ann as a tenant in common if the grant had been so worded; then Bob or Carl would take the other's share by survivorship, but there would be no survivorship to the two large halves.

3. *False.* The presumption today is in favor of a tenancy in common. Most states require that the intent to create a joint tenancy be expressed in the deed, and several add the deed also recite that there is to be survivorship.

4. *True.* When Ann dies, Bob and Cal become joint tenants, each owning half of the property by survivorship. When Bob dies, Cal survives to that entire share, becoming the sole owner.

5. *False.* Cal's conveyance severed the joint tenancy as to Don, making Don a tenant in common. It did not sever the joint tenancy between Ann and Bob, so that Bob took Ann's share by survivorship on Ann's death. Thus Bob owns two-thirds, Don owns one-third, and they are tenants in common.

6. *False.* Each cotenant has an undivided right to possess the whole property, and therefore that possessory right may be transferred to a third person. The lease will not, however, entitle the lessee to exclude the nonsigning coowner.

7. *False.* Only payments made to preserve the title, e.g. taxes and mortgage payments are directly recoverable. Other expenditures will, at best, be made the subject of adjustment in the division of any partition proceeds or accounting of the profits.

8. *False.* Property is not recharacterized on marriage. Community property consists only of what is acquired during the marriage.

IV. LANDLORD AND TENANT

1. *True.* At the landlord's election a holdover tenant may be converted into a periodic tenant. An election to that effect was made here since Laura

accepted Tom's rent. The period appears to be yearly rather than monthly, based upon the fact the rent seems payable on a yearly basis.

2. *False.* Destruction of the premises does not terminate a common law tenancy. A periodic tenancy is terminated only by timely notice (usually given six months in advance in a tenancy from year to year). Tom's quitting is not notice. Tom has therefore not terminated his estate and it will renew the following year, and thereafter, until Tom gives proper notice of termination.

3. *False.* Laura was entitled to terminate the tenancy for Tom's breach in most states, but the effect is to end Tom's rent liability as well. If Laura wants to hold Tom to the rent she must not terminate his right of possession.

4. *True.* Laura can ignore Tom's abandonment and sue for the entire rent, but not before it falls due. She must wait until the end of the term if she wants to sue just once for all of the rent. If she sues earlier than that she can only recover the rent then actually due.

5. *False.* Laura is obliged to give Tom quiet enjoyment but this does not make her an insuror against the acts of strangers. Tom is excused from the rent only if his loss of possession is the result of Laura's act. Tom is the one who must seek relief against the strangers, and his rent liability to Laura continues whether or not he does so.

6. *False.* Tom takes the premises "as is" and the doctrine of caveat emptor applies. Laura has a duty to disclose hidden defects known to her, but this defect was unknown.

7. *True.* Laura has no obligation to keep the premises tenantable for Tom, and Tom's duty to avoid waste does not include a duty to rebuild after total destruction. At best either party may elect to terminate the tenancy if there is a statute permitting termination after destruction. But such statutes do not impose a duty to restore on either party.

8. *False.* When a tenant's use generates additional code requirements, the burden of compliance is on the tenant. This does not mean that Laura can compel Tom to add the washrooms, but it does mean that Tom cannot terminate the lease merely because the authorities shut him down.

9. *True.* Laura has no duty (unless imposed by some statute) to furnish heat. Therefore there was no breach of covenant by her and Tom cannot claim constructive eviction. Tom has merely abandoned and one

remedy open to a landlord when the tenant abandons is to continue to hold the tenant for the rent as it falls due.

10. *False.* The breach of covenant would probably make Laura liable to the guest if the guest chose to sue her. But as occupier of the premises Tom owed certain nondelegable duties of care to his guests and a jury could find that he was negligent in failing to fix the faucet himself or in failing to warn the guest about the faucet.

11. *True.* Tom's wrongful assignment permits Laura to terminate the tenancy. But if Laura does not terminate it then the assignment is valid and Ann has the benefits of all covenants made by Laura to Tom. The benefit of this particular covenant plainly runs with the land (with the leasehold estate) to Ann.

V. EASEMENTS

1. *False.* An implied easement can arise only where express language could have validly created the same easement. Since the facts do not indicate that Dita herself had an easement over Steve's land, Dita could not create in Ann an easement over Steve's lot. Since Dita could not expressly give Ann an easement over Steve's property, she could not do so by implication either.

2. *False.* Dita's initial use was adverse, and Steve could not convert it into permissive use by unilaterally attempting to consent to it. But once Dita accepted Steve's offer, her further use was carried on under his permission and was therefore not adverse. Had Dita replied to Steve that she did not need his consent to continue crossing then her use would have remained adverse.

3. *False.* An easement of support is a negative, not an affirmative easement. Negative easements cannot be acquired by prescription because there is no adverseness during the prescriptive period. Steve had no cause of action against Dita for the 25 years that her building stood, and therefore Steve has lost no rights by not suing. Dita was privileged to build her building and Steve was privileged to excavate. Steve's failure to exercise his privilege does not cause him to lose it, and Dita's continued exercise of a "privilege" does not convert it into a "right."

4. *True.* Dita had an easement appurtenant, which cannot be converted into an easement in gross. If Ann happens to own some adjacent property (to which the road might be deemed appurtenant) the transfer still is bad

because that would constitute an impermissible enlargement of the dominant tenement.

5. *True.* Dita had an easement appurtenant, which is transferred along with a transfer of the dominant tenement. The easement therefore passed to Ann since it was not expressly excepted from the grant to Ann.

6. *False.* The grant of an easement or profit does not deprive the servient tenant from making a similar use of the property or permitting others to make a similar use, so long as it does not unreasonably interfere with the prior use. For Dita to stop Ann she must show that Ann's drawing water will impair her own right to do so.

7. *True.* Dita originally had an easement over Steve's property but it was extinguished by a merger when Steve acquired Dita's property and its easement over his own property. However there was still a quasi-easement in existence which was apparent, continuous and necessary at the time that title to the two parcels was later reserved, so that Ann may claim that she received an easement by implied grant when Steve conveyed Dita's lot to her.

VI. COVENANTS RUNNING WITH THE LAND

1. *False.* The covenant is purely personal because neither the burden nor the benefit touches and concerns land (as explained in the text). A "collateral" covenant, such as this, will not run with land even though there is privity and even though the parties state that it should run.

2. *False.* The covenant does not run at law because there was no privity of estate between Prudence and Pete at the time the covenant was made (in most states). Had the covenant been included in the deed to Prudence there would have been privity. But since the covenant came later, it was made at a time when Prudence and Pete were merely neighbors and thus not in privity of estate. Only if the jurisdiction requires no privity whatsoever is the covenant enforceable at law.

3. *True.* There was privity of estate between Prudence and Pete at the time that Prudence covenanted because they both had interests in the same property (Pete had a servient estate and Prudence had a dominant estate). It does not matter here that the deed to Prudence was a month earlier, since the easement constituted a privity of estate between them after that.

4. *False.* There is no vertical privity between Prudence and Al, since Al has not succeeded to Prudence's entire estate, and therefore the burden of

the covenant does not run to her. (The benefit of the covenant probably does run to Barbara since vertical privity is not there required, but it does no good here if the burden does not also run.)

5a. *False.* Unless the jurisdiction follows the theory of implied reciprocal servitudes. In that case a court will say that when Ann agreed to restrict her lot, Pete impliedly agreed to reciprocally restrict all retained lots and this restriction ran with retained lot 2 into the hands of Bob. It may be necessary to show a common plan for this theory to apply.

5b. *True.* Under third party beneficiary theory or implied reciprocal theory. The implied reciprocal theory leads to the same result as it did in the previous case of Bob, since lot 3 was also a retained lot when Ann made her covenant. Third party beneficiary theory treats Ann as the beneficiary of Carol's promise to Pete. It may be necessary to show a common plan for this theory to apply.

5c. *True.* Bob would enforce the covenant as the successor to Pete who received the benefit of Ann's covenant in favor of retained lot 2, which benefit then ran to Bob. But it might be necessary to show a common plan for Bob to be able to enforce a burden on another lot when his lot is not similarly burdened.

5d. *True.* Under third party beneficiary theory, Bob may be able to show that he is as much a third party beneficiary of Carol's promise as Ann was. No implied reciprocal theory can be used, since Bob himself made no covenant from which a reciprocal could be implied. Nor could Bob claim to be the beneficiary of any covenant reciprocally implied out of Ann's covenant to Pete.

5e. *True.* Since Ann's covenant benefitted the common grantor's retained land and that benefit ran to her with the conveyance of lot 3, Carol can restrict Ann just as Bob could.

5f. *False.* Bob made no covenant himself from which the benefit could run to Carol or from which Carol could claim to be a third party beneficiary. Carol cannot claim any implied reciprocal out of her own covenant to Pete since he did not own lot 2 at the time Carol covenanted, and an implied reciprocal can work only as to land the grantor still owns. Possibly Bob's lot is subject to an implied reciprocal of Ann's covenant, but it would be hard to show that Carol is the beneficiary of that implied reciprocal.

PART TWO: CONVEYANCING

VII. CONTRACTS FOR THE SALE OF LAND (VENDOR–PURCHASER)

1. *True.* Since the option is valid, Van's title is not marketable. Were Pearl to accept his deed, knowing of the option, she would later be compelled to honor the option if Ann chose to exercise it, thus being forced to permit Ann to purchase the property from her.

2. *False.* Van is not required to have a marketable title until the time for completing the contract. Van can use the purchase price received from Pearl to pay off the mortgage and thereby deliver to her a marketable title free of the mortgage.

3. *False.* Pearl's right to a marketable title, implied in the contract (or even expressed), was a contract right which did not survive the consummation of that contract. Once Pearl accepted the deed, her contract right to marketable title expired. She should have investigated to discover the easement before accepting the deed. Had she done so, she could have refused to complete the contract unless the easement was removed. But now it is too late.

4. *True.* The Act puts the risk of loss on the vendor unless the purchaser takes possession or title. Since neither has yet been transferred to Pearl, Van bears this risk.

VIII. CONVEYANCES (TRANSFER OF TITLE BY DEED)

1. *False.* Grace's note indicates an intent that the deed not operate until after her death (in effect, a will substitute). Therefore she had no present intent at any time while she was alive to commit a binding legal act, and the deed has never been delivered.

2. *True.* Grace committed a binding legal act by irrevocably delivering the deed into escrow. The later return of the deed to her is irrelevant. It has no more effect than would result if Grace had delivered the deed to Gene directly and later he had honored her request to give it back to her; title would not go back with it.

3. *False.* Relation back applies only when necessary to do justice. Its application in this case would be unjust and the doctrine will therefore not be applied. Instead the second delivery will be taken as the significant one, since at that moment Grace did have a title to pass.

IX. PRIORITIES (THE RECORDING SYSTEM)

1. *True.*   Although Owen divested himself of the title when he first conveyed to Ann, nevertheless Ann's failure to record left him with an *apparent* title and the power to divest her by conveying to a bona fide purchaser. When Owen died, real title did not descend to Bob (since Owen had no title), nor did Bob qualify as a bona fide purchaser (having paid no value), but the power to divest Ann did pass to Bob because he then appeared on the records as the apparent owner. When Bob thereafter conveyed to a bona fide purchaser (Carol) the recording act protected Carol and divested Ann.

2. *True.*   Bob prevails in notice states because he purchased without notice. But in all other states he must record first. Even in a notice-race state, Bob loses since he has not been the first to record; lack of notice is necessary but not sufficient.

3. *False.*   Since Bob qualified as a purchaser for value without notice who recorded first, he has divested Ann of title. Bob became the true owner of the property and had a real title. His deed to Carol transferred that title. Carol need not qualify as a bona fide purchaser because she dealt with a true owner, not an apparent owner. She wins under any recording act.

4. *True.*   Although the deed to Bob did not divest Ann, since Bob had notice, nevertheless it did transfer apparent title to him, giving him the power to divest Ann by conveying to a bona fide purchaser. Since Carol was such a person, the deed to her divested Ann. This is quite similar to the situation in problem 1 above.

5. *True.*   Bob gave value in reliance on the records. He had a right to receive $10,000 from Owen, which he gave up because Owen appeared to own the property he transferred to Bob. Although as a creditor Bob would not have been protected, he has since become a purchaser who is protected because of the value given (cancellation of a preexisting debt).

6. *False.*   Probably. Since the statute does not refer to "actual" notice, it should permit application of the doctrine of constructive notice. Bob was therefore charged with notice of the rights of persons in possession when their possession was not consistent with the record title. Thus he was charged with notice of Tom's possession, and the fact that Tom claimed under a lease from someone other than Owen. These suspicious circumstances gave Bob an obligation to investigate and further charged him with the results of a reasonable inquiry. It is probable that such an inquiry would have led to the discovery of Ann's interest in the property.

X. TITLE ASSURANCE

1. *False.* The title insurance policy will not eliminate a valid encumbrance on the title. All that Gene will obtain from his policy is a statement that the title is vested in him subject to the easement of record. If he does not want encumbered property, he should decline to complete the contract.

2. *True.* Title insurance insures whatever interests the insured party purports to have. A mortgagee's title insurance policy will therefore insure not only that the mortgage is a valid lien on the property, but its priority as well. If the records revealed that Marie's mortgage was inferior to some other recorded mortgage, the title report should have so stated. Its failure to do so will make the insuror liable for any damage Marie suffers by virtue of her junior position.

3. *False.* Neither matter concerns title. Gene still has a perfect title to the property, regardless of its deficient physical condition.

4a. *False.* Zoning and other land use restrictions are not burdens upon title as shown in the official record. Therefore, they are not covered by title insurance.

4b. *False.* A prescriptively acquired right does not appear of record and is therefore not insured against (unless it has been established by a recorded judgment).

4c. *False.* The mortgage would not be effective against a bona fide purchaser since it has not been recorded. Title policies exclude claims which are valid only because of the actual knowledge of the insured.

4d. *False.* The judgment did not become a lien upon the title until after the title policy was issued. Therefore, there was no way for the policy to cover it. Title policies insure only against matters affecting the title as of the time when the policy was issued.

XI. MORTGAGES

1. *True.* The equity of redemption is generally available to all parties having an interest in the mortgaged property whose interest would be lost by a foreclosure. Thus, Sid may cure the default or redeem in order to

prevent a senior foreclosure sale from destroying his junior mortgage. (He may then declare a default under his own mortgage and commence junior foreclosure proceedings.)

2. *True.* The transaction appears to be a mortgage disguised as a sale and option to repurchase. The disparity between the "purchase price" and fair market value, the similarity between the option and a loan of principal and interest ($100,000 for 3 years at 7%), and the rent-free possession all indicate that the transaction is in fact a loan. As a mortgagor, Mort has an equity of redemption and may pay, i.e., exercise the option, late.

3. *True.* The lien or title given to a mortgagee is protected by all of the land given as security until the obligation is entirely paid. Mort should have insisted, at the outset, that the mortgage contain a *release* clause, permitting some of the property to be discharged as the debt is reduced. Release clauses are common in large development projects.

4. *False.* A mortgage may not be unilaterally enlarged by the mortgagee to include other debts. Marie should have, at the outset, included a *dragnet* clause in her mortgage, providing that it secured not only the basic obligation but any other obligations as well. However, not all courts will enforce a clause so broadly worded.

5. *False.* The equity of redemption was created by the courts independently of and in opposition to the language of the mortgage. Courts of equity assume that a necessitous debtor will sign any document demanded by the creditor and therefore prohibit the mortgagee from *clogging* the equity of redemption by language in the mortgage.

6a. *True.* Mort can sell his equity in the property, which is equal to the market value of the property ($100,000) less the liens imposed on the property ($80,000).

6b. *False.* Marie, as senior mortgagee, can sell a title free and clear of all junior liens. Thus, a bidder should be willing to pay $100,000 for the property.

6c. *False.* The mortgagee can sell the mortgagor's entire title to the property, including the owner's fee interest. The bid should be $100,000, of which the first $50,000 should go to Marie, the next $30,000 to Sid, and the remaining $20,000 to Mort.

6d. *False.* A junior mortgagee cannot foreclose and sell a title free of the senior mortgage. Thus, the bid should be $50,000, because the purchaser will acquire a title subject to Marie's mortgage. The $50,000 should be allocated $30,000 to Sid and the remaining $20,000 to Mort.

6e. *False.* Either mortgagee may foreclose independently, as described above.

PART THREE: RIGHTS RELATING TO LAND

XIII. MISCELLANEOUS PROPERTY DOCTRINES

1. *False.* This is backwards. Nora may safely cause Owen's land to subside only if she can show that it happened because of the extra weight of his house. If his lot would have subsided even if it were unimproved, she is liable.

2. *False.* Coming to the nuisance is not a defense. If Nora's burning unreasonably interferes with Owen's enjoyment of his land it does not matter that she started first.

3. *False.* Mistake is no defense to a trespass. Nora intends to be where she is, which is enough to make her liable.

4. *True.* As an upstream riparian not affected by alterations of the flow resulting from Nora's diversion, Owen has no cause of action against her. Only downstream owners may take action against her.

5. *False.* A trespass may occur above or below the surface. Owen's title and possessory rights extend above the surface into his overhead airspace. He may bring ejectment against her.

6. *True.* Perhaps. The shed may have become a fixture, with title passing to Owen as landowner, but Nora is nevertheless entitled to remove it under the trade-fixture exception if it so qualifies.

7. *True.* As a tenant, Nora may not commit active waste. Her alteration of the surface by removing the shed is therefore actionable.

XIV. LAND USE

1. *False.* The mere diminution of value does not constitute an impermissible taking of land. Some rezonings have been upheld even though they produced value losses in excess of 80–90% of the original value.

2. *True.* Most jurisdictions now permit cities to engage in legitimate growth techniques, so long as it is not done for an exclusionary or otherwise discriminatory purpose and is merely designed to enable the city to control its population increase in a sensible fashion.

3. *False.* The amendments to the ordinance appear to be intended to accomplish an exclusionary purpose, i.e., the exclusion of lower and middle income persons from the community. Many jurisdictions now prohibit zoning for such purposes and might hold this scheme invalid.

4a. *False.* A subdivision permit entitles the owner of a parcel of land to divide it into smaller parcels and does not, by itself, entitle him to build upon a parcel.

4b. *True.* A variance entitles an owner to deviate from a land use restriction, such as is involved here. In this case, the owner would seek a bulk variance.

4c. *False.* A conditional use permit entitles the owner of property to make certain specified uses of his property and does not deal with building size.

4d. *False.* Mandamus is a form of action frequently brought by a property owner to challenge a land use regulation. (It might be an appropriate remedy for the owner to consider if his application for a variance were denied.)

4e. *False.* The property owner is not burdened by a zoning classification (as to whether it is residential, commercial, etc.), unless the land use ordinance ties building size to use classification.

4f. *False.* A nonconforming use is a structure or activity which preceded the zoning ordinance and is therefore permitted to continue. In this case there is no existing building.

5a. *False.* Assuming that there is a valid building permit for the structure and that substantial construction activity has occurred, the owner of the office building has a "vested right" to complete it, and then to continue it as a nonconforming use.

5b. *False.* The office building preceded the zoning ordinance and therefore has nonconforming use protection. Immediate application of the ordinance to it would constitute an impermissible taking of property.

5c. *True.* There is nonconforming use protection for activities as well as structures, but in the situation here it was lost by the abandonment.

6a. *False.* Cities may regulate billboards in order to eliminate light and visual clutter and to promote public safety. First Amendment considerations limit municipal power in this respect, but do not prohibit it absolutely.

6b. *False.* No federal constitutional violation is committed by an ordinance limiting the number of unrelated persons who may reside in a single family house unless the ordinance intrudes too far into certain forms of familial association. (However, some state courts do invalidate these ordinances on associational grounds.)

6c. *False.* The conversion of an apartment building into a condominium constitutes a subdivision activity, thereby bringing it within local land use controls.

6d. *False.* So long as it is done to manage and control growth, and not for an exclusionary purpose, a city may pass a growth restricting ordinance.

6e. *False.* A height limit is plainly a matter of local land use control and may be done by initiative so long as it is not confined to an individual parcel, unless the state prohibits all land use regulation by initiative.

*

APPENDIX B

PRACTICE EXAMINATION

There are two parts to this exam. The first part consists of twenty three multistate-type questions. Questions 1 through 10 are taken, with minor modifications, from publicly disclosed Bar Examination questions, although the answers to them were prepared by me rather than by the bar examiners. The remainder of these short questions are original and are designed to interrelate different sections of this book.

The second part consists of three very long essay questions, also intended to force you to interconnect diverse fields of Property law. They also incorporate different styles of questioning; note carefully the call of each question. In lieu of model answers, I prepared grader's notes, giving you the issues an instructor would probably be expecting to see covered in an answer (although this always varies from instructor to instructor).

This does not purport to be a "sample" exam in the sense that you would be likely to get an exam like this in law school. It is far too long and complex, and it contains no intermediate length questions (questions of that nature appear at the end of each chapter). While each of these questions is, individually, typical of the kinds of questions most law professors write, they are, collectively, an enormous batch. I do not expect you to sit down and answer them all at once; they are more intended to serve as additional study aids in your review of Property.

SAMPLE MULTISTATE QUESTIONS

Questions 1 through 7 are based on the following fact situation:

By way of a gift, Pat executed a deed naming his son, Mike, as grantee. The deed contained descriptions as follows:

(1) All of my land and dwelling known as 44 Main Street, Midtown, United States, being one acre.

(2) All that part of my farm, being a square with 200-foot sides, the southeast corner of which is in the north line of my neighbor, John Brown.

The deed contained covenants of general warranty, quiet enjoyment, and right to convey.

Pat handed the deed to Mike who immediately returned it to his father for safekeeping. His father kept it in his safe deposit box. The deed was not recorded.

The property at 44 Main Street covered ⅞ of an acre of land, had a dwelling and a garage situated thereon, and was subject to a right of way, described in prior deeds, in favor of Jack, a neighbor. Pat owned no other land on Main Street. Jack had not used the right of way for ten years and it was not visible on inspection of the property.

1. The description of 44 Main Street was:

   a. Not sufficient, because it contained no metes and bounds.

   b. Not sufficient, because the acreage given was not correct.

   c. Not sufficient, because a deed purporting to convey more than a grantor owns is void *ab initio*.

   d. Sufficient, because the discrepancy in area is not fatal.

2. The description of part of Pat's farm:

   a. Is insufficient because of vagueness.

   b. Is sufficient if consideration has been paid.

   c. Is sufficient because no ambiguity therein appears on the face of the deed.

   d. Could be enforced if the deed contained a covenant of seisin.

3. Ignoring any question of the adequacy of description, the deed:

    a.   Was not delivered to Mike because Pat maintained custody of the deed.

    b.   Transferred nothing to Mike because it was not recorded.

    c.   Transferred nothing to Mike because it was never accepted by him.

    d.   Transferred a property interest to Mike which he could enforce against Pat.

4. Mike made a title search a few months after Pat handed him the deed and discovered the existence of Jack's right of way. Mike could recover substantial damages from Pat for breach of the covenant of:

    a.   Right to convey.

    b.   Right to convey if Jack has commenced using the right of way and if Mike had given consideration for his deed.

    c.   Quiet enjoyment if Jack has commenced using the right of way and if Mike had given consideration for his deed.

    d.   Quiet enjoyment.

5. Assume that Jack continues not to use his right of way as such but erects a tool shed within the boundaries of the right of way on Mike's lot. Which of the following statements is most accurate?

    a.   Mike can compel Jack to remove the shed.

    b.   Jack is entitled to maintain the shed on the right of way so long as it does not become a fixture.

    c.   Jack will be ordered by a court to remove the shed only if Mike can show that he is unreasonably harmed by it.

    d.   Mike can recover from Pat for breach of the covenant of quiet enjoyment.

6. Assume Pat had agreed with Jim, who had sold 44 Main Street to him, never to convey that property to Mike. The agreement between Pat and Jim was in writing and was known to Mike but was not recorded. Mike conveyed 44 Main Street to Joe for a valuable consideration, telling Joe of Jim's agreement, but saying he did not think Jim intended to enforce it. Mike's deed contained only a covenant of right to convey. Which of the following statements is most accurate?

a. Joe has no title to the property because Pat's agreement with Jim runs with the land and invalidates any title purporting to pass through Mike.

b. Jim may recover damages from Pat for breach of the agreement but may not set aside the conveyance.

c. If Jim brings suit to set aside the conveyance, Joe can hold Mike liable on the covenant of right to convey.

d. Joe's knowledge of Jim's agreement did not prevent him from being a bona fide purchaser.

7. Assuming the same facts as in question 6, which of the following statements with respect to the covenants in Pat's deed is most accurate?

a. The covenant of right to convey in Pat's deed could be enforced by Joe because of its repetition in Mike's deed.

b. The covenant of quiet enjoyment in Pat's deed ran with the land as far as Mike but not as far as Joe.

c. The covenant of quiet enjoyment in Pat's deed may be enforced by anyone having a privity of estate.

d. The covenant of quiet enjoyment is implied in every conveyance and need not be recited therein.

Questions 8 through 10 are based upon the following fact situation:

In 1945, Owen executed and delivered a deed by which he conveyed Blackacre as follows: "To Alpha and his heirs as long as it is used exclusively for residential purposes, but if it is ever used for other than residential purposes, to the American Red Cross." In 1950, Owen died leaving a valid will by which he devised all his real estate to his brother, Bill. The will had no residuary clause. Owen was survived by Bill and by Owen's son, Sam, who was Owen's sole heir.

For the purpose of this set of questions, it may be assumed that the common law rule against perpetuities applies in the state where the land is located and that the state also has a statute providing that, "All future estates and interests are alienable, descendible, and devisable in the same manner as possessory estates and interests."

8. In 1955 Alpha and Sam entered into a contract with John whereby Alpha and Sam contracted to sell Blackacre to John in fee simple. After examining title, John refused to perform on the ground that Alpha and Sam could not give

good title. Alpha and Sam joined in an action against John for specific performance. Prayer for specific performance will be:

a. Denied, because the American Red Cross has a valid interest in Blackacre.

b. Granted, because Alpha alone owns the entire fee simple in Blackacre.

c. Denied, because Bill has a valid interst in Blackacre.

d. Granted, because Alpha and Sam together own a fee simple absolute in Blackacre.

9. In 1946 the interest of the American Red Cross in Blackacre could be best described as a:

a. Valid contingent remainder.

b. Void contingent remainder.

c. Void executory interest.

d. Valid executory interest.

10. In 1951 the interest of Bill in Blackacre could best be described as:

a. A possibility of reverter.

b. An executory interest.

c. An executory interest in a possibility of reverter.

d. None of the above.

Questions 11 through 13 are based on the following fact situation:

Owen, an owner in fee, leased a house and lot to Tina for ten years. By the terms of the lease, Tina, for herself, her heirs, executors, administrators, and assigns, expressly covenanted to pay rent and to pay the taxes on the premises during the term of the lease. Two years later Owen conveyed his interest in the premises to Larry. About the same time, Tina assigned her lease to Annie by a written assignment in which Annie expressly assumed the obligation of the covenant to pay rent but said nothing concerning the payment of taxes.

11. Annie refused to pay taxes and Larry, after paying the same, brought an action against Annie for the amount paid. Judgment for:

    a.   Annie, because the covenant to pay taxes is a collateral covenant not touching or concerning the land.

    b.   Larry.

    c.   Annie, because Annie has made no contract concerning payment of taxes and is not liable upon contracts she did not make.

    d.   Larry, but only if Owen expressly assigned the covenant to him.

12. If no one pays the rent to Larry after Tina has assigned the lease to Annie, which statement is most accurate:

    a.   Larry will not prevail in a suit against Tina for the rent because Tina assigned rather than sublet to Annie.

    b.   Larry will prevail in a suit against Annie for the rent because the burden of the covenant ran to Annie.

    c.   Larry will not prevail in a suit against Annie for the rent because it is only Tina who can enforce Annie's assumption agreement.

    d.   Tina would prevail in a suit against Annie for the rent because the benefit of the rent covenant made to Owen ran to Tina when Tina assigned to Annie.

13. If a customer of Annie's is injured while on the premises, due to a defective condition there, which statement is most accurate:

    a.   The customer may not recover from Larry if Larry can show that the injury occurred in a common area.

    b.   The customer may recover from Tina on the ground that Tina had a duty to inspect the premises prior to assignment to Annie.

    c.   The customer may not recover from Annie if Annie can show that the lease contained a covenant by the landlord to make repairs.

    d.   The customer may recover from Owen if s/he can show that the injury was caused by a latent defect in the premises which Owen knowingly failed to disclose to anyone.

Questions 14 through 17 are all based on the following fact situation:

On January 10, Van and Paul signed the following contract:

"Van hereby agrees to convey Blackacre to Paul and Paul hereby agrees to pay Van the sum of $25,000.00, all cash, for the property. This agreement shall be performed by both parties on February 15."

14. Which statement is most accurate as of January 11:

    a.   Van is required to tender a deed conveying marketable title to Blackacre on February 15.

    b.   This agreement does not prohibit Van from removing the barn, which is presently situated upon the land, prior to February 15.

    c.   Paul is now a bona fide purchaser who will prevail over any prior unrecorded instruments in a notice jurisdiction.

    d.   Paul is now entitled to take immediate possession of the property under the doctrine of equitable conversion.

15. If, at the time of signing the contract, Ann has been in wrongful possession of part of the property the past two years, and the statutory time period for adverse possession is ten years, which statement is most accurate as of January 11:

    a.   Paul may immediately withdraw from the contract because of Ann's presence.

    b.   Paul must accept a deed from Van if Van ejects Ann prior to February 15, or within a reasonable time thereafter.

    c.   If Paul accepts a deed from Van, Ann will be required to spend at least ten more years in actual possession before she will acquire any title thereby.

    d.   Paul may accept a deed from Van because when and if Ann ever does acquire title by adverse possession, Paul will be protected by his title insurance policy.

16. If, at the time of signing the contract, Betty had been in wrongful possession of a part of the property for over 25 years, which statement most accurately describes the parties' rights after Paul accepts a deed from Van:

    a. Paul will prevail over Betty's claim of adverse possession if he can show that the color of title under which she possessed this property actually described land somewhere else.

    b. Paul will prevail over any claim of adverse possession by Betty in a notice-race jurisdiction, if he can show that he took his deed without notice of her and immediately recorded it.

    c. If Paul loses to Betty's claim of adverse possession, he may recover against Van in an action based upon the implied condition of marketable title in the contract of sale.

    d. If Betty prevails over Paul in her claim of adverse possession, she may then take a vacation and leave the property vacant for a year without fear of losing her claim upon it.

17. If a title search by Paul prior to the close of escrow reveals that Van holds title in joint tenancy with Wanda, which statement is the most accurate:

    a. A deed signed by Van alone will convey no interest whatsoever in the premises.

    b. Van must give Wanda one-half of the proceeds received by Paul for a deed signed by Van alone.

    c. A deed signed by Van alone will make Paul a joint tenant with Wanda.

    d. Wanda cannot exclude Paul from any part of the premises even though he holds under a deed which has been signed by Van alone.

Questions 18 through 20 are based upon the following fact situation:

ABC Corporation owns 100 acres of undeveloped land. It intends to subdivide the property and to offer individual unimproved lots for sale. Its present intent is to create a strictly residential subdivision and to permit no non-residential use of any lot.

18. In considering what sort of mechanism to employ in order to maintain a residential community, which statement is most accurate:

    a. Imposing residential restrictions by way of inserting them as conditions in all deeds, so as to create conditional fees in the buyers of lots, would have the drawback that enforcement of such conditions would depend upon a court finding that there is a "common plan."

b. Imposing residential restrictions by way of inserting them as easements in all deeds would not be enforceable in a jurisdiction which held that there is no "privity" in a grantor-grantee relationship.

c. Imposing residential restrictions by way of inserting them as covenants in all deeds would have the drawback that a court could decline to enforce them if it found that "changed conditions" had since occurred.

d. Imposing residential restrictions by way of a zoning ordinance would have the drawback that the ordinance could never subsequently be modified if conditions did change.

19. If ABC imposes the restrictions by way of covenants in the deeds restricting all lots to residential use, which statement is most accurate with regard to enforcement of the covenant made by the purchaser of the third lot sold.

a. ABC may itself enforce the covenant against the purchaser if it can show that it made a reciprocal covenant to the purchaser, and that it still owns some property in the subdivision.

b. The first and second purchasers from ABC may enforce the covenant made by the third purchaser if they establish both that they are third party beneficiaries of that promise and that ABC made a similar covenant to them.

c. Subsequent purchasers of lots from ABC may enforce the covenant made by the third purchaser by showing that the benefit of that covenant ran to them and that they have not failed to enforce it against other violators.

d. The municipality cannot enforce the covenant itself because this would constitute state action in violation of the Fourteenth Amendment.

20. If ABC has the residential restrictions imposed by way of a municipal zoning ordinance designating the area as residential, which statement is most accurate:

a. If the city fails to enforce the ordinance against a violator, any resident of the subdivision may bring suit against the violator to enforce the ordinance.

b. In order later to sell any lot free of the residential restriction, ABC must first obtain a special use permit from the appropriate agency by showing unnecessary hardship resulting from strict enforcement of the ordinance.

c. If the ordinance permits multi-family residential uses, any subsequent covenants in deeds to the subdivision restricting use to single family residential would be unenforceable.

d. If there is any non-residential structure existing on any lot in the subdivision prior to enactment of the ordinance, the city may allow it to continue as a nonconforming use.

Questions 21 and 22 are based on the following fact situation:

Nina, Oren's neighbor, dug a well and begun to pump out water from an underground basin below her land.

21. Which of the following statements is correct:

a. Nina will not be liable in nuisance to Oren for any noise the well makes when it is operating so long as the well itself is located solely upon her own land.

b. If the underground basin of water lies below Oren's land as well as Nina's, she has no right to pump any of the water out without his consent.

c. If the well was dug at a slanted angle so that—as its lowest point—it is below Oren's land rather than Nina's, she is not liable to him in trespass so long as—at the surface—the well is solely on her land.

d. If Nina's pumping of the water causes Oren's land to subside, she is liable to him for loss of support even though she has not removed any soil from his or her land.

22. Which of the following statements is correct:

a. If the water Nina draws up overflows and floods Oren's land, she is liable to him for waste.

b. The assessor may increase Nina's real estate taxes because of the well since it is merely a fixture and, therefore, not real property.

c. County officials may enjoin Nina's operation of the well if Nina failed to make an environmental analysis or obtain a use permit as has always been required by local ordinances, even though Nina's well has been in operation for the past month.

d.   If Nina's pumping keeps the surface of Oren's land dry and free from ponding for a long enough time, Oren will acquire a prescriptive easement against Nina to have this condition maintained.

Ann and Bob owned a parcel of land in joint tenancy. Ann gave the bank a mortgage on her interest.

23. Which of the following statements is correct:

a.   As a result of the mortgage, some courts might hold that the joint tenancy has been severed.

b.   If Ann does not pay the mortgage and the bank forecloses, it will sell the entire fee to the property.

c.   If the bank forecloses and sells only Ann's interest, the purchaser at the foreclosure sale will become a joint tenant with Bob.

d.   If Ann dies before the mortgage is paid off, the bank's mortgage will attach to Bob's interest in the property.

ESSAY QUESTIONS
QUESTION I

Lil comes to your law office and tells you the following story:

She owns a house in the small town of Mt. Petal, which she rented to Tess recently for a term of five years. (The lease contained no significant provisions relating to the problems raised below.)

Shortly after Tess moved in, she began to conduct meditation classes for hire inside the house. This prompted some of the neighbors to visit Lil and inform her that the classes were illegal because they violated deed restrictions common to the neighborhood. (All of the neighbors' deeds recited, "In consideration of there being similar restrictions on all other property in the subdivision, grantee covenants not to conduct any commercial activities upon the premises; this covenant is intended to run with the land.") Lil then investigated her own title and learned that neither her deed from Pete (her predecessor), nor Pete's deed from ABC Corp. (the developer) contained this restriction.

Lil decided to ignore the neighbors' demands. As a result she has since received threatening letters from the lawyer for the neighborhood association and from ABC. Furthermore the neighbors petitioned the town council to amend its zoning ordinance to expressly bar conducting meditation classes for hire in areas zoned single family residential (this neighborhood being the only area in town so zoned). The town council held a hearing and made findings that conducting such classes in a single family residential area would disturb the peace and quiet and neighborhood character of the area, and amended its zoning ordinance as requested. As a result of this action, both Lil and Tess have received letters from the town's zoning administrator ordering the classes to stop. Tess has informed Lil that she will move out if she cannot continue conducting the classes.

Advise Lil as to her legal position. Tell her what additional facts you need to know, if any, and how they will bear on your opinion. Meanwhile, make the most sensible assumptions you can about any missing data in giving her your opinion.

QUESTION II

Amy and Bella owned a piece of land in joint tenancy. They entered into a binding contract to sell it to Calvin for $100,000 cash, through an escrow to close in 60 days. Calvin deposited the cash into escrow and Amy and Bella deposited separate deeds conveying each of their interests to Calvin, with instructions to the escrow agent to deliver the deeds to Calvin when escrow closed and the money was paid to them. They told the escrow agent to issue a single check payable to them jointly.

However, Bella died before the 60 days had passed. The next day Calvin was contacted by Amy's attorney who told him that Amy, as the surviving sole owner was prepared to honor the contract and had deposited a new deed to the entire estate into the escrow. However, Calvin was also contacted by an attorney for Harry, who informed him that Harry was Bella's sole heir and claims to have inherited Bella's half of the property because the joint tenancy had been severed by the sales contract. Harry's attorney advised Calvin that Harry did not wish to sell his half interest in the property.

Calvin now visits you, his attorney. He wants to know what to do. Should he accept Amy's deed? Should he demand that Bella's deed also be delivered to him? Or should he withdraw from the contract on the ground that title is unmarketable unless Harry also executes a deed?

In researching this matter you discover that there are no probate problems to be concerned with, i.e. either Amy or Harry—whoever owns—is free to execute a deed immediately without probate court approval. As to which of them does in fact own, you discover the following two cases (which may or may not be helpful):

Pam v. Ned, 1961 In this case Mike and Ned were joint tenants. Mike gave Pam an option to purchase his half-interest but then died before Pam had exercised the option. Pam sought to exercise the option thereafter but Ned refused to honor it. The court held that the option had not severed the joint tenancy, that Ned had survived to the entire estate and was not subject to the option. The court said "Pam's option was only an option on Mike's interest. When Mike died, the option died along with it, since Mike did not have an estate of inheritance unless he outlived Ned. It is absurd to contend that this option severed the joint tenancy so as to make Mike's interest exempt from the doctrine of survivorship. This is a far cry from a deed by one joint tenant actually conveying his interest in the property and thereby severing the joint estate."

Sally v. Walt, 1978 In this case Rose and Sally were joint tenants who conveyed their property to Ted by a single deed and took back a single promissory note for the price, which was payable to both of them and was secured by a mortgage on the property. Before the note fell due Rose died and Sally claimed that she was entitled to receive the entire proceeds of the note. The court held that Rose's heir, Walt, rather than Sally, was entitled to Rose's half of the proceeds. The court said "The joint tenancy in the land was terminated when Sally and Rose conveyed their property and it is absurd to say that they held the note in joint tenancy thereafter since nowhere did the note or mortgage say that they were to be treated as joint tenants with regard to payment. Pam v. Ned is quite different since it involved an option which was never exercised."

Please advise Calvin as to what you think a court will do in this case. Explain to him how you see either or both of the cited cases as resolving his problem.

QUESTION III

Owen owned a parcel of land which contained a large cave underground reached by a long tunnel. He had built a medium size house and two other houses on the surface of his land. The big house sat directly over the cave, the medium house was over the tunnel, and the little house was near the tunnel entrance. A pictorial description follows. (The dotted vertical lines indicate how the land was subsequently subdivided, discussed in the next paragraph).

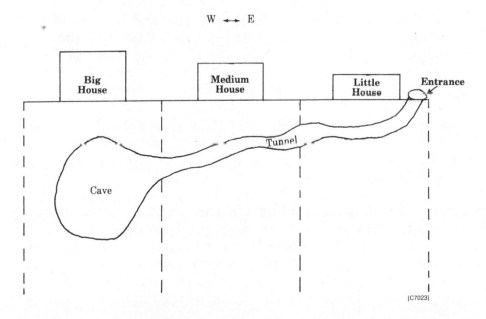

Owen subsequently subdivided his property into the three parcels shown and, in 1972, he sold the east parcel (the one with the little house) to Ed and Fred, who took title as joint tenants. In 1973, he sold the middle parcel (with the medium house on it) to Minnie. Finally, in 1974, he sold the west parcel (with the big house) to Wes. Each sale was properly consummated, and each deed was properly executed, delivered and recorded.

As a boy, Owen had often wandered down the tunnel and played in the cave, but this had ended with his adulthood and, in fact, he had forgotten entirely about the tunnel and cave when he sold the three parcels. Consequently, no mention of their existence was made to any of the buyers.

For the next several years, the owners all resided peacefully in their respective houses, except that Ed and Fred had a falling out in 1974 and Fred suddenly vanished one day, leaving no explanation other than a note on the sink saying, "Ed, I have went. (Signed) Fred."

In 1975, Ed discovered the tunnel entrance and wandered down it until he came upon the cave. The route was so circuitous that Ed was unsure as where he was precisely, but he believed that the cave was directly below his own house. He saw commercial possibilities with the cave and set to work installing electric lights and hanging pictures of his family in the tunnel and cave. He opened it up as a tourist attraction in 1976 and sold admissions to eager visitors, grossing an average of $44,322.39 yearly over the next several years.

Meanwhile, in 1977, Fred visited an attorney who explained to him what it meant to be a joint tenant of the east parcel. Since Fred was considerably older than Ed, Fred promptly conveyed his interest in the property to his girlfriend Gina.

In 1978, Fred and Gina were travelling in the vicinity and learned about Ed's cave. They went to see it and met Ed there. Ed said that they should make a tour of it, and insisted that Fred go in free. Fred did not want Ed to know anything about the deed to Gina, so he insisted that Gina buy a ticket for herself before entering, which she did ($2.15, including tax).

Also during these years Minnie and Wes occasionally brought their friends over to visit the cave. Since they all assumed that the cave was entirely on Ed's property, they gladly paid the reduced admission fee which Ed offered to charge them as good neighbors ($1.95, including tax).

In 1982, Ed decided to enlarge and straighten the tunnel in order to charge a higher admission price. He enlarged and slightly relocated the tunnel. This activity, although done carefully, caused Minnie's parcel to sink slightly and her house began to crack as a result. (There was no subsidence to Ed's or Wes's lot.)

Minnie discovered that the tunnel ran underneath her house when she called in engineers to explain the cracks in her house. The engineers also reported to her that the cave was under Wes's house, and she relayed this information to Wes. Wes was very concerned, because he had planned on enlarging his residence and his architect now advised him that the additions might add so much weight to the surface as to cause the cave underneath to collapse, taking the house along with it.

Minnie and Wes filed appropriate actions against Ed, seeking to enjoin him from using the cave or altering it, and claiming a share of his past profits. Ed answered and cross-complained against Wes, seeking to enjoin him from enlarging his house. Fred and Gina learned of the litigation and filed their own complaint against Ed, Minnie and Wes, seeking appropriate relief. All actions were consolidated.

The relevant statute of limitations for all claims involved here is 5 years.

Assume that all relevant claims have been properly raised and pleaded. What results? Discuss.

ANSWERS TO MULTISTATE QUESTIONS

Question 1

a.   Incorrect, since a deed may describe the property according to any one of several standards or measures.

b.   Incorrect. A reference to the area is unnecessary if there is some other way of identifying the land. Since the deed refers to "all my land," and "44 Main Street" allows that land to be located, the "being one acre" will be ignored.

c.   Incorrect. If the acreage reference is ignored, the deed does not convey more than Pat owns. (In any event, a deed which describes more than the grantor has still works to convey what in fact he does own).

d.   Correct, for the reasons which make the others incorrect. None of the three alleged defects mentioned above invalidates the description.

Question 2

a.   Correct. The southeast corner can start anywhere along Brown's north line. Thus the square portion can be in any number of places, all along Brown's north line. The description is therefore insufficient.

b.   Incorrect. Consideration is unnecessary to a deed, and even when present, cannot overcome an insufficient description.

Bernhardt–Property, 2d BLS—13

c. Incorrect. This ambiguity is apparent from the face of the deed. One need not make a survey in order to know that something is wrong.

d. Incorrect. A covenant of seisin cannot compensate for a bad description. Even if the grantor was seised of the entire farm, which part of it is being conveyed?

Question 3

a. Incorrect. When Pat handed the deed to Mike it was thereby delivered. Its return to Pat does not amount to a redelivery. (A deed cannot be redelivered; the grantee must prepare a new one and deliver that). This was merely a case of Pat holding Mike's deed.

b. Incorrect. A deed must be delivered to be valid, but it need not be recorded. Recordation deals with protection against subsequent bona fide purchasers, not with the question of delivery.

c. Incorrect. Acceptance is presumed when the deed is beneficial, unless there is an express repudiation. Mike's returning the deed for safekeeping was the opposite of a repudiation.

d. Correct. Since the deed was effective to pass title, Mike immediately became owner of the property, and Pat became merely the former owner. Thus, Mike could, e.g., eject Pat.

Question 4

a. Incorrect. Pat did have the right to convey. That fact that his property was subject to an easement meant that he was conveying only a servient tenement, but he did have the right to convey that.

b. Incorrect. Pat still had a servient tenement to convey.

c. Correct. The covenant of quiet enjoyment is breached when there is an actual "eviction" (Jack's using the right of way). Since recovery for breach of this covenant is limited to the price paid, it is also essential that Mike have given consideration for the deed.

d. Incorrect. Since this answer omits the requirement of eviction.

Question 5

a. Correct. Jack has gone beyond the use privileges originally given to him and is now doing acts of possession on Mike's property, As holder of the possessory right, Mike may have the shed removed.

b.   Incorrect. The doctrine of fixtures is irrelevant to Jack's right to maintain the shed. Whether or not it becomes a fixture depends upon how it was initially affixed, and has nothing to do with subsequent acts. If it is a fixture, Jack may lose the right to remove it, but that does not mean that he thereby acquires the right to maintain it.

c.   Incorrect. The servient tenant may have to show unreasonable harm when the question is whether the dominant tenant may make some new use not mentioned by the easement. But when the dominant tenant undertakes acts of possession rather than use, the servient tenant may automatically obtain relief. Acts of possession by the dominant tenant dispossess the servient tenant and will lead to title by adverse possession if the servient tenant does not bring a timely suit in ejectment. Ejectment will lie based upon the mere fact of dispossession; harm is not required.

d.   Incorrect. Since Jack's actions are not authorized by the easement Pat gave him, Pat is not responsible for them. The covenant of quiet enjoyment does not warrant against acts by strangers or acts never authorized by any instrument in the chain of title.

Question 6

a.   Incorrect. It does not appear that the parties agreed that any conveyance to Mike would be automatically invalid. Even if they had made such an agreement, disabling restraints of this sort are unenforceable. Thus, title did pass to Mike and then to Joe.

b.   Correct. Jim cannot invalidate the deed to Mike, since a disabling restraint would be unenforceable. But as a promissory restraint, it will make Pat liable to Jim for breach of his promise.

c.   Incorrect. If Jim sues to set aside the conveyance, he will lose. Joe has no cause to sue Mike. Mike did have the right to convey.

d.   Incorrect. Joe's knowledge would prevent him from being a bona fide purchaser were it necessary for him to be one. However, since Mike had an actual title to convey and the right to convey it, Joe takes Mike's title regardless of what he knows. This is not a recording act problem.

Question 7

a.   Incorrect. The covenant of right to convey is a present covenant and therefore does not run with the land. Pat's covenant ran only to Mike; Mike's covenant to Joe gave Joe a right to sue Mike but not Pat. Mike cannot covenant on behalf of Pat.

b.   Incorrect. The covenant of quiet enjoyment is a future covenant and does run with the land. Therefore Joe or Mike can sue Pat on it.

c.   Correct. Since this covenant does run, anyone who holds the estate benefited thereby may enforce it.

d.   Incorrect. The covenant of quiet enjoyment is implied in all leases but not in deeds. It must be recited in a deed.

Question 8

a.   Incorrect. The Red Cross' executory interest is void under the rule against perpetuities. It is possible that the violation of the residential clause would not occur until more than 21 years after the death of all parties now living. (The exception for charities does not apply here, since it requires that both parties be charities, and Alpha is not).

b.   Incorrect. Alpha's interest remains a determinable fee even after the executory interest following it is stricken. Alpha's estate did not enlarge into a fee simple absolute, but remained determinable.

c.   Correct. Alpha's determinable fee was subject to a possibility of reverter in Owen. This realty interest passed under the will to Bill.

d.   Incorrect. Since the possibility of reverter was devised to Bill, Owen was left with no interest in Blackacre which could pass to Sam. Sam has no interest in the property.

Question 9

a.   and b. Incorrect. The Red Cross did not take a contingent remainder, since it would not take upon the natural expiration of the prior estate. Alpha held a fee simple which could be cut short upon the happening of an event, and the Red Cross would take by virtue of divesting Alpha. Contingent remainders do not divest precedent estates.

c.   Correct. The Red Cross held an executory interest which would divest Alpha when and if it ever vested in the Red Cross. However, as the answer to the previous question indicated, the fact that this non-vested interest could possibly vest after the period allowed by the rule against perpetuities meant that it was void.

d.   Incorrect. Since the Red Cross' executory interest violates the rule against perpetuities, it cannot be valid.

Question 10

a.   Correct. As shown in question 8, Owen held a possibility of reverter in Blackacre by virtue of the invalidating of the Red Cross' executory interest. When this interest passed to Bill, its character (and label) were unchanged.

b.   Incorrect. Had this interest been originally created in Bill, rather than transferred to him at a later date, it would have been a (void) executory interest. However, since Bill received merely the interest which Owen had, he took a possibility of reverter. The difference between an executory interest and a possibility of reverter is that the former is created in a third person whereas the latter is created in the grantor.

c.   Incorrect. There is no such interest. It is a nonsense combination of terms.

d.   Incorrect, since a. is correct.

Question 11

a.   Incorrect. Covenants to pay taxes are generally held to touch and concern land because they protect titles from loss due to tax sales. Taxes are a lien if unpaid, and so covenants to pay them keep the title free from liens. (This includes even the burden of the covenant, although the act of paying money would not normally appear to be related to land).

b.   Correct. Since the covenant to pay taxes does touch and concern land and therefore generally runs with the land, its benefits and burdens fall upon the present holders of the relevant estates, Larry and Annie. Thus, Larry may recover from Annie.

c.   Incorrect. When a covenant runs, it binds the holder of the burdened estate without the need for his or her assent. Assent of the remote taker is necessary only when the covenant does not run.

d.   Incorrect. The benefit as well as the burden of this covenant runs. Thus, the benefit passes to Larry without the need for any assignment.

Question 12

a.   Incorrect. Tina remains liable for the rent because of her original promise to pay it. Burdens cannot be assigned away. Tina is liable regardless of whether she assigns or sublets.

b.   Correct. The covenant to pay rent touches and concerns land, and both its burden and benefit run. As successor to the burdened leasehold estate, Annie must now pay rent to Larry who is the successor owner of the benefited reversion.

c.   Incorrect. Larry can probably enforce the assumption agreement as a third party beneficiary, if need be. However, since the covenant runs and binds Annie in any event, the assumption agreement is irrelevant.

d.   Incorrect. Tina might well be able to recover the rent from Annie, especially if she had been compelled to pay Larry. However, Tina's rights arise from the assumption agreement and not because the burden of Tina's promise to pay rent to Owen was ever converted into a benefit to receive rent from Annie. A covenant may run, but while doing so it does not convert itself from burdensome to beneficial.

Question 13

a.   Incorrect. Larry, the present landlord, has responsibility to maintain the common areas, which remain in his possession. The worst thing Larry could do is show that the injury occurred in a common area; Larry should try to show that the defect was in premises under the exclusive possession of the tenant.

b.   Incorrect. Tina, as former tenant and "seller" of the leasehold to Annie had no duty to inspect for defects prior to sale. Even a landlord has no such duty prior to leasing to a tenant.

c.   Incorrect. The covenant is no defense for Annie the present tenant. As possessor, Annie owes certain duties of care toward invitees, which cannot be escaped by having third parties undertake them. The covenant may make the landlord also liable to the customer, or may allow Annie to cross-complain against the landlord for indemnity, but it does not allow Annie to avoid her general duty of care.

d.   Correct. A landlord does have a duty to disclose to the tenant latent defects known to him/her on pain of being liable for personal injuries resulting from nondisclosure. This duty probably survives the transfers of the estates involved, although some states might hold that lack of privity is a defense.

Question 14

a.   Correct. There is an implied condition of marketable title in every contract for the sale of land unless expressly waived. Van's obligation is to convey such at the time of closing.

b.   Incorrect. As a fixture, the barn is part of the realty and therefore has been sold to Paul.

c. Incorrect. Paul has not yet paid the price and in fact can withdraw from the contract if he learns of any title defects prior to the consummation of the contract. Thus he is not yet within the protection of the recording acts.

d. Incorrect. Possession passes with legal title. Equitable conversion gives Paul a right to compel delivery of the legal title (by suing for specific performance), but not prior to the date contemplated by the parties for performance.

Question 15

a. Incorrect. Van's obligation as to marketable title is not required to be performed prior to February 15. Therefore Paul must wait until then.

b. Correct. If Van has disposed of Ann by February 15th, then he is capable of passing marketable title to Paul at that time. Unless time is of the essence, Van will be allowed additional reasonable time to get rid of Ann.

c. Incorrect. The transfer of title from Van to Paul would not interrupt Ann's possession. She would need only eight more years.

d. Incorrect. Paul's title policy would not insure him against subsequent threats to his title. So long as he had a good title as against Ann when he took Van's deed (i.e., he could eject Ann), his loss is strictly his own.

Question 16

a. Incorrect. An adverse possessor never has a good deed to the property possessed, since that would be owning rather than adversely possessing it. The wrong description bars Betty's deed from being color of title to this land, and thereby acquiring constructive adverse possession to any extra land, but it does not defeat her basic adverse possession claim.

b. Incorrect. The recording acts do not apply to adverse possessors. And Paul will probably be charged with constructive notice of Ann by virtue of his duty to inspect the land as well as the records.

c. Incorrect. Paul's contract right to a marketable title ends when he accepts Van's deed. Thereafter, his rights, if any, against Van depend strictly upon language in the deed.

d. Correct. Once Betty acquires title by adverse possession, she is a full owner. An owner does not lose her title by failing to possess her property for a short time.

Question 17

a.   Incorrect. As a joint tenant, Van may convey his half interest without Wanda's consent or signature. His interest is freely alienable.

b.   Incorrect. A deed by Van will convey his one-half interest and will convey none of Wanda's interest. Therefore, he alone may keep the proceeds.

c.   Incorrect. The deed will make Paul into a tenant in common with Wanda. They cannot be joint tenants because Paul has taken his title at a different time and from a different source (no unity of time or title).

d.   Correct. As tenant in common, Paul has the right to possess the entire property subject only to Wanda's equal right to do the same. Neither may exclude the other.

Question 18

a.   Incorrect. Covenants sometimes require a common plan in order to be enforced in equity, but this is no requirement for conditions in deeds. If a condition is properly written, it will be enforced upon a mere showing of violation.

b.   Incorrect. Easements differ from covenants in that they do not require privity as a condition of their creation. Any two persons may create an easement between them.

c.   Correct. Equity will not enforce covenants when it is no longer equitable to do so, i.e., when changed conditions render the benefit too doubtful to warrant continued imposition of the burden.

d.   Incorrect. Zoning ordinances may be modified by the proper political process at any time. Of all the mechanisms listed, zoning ordinances are the easiest to alter.

Question 19

a.   Incorrect. Sometimes it is required that the subdivider continue to own some benefited property in the subdivision in order to enforce the covenant. But no jurisdiction requires the subdivider to make a reciprocal covenant as a condition for enforcement of the purchaser's promise.

b.   Incorrect. Prior grantees may enforce on either a third party beneficiary theory *or* by showing that the benefit of covenants they received ran with the land to bind the subsequent purchaser. But the two theories are different, and do not depend on one another. Thus it is not necessary to show both.

c. Correct. Subsequent grantees do enforce by showing that they have succeeded to benefited property. In order to avoid the defense of acquiescence, they must enforce it against all violators.

d. Incorrect. The Fourteenth Amendment is not violated by a residential covenant which does not exclude any particular class of persons. The municipality probably cannot enforce a covenant to which it is not a party, but this has nothing to do with the Constitution.

Question 20

a. Incorrect. Zoning enforcement is vested exclusively in public officials. Aggrieved individuals may request the government to act and may even sue to compel the government to do so but have no standing to enforce the ordinance directly against other individuals.

b. Incorrect. ABC needs to obtain a variance, not a special use permit.

c. Incorrect. Covenants may impose restrictions greater than those created by a zoning ordinance, so long as there is no inconsistency between them. In this case, single family use does not violate a multi-family residential zone, so the two are compatible.

d. Correct. Zoning is basically prospective. An attempt to stop a previously lawful use might constitute an unconstitutional taking of property, which the city may avoid by tolerating nonconforming uses.

Question 21

a. Incorrect. A private nuisance always results from activity conducted upon private property. The issue is whether the activity causes unreasonable harm, not whether it is on one's own land.

b. Incorrect. Overlying owners have at least correlative rights to pump from common underground basins. Oren may be able to limit Nina's pumping, or to pump himself, but he may not categorically stop her from pumping.

c. Incorrect. A trespass can occur above or below the surface. The owner's boundary lines are not vertically limited except at extreme distances.

d. Correct. Actionable removal of support can occur by withdrawal of water. Her activities on her land have deprived Oren of the natural support he once had, and she is liable.

Question 22

a. Incorrect. The avoidance of waste is a duty owed to others who hold interests in the same property, e.g., cotenants or holders of future interests. It does not apply to neighbors. Oren may have a cause of action in tort for the wrongful discharge of surface waters onto his land, but the theory is not waste.

b. Incorrect. A fixture is real property. It should be taxed as such.

c. Correct. Nina is not entitled to nonconforming use protection if the rules involved were in effect at the time her activity commenced. She has, at best, a defense of laches if the county knew of her activities and failed to act in a timely fashion.

d. Incorrect. At no time in the past did Nina ever have a cause of action against Oren because his land was dry; therefore she cannot have lost any such one by failing to sue. Her privilege to pump cannot be converted into a duty to pump by the passage of time.

Question 23

a. Correct. If the jurisdiction treats a mortgage as conveying a title to the mortgagee, then the execution of one works a severance, as does any conveyance by a joint tenant.

b. Incorrect. Ann has mortgaged only her fractional interest in the property (regardless of whether the mortgage is treated as a lien or a title). On foreclosure, the mortgagee will acquire only what she had.

c. Incorrect. The foreclosure purchaser has neither unity of time nor title with Bob, having taken at a different time and by a different instrument than did Bob. Again, the result is independent of whether the original mortgage was treated as a title or a lien.

d. Incorrect. If the mortgage gives the mortgagee a title and severs the joint tenancy, then the mortgagee has an interest on a tenancy in common estate. Upon Ann's death, the mortgage will follow the transfer of her interest to her heirs or legatees, but will not affect Bob's interest. If the mortgage is a lien and does not sever the joint tenancy, then Bob will take the entire estate by survivorship on Ann's death, free and clear of the mortgage, and the mortgagee's interest in the property will be destroyed. In neither event is Bob's share of the estate subject to the mortgage.

ANSWERS TO ESSAY QUESTIONS
QUESTION I

The question raises three sets of issues for you to cover: (1) Lil's problems with the neighbors (and ABC); (2) her problems with the zoning administrator; (3) and her problems with Tess. The discussion of Tess's right should come last, because it is dependent upon the other two matters. The other 2 issues can be discussed in either order.

(1) *Lil v. The Neighbors.* The issue you must discuss here is whether Lil's land is restricted the same as are the neighbors' lots. Although the deeds in her own chain of title do not contain any such restrictions, the neighbors or the neighborhood association may be able to impose such a restriction on her anyway. If some of the neighbors took deeds to their lots from ABC *prior* to the deed to Pete being delivered, they may be able to claim that all of the land ABC still held at the time it conveyed their lots to them was similarly restricted by virtue of the first clause of the covenant. So you need to ask when, in order of sales from ABC, Pete acquired his lot. (For those neighbors who acquired lots from ABC *after* Pete, such a theory would not work because, it was by then, too late for ABC to restrict land which it had already conveyed to Pete.) The standing of the neighborhood association is also an issue and you should want to know whether it holds any land itself, especially whether or not it holds any lot which was conveyed to it prior to the conveyance to Pete, and also whether the deed of such a lot from ABC to the association restricted the rest of the subdivision for the benefit of the association lot. (ABC itself appears to have no basis of enforcement since Pete never promised ABC to restrict this lot.)

A series of other questions follow for you to discuss. Do the provisions in the other deeds actually restrict ABC's retained lots? They are not worded as express covenants by ABC and a court would need to construe them favorably to the neighbors in order to impose such restrictions on ABC's retained land. A general plan would be helpful to the neighbors here, and you should consider investigating how many lots in the entire subdivision really are similarly restricted.

The restriction appears clearly to touch and concern land, but you can raise a question as to where the benefit is. The neighbors will have to show that the effect of the common clause was not only to restrict ABC's retained lots but to confer the benefit of the restriction upon each of their lots; perhaps they might need to show that they relied upon the promised imposition of a reciprocal restriction as a condition for agreeing to restrict their own lots.

Horizontal privity requirements are probably satisfied, since these are covenant in deeds (which is generally sufficient). But there is a vertical privity problem: although Pete succeeded to ABC's entire estate in the lot, and Lil succeeded to Pete's entire estate, Tess only took a leasehold estate from Lil, and is therefore not in vertical privity with her. Consequently, the burden might not run at law to bind her. But you must also consider whether the restriction is enforceable against Tess as an equitable servitude (without the need for vertical privity) and, if so, whether there is a defense if either Tess or Lil took without notice of the restriction. You should find out what either of them knew. (For instance, if Lil obtained a policy of title insurance when she purchased the property, did it mention the existence of neighborhood restrictions? Even if it did not, does the jurisdiction require each purchaser to search "deeds out" by a common grantor to see if deeds to other properties restrict the grantor's retained land? Or, is the neighborhood itself so uniform as to impose upon a purchaser the duty of inquiring as to the existence of such restrictions? You have no facts on any of this, so you will have to create the kind of information you wish to acquire.)

Finally, even if the neighbors or neighborhood association do have an equitable theory of enforcement, are there any affirmative defenses which Tess or Lil can raise? It is difficult to construe the covenant as not applying to commercial meditation, but if other neighbors are engaged in commercial activities in their houses defenses of unclean hands or acquiescence or changed conditions may be available. This will entail an investigation by you of the current nature of the neighborhood.

(2) *Lil v. The Zoning Administrator.* Even if the neighbors are unable to enforce the covenant, Lil must worry about whether the zoning administrator can stop the meditation classes. This depends upon the validity of the ordinance. You should investigate whether all of the procedural requirements for the enactment of zoning ordinances were met (e.g. notice, opportunity to be heard, etc.). The ordinance should also be compared to the town's master plan for consistency and may fail if it imposes a restriction incompatible with the plan. Furthermore, you can possibly attack it as spot zoning because it singles out only one neighborhood for the imposition of the restriction. You need to know the character of the rest of the town, the restrictions imposed elsewhere, and the reasons the city gives for confining this restriction to one zone. You can also consider claiming that the restriction is arbitrary and capricious, since meditation, by its nature can hardly disturb neighborhood peace and quiet; perhaps the lack of any findings regarding vehicle or pedestrian traffic to and from the house might help. Finally, there is the question of retroactvity. Tess' classes commenced prior to the ordinance and may, therefore, be entitled to continue, as a valid nonconforming use, if you can demonstrate that she has a "vested right". If so, immediate enforcement of the ordinance against her would constitute a taking of her property. (These defenses are mostly Tess', but perhaps Lil can raise them for her.)

(3) *Lil v. Tess.* If either the neighbors or the city can stop Tess, Lil faces the problem of Tess' threatened abandonment. Is Tess entitled to leave merely because she cannot conduct meditation classes? The lease neither prohibits her from engaging in such activity nor guarantees her the right; thus she is

free to make other uses of the property. You can probably conclude that Tess is therefore not entitled to terminate the lease just because one activity is foreclosed to her. If she does leave, her departure will be an unjustified abandonment. You should advise Lil that at common law this does not relieve Tess from her rent liability and that Lil might allow the premises to remain vacant and sue Tess for the rent as it falls due (unless the jurisdiction requires Lil to mitigate her damages). Alternatively, Lil could elect to accept a surrender by reentering on her own behalf and resuming control of the premises. Finally, if the jurisdiction permits, Lil can reenter as Tess' agent and relet the premises for Tess' account, suing Tess for the difference between the rent reserved in her lease and what Lil is able to collect from the new tenant over the balance of the term. If your jurisdiction has special statutory provisions on this matter which were covered in class, review those too. (On the other hand, if Tess is entitled to quit, then her departure will work a termination of the lease and Tess would be free of further rent liability.)

Finally, you should advise Lil that she herself should probably not seek to enforce the restriction against Tess, lest she be accused of constructively evicting Tess since the lease itself gives Lil no right to stop Tess from this activity. If there were a constructive eviction, then Tess could quit and stop paying rent.

QUESTION II

Your answer to this question should first analyze the issue of whether or not the joint tenancy was severed by the contract, followed by a discussion of the consequences for each of the two possibilities.

Severance. The authorities cited would let you conclude either way. Each of the cited cases has similarities and differences with the issue at hand and an answer should point these out. *Pam v. Ned* does say that a deed is required to work a severance, but it involved an option rather than a binding contract, the option was given by only one of the two joint tenants and it was never exercised. Creation of an option does not generally work an equitable conversion, (shifting equitable title to the optionee) and the case can be readily distinguished from the specifically enforceable bilateral contract involved here. *Sally v. Walt* seems to hold that sale by the joint tenants produces a severance, but it too can be easily distinguished. That transaction involved a completed transfer of title; Rose and Sally had no ownership interest in the property after the conveyance and the court's opinion may be treated as merely refusing to continue a joint tenancy from the title over to the funds. (If you want to play around with this even more, you can consider whether the case is more or less useful in a jurisdiction which follows a title rather than a lien theory of mortgages.) There is plainly no single correct resolution to the role of these two cases, and this part of your answer will be judged far more for what you make of these cases than on the particular conclusion you draw.

In the case here, there was a binding contract and therefore Amy and Bella held the legal title only as security for Calvin's performance of the contract. Their execution of separate deeds may indicate an intent to sever their joint tenancy, especially since they have been deposited in escrow (irrevocably?). And the doctrine of relation back might allow a court to treat the transaction as having constructively closed, with a severance therefore having occurred. On the other hand, Amy and Bella are still the legal owners of the property and title has not passed, and they may well have intended that no severance occur until funds are received, or perhaps even thereafter. The fact that their escrow instructions called for a single check payable to them jointly might corroborate this intent, although it could also be in order to permit them to make a fuller accounting between themselves later on.

Consequences. In light of the doubtfulness of either conclusion, a good answer should consider both possibilities. If a court concludes that there was no severance, then Amy holds the entire fee simple by virtue of the doctrine of survivorship and the deed she tenders should be sufficient. (Alternatively, in light of the doctrine of relation back, it would be harmless if the original two deeds were used instead.) Amy would be entitled to all of the funds and Calvin would not be entitled to withdraw from the contract since her deed does convey a marketable title.

On the other hand, if the court concludes that a severance did occur, Harry is a tenant in common with Amy. A deed from Amy alone is insufficient since it would convey only ½ of the title. Calvin would certainly not be required to complete the contract and pay the price for such a partial title; nor could Amy force him to take her tenancy in common interest for ½ the price since that is not what he bargained for. Her title is unmarketable and he may withdraw. However, the severance might be offset by a relation back doctrine, if the court used it to validate Bella's earlier delivery of her deed into escrow (especially if it were irrevocably put into escrow). Then the two earlier deeds would furnish Calvin with the title his contract called for, and he would be bound to pay the full price. The sales proceeds would probably be divided between Amy and Harry in this situation, but that is of no concern to Calvin. None of these consequences is much in dispute (after the basic severance issue is resolved) and the bulk of your writing and analysis should probably be devoted to the question of severance. However, it would be unwise on your part not to cover all of the consequential possibilities.

QUESTION III

This is a very complicated question and organization will probably play a significant role in the professor's evaluation of your answer. A substantial amount of time should be spent on reading and rereading the problem (and possibly making a factual outline of it for yourself); an even more substantial period of time should be spent on outlining the answer and making sure that every small point is covered somewhere before you start writing.

There are three possible ways to go about organizing an answer to this question: (1) chronological—where a legal analysis is made of each new fact as it arises; (2) topical—covering one broad issue at a time; (3) litigational—discussing all of the issues that pertain to each of the separate conflicts between the parties. The third is probably the easiest to follow because it involves less circularity and repetition than do the others. My comments are organized that way but a good answer could easily be differently arranged.

Wes v. Ed. The first issue which must be discussed (because almost everything else depends on it) is ownership of the cave. Obviously, record title to the cave itself is in Wes since he owns the surface. But the facts require a discussion of adverse possession, because Ed has been using the cave for over five years. (A prescriptive easement might also be considered, but should probably be rejected since the charging of admission by Ed for entry is a fairly possessory act.) The elements of adverse possession which are in doubt here are openness and hostility. Openness (and notoriety) are in issue because Wes was not aware of the fact that Ed was in a cave under his property. The requisite hostility may be missing in those jurisdictions which do not permit an adverse possession to be founded on mistake (since Ed thought he was under his own property). These two points should receive extensive treatment. A minor adverse possession issue would be the payment of taxes, if the jurisdiction required it.

If you conclude that Ed's claim of adverse possession fails, then Wes does own the cave and you should discuss his remedies. He should be able to eject Ed from the cave and should also be entitled to some portion of the profits Ed made from selling admissions to the cave. (If you have time, you can speculate as to a method of allocating the profits.) Since admission fees were also derived from the tunnel and its entrance as well (which do not belong to Wes), some apportionment of profits might be in order. You might also go further and inquire whether or not Wes has some entitlement to enter into his cave through the entrance on Ed's land; perhaps an easement by implication or by necessity?

If, on the other hand, you conclude that Ed has met the requirements of adverse possession, that will dispose of Wes's claims for ejectment, accounting, and entry, but it raises its own problem of support. If Ed does own the cave beneath Wes's house, he has a duty of furnishing subjacent support to the house. However, since the facts do not indicate any plans by Ed to alter the cave (only the tunnel), this matter is technically not an issue in this question. You should only go into it if you know your professor wants you to search for remote issues; otherwise it deserves only a mention.

As a matter of wisdom, you should try to cover both alternatives (adverse possession or no adverse possession), in order to cover more issues, rather than pinning all on the hope that you have reached the "correct" conclusion as to adverse possession.

Ed v. Wes. This case is pretty much the converse of the previous one, and many of the points you have raised earlier need merely be referred to here. If Ed is a successful adverse possessor, then he should be entitled to a quiet title decree to the cave as against Wes. Furthermore, he may have some right to demand that Wes not put too much weight on the surface so as to jeopardize the integrity of the cave. (You may have to invent a theory here, since this is not a situation involving conventional notions of lateral or subjacent support.) If Ed fails in his claim of adverse possession, then he is obviously not entitled to quiet title or demand support, but he still owns the tunnel entrance and may be able to insist that Wes not enter upon his land to get into the cave.

Minnie v. Ed. Most of the issues are the same here as in the previous cases and much can thus be incorporated by reference. Whether Ed has successfully established adverse possession to the tunnel involves the same issues as were involved in his claim of adverse possession to the cave. If he doesn't have a good claim of adverse possession then Minnie owns the tunnel, can eject him, and can claim some of his past profits. (Again, if time permits, devise a theory for allocating them.) If he does have a good claim then he owes the same duty of subjacent support to her as he did to Wes. The subjacent support issue is more serious here, because actual damage has been done to Minnie's house as a result of Ed's activities, and since this duty is absolute, his carefulness in this respect is irrelevant. You should discuss his liability for her injury. As with Wes, if Minnie owns the tunnel she may have some right of access through Ed's entrance. There is also one new issue here, which involves the fact that Ed is improving and relocating the tunnel. If he owns the tunnel, he is free to improve it, but relocating it might constitute a trespass if it travels under different parts of Minnie's land, and she might enjoin that. If you conclude that Ed has an easement in the tunnel, is this a permissible variation of it?

Ed v. Minnie. You should quiet Ed's title to the tunnel if you conclude he is an adverse possessor. Since there is no indication that Minnie is doing anything to her house, there appears to be no issue of "superjacent" support involved here. If Ed is not an adverse possessor, he may still be able to retain some of the profits for the tunnel.

Gina v. Ed. On the records, Gina has a tenancy in common interest in Ed's property, since her predecessor in title, Fred, was a joint tenant with Ed. As such, she may have a claim to share in Ed's profits resulting from use of the common property (recall the Statute of Anne). But this claim involves two difficulties which you must discuss.

First, has Gina lost her claim against Ed by virtue of the statute of limitations? Even if you concluded that Ed was a successful adverse possessor against Wes and/

or Minnie, this is a different matter because successful adverse possession against a co-tenant requires an ouster. Was there one here? The facts for you to work with are that Ed did not charge Fred admission (who, for all he knew, was still his joint tenant) and that Gina did pay the admission fee. But it is very confused because perhaps Ed let Fred in free out of friendship rather than in recognition of any right he thought Fred had, and Gina's payment is equivocal in light of the fact that Ed didn't know she had succeeded to Fred's title and she had other reasons for not telling him. There is also the fact that Fred had previously abandoned the property which, while not in itself sufficient to pass a title to Ed, might support the finding of an ouster later on. However, the visit by Fred and Gina perhaps occurred less than five years ago and, if that is when the clock first started running, it might be too recent. If you conclude that Ed has established adverse possession against Gina, that should dispose of any claims she has against him, either to assert her title to the land or to share in his profits.

Second, even if you conclude that Ed did not establish adverse possession against Gina, there is the question of how much she owns. Her claim to the surface is still good, but should she share in Ed's ownership of the tunnel and cave (if you have concluded that he had acquired them by adverse possession against Wes and Minnie)? Ed's adverse possession of the tunnel and cave resulted from his own acts in those places, but his entry to them was through the tunnel entrance, which was on the commonly held property. So perhaps you want to work out some accounting that would give Gina a share of the past profits only. And you will have to decide whether, if Ed did establish adverse possession against Wes and Minnie but not against Gina, she is a tenant in common to the tunnel and cave, or merely to the entrance to it.

Don't expect to have figured all this out on your own under exam pressures; I doubt that any professor would expect this much.

*

APPENDIX C

TEXT
CORRELATION CHART

Bernhardt Property Black Letter	Browder, 5th Ed.	Casner, 3rd Ed.	Cribbett, 6th Ed.	Donahue, 2nd Ed.	Dukeminier, 2nd Ed.	Haar, 2nd Ed.	Rabin, 2nd Ed.
Chapter I Adverse Possession	44–96	52–64	139–156	108–162	86–130	66–88	745–790
Chapter II Estates in Land	202–327	183–352	209–579	506–694	143–539	201–255; 483–560	165–374
Types	207–241	205–352	209–435	509	156–373		165–229; 260–279
Rule Against Perpetuities	246–252	335–352	302–321	594–610	250–277	611–648	229–260
Rule in Shelly's Case	242–243	302–310	281–285	551–552	241–244	498	
Doctrine of Worthier Title	244–245	310–316	285–291	551–552	244–246	498	178–180
Restraints on Alienation	249–265	973–978	302–304	569–616	140–202	203–225	279–297
Marital Estates	266–277	219–243	332–342	557–559	324–373	863–908	246–374
Chapter III Concurrent Ownership	277–327	251–284	322–425	559–568; 617–694	279–373	853–908	297–345; 374–399
Chapter IV Landlord and Tenant	328–513	353–662	426–579	787–1035	375–539	255–482	21–164
Types of Tenancies	328–354	243–250	426–435	787–826	377–383	255–259	119–130
Possession	370–406	423–626	436–579	827–907	391–397; 431–454	259–286	21–44
Condition of the Premises	407–477	359–422	456–480	936–1017	417–486	330–350	45–118; 131–148
Tort Liability	478–513	375–395	481–494	936–990	487–499	294–329	
Transfers by the Parties	355–369	553–586	564–579	1017–1021	383–415	259–268	149–164
Chapter V Easements	514–595	1056–1114	580–647	1078–1142	825–889	909–933	400–479; 790–822
Creation	537–567		582–629		829–863	909–933	400–418
Express Easements	537–541	1058–1060	582–600	1080–1120	829–841		418–434
Implied Easements	542–556	1060–1068	601–612	1121–1139	842–871	88–101	463–479
Prescriptive Easements	557–567	1069–1082	613–629	1121–1139	842–863	88–101	790–822
Scope of Easement	568–587	1083–1097	630–643	1078–1139	864–871		418–434
Transfer and Subdivision	588–595	1098–1100	630–643				434–446
Termination	588–595	1101–1105	644–647	1140–1142	942–964	920	447–462
Chapter VI Covenants	596–689	987–1055	648–715	1143–1220	890–985	934–1089	480–524; 527–575
Requirements	596–624	987–1013	649–666	1143–1202	890–941	934–958	480–510; 527–575
Equitable Servitudes	629–687	1013–1029	667–689	1153–1220	897–964	958–976	527–575
Subdivisions	631–689		801–819	1185–1220	964–985	977–1071	
Defenses	683–686	1052–1055	690–715	1204–1220	942–963		511–524

Bernhardt Property Black Letter	Browder, 5th Ed.	Casner, 3rd Ed.	Cribbett, 6th Ed.	Donahue, 2nd Ed.	Dukeminier, 2nd Ed.	Haar, 2nd Ed.	Rabin, 2nd Ed.
Chapter VII Brokers	915-946	667-712	1122-1140	697-714; 770-781	543-554	651-668	921-968
Chapter VIII Contracts for Sale	915-993	663-738	980-1121	765-786	548-588	672-778	834-849; 991-1006 1111-1132
Elements	915-946	663-692	981-1021	713-769	548-566	672-690	834-849
Marketable Title	947-972	716-723	1059-1071	736-751	545-564	716-720	991-1006
Risk of Loss	973-980	724-738	1107-1121		566-573	690-692	1111-1132
Chapter IX Deeds	749-809	755-800	1141-1202	462-505	601-649	748-758	823-833; 850-877 888-905
Elements	749-780	755-800	1149-1162	462-487	601-607	748-758	823-833; 850-877
Delivery	781-809	762-775	1163-1202	488-505	608-644		888-905
Chapter X Priorities	810-847	801-868	1203-1267	727-735	646-689	694-746	1007-1064
Recording Acts	810-847	801-876	1203-1233	727-735	690-733	697-701	1012-1013
Value	819-821	859-868			745-781		
Notice	815-823	843-868	1234-1259		705-744		
Chapter XI Title Assurance	848-914	869-918	1268-1434	727-769	645-781	720-778	906-920; 1065-1110
Title Covenants	848-855	869-900	1268-1336	471-474; 507-510	646-669	758-776	906-920
Title Insurance	862-890	919-938	1367-1434	751-764	670-689	720-725	1065-1110
Chapter XII Mortgages	933-946	739-754	1032-1058	713-727	588-601	781-850	1149-1217
Chapter XIII Miscellaneous Doctrines:							2-20; 206-228 576-616; 878-887
Water	148-188	1205-1226	747-787	322-359	29-31	133-200	605-616
Support	189-201	1195-1204	733-746	686	796-797		598-604
Trespass				1037-1048	67-77		2-20
Nuisance	112-131	1444	716-732	1038-1077	783-824		576-597
Airspace	132-147	1227-1242	764-787	375-395	872-890	1151-1181	
Fixtures	511-513	607-626	534		114		878-887
Waste	253-261	731	244-248	520-528	175-181	239-244	206-228

Bernhardt Property Black Letter	Browder, 5th Ed.	Casner, 3rd Ed.	Cribbett, 6th Ed.	Donahue, 2nd Ed.	Dukeminier, 2nd Ed.	Haar, 2nd Ed.	Rabin, 2nd Ed.
Chapter XIV							
Land Use	1109–1376	1115–1192	820–889	1221–1342	987–1259	1089–1328	617–744
Zoning	1109–1231	1115–1165	788–876	1237–1308	1115–1259	1089–1262	617–639
Other Forms of Regulation	1303–1376	1166–1192	801–819	1309–1342	987–1113	1265–1328	705–722
Judicial Review	1232–1302		829–870	1242–1342	987–1259	1263–1328	640–704; 723–744

APPENDIX D

GLOSSARY

INTRODUCTION

I have prepared this glossary by going through the text and picking out all of the technical words which lack a common sense meaning. The definitions given here are not taken from a law dictionary but have been written by me to conform to the text discussion of the appropriate concepts. (The relevant chapters are shown in parentheses following the words.) This glossary can also be used as a quiz or refresher to check your understanding of some—although not all—of the matters discussed in this book.

A

Accretion (Conveyances) The alteration of a boundary line due to the gradual addition of land to one side of the stream which serves as the boundary.

Active Waste See Affirmative Waste.

Adverse Possession The act of wrongly possessing property owned by another so as to trigger the running of the statute of limitations against the true owner. Alternatively, the completion of such wrongful possession such as to bar the true owner's cause of action in ejectment by virtue of the statute having run.

Affirmative Easement The privilege of engaging in activity on land possessed by someone else which would otherwise be unprivileged.

Affirmative Waste (Miscellaneous Doctrines) Activity by a possessor of land which unreasonably impairs the value of other estates in the same land.

After-Acquired Title (Title Assurance) Title acquired by a grantor after he has conveyed or mortgaged the subject property.

Architectural Review See Design Review.

Assumption (Landlord-Tenant; Mortgages) A promise by an assignee or subtenant made to a tenant to perform (i.e., assume) the obligations owed by the tenant to the landlord. Alternatively, a promise by a purchaser of land to the seller to perform the obligations owed by the seller to a mortgagee.

Avulsion (Conveyances) The sudden addition or removal of land from one side of a stream; boundary lines marked by the stream are not thereby affected.

C

Chain of Title (Contracts, Priorities) The history of ownership of a parcel of land from its original source, usually the government, through the various intermediate owners, up to the present holder of title.

Closing See Settlement.

Cluster Zoning (Land Use) An ordinance which permits the owner of a large parcel of land to ignore the density requirement otherwise applicable to individual lots, so long as the entire project is within the limits specified by the ordinance.

Collateral Covenant (Covenants) A covenant which does not touch and concern land, i.e., is not "real", and therefore does not run with the land.

Comprehensive Plan See Plan.

Condominium (Concurrent Ownership) Ownership of common areas of a project in common with other owners and separate own-

ership of the individual unit in the condominium project.

Community Property (Concurrent Ownership) Property in some western states which is acquired by spouses during their marriage.

Condition Subsequent (Estates) An event which, if it occurs or fails to occur, terminates an existing estate.

Conditional Use (Land Use) A use which is permitted in many zones, so long as conditions are met to ameliorate its adverse impact on the neighborhood. Also known as a special exception.

Constructive Eviction (Landlord and Tenant) The right of a tenant to quit the premises and cease paying rent when his quiet enjoyment of the premises has been rendered impossible by some breach of obligation owed to him by the landlord.

Constructive Notice (Priorities) Notice charged to a purchaser of land, even in the absence of actual knowledge, by virtue of information properly recorded in the official records (or visible from the fact of possession).

Constructive Possession (Adverse Possession) Land which a person may acquire by adverse possession even though he has never had actual possession of it, where he does have a color of title to it and has actually possessed some part of it.

Contingent Remainder (Estates) A remainder which has either been given to an unascertained person or which is subject to some condition precedent, other than the natural termination of a preceding estate.

Contract Zoning (Land Use) An arrangement whereby a local government grants a zoning entitlement to a property owner in return for some promise or consideration by the owner.

Covenant Against Encumbrances (Title Assurance) A grantor's covenant that there are no encumbrances against the title.

Covenant of Further Assurance (Title Assurance) A grantor's covenant to take all steps necessary to protect the grantee's title.

Covenant of Good Right to Convey (Title Assurance) A grantor's covenant that she is entitled to convey the property.

Covenant of Quiet Enjoyment (Landlord-Tenant; Title Assurance) A grantor's or landlord's covenant that the grantee or tenant shall enjoy the property free of disturbance by lawful claims by others.

Covenant of Seisin (Title Assurance) A grantor's covenant that she is seised of the property which she purports to convey.

Covenant of Warranty (Title Assurance) A grantor's covenant to defend the grantee's title against claims of third persons.

Covenant Running With the Land A promise made with respect to land which burdens one parcel and/or benefits another and is binding not only upon the original parties to the promise but also upon their successors in interest to the parcels involved as well.

Cumulative Zoning (Land Use) A form of zoning which permits any "higher" use to exist in a lower zoned district.

Curtesy (Estates) An interest in the wife's property given at common law to a husband by virtue of marriage.

Curtesy Consummate (Estates) The nature of a husband's curtesy interest after the birth of children and the death of his wife, i.e., a life estate in all of her freehold property.

Curtesy Initiate (Estates) The nature of a husband's curtesy interest after children were born alive and before death of his wife.

D

Deed (Conveyances) The instrument by which title to an interest in land is passed from one party to another.

Deed of Trust See Mortgages.

Defeasible (Estates) An estate which is not absolute, i.e., one which is determinable or subject to an executory limitation or condition subsequent.

Deficiency Judgment (Mortgages) The monetary claim a mortgagee has against a mortgagor when a foreclosure sale of the property fails to produce sufficient funds to satisfy the secured obligation.

Delivery (Conveyances) The transaction which makes a deed effective to pass title.

Design Review (Land Use) A process whereby a building permit is not issued until the proposed building is determined to comply with the design or architectural standards established by the land use regulation.

Destructibility (Estates) A characteristic of contingent remainders which requires them to have become vested remainders on or before the time they are to become possessory or else suffer total destruction.

Divestment (Estates) The complete loss of an interest in land (total divestment) or the partial loss of it by virtue of others sharing it (partial divestment).

Dominant Tenant (Easements) The person who holds the benefit of an easement.

Dominant Tenement (Easements) Land which is benefitted by an easement.

Dower (Estates) A life estate given to a widow in ⅓ of the property of which her husband had been seised sometime during the marriage.

Dower Consummate (Estates) The nature of a wife's dower interest after the death of her husband, i.e., a ⅓ life estate in eligible property.

Dower Inchoate (Estates) The status of the wife's dower interest at common law, prior to the death of her husband: an interest not subject to fraudulent conveyance, alienation, or seizure by creditors.

Duty (Easements) In Hohfeldian (and Restatement) usage, a duty means that a person is under a legally enforceable obligation to do or not do a certain act at the demand of another person (who holds the corresponding right). In the absence of a duty, the person is privileged to do or not do the act, without complaint by the other person (who then has no right). A negative easement imposes upon the servient tenement a duty to not do some act on her land which would otherwise be privileged. (See also Right and Privilege.)

E

Easement A nonpossessory interest in land, consisting of either a privilege to make some use of land possessed by another (affirmative) or of the right to restrain the possessor from making some use which would otherwise be privileged (negative).

Easement Appurtenant An easement which benefits the owner of some other property in her capacity as owner of that property rather than as an individual.

Easement by Implication An easement created because the circumstances surrounding a division of land justify a court in inferring that the parties intended that one of the resulting parcels have an easement over the other.

Easement in Gross An easement which benefits a person as an individual rather than as possessor of some other property.

Ejectment (Adverse Possession) A cause of action in favor of a person entitled to possession of land against anyone guilty of wrongful dispossession.

Environmental Impact Report/Statement (Land Use) A study prepared by a government agency concerning the environmental impact of any project which it intends to undertake or to approve.

Equitable Conversion (Contracts) The doctrine that, since equity regards as done what ought to be done, once parties have executed a binding contract for the sale of land, equitable title vests in the purchaser and the vendor holds legal title only as security for payment of the balance of the purchase price.

Equity of Redemption (Mortgages) The right given by courts of equity to delinquent mortgagors permitting them to pay their debts late and thereby avoid forfeiture of their property.

Escrow (Conveyances) The handing of a deed from a grantor to a third party, irrevocably, with instructions to the third party to hand the deed to the grantee at a future time or if some condition occurs.

Estate for Years See Tenancy for a Term.

Estoppel by Deed (Title Assurance) A doctrine which provides that any title subsequently acquired by a grantor who has warranted the title to the grantee passes directly to the grantee by virtue of the warranty.

Executory Interest (Estates) A future interest in a third person which cuts off a prior interest. It may either "spring" out of the grantor's reversion or may "shift" the seisin from the preceding estate to it.

Exclusionary Zoning (Land Use) The process by which a community employs its land use regulations to exclude persons because of race, income level, etc.

F

Fee Simple (Estates) An interest in land which endures until its then current holder dies without heirs.

Fee Tail (Estates) An interest in land which endures until its then current holder dies without issue.

Fixtures (Miscellaneous Doctrines) A chattel which becomes realty by virtue of affixation to land.

Fixture Filing (Miscellaneous Doctrine) The recording in the real estate records of a security interest in a chattel which is intended to become a fixture.

Floating Zone (Land Use) A zoning category which is described in the ordinance but which is not prelocated on the zoning map for the territory.

Foreclosure (Mortgages) The process by which a mortgagee reaches the mortgagor's property when the obligation is not performed. If the property passes directly to the mortgagee, it is strict foreclosure; if the property is sold in order to satisfy the obligation, it is sale foreclosure.

Freehold (Estates) A common law estate, either a fee simple, fee tail or life estate, which has no ascertainable termination date.

G

General Plan See Plan.

Grant Deed (Conveyances) A deed containing or having implied by law some but not all of the usual covenants of title.

Grantee-Grantor Index (Priorities) A set of indexes organized alphabetically according to the names of all the grantees of documents in the official records.

Grantor-Grantee Index (Priorities) A set of indexes organized alphabetically according to the names of all the grantors of documents in the official records.

Growth Management (Land Use) An ordinance which regulates the rate of growth by a community through restrictions upon the issuance of residential building permits.

H

Historic Preservation (Land Use) An ordinance which prohibits the demolition or exterior alteration of certain historic buildings or of all buildings in an historic district.

Holding Zone (Land Use) A form of low density zoning employed for a temporary purpose until the community decides how to rezone the area.

I

Index (Priorities) A book or set of books organized by the names of the parties or the location of land, indicating where, in the official records, all documents referred to may be found.

Implied Reciprocal Servitude (Covenants) A situation where a court will presume that, in return for a promise made by one party to another respecting land, the promisee has impliedly made a reciprocal promise to the promissor respecting the other land.

Initiative (Land Use) The process by which citizens enact laws directly rather than through their legislators.

Innocent Improver (Miscellaneous Doctrines) A person who innocently improves land of another, thereby possibly losing title to the improvement, under the doctrine of fixtures.

Inquiry Notice (Priorities) Information which is charged to a person where a duty is imposed upon him by law to make a reasonable investigation: the information which such investigation would have revealed is imputed to him.

Inverse Condemnation (Land Use; Miscellaneous Doctrines) A claim for monetary damages by a landowner aggrieved by governmental activities or regulation, on the ground that the government in fact has already taken the property and now must pay for it.

J

Joint Tenancy (Concurrent Ownership) An estate shared by two or more persons who have taken at the same time and through the same instrument, and with equal interests and rights of possession, and subject to the principle of survivorship.

Junior Mortgage (Mortgages) A mortgage which is lower in priority than some other mortgage and which will, therefore, be eliminated by a foreclosure of the senior mortgage, entitling the junior mortgagee only to receive the surplus, if any, from the senior sale.

Jure Uxoris (Estates) The nature of the husband's curtesy interest after marriage and before children were born.

L

Lateral Support (Miscellaneous Doctrines) The support which any parcel of land receives from the surrounding parcels of land.

License (Easements) A privilege of engaging in some activity upon another person's property, which is revocable at will by the owner of the land.

Life Estate (Estates) An interest which endures only so long as its holder (or whoever serves as the measuring life) lives. Where someone other than the life tenant is the measuring life, it is a life estate per autre vie.

Littoral (Miscellaneous Doctrines) Land adjacent to a lake.

M

Marketable Title (Contracts) A title which is free of defects and doubt and covers the entire estate which the vendor has purported to sell.

Master Plan See Plan.

Mortgage A promise by an owner of property that, if some obligation is not performed, the creditor may reach the property in order to satisfy it. In many jurisdictions a deed of trust is the conventional form of mortgage.

N

Negative Easement The right to restrain a possessor of land from engaging in activity which would otherwise be privileged.

Nonconforming Use (Land Use) A use which is impermissible under current land use regulations but which is allowed to continue because it preceded the enactment of the regulation.

Nonfreehold (Estates; Landlord-Tenant) A tenancy for a term, periodic tenancy, or tenancy at will; at common law the holder of such an estate had possession but not seisin.

Notice Act (Priorities) A statute which provides that an unrecorded instrument is void as against any subsequent purchaser or encumbrancer for value who takes without notice of it.

Notice-Race Statute (Priorities) A statute which provides that any unrecorded instrument is void as against any subsequent purchaser or encumbrancer for value who takes without notice of it and records first.

Nuisance (Miscellaneous Doctrines) An activity on one's property which unreasonably interferes with the use and enjoyment of another's property. This is also known as a private nuisance.

O

Ouster (Adverse Possession) The event which starts the statute of limitations running when a formerly permissive possessor becomes hostile to the owner or to other persons having possessory rights in the land.

P

Partition (Concurrent Ownership) The division of concurrently owned property into divided interests, separately owned by the parties.

Passive Waste See Permissive Waste.

Periodic Tenancy (Landlord-Tenant) A nonfreehold estate of specified duration which automatically renews itself continuously at the end of each period unless either landlord or tenant gives proper advance notice of an intent to terminate it.

Permissive Waste (Miscellaneous Doctrines) The failure of a possessor to make normal repairs to property so as to protect it from substantial deterioration.

Plan (Land Use) A document by which government sets forth its method and goals for the physical development of the region. Also known as the comprehensive plan or the master plan or the general plan.

Planned Unit Development (Land Use) A zoning principle which permits a developer to organize density and use allocations of property on a large parcel of land such that individual lots may violate the land use restrictions but, overall, the project is within the limits set by the ordinance.

Possibility of Reverter (Estates) A future interest retained by a grantor after the grant of a determinable estate which, if it takes effect, revests the property automatically in him.

Power of Termination (Estates) A future interest retained by a grantor after the conveyance of an estate subject to condition subsequent which, if it takes effect, does so only after he so elects.

Preliminary Title Report (Title Assurance) A report by a title company as to the existing state of the title, and indicating the willingness of the company to issue an insurance policy confirming the accuracy of its search.

Prescription (Adverse Possession; Easements) The running of the statute of limitations against a cause of action for the recovery of some interest in land.

Prior Appropriation (Miscellaneous Doctrines) A principle of water regulation in the western states, allocating rights to draw water according to a permit system based upon time of application.

Private Nuisance See Nuisance.

Privilege (Easements) In Hohfeldian (and Restatement) usage, a privilege indicates that the person is not under a duty to do or not do some particular act, i.e., another person has no right to compel her to act or not act. A person holding an easement of right of way has a privilege to cross the owner's land, without protest by the owner, which she would otherwise be obliged not to do. (See also Right and Duty.)

Privity of Estate (Landlord-Tenant; Covenants) The relationship between owners of land when a covenant is made, (horizontal) or between the original owners and their successors in interest to the parcels involved (vertical), which state law may require to exist in order that a covenant run with the land at law. Also the relationship which exists between a landlord and tenant or landlord and assignee, but not between landlord and subtenant.

Profit (Easements) The privilege of removing some mineral or soil from land owned by another.

Public Nuisance (Miscellaneous Doctrines) A nuisance which adversely affects the entire community, rather than merely the neighboring landowners.

Q

Quasi Easement A relationship of burden and benefit between two parts of a single parcel of land such that there would be an easement if these were separately owned parcels.

Quiet Enjoyment (Landlord-Tenant, Title Assurance) The use and enjoyment of an estate in land undisturbed by lawful claims asserted by the grantor or the landlord or by persons acting under them or by persons with a title paramount to them.

Quitclaim Deed (Title Assurance) A deed in which the grantor makes no representations concerning the state of title.

R

Race Act (Priorities) A statute which provides that an instrument is void as against other instruments which are recorded before it is recorded.

Race-Notice Act (Priorities) See Notice-Race Act.

Redemption (Mortgages) Payment of the mortgage debt, which then eliminates the mortgage as a charge on the property.

Referendum (Land Use) The process by which citizens, through the electoral process, repeal legislation enacted by the legislature.

Reliction (Conveyances) The alteration of a boundary line due to the gradual removal of land by a stream serving as the boundary.

Remainder (Estates) A future interest created in a third person to take effect upon the natural termination of a prior estate created in the same instrument.

Reserved Easement An easement created by the grantor of property, benefitting the retained property and burdening the granted property. Restraint on Alienation Language in a deed or similar instrument which restricts the power of the grantee to transfer the property to others. Common versions of modern restraints include no-assignment clauses in leases (usually requiring the landlord's consent for any assignment or sublease) and due on sale clauses in mortgages (entitling the mortgagee to accelerate all remaining installment payments due on the debt if the mortgagor transfers the security).

Reversion (Estates) A future interest retained by a grantor after the conveyance of a present estate of a smaller duration than his own.

Right (Easements) In Hohfeldian (and Restatement) usage, a right refers to the legally enforceable demand one person has towards another to make her do or not do a certain act. With respect to land, an owner generally has the right to tell all others not to trespass, but if she gives someone an easement to cross, she has no right to exclude her thereafter when she crosses. (See also Duty and Privilege.)

Riparian (Miscellaneous Doctrines) Land adjacent to a stream.

S

Sale Foreclosure See Foreclosure.

Seisin (Estates; Title Insurance) The common law characteristic of being in lawful possession of a freehold estate.

Servient Tenant (Easements) The person whose land is subject to an easement.

Servient Tenement (Easements) Land which is subject to an easement.

Settlement (Contracts) The completion of a contract for the sale of land by virtue of the vendor conveying the property and the purchaser paying the price. Also known as closing.

Severance (Concurrent Ownership) The conversion of a joint tenancy into a tenancy in common.

Special Exception See Conditional Use.

Spurious Easement The right to compel a possessor of land to do an act which he would otherwise be free not to perform.

Strict Foreclosure See Foreclosure.

Subdivision (Land Use) The division of a parcel of land into smaller lots.

Subdivision Exaction (Land Use) A charge of land or money which a community imposes upon a subdivider as a condition for permitting recordation of the subdivision map and sale of the subdivided parcels.

Subdivision Map (Land Use) A map showing how a larger parcel of land is to be divided into smaller lots, and generally also showing the layout of streets, utilities, etc.

Subjacent Support (Miscellaneous Doctrines) The support which the surface of land receives from the soil beneath it.

Sublease (Landlord-Tenant) A transfer by a tenant of an estate of lesser duration than the leasehold estate held by the tenant.

Surrender (Landlord-Tenant) A conveyance of a present estate to the holder of a future interest in the same property. A "surrender by operation of law" occurs when the tenant abandons the premises and the landlord reenters.

Survivorship (Concurrent Ownership) A feature of joint tenancy and tenancy by the entirety, whereby the surviving co-owner takes the entire interest in preference to heirs or devisees of the deceased co-owner.

T

Tacking (Adverse Possession) The joining together of times of possession of different persons so as to total a period of wrongful possession in excess of the statute of limitations.

Tenancy at Sufferance (Landlord-Tenant) The status of a tenant who has held over after the expiration of his term and as to whom the landlord has not made an election either to compel him to leave or to require him to stay as a periodic tenant.

Tenancy at Will (Landlord-Tenant) A nonfreehold estate which has no set termination date or regular rent and which may be terminated at the election of either party at any time.

Tenancy by the Entirety (Concurrent Ownership) A joint tenancy between spouses and which cannot be severed.

Tenancy for a Term (Landlord-Tenant) A nonfreehold estate lasting for some definite time, from one day up to 999 years. Also known as an estate for years.

Tenancy in Common (Concurrent Ownership) A form of co-ownership requiring only that the parties have undivided interests in the property, i.e., equal rights to possess all of it.

Tenancy From Period to Period (Landlord-Tenant) See Periodic Tenancy.

Title Insurance (Title Assurance) A policy issued by a title company after searching the title, representing the state of that title and insuring the accuracy of its search.

Title Policy See Title Insurance

Touch and Concern (Covenants) A requirement of covenants that they be "real" rather than "collateral," i.e., relate to the land rather than to persons, before they will be permitted to run with the land.

Tract Index (Priorities) A set of indexes organized according to the location of all parcels of land described in documents in the official records.

Trade Fixture (Miscellaneous Doctrines; Landlord-Tenant) A fixture installed by a tenant for the purposes of trade, which is therefore removable by the tenant at the expiration of the term.

Transferable Development Right (Land Use; Miscellaneous Doctrines) Permission granted by a government to a property owner to build a taller or larger building elsewhere as compensation for building restrictions imposed upon the subject parcel.

Trespass (Miscellaneous Doctrines) An unprivileged intentional physical intrusion upon land possessed by another.

Trespass to Try Title (Miscellaneous Doctrines) An action in trespass brought to recover nominal damages and primarily intended to establish the title of the plaintiff to the land.

V

Variance (Land Use) A permit entitling a landowner to depart from some zoning requirement by virtue of unique hardship due to special circumstances regarding her property.

Vested (Estates) An indication either that an interest is certain to take and is not contingent (vested in interest) or else that an interest has become possessory (vested in possession).

Vested Remainder (Estates) A remainder which has been given to an ascertained person and is subject to no condition precedent other than the natural termination of prior estates.

W

Warranty Deed (Title Assurance) A deed containing numerous covenants of title by a grantor.

Waste (Miscellaneous Doctrines) Action or inaction by a possessor of land causing unreasonable injury to the holders of other estates in the same land. This includes the obligation to make minor repairs to keep the premises windtight and watertight.

Wild Deed (Priorities) An instrument which is recorded but, because some previous instrument connecting it to the chain of title has not been recorded, will never be discovered in the indexes.

Words of Limitation (Estates) Language in a deed indicating how long the estate granted is to endure.

Z

Zoning (Land Use) The division of a region into separate districts with different regulations as to height, bulk or use in the districts; within each district the requirements are uniform.

APPENDIX E

TABLE OF CASES

*

APPENDIX F

INDEX

†